THE
IDEA OF PERFECTION
IN CHRISTIAN
THEOLOGY

THE
IDEA OF PERFECTION
IN CHRISTIAN
THEOLOGY

AN HISTORICAL STUDY OF
THE CHRISTIAN IDEAL FOR
THE PRESENT LIFE

By R. NEWTON FLEW

M.A., D.D. (Oxon.)

Tutor and Lecturer in New Testament
Language and Literature, Wesley House
Cambridge

HUMANITIES PRESS

New York 1968

First published in 1934

Reprinted 1968 by

HUMANITIES PRESS, INC.

New York, N. Y. 10010

Printed in U.S.A. by

NOBLE OFFSET PRINTERS, INC.

NEW YORK 3, N. Y.

To W. F.

Take them, Love, the book and me together:
Where the heart lies, let the brain lie also.

ROBERT BROWNING: 'One word more'..

PREFACE

IN this long journey through the centuries the writer has naturally walked with many guides. Necessary acknowledgement has been made in the footnotes, though no attempt has been made to chronicle all the books read in a study of the history of Christian spirituality which has now been pursued for many years.

There are three useful historical sketches of the doctrine of perfection, all by Wesleyan writers: W. B. Pope, *Compendium of Christian Theology* (2nd ed., 3 vols., 1879), iii. 28–99; H. W. Perkins, *The Doctrine of Christian Perfection* (1927); F. Platt, art. 'Perfection (Christian)' in *E.R.E.* ix. 728–37. I have not found Dr. Pope's assumption justified, that Wesley's doctrine of perfection was indebted to the Arminian divines. Of the Tridentine doctrine there is an outline in Dr. Platt's article. For Roman Catholic views, Deharbe, *Die vollkommene Liebe Gottes* (1856), Pourrat, *La Spiritualité chrétienne* (4 vols., 1918–28), Garrigou-Lagrange, *Perfection chrétienne et Contemplation* (2 vols., 1923), also the periodical *La Vie spirituelle* (from 1919 onwards), have been found especially useful. Dr. K. E. Kirk's great book, *The Vision of God* (1931), should be constantly used by all students of this subject, though in the realm of Protestant spirituality it will not be found a sympathetic guide. For modern perfectionist movements see B. B. Warfield, *Perfectionism* (2 vols., 1931–2).

A student of New Testament theology must acknowledge debt to the monumental *Lehrbuch* of H. J. Holtzmann (2nd ed. 1911, ed. Jülicher and Bauer). A footnote (vol. ii, 166–7) introduced me to the indispensable work of Windisch (1908) which is often cited in the following pages: *Taufe und Sünde im ältesten Christentum bis auf Origenes*. The scanty references to this book in English writers up to 1928 give no hint of the important question which Windisch had treated; but it was pointed out by Dr. K. E. Kirk in *Essays on the Trinity and the Incarnation* (1928). Early Christian literature, and the Pauline writings in particular, contain passages which seem to assume that the Christian should, and can, live a sinless life. Dr. Kirk's view is (p. 230) that the problem thus created is perhaps the greatest which the Pauline writings have bequeathed us. Windisch felt the need, as his last chapter shows, of providing some analogies in history for the disconcerting phenomena of the New Testament, and he sees that there is a real analogy in the teaching and aim of the early Methodists.

My thanks are due to the Editor of the *London Quarterly Review* and to the S.C.M. Press for permission to reprint parts of two essays, the one on St. Augustine, the other on Clement of Alexandria.

It is a particular pleasure to be able to record my gratitude to many who have helped me; first, to Dr. H. L. Goudge, Regius Professor in the University of Oxford, for most generous encouragement and wise advice during the last eleven years; to the Divinity Professors of an earlier date, especially the late Canon Scott Holland, who by an election to a travelling scholarship gave a Methodist preacher the opportunity of further study of historical theology in Fribourg-en-Suisse and at Rome; to Dr. F. C. Burkitt, Norrisian Professor in the University of Cambridge, for constant stimulus, especially in the study of early Christianity; to Dr. W. Russell Maltby, Warden of the Wesley Deaconess College, Ilkley, for permission to use his paraphrase of Romans viii, and for many an inspiration; to my beloved colleague Principal H. Maldwyn Hughes, for continued encouragement and wise advice; to my brother-members of the London Society for the Study of Religion, before whom parts of this book have been read; to Father M. J. D'Arcy, S.J., of Campion Hall, Oxford, and to my old friend Professor J. Arundel Chapman, of Wesley College, Headingley, Leeds, for reading and criticizing various portions of the book; to the Reverend R. T. Fleming, B.A., for careful help in the revision of the proofs; to the officials of the Clarendon Press for their courtesy and patience; to Mr. Charles J. Barker, M.A., of Preston, formerly Scholar of Christ Church, who has read the manuscript again and again, and the proofs, and has also made invaluable suggestions as to the style and content of the book; and to her to whom the book is dedicated.

But the chief and quite incalculable debt for anything fresh or living which may be found in these pages is due to some who have passed 'within the veil', who proved how rich, how vivid, how human, how gay, was true saint-liness. Among many I may be allowed to name my father, who led his son to Christ, and Friedrich von Hügel, who in his intense and affectionate interest in younger men, encouraged the writer to study more closely the type of piety revealed in the autobiographies of the early Metho-dists. Of these two, the one was a Wesleyan Methodist Minister, who wrote only two short books, but whose life-work was to write in souls; the other was a Roman Catholic layman whose massive writings and prophetic insight will continue to point forward to a richer Catholicism of the future. The two men met only once, but immediately they understood one another. *Deep calleth unto deep.* Both knew that the ultimate attitude of the soul must be that of adoration. Of either of the two the word is true: *Defunctus adhuc loquitur.*

R. N. F.

WESLEY HOUSE, CAMBRIDGE.

February 1934.

CONTENTS

INTRODUCTION

WHAT is the Christian ideal for the present life? And is it the will of God that by His grace we should attain to it? These are questions which ought to be raised incessantly, and for which Christian theology may reasonably be expected to provide an answer.

The following chapters are an attempt to sketch the chief answers which have been given to these questions in Christian history. The idea of perfection has taken varying forms; the leading and characteristic forms will be investigated, and in the last chapter some conclusions will be drawn. If I may be permitted to borrow a distinction from Roman Catholic theology, I would ask my readers to regard this book as an essay in *Theologia Spiritualis*. As formulated by the learned M. l'Abbé Pourrat, 'spiritual theology' is to be distinguished from 'dogmatic theology' and 'moral theology'. It is 'above them, but based upon them'. I would rather say that the *Theologia Dogmatica* of the future which may be different from previous structures must be built on the *Theologia Spiritualis* of the past. But in any case, the principles of the life of prayer, the conditions, rules, and graces of holy living, the nature of the goal at which we are to aim—all these are surely as worthy of the attention of the theologian as of the last convert to be admitted into the Christian Church. But apart from many excellent books on Mysticism (especially that of Dean Inge), and the recent great works of Professor Friedrich Heiler and Dr. Kenneth E. Kirk, it is surprising how little systematic work has been accomplished by non-Roman writers in this field. The present writer knows that his book is unworthy of its high theme, but he has endeavoured to treat it with reverence; and he has paid especial attention to Protestant spirituality, and to the theory of sanctity in the communion to which he owes his soul.

The subject has been carefully limited. The book is concerned with the content of the ideal, and does not attempt any account of the different methods employed for the realization of the ideal. There is one question by which all talk of perfection is often swept aside: 'Have you ever known any one, except our Lord, who attained to perfection, or sinlessness, in this life?' As a criticism this question is really irrelevant. There may be an ideal which, according to God's will, we should attain in the present life, even if no one has yet attained it. Even St. Augustine[1] admitted the possibility of attaining to a sinless state in this life, though only through a miraculous exertion of the power of God. And after all, to judge the saints is not our business. Every one of them has the right to say to us: 'It is a very small thing that I should be judged of you, or of man's judgement: . . . but he that judgeth me is the Lord.'

But it will be observed that in the following pages the idea of perfection is not regarded as synonymous with sinlessness. Freedom from sin must be an element in the ideal. But the idea of perfection should be stated positively rather than negatively; it is far larger and more inclusive than it has been made to appear in the teaching of many 'perfectionists' of the nineteenth century. For this reason the primary and determinative description is to be sought in the teaching of our Lord about the Kingdom of God, as recorded in the Synoptic Gospels. Perhaps in the attempt at a synthesis of the various elements in that teaching, and in the treatment of it as containing an ideal realizable in some measure in this world, may be found a new setting for the idea of perfection. Hitherto it has been regarded as the peculiarity of various sects. The doctrine of perfection, writes my friend and former colleague Dr. Frederic Platt,[2] 'is a bypath in Christian theological systems'. I hope to have shown that, when it is not simply identified with sinlessness, it is veritably the King's highway.

Of course, the word 'perfection' when applied to any

---

[1] *De spiritu et littera*, 7; Migne, xliv. 204. Cf. J. B. Mozley, *Lectures* (1883), 166; Lecture xi, on 'Perfectibility'.

[2] Quoted in H. W. Perkins, *The Doctrine of Christian Perfection*, viii.

attainment in this life is strictly incorrect, and the phrase 'relative perfection' contains a contradiction. But we can hardly avoid some such phrase. On the one hand, we must hold fast the truth that the ideal attainable in this life can never be the Christian's ultimate goal; on the other hand, the words 'perfect' or 'perfection' as applied to a certain degree of attainment in this world are enshrined in the Sermon on the Mount, in the Epistles of St. Paul, in the Epistle to the Hebrews, and have had a long and honourable history in the Catholic tradition. But the word 'perfection' has during the last century encountered in overflowing measure the unmerited fate of other great Christian words—to be distrusted because of some unworthy advocates. There may be something said in the following pages to rescue from contempt or neglect both the word and the ideal which it conveys.

I may be forgiven for insisting that the book is not academic in its origin. Many of us, who were comparatively fresh to pastoral work when the Great War broke out, were dismayed by the spiritual unpreparedness of the Christian Church. As Bishop Neville Talbot wrote: 'we were all overtaken in a state of great poverty towards God'. Amid the inward conflicts of those years of war, some of us stumbled on the principle of John Wesley, which was of immediate value as a guide in practical work—that the truest evangelism is to preach the full ideal for which power is offered in the present life. 'The work of God does not prosper', said John Wesley, 'where perfect love is not preached.' Those who dislike the phrase or who suspect the maxim may yet bear with an attempt to penetrate to the spiritual value of the principle. The surest way to victory over the many is to begin with the few. A vast evangelistic advance can only be sustained if the Christian ideal for this life is steadily set forth in all its beauty and its fullness as being by the grace of God something not impossible of attainment. If this principle be valid, it is likely that the ignoring of it will bring impoverishment and arrest. In the following pages, for example, it is suggested that it was a defect in the Reformation divines that they were not at home with this principle, and that the sectarian reactions of Quakerism, Pietism, and Methodism were, in spite of all appearances, symptoms of a return to the larger and more truly Catholic view. At all events, the principle of Wesley was that of our Lord, who chose Twelve that they might be with Him, whose last journey to Jerusalem was based on His own missionary tenet: *Let the children first be filled.* Holiness is not only (as Newman said) necessary for future blessedness. It is essential to the vitality and advance of the Christian message in this world.

There is a second principle which has governed the choice of material for this essay, and this, too, arises out of the practical needs of our own day. It has been stated by Troeltsch as a valuable historical generalization. Genuine religious reformations (*Neubildungen*), he says, do their work in a double way and are of two kinds. On the one hand they proceed from the serene heights on which thinkers and cultivated people live; they are expressed in the form of criticism and speculation; their significance depends on the depth of religious vitality concealed beneath this criticism, this speculation. Platonism and Stoicism are examples of this type. But they never achieve the specifically religious power of a faith founded on revelation. On the other hand the really powerful movements in religion come from the lower classes. At this level alone do we find simplicity of feeling, a non-reflective habit of mind, a primitive energy, an urgent sense of need. From such a soil alone spring unconditioned faith in an authoritative divine revelation, simplicity of surrender, unshaken certainty. In such faith, self-abandonment, and certainty, lies the transforming power of popular religious movements, such as early Christianity, Methodism, modern missions in India and the Far East. 'Christians—the dregs of the kettle!' was the gibe of a heckler at an open-air meeting of a Sinhalese preacher. 'Yes', was the retort, ' but the kettle boils from the bottom up!'

Troeltsch observes that this type of religious movement, with its deep spiritual experience, must sooner or later come to terms with the other type, with its reflectiveness and religious sincerity. 'Apart from this fusion faith would be broken.' As applied to historical theology, the acceptance of this generalization would mean, first, that we should expect to find those theologians the most significant and influential who are applying themselves to this task of fusing the deep religious experience of popular Christianity with the other type of religious movement which works from the heights of reflection and speculation. That is what we do find in Clement of Alexandria and Origen, in Augustine and Aquinas and Schleiermacher. Augustine, for example, is working with the new religious impulse given by the popular lay movement of Monasticism, and he is attempting to reconcile the power of this movement with the culture of the ancient world and the reflective mysticism of Plotinus. Schleiermacher is fusing the piety of the Moravians with the new ideas of the age of the Enlightenment.

In the second place, since these popular movements are working, as I hope to show, with a passion for a holiness which can be attained in this world, the principle of Troeltsch implies that sooner or later the popular ideal must be widened to include the culture of this world. There are realms of the spirit which are not specifically, and in their origins, religious, but which yet must be brought into the Christian experience as part of the soul's ideal. Clement sees this in the second century, Schleiermacher, nearer our own time.

These two principles, the one from Wesley, the other from Troeltsch, may serve to explain the choice of the writers and movements handled in the following essay, and to demonstrate how the best Christian thinking is deeply rooted in the spirituality of the Church.

THE
IDEA OF PERFECTION
IN CHRISTIAN
THEOLOGY

CHAPTER I

THE TEACHING OF JESUS

'Take My yoke upon you . . . and ye shall find rest.'
Ubi Christus, ibi Regnum Dei.

'WHOEVER would act wisely,' said Plato, 'whether
in public or in private life, must set the Idea of Good
before his eyes.'[1] The same canon is proposed to His followers by One greater than Plato, and the Idea of Good is
presented in a richer, more personal, more comprehensive
picture than the Platonists ever knew. In Christ,

> the golden hope of the world, unbaffled
> Springs from its sleep, and up goes the spire.

There is a new shrine for the immemorial hopes of man,
and the name of it is the Kingdom of God.

But it is not a simple ideal. The simplicity of the
Gospels is an axiom of the modern evangelist. But, like
all other axioms, the assumption must be examined by the
theologian. The religious temper longs for simplification,
but any premature simplification of the message of Jesus
may cut the nerve of the Gospel to be preached. 'Consider', says Johannes Weiss,[2] 'the simplicity of Jesus, His
objectivity, His warmth, how these speak to every child,
and yet have something to say to the profoundest thinker.'
And any one who attempts a synthesis of the various
elements in the teaching of Jesus is confronted by obstacles
wellnigh insurmountable.

There have been two main difficulties in recent studies.
The first has been historical and the second practical. In
the first place the examination of the apocalyptic writings
of the period between the Old Testament and the New has
raised new problems for traditional belief. According to
the Apocalypses, the kingdom would be established by a
violent cataclysm and overthrow of the existing order.

---

[1] *Republic*, vii. 517.   [2] *Das Urchristentum*, 322.

The end would come by the intervention of God. Then the new realm would be inaugurated on the earth.[1]

There can be as little doubt that Jesus shared these expectations, as that He transcended them. He filled the old forms with a new content. He rearranged or rejected some popular beliefs. But the facts are too stubborn to be explained away. He seems to have believed that the end of the world was not far away, and that His own Parousia in glory was imminent.[2]

It was Albrecht Schweitzer, as is well known, who, following in the wake of the still more original work of Johannes Weiss, first forced these questions on the notice of the students of the life of Jesus. He insisted on unlocking every door with this eschatological key. The kingdom of God was wholly in the future; the ideal for which Jesus lived and died was wholly apocalyptic. The ethical teaching was only for the interim between the dark present and the glorious unveiling. There is a rigidity, a one-sidedness, an exclusiveness in the interpretation of Schweitzer; and his reading of the life of Jesus has failed to win general assent. But no longer can we rest easily either in the liberal Protestant delineation of Jesus, which dominated the minds of scholars at the beginning of this century, or in the traditional explanations in their older forms. The message of Jesus is set in an eschatological framework. There are sayings enough to prove the predominance within His teaching of the apocalyptic hope.

If His ruling idea is intertwined with a prediction which has been falsified by history, how can He maintain His place as the Lord of time and of eternity, the Lord of thought as well as the Saviour of every human soul? Was He not a victim of a sublime illusion? Was He not a visionary hovering between two worlds, one dead, the other powerless to be born?

Ein schöner Traum!—indessen sie entweicht.

It is at this point that the other and even more pressing

[1] Cf. E. F. Scott, *The Kingdom of God in the New Testament* (1931), 55–71.   [2] Mark ix. 1; xiv. 61, 62.

difficulty of practical men becomes one with the doubt
of the historians. The ultimate question for all of us is
whether the teaching of Jesus is not too high, too ideal to
be incorporated in the realism of this stubborn, practical
world. 'Ye therefore shall be perfect, as your heavenly
Father is perfect.' If the message of the imminence of the
Kingdom sounds like an old Jewish dream, the counsels
of perfection seem to stamp the ethical teaching of Jesus
as impracticable and remote.

In the following pages an attempt will be made to
answer both these difficulties, first by combining them and
then by seeking a solution at the very point where the
difficulties press most hardly. In effect, the final answer
will be that the proclamation by Jesus of the Reign of God
carried with it a doctrine of the ideal life which might be
lived out in the present world.

First of all I shall state the preliminary evidence which
renders this view intrinsically probable. Secondly will
follow an analysis of the idea of the 'Kingdom' of God;
and finally will come an exposition of the main elements of
the ideal which our Lord holds up for mankind.

I. There are several reasons which justify us in interpreting the Synoptic teaching of the 'Kingdom of God'
as an ideal of Perfection.

(i) The preservation of the sayings of Jesus by the
early Christian community.

Every word of Jesus in the Collections of Logia which
have been preserved to us in the first three Gospels is a
witness for an Ideal or a conviction of the primitive community.[1] This is true of any saying the authenticity of
which may be doubted. Indeed the more doubt we may
have that the saying derives from Jesus Himself, the more
certain we may be that the saying proves the existence of
a conviction in the community.

Any one who really understood the Beatitudes must
have seen that it was not the exemplary pious people who
were called, but the poor in spirit, who hungered and
thirsted after the righteousness of God. But he must have

[1] Cf. Johannes Weiss, *Urchristentum*, 56.

felt quite clearly that far more was expected from him than the common ideal of the Scribes. 'The proud feeling of daring to reckon oneself with the few who were chosen (Matt. xxii. 14), with the little flock (Luke xii. 32), is only morally possible when it is bound up with the consciousness of being pledged to do extraordinary deeds.'[1]

The sayings in the Sermon on the Mount are set in an eschatological framework.[2] But they are witnesses to the fact that from the earliest days of the Christian Church there were certain communities which believed that such an ideal life could be lived in this world.[3]

So far we have not discussed the *logion* which has played so influential a part in the history of Christian spirituality.

Ἔσεσθε οὖν ὑμεῖς τέλειοι, ὡς ὁ πατὴρ ὑμῶν ὁ οὐράνιος τέλειός ἐστι. (Matt. v. 48.)

Some have maintained that the Lucan form of the *logion* is more original (so Wellhausen, Marriott, Creed, and others).

γίνεσθε οἰκτίρμονες καθὼς ὁ πατὴρ ὑμῶν οἰκτίρμων ἐστίν. (Luke vi. 36.)

The chief reason is that the word τέλειος is found in Matthew only of the evangelists, and he inserted it in his version of the words of Jesus to the Rich Young Ruler. On the other hand it has been suggested that the divergence goes back to the original Aramaic.[4] The Aramaic word does not mean merciful, and therefore if this argument is pressed, it is possible that Luke or his authority mistranslated the Aramaic original, and that the Matthaean version is more reliable. There are parallels in the Old Testament to this summary of the Sermon on the

---

[1] Cf. Johannes Weiss, *Urchristentum*, 56, 57.

[2] For the detailed proof of this see Windisch, *Der Sinn der Bergpredigt*, 9–20.

[3] Windisch, ibid., 131.

[4] Moffatt, *Introd. to the Literature of the N.T.*, 195, 196. שלם has the sense of completeness in Biblical Aramaic. See Brown, Driver, Briggs, *Lexicon*, 1115, 1116. Compare Dalman, *The Words of Jesus*, 66.

Mount. The LXX of Deut. xviii. 13 has τέλειος ἔσῃ ἐναντίον Κυρίου τοῦ θεοῦ σου.

But whether the word 'perfect' was used by Jesus or not, there were those in the early Church who could accept the *logion* as given by Matthew as a just summary of their task. For us, perhaps, it is difficult to imagine a community where that *logion* could be taken seriously. Here it dominates the thought. Like some phrase of music which summarizes and concludes a symphony, so the aspiration after perfection gives unity and harmony to the whole discourse. The phrase is evidence for the existence, at least in some unknown early community, of an ideal of life which was pure, unmerited, persistent overflowing love, as vast and immeasurable as the love of God.[1]

(ii) For the early Christian the Kingdom was indissolubly bound up with the person of Jesus Himself. He had already come once, and to their minds the Kingdom was already present.

If I by the finger of God cast out demons, then is the Kingdom of God come among you.

I saw Satan fallen like lightning from heaven.

Blessed are your eyes because they see, and your ears because they hear.

These sayings[2] are usually (and with justice) taken to prove that Jesus did not conceive of the kingdom as purely eschatological. With even greater certainty they prove that from the earliest days of the Christian Church there were certain communities which were attempting to live a life in accordance with these words of our Lord. They had already tasted the powers of the world to come, for He had come. He was to come again, and therefore the full manifestation of the Kingdom was set in the future, at the end of the Age. The Kingdom was perfection because He was at the centre of it. *Ubi Christus, ibi Regnum Dei.*

(iii) If, as they believed, they had a new law and a new

---

[1] Cf. Johannes Weiss, *Die Schriften des N.T.* (1907), i. 281.

[2] Matt. xii. 28; Luke x. 18; Matt. xiii. 16 (Luke x. 23, 24); see also Luke xvii. 20–1; Matt. xi. 4–11 (Luke vii. 18–28).

Lawgiver, they had a new doctrine of grace. The evangelist who has been accused of conceiving Christianity merely as a New Law closes his work (Matt. xxviii. 20) with the promise of the presence of the Risen Lord, to enable His disciples for their impossible mission. It is probably to that evangelist that we owe the word τέλειος in the story of the Rich Young Ruler. There it must mean 'utterly devoted to God.'[1] Is this devotion possible? The Synoptists tell us that the disciples doubted it, that then the answer came: *With men it is impossible, but not with God. All things are possible with God.*

The preservation of this saying in such a context means that the evangelists, and the churches who endorsed their work, recognized that the new religion offered immeasurable power to meet the heightened moral demands made by their Lord.[2]

(iv) This introduction of God's will, God's love, as the standard whereby man may measure the moral demands made on him, means that the ideal is not fixed or static but illimitable. This is recognized in another *logion*[3] preserved to us by Luke (xvii. 10). *When you have done all that is commanded you, say, We are unworthy servants; we have done what we ought to have done.*

There is a spiritual law, discernible in the supreme creative achievements of art or literature, that nothing enduring is brought forth save by one whose aim is illimitable and whose standard is perfection. An artist is an artist because he attempts more than he can ever do. All the incalculable beauties of poetry come from the poet's attempt to say more than he can say. So, too, in religion the ultimate aim of the soul must be in its very nature illimitable. Our physical activities are limited. We know, to within a few inches, the farthest that a man can jump;

---

[1] Moffatt, *Love in N.T.* (1929), 67.

[2] B. W. Bacon, *Studies in Matthew* (1930), 240, who expounds the Marcan *motif* in this sense, though he brands Matthew as a 'neo-legalist'.

[3] Bultmann admits the authenticity. I follow J. M. Creed, *St. Luke*, 216 in keeping ἀχρεῖοι and translating 'unworthy' rather than 'useless'. So in 2 Sam. vi. 22, LXX.

we do not know at all what limits there are to any spiritual excellence. A man keeps his passion of discovery and adventure only because he knows that there is an impossible infinity of achievement before him. The moment he believes that his art is final in its accomplishment, or his truth perfect in its grasp, he ceases to be a man of science or an artist.

Perhaps in this principle we may find some solace as we read the words of Figgis: 'Christian holiness is not only never achieved in perfection, but it is far less nearly and less frequently achieved than the ethical ideals of Pagans or Mohammedans.'[1] At all events this principle will explain two characteristics of the Christian ethic which are everywhere noticeable in the Synoptic Gospels. On the one hand, the supreme enemy of Christianity is the sin of spiritual complacency. The temper now called Pharisaism[2] is the besetting danger of an advanced stage of civilization. It shelters behind virtues such as discipline, chastity, benevolence, generosity; for the real virtues of one age readily become the spurious virtues of the next. The root of this temper is the tendency to rest in the truth already possessed as final and imperfectible. The devotees of a religious legalism tend to be content with their attainment. On the other hand, the Synoptic Gospels, because the framework of their teaching is eschatological, ever point forward to the ultimate goal, the complete victory of God. The Transfiguration story, which perhaps bears on it traces of the devout imagination with which the early Christians embellished the original incident, is a sign that all that they had learnt of God in Christ was but a preparation for the beatific vision in the next world.[3] Hence there is a paradox at the heart of the Christian experience. 'I saw Him and I sought Him; I had Him and I wanted Him', said Mother Julian of Norwich.[4] 'And this is and

---

[1] *Churches in the Modern State*, 3, 4.
[2] See the classical study of Pharisaism in J. B. Mozley, *University Sermons*, 25–45. Also A. L. Lilley, *Religion and Life*, 11–18.
[3] See Kenneth E. Kirk, *The Vision of God* (1931), 97–101.
[4] *Revelations of Divine Love* (ed. Grace Warrack, 1907), 22. Cp. E.

should be our common working in this life, as to my sight.'
We shall therefore be prepared to believe that at the heart
of the teaching of Jesus was an ideal attainable in this
world, while the ultimate goal of all aspiration was set in
the age to come.

II. In what sense is the main theme of Jesus, 'The
Kingdom of God,' to be understood?

In the later years of his life Johannes Weiss recognized
whole-heartedly that, in many sayings, the Kingdom could
not be interpreted in a purely eschatological sense. 'The
problem of the relation of the eschatological to the non-
eschatological sayings of Jesus has not yet been solved.'[1]
It would be presumptuous to say that the problem has now
been solved, but recent discussions seem to have brought
a solution nearer.

The solution is to be found primarily in the conception
of the God Whom Jesus proclaimed,[2] and, secondarily,
in defining with greater precision the relation of the Kingdom of God to the society of disciples which was to grow
into the Christian Church.

The conception of God in the Old Testament is of a
Personal Being who is Active Will: *Purus actus* would be a
not inapt description. 'The idea of God was eminently
personal. He was supramundane, but not extramundane;
exalted but not remote. He was the sole ruler of the world.
He had created and he ordered all things in it in accordance with his character.'[3] It is difficult for those who
have always lived under a kingship whose powers of action
are severely limited to interpret kingdom save as the realm

Underhill, *Mysticism*, 107. The same paradox reappears in the poetry of
Kabir (tr. R. Tagore, 1918), iii. 2–3, and in the confession of St. Paul, *I
press on . . . because I have been apprehended by Christ Jesus.*

[1] *Das Problem der Entstehung des Christentums*, in the *Archiv für
Religionswissenschaft*, Band xvi, 449. The statements here are stronger
than the retractations in the second ed. (1900) of the *Predigt Jesu.*

[2] So, e.g., E. F. Scott, *The Kingdom of God* (1931), 65; Gerhard Gloege,
Reich Gottes und Kirche (1929); H. D. Wendland, *Die Eschatologie des
Reiches Gottes bei Jesus* (1931); so Bultmann, *Jesus* (1926), 49; K. L.
Schmidt, C. H. Dodd, and G. Kittel in *Theology* (May 1927).

[3] G. F. Moore, *Judaism*, i. 423.

or as the society over which a king rules. But the primary notion in βασιλεία, as in the Hebrew malkuth, is the active rule, or kingly working of God. The idea of God is dynamic and not static. 'The first consideration in the Jewish view is that the sovereignty of God is an eternal one.'[1] God has been active in the world since its creation, and He is king even though there are wicked on the earth and the rulers set themselves to take counsel together against the Lord.[2]

In the later literature of Judaism appears the conception (perhaps under the influence of Persian ideas) of a kingship of evil rearing itself against the rule of God. The faith of the Jew was that the inevitable conflict of these two rules would ultimately result in the 'coming' of the undisputed Reign of God. This clash involves catastrophe for the existing world-order. Jewish Apocalyptic, like Hebrew Prophecy, rests on the view that civilization is not an end in itself. There are evil elements in it as well as good, and the final disaster overwhelms a corrupt order because God's purpose is supreme and works for moral ends. 'Good is as active as evil; calamity is as much for the manifestation of good as for the destruction of evil.'[3]

The central idea of apocalyptic is thus seen to be a development of the faith in the eternal sovereignty of God. 'The omnipotence of God is thus interlocked with the teleology of history.'[4] The Rule of God is above time in the sense that it is eternal. It goes back to Abraham, and farther still to the foundation of the world. But it operates in time, and will be completely manifested at the end of the age, when the 'Kingdom shall have come', and God shall have achieved His final victory. And because the final victory is certain, it determines the present, not

[1] Dalman, *The Words of Jesus*, 96 ff., where evidence is given. Further proof in G. F. Moore, *Judaism*, i. 401, note 2. Particularly interesting is the citation of Psalms of Solomon xvii. 4, and Enoch lxxxiv. 2 by T. W. Manson, *The Teaching of Jesus* (1931), 136.

[2] Psalm ii; cxlv. 13.

[3] John Oman, in *The Churchman* (July 1932), 184–91.

[4] G. F. Moore, i. 375.

merely because the proclamation of its nearness forces
man to an immediate decision,[1] but because God in His
eternal sovereignty, which one day will be owned by all,
is ruling now, and gives present evidence of His final
triumph to those who have eyes to see. The God who feeds
the sparrows and clothes the flowers of the field also
watches over His children, and calls them to share the
light burden, the easy yoke of the Kingdom, which Jesus
bears. 'With this intense realization of God as a living
and all-sustaining presence, it was impossible for Jesus to
see the Kingdom as wholly in the future.'[2]

So far we have interpreted βασιλεία as meaning the
'rule', or kingly working of God. This meaning fits the
parables in Mark iv and parallels, where the βασιλεία is
likened to a man *doing* something. Such sayings as that
about receiving the Kingdom of God as a child are
meant for those whom Jesus sets face to face with God
and His rule.

Naturally the Rule of God does not operate in the void.
It is not abstract. God rules over nature and the world of
men. Does the word sometimes mean, by a natural
transition, the 'realm' or the sphere in which the rule is
exercised? That would be a possible meaning for the passages which speak of 'entering into', or 'inheriting' the
Kingdom.[3] In most of these references the Kingdom is
thought of as the coming age, and may well signify the
whole order established there by God and completely
obedient to His will. All the emphasis is on God's rule,
even if it would be permissible to translate βασιλεία in
these instances by 'realm'. On the other hand where
βασιλεία refers to the Rule of God which is present and
may be accepted now, the meaning 'realm' is unsuitable.
The common phrase of Jewish piety was 'to take the kingdom' or 'the yoke of the kingdom upon oneself'.[4]

---

[1] As Bultmann, *Jesus*, 49, maintains.
[2] E. F. Scott, *The Kingdom of God* (1931), 69. See also C. H. Dodd in
Theology (May 1927), 259.
[3] Matt. v. 20; vii. 21; xviii. 3; xxv. 34.
[4] Evidence in Strack-Billerbeck, i. 176–180. See the petition in the

But while 'realm' is only to be accepted (if at all) as a subordinate and limited meaning, the interpretation of 'kingdom' as a 'community' should be rejected altogether. The Rule of God implies a community ruled, but it is never to be identified with the human beings who enter that rule. Hence the Kingdom is always to be distinguished from the *ecclesia*; and the influential Ritschlian interpretation which defined the Kingdom as 'the organization of humanity through action inspired by love'[1] is almost as far from the truth as the Roman view which identifies Kingdom and Church.

The passages (Matt. viii. 11; Luke xxii. 29–30; xiv. 15 ff.) which speak of sitting at table, eating and drinking in the Kingdom of God are strictly eschatological. They imply a perfected society which will be the object of God's Rule in the coming age.[2] But the social meaning is only derivative. The primary meaning is the perfect communion with God to be enjoyed in the coming age. There is no evidence in the sayings of Jesus that the society formed by those who were called by Him was regarded as the fulfilment or even as the partial fulfilment of the eschatological hope. The community 'seeks' the Kingdom, will 'enter' or 'inherit' the Kingdom, will be 'given' the Kingdom, but is not itself the Kingdom.[3]

The phrase *the Kingdom of God* has been called kaleidoscopic, but the vast and varied figures seen in it are symmetrical and together form a coherent and intelligible picture. Jesus chose the term for His preaching to His own people, because it was their name for the noblest hope

---

Alenu of the *Authorised Jewish Prayer Book* (ed. Singer), 77; the *Alenu* is 'probably pre-Christian in date' (Israel Abraham's note on p. lxxxvii).

[1] *Justification and Reconciliation* (E. tr.), 12. The attempt of T. W. Manson to equate the coming of the Kingdom with Peter's Confession rests on the view that the kingdom may be 'defined as a community whose faith envisages God as their King'. See *The Teaching of Jesus*, 130, 195, 294.

[2] Evidence in Joachim Jeremias, *Jesus als Weltvollender* (1930), 75.

[3] The passages adduced, e.g., by v. Hügel, *Eternal Life*, 62–3, or Holtzmann, *Lehrbuch der N.T. Theologie*, i. 265–74, do not affect this conclusion. See the judgement of H. D. Wendland, op. cit., 142–3.

they had. He emptied it of its unworthiness. He purged it of its merely nationalist or political implications, but endorsed and spiritualized its basic ideas. Because Jesus was a Jew, the phrase to Him still carries the meaning which it had for prophets and apocalyptists. In the north of Switzerland there lie the considerable remains of a Roman theatre. To the visitor who approaches the ruins for the first time they present some most perplexing features. The perplexity deepens till the truth breaks in on him that here he has not one ancient theatre alone, but a theatre which was in course of time remodelled as an amphitheatre and then again altered and used once more as a theatre in later Roman times. So it is with the Kingdom. The term carries with it traces of all the divers uses to which it had been put in the course of time, but when its history has been disentangled, the dominant meaning is clear. The Kingdom for Jesus was the rule of God. It was both eternal and yet only to be fully manifested at the consummation of the present age. It was present, and yet only fully to be realized in the future. It was both moral and religious. It was to be sought and to be given, to be striven for and yet awaited. It was the supreme ideal which spanned both the present age and the age to come. With all the perplexities which for our finite minds still remain clinging to it, the ideal which Jesus Christ proclaimed is the standard by which all Christian theories of perfection are to be measured and judged.

III. The main elements in the ideal of our Lord.

The real problem that faces any reader of the first three Gospels is whether he can unify all the apparently disparate facts that meet his gaze. This is what is meant by 'the attempt to make the portrait of the historical Jesus psychologically intelligible'.[1] It is an attempt to see how all the main elements in the Synoptic tradition cohere in a single personality. But we begin with the presupposition based on the experience of the centuries—that Jesus is a Friend, that He may be known. As an illiterate Indian woman in our own day said when for the first time she had

[1] Bultmann, *Jesus*, 9–10.

heard the story as St. Mark tells it: 'That is what I have been waiting to hear all my life.' The Jesus of the first three Gospels is not altogether a Stranger. Human beings in all centuries and everywhere have found that, after all their wanderings, coming to Jesus is like coming home.

Let us, then, set down eight main elements in the ideal which Jesus held out to mankind.

1. The Kingly Rule of God means the final Victory of Love.

The Rule of God is at hand.   Both for Jesus and His contemporaries, this message meant first of all that the time was near when the God of their fathers, Who had guided the whole course of their history, would win His final victory. As against the opposing domination of the evil power His might would be made manifest. Everything here depends on how Jesus interpreted the character of the working of God.

Schweitzer thinks[1] that Jesus believed in predestination. It is an eccentric view, and the reasons given are flimsy. It is equally difficult to hold that Jesus, or indeed the Apocalyptists, believed in the use by God of the weapon of sheer overwhelming force to bring in the kingdom.[2] Jesus Himself rejected the temptation to coerce men, or even to force their belief by a display of supernatural power. The way left to Him was persevering love. He chose that way because it was God's way. It is true that He rarely used the word, perhaps, as Ritschl[3] said, because in common use the term did not include the particular traits which characterize the true relationship of man with God. That relationship is absolute dependence; we men can never be to God what God is to us. But the divine love determines the parables[4] as well as the practice of Jesus, for every parable is an appeal, and 'a mode of

[1] *Quest*, 352–3; also *Mysticism of Paul*, 102. But it is a predestination that does not really predestinate! See 180, 106, where it is described as not unalterable. For a clearer explanation of predestination in the Beatitudes see H. M. Hughes, *The Kingdom of Heaven* (1922), 85.

[2] Oman, loc. cit.   [3] *Rechtfertigung u. Versöhnung* (3rd ed.), ii. 99–101.

[4] Luke xv; xi. 1–13; cp. Moffatt, *Love in N.T.*, 79–82. Matt. xx. 1–16; for a true interpretation see Anders Nygren, *Agape and Eros* (1932), 61–4.

religious experience . . . its object is not to provide simple theological instruction but to produce religious faith'.[1] The parables, therefore, both provide an example of the method of love in winning men, and contain a revelation of the meaning of the sovereignty of love. The astounding quality of God's love for sinners and the forgiveness which flows from it, can only be seen against the eschatological background of judgement and ultimate victory over evil which are essential elements in the idea of the Kingdom. God is the God of all power and glory. Even in the Lord's Prayer the name of Father is only given to Him when it is joined with the thought of His heavenly seat. It is not an accident that the next phrase in the Prayer is a cry of adoration.[2] There is no place in the teaching of Jesus for a merely immanent God. The very conception of the Kingdom means that Jesus lays the chief emphasis on the transcendence of God.

There is a place near Chamonix in the high Alps where in June the Alpine flowers bloom in profusion—saffron, purple, crimson. The marvel of this garden is not the perpetual wonder that flowers bloom at all, but that such beauty may be seen in those perilous distances, at that height, amid the awful purity of the snow. So, too, the doctrine that God is love is not unknown in other religions, but set against the austere background of perfect purity and transcendent power it becomes a marvel of marvels beyond all telling wonderful. A modern preacher[3] could say: 'Nothing is inexorable but love. Love which will yield to prayer is imperfect and poor. Nor is it then the love that yields, but its alloy. . . . Love is one, and love is changeless. For love loves unto purity. Love has ever in view the absolute loveliness of that which it beholds. . . . it strives for perfection.'

[1] Manson, *Teaching of Jesus*, 73.

[2] Cf. Titius, *Die Neutestamentliche Lehre von der Seligkeit*, i. 105; Wendt, *Die Lehre Jesu* (2nd ed. 1901), 362.

[3] Geo. Macdonald, *Unspoken Sermons*, i. 26. Cp. Frick, *Die Geschichte des Reich-Gottes-Gedankens*, 6–7, and some fine sentences on the latter page. Leipoldt, *Die Gotteserlebnis Jesu* (1927), 35, finds in this *Doppelseitigkeit* the perfection of Christ's idea of God.

From this conception of God, it follows, first, that His complete victory will be the victory of perfect love (Matt. v. 43–8). In the teaching of Jesus there is no setting of love over against holiness, as though one attribute were separate from another in the character of God. Both are fused together in an indissoluble personal unity. A love that was not holy would not be perfect love. And yet there is a certain tension, a bracing austerity, both in the personality and the teaching of Jesus. It is because the grace He declares to men, the flower of eternal life He offers, blossoms at that unearthly inaccessible height. So it was that in the time of His earthly life He preserved His own secret; μυστήριον ἐμὸν ἐμοί. There was something strangely sublime about Him even to the sons of His own house.[1]

> And they were in the way, going up to Jerusalem; and Jesus was going before them: and they were amazed;
> And as they followed they began to be afraid.

And yet He came to fulfil the law, to love perfectly as the Father loves, to bind up the broken-hearted and declare the acceptable year of the Lord.

Second, the victory is to be won in this world.

Thy Kingdom come, Thy will be done, As in heaven so on earth. The prayer is evidence that Jesus taught and expected that this life is to be transformed in the Messianic age. Further, the power of evil is already being brought low; God's victory is already being manifested in the wonders worked by the disciples (Luke x. 18). It is probable, too, that the saying *the Kingdom of Heaven is among you* means that men may enjoy in their hearts the life of the Kingdom which will be vouchsafed hereafter.[2] The ethical sayings are essentially connected with the victory over evil to be won in the present world. The presence of Jesus Himself in His victorious power over the forces of evil is a sign of the actuality of the Kingdom.[3]

---

[1] Mark x. 32; cf. a magnificent paragraph in Jülicher, *Kultur der Gegenwart*, 58.

[2] So E. F. Scott, *The Kingdom of God* (1931), 94, 95; cf. C. H. Dodd, in *Theology* (May 1927), 258.

[3] Matt. xii. 28; 'The parallelism in the Gospels of Parousia-language

Third, the Kingdom is actualized through miracle.

Jesus compared the Kingdom to the ordinary processes of nature, even these are mysterious—'as if . . . the seed should spring up and grow, he knoweth not how'. The common work and life of man are not denied, but ratified and transformed.

But, on the other hand, life in the Kingdom can only be lived on a supernatural level. The ideal is so vast that miracles are demanded to give it actuality and presence. This contrast is but another example of the power to hold in poise the twofold thought of the Kingdom as both Now and Then, of God as both immanent and transcendent. Just because God is infinitely more than visible Nature and the life of man, He must be Master in His own world. And this mastery is shown in miracle. For our present purpose it is immaterial to discuss the authenticity of the miracles recorded in the Synoptic Gospels, or to distinguish between nature-miracles and healing-miracles. Let it once be granted that one of the accounts of the supernatural has at the heart of it an historic happening, some kernel of truth which transcends the ordinary experience of men; and that is enough to prove the validity of the teaching of Jesus at this point. For example, take the conclusion of Johannes Weiss. In his discussion of the Resurrection he reaches many results which are contrary to the cherished convictions of the Church Catholic. But for the origin of the Church he is forced to fall back on the theory of 'visions'. He holds to it that the disciples experienced real 'visions' of the glorified Lord, and that God deliberately chose this way to make the reality of the Living Christ the rock on which the Church was built.[1] And that very belief of his implies the use by God of the supernatural. God enters into History, proves Himself Master of it, breaks the ordinary sequence

and of words, implying the consciousness of αὐτοβασιλεία (Luke iv. 21: σήμερον; Matt. xi. 5; cf. also Mark ii. 20 νυμφίος) signify, once for all, the parallelism of an eschatology operative in time and beyond time.' G. Kittel, in *Theology* (May 1927), 261; and in *Spätjudentum u. Urchristentum* (1926), 130, 131.   [1] *Das Urchristentum*, 21.

of the expected, hints at the unspeakable riches of the Wisdom and Power which lie beyond our ken, raises frail human nature to a new level of possibility. The conversion of Zacchaeus is regarded by the evangelist as a miracle of God. There is a connexion between the miracle of forgiveness and the miracle of making the paralytic walk. Titius has called Miracle the *integrirendes Moment des Reiches Gottes*. Jesus lived and worked with this conception. Miracle is the moment wherein the future Kingdom achieves a present reality, and so unifies and binds the achievement of the present with the hope of the future, the perfect manifestation of the reign of God.

If I by the finger of God cast out devils then is the kingdom of God come upon you.

The distinction of the Synoptic stories of the miraculous from those recorded in the legends and sagas of other wonder-workers is that these supernatural powers of which Jesus was conscious were used, not as a weapon to compel belief, but in compassion, for the love and service of men.[1] It is possible, too, that behind the Synoptic stories lies the belief that the new creation, which was one of the signs of the Messianic age, had already begun in the miraculous activities of Jesus.[2] 'Behold I make the last things like the first things, saith the Lord.'[3]

2. The Givenness of the Kingly Rule of God.

The Kingdom in the sayings of Jesus appears primarily as offer rather than demand. 'It is not a seeking of something for God, but has as its end the blessedness of men.'[4] It is 'given'.

---

[1] Cf. Titius, i. 55. The evidence above is from Luke xix. 9; Mark ii. 10, 11; Matt. xii. 28. Cp. Matt. xi. 3–5; Luke x. 18, and xii. 54–6.

[2] The case for this is set out by Joachim Jeremias, *Jesus als Weltvollender* (1930), 9–10, and *passim*. One may add that the παλινγενεσία (Matt. xix. 28) corresponds with the creation anew of the heavens and the earth (Enoch xci. 16–17). Cf. Schweitzer, *Mysticism of Paul*, 79–80; Rawlinson, *N.T. Doctrine of Christ* (1926), 144, n. 8; Windisch, *Taufe u. Sünde*, 146 ff.; also *Der zweite Kor. Brief*, 189.

[3] *Ep. Barnabas*, vi. 13; see Bauer, *Das Leben Jesu im Zeitalter d. N.T. Apokr.* (1909), 403.   [4] See Strack-Billerbeck, i. 180–1.

Both the final victory and the present anticipation of it are not to be explained as developments within human history. They come from above.

The Givenness of God, as Friedrich von Hügel uses the phrase,[1] means, first, that like all other correspondences with the real, religion begins and ends with what is given. God is reality, though men may not perceive Him. Jesus never attempts to prove the existence of God. God is there—there in the sparrow's fall, there in the sunrise, there in the hard decision, in the taking up of the cross, behind the closed door. Secondly, the Givenness of God is the Grace of God. At the secret centre of all true communion with God is the humbling conviction that God Himself took the initiative. The Grace of God means that we poor frail human beings have been drawn by Him into an awareness of God, into a marvellous intercourse. And that awareness of God, that intercourse, is the end for which our souls were made, without which we must go blinded and hungry all our days; which owes nothing whatever to our own achievement or deserts, but everything to His mercy. Everything in the religious life is given; all things are of God. And this operative religious conviction is encountered wherever we open a book of first-hand experience of God—in the hundred and thirty-ninth Psalm, in the lyrics of Tuka Ram or of the fourteenth-century Kabir, in the hymns of the Wesleys, in the letters of St. Catherine of Siena, in the Sufi mystics, or even in ancient Babylonia, in some far-distant song of praise to the Moon God of Ur.

The essential truth in the eschatological teaching of Jesus is that the Kingdom is not a human achievement, but a pure gift of God.[2] The *summum bonum* is not in this world. Our destiny, our true home, is in that other world which descends out of heaven from God.

Let us apply this conception to the ethical teaching of Jesus.

It is an old difficulty that the Kingdom is presented as 'Gabe' and as 'Aufgabe', as an offer and as a demand. If we

---

[1] *Essays and Addresses*, i. xiii, xiv; 56, 57; *Eternal Life*, 57, 64.
[2] Cf. von Hügel, *Essays*, i. 121, 130; *Eternal Life*, 56–9.

examine the demands carefully, they are so incredible that
they can only be thought of as the gifts of God. The area
of sin is widened to embrace the intention as well as the
outward act; anger is classed with homicide. The goodness of His followers is to exceed the goodness of the
Scribes and Pharisees. They are to love to the uttermost
with a love as persevering as the love of God Himself.
They must take up the Cross. The perfect life may involve
an asceticism of poverty or celibacy. When the disciples
are haled before tribunals they are to have no fear of those
who can only kill the body. Sayings such as these make
us wonder if we have ever known a community where
they could be taken seriously. Self-sacrifice, the uttermost
fearlessness, joy in God, compassion, pity, forgiveness of
enemies, infinite love—all are expected, all are demanded
by this inexorable leader. 'The ethical teaching of Jesus
is an ethical teaching for heroes.'[1] But perhaps the most
impossible of all demands is the condition set for all who
would fain come beneath the rule of God—that they
should become as little children. 'Know you what it is to
be a child? It is to be something very different from the
man of to-day. It is to have a spirit yet streaming from the
waters of baptism; it is to believe in love, to believe in
loveliness, to believe in belief. . . . It is

> To see a world in a grain of sand,
>   And a heaven in a wild flower:
> Hold infinity in the palm of your hand,
>   And eternity in an hour.'

But childlikeness such as this is beyond our willing and
our striving. It can only be given by God.[2]

On the other hand there are the parables of quest, and
the swift, sharp statements of His mission, pulsating with
the energy of the grace of God.[3] Both these sets of passages are essential to the full understanding of the message

---

[1] C. G. Montefiore, *The Old Testament and After* (1923), 241.

[2] See the fine exposition of Johannes Weiss, *Die Predigt Jesu* (1900),
132, 133; cf. Frick, *Reich-Gottes-Gedanke* (1928), 8. The quotation in the
text is from Francis Thompson's *Shelley*.

[3] Mark i. 38; Luke xix. 10.

of Jesus. But there can be no doubt that the offer is the foundation of the demand. The call to action is set within that framework of grace. The kingdom is to be given.

The soul's perfection is thus practised and proclaimed by Jesus as its complete self-donation to the service of man for God, and of God in man. And this self-donation is effected in utter dependence upon God's aid, and yet with the fullest actuation of all the feelings, motives, and passions of chaste fear, tender pity, manly wrath, child-like simplicity and humility, homely heroism, joy in God, love of our very enemies, sense of and contrition for sin, and trust in God's fatherly care even in deep desolation and an agonizing death. . . Plato's wisely wide acceptance of the *Thumos* is here far surpassed by the delicacy, elasticity, and depth with which the entire gamut of the soul's impulsions and necessities is utilized, cultivated, and organized.[1]

There has been a tendency to deny that the teaching of Jesus contains anything new. But surely this ideal of the perfection demanded by God, and given by God to sinful men, has no parallel. It is the quality of the doctrine of grace that is so original.[2] Karl Holl says that he has never understood how any one could doubt that Jesus brought a new conception of God. In the Old Testament God is Father, but Jesus teaches a new kind of divine love, a love that seeks out the sinner, 'A faith in God as Jesus preached it, whereby God gives Himself to the sinner— that was the death of all earnest moral striving, that was nothing else but blasphemy against God. For that the Jews brought Jesus to the Cross.'[3] Let us add to this statement the offer made by Jesus to sinners thus sought

---

[1] Fr. von Hügel, *Eternal Life*, 64–5.

[2] Cf. Moffat, *Grace in the New Testament* (1931), 72.

[3] *Gesammelte Aufsätze*, ii. 10, 11. Cf. for the new thing in the Gospels, Montefiore, op. cit., 253; also *Beginnings of Christianity*, i. 79; *Synoptic Gospels*, ii. 520 ff. Bultmann, *Jesus* (1926), 123 ff., 139 ff., would not agree as to the novelty of Jesus' conception of God. But he sees the distinction of the teaching in the radical way in which Jesus conceived of the grace of God in relation to the sin of man; 133 ff., 183. Cf. H. D. Wendland, *Die Eschatologie des Reiches Gottes bei Jesus*, 11–14, and the excellent treatment in Nygren, *Agape and Eros* (1932), 45–56.

out and brought back—an offer of a new life on a supernatural level. If it be true that in the Synoptic Gospels we
see a heightening of the moral demands on the disciples,
due to the fact that they are measuring their lives by the
character of God Himself, if it be true that these demands
are set in the framework of a gospel of God's grace which
is directed to the sinner, lost and in moral need, it must
follow that these two facts have an inner connexion. With
every divine demand there goes a divine promise. Goguel
appeals to the saying (Matt. v. 48) enjoining perfection to
prove this old precept of evangelicalism. 'Il aurait pro-
noncé une parole entièrement dénuée de sens, si la
perfection divine n'était pas directement accessible aux
hommes.' This means that the God of majesty who once
spoke to the fathers in the thunder and lightnings of
Sinai is also the God within, who reveals Himself in the
heart of those of His children who wish to fulfil His will.
'Jesus does not admit that the life of man cannot be, in its
totality, obedience to God.'[1]

3. The Kingly Rule of God implies the communion of
the individual soul with God.

There is a radical individualism[2] underlying all the
preaching of Jesus, for the ultimate goal in the life beyond
is the vision of God. This implies a fellowship with God
in the present world.

Chief among the gifts of the Messianic age, according
to the prophetic tradition, is forgiveness.[3] And forgiveness as mediated through Himself was a thought present
with Jesus from first to last. The offer was implicit in the
first call to repentance (Mark i. 14–15; cf. Matt. vi. 12).
Various stories prove how deeply embedded in the
Synoptic tradition was the fact of forgiveness as the pre-
rogative of the Son of Man.[4] At the Last Supper, the

---

[1] Maurice Goguel, 'Jésus et les origines de l'universalisme chrétien' in
Revue d'histoire et de philos. religieuses (Mai/Juin 1932), 204, 205.

[2] Cf. Troeltsch, *Social Teaching* (E. tr. 1931), 51–5.

[3] Micah vii. 18–19; Isaiah i. 18; xxxiii. 24; xliii. 25.

[4] See the treatment by H. Windisch, 'Das Erlebnis des Sünders in den
Evangelien' in the *Festgabe für Wilhelm Herrmann* (1917), 292–313.

laying down of His life is expressly connected in His mind with the forgiveness of sins.

He was able to look away from the death whose approach troubled Him to the moral need of men held captive by the consciousness of guilt, so deeply did He feel the horror of that need. . . . In the hour when the conscience of every man who is morally alive inexorably sums up his life, this Man could conceive of His own moral strength and purity as that power which alone could conquer the sinner's inmost heart, and free him from the deepest need.[1]

So far many would agree with us. The forgiveness of sins is one of the chief gifts of the Messianic age. But this admission carries us farther than is generally recognized. In the teaching of Jesus, says H. J. Holtzmann,[2] forgiveness does not depend on sacrifices, but 'on the one condition of moral conversion, a cleansing of the heart and obedience'. The inference is often made that this discovery renders unnecessary anything like the traditional doctrine of the Atonement. This would miss the chief problem which preoccupied the mind of Jesus.[3] Doubtless repentance is the one condition of forgiveness. But is repentance, then, so easy? What if your hearers do not repent? Repentance includes 'moral conversion, cleansing of the heart, obedience'. But even before these are given a man must see himself as he really is. The majority of men do not yet admit that they need repentance. And when their eyes are opened to see themselves as they really are, the work is but begun. How are they to be delivered from that which they themselves are?

The difficulty of repentance is becoming vaster. And vaster, too, becomes the meaning of forgiveness.[4] For Jesus forgiveness could not mean a mere remission of a penalty. Titius[5] has well noted that all the usual expressions—forgiveness of sins, salvation, redemption—are quite inadequate to express what was meant for Jesus by the forgive-

---

[1] Herrmann, *Communion with God* (E. tr. 1906), 89.

[2] *Lehrbuch*, i. 255.

[3] Compare Mark iv. 12 with its reference to Isaiah vi. 9 and 10.

[4] I have tried to work this out in *The Forgiveness of Sins* (1916). See H. R. Mackintosh, *The Christian Experience of Forgiveness* (1927), 187–9.

[5] i. 128.

ness of sins. These formulae are negative. The thing they imply is positive. They mean that the repentant sinner has been freely given all the good things of the Kingdom of God that can be given in the present. He knows the Grace of God. Forgiveness means the reception of the sinner into a personal relationship with God; and means, too, that this relationship is richer than it was before the relationship had been broken.[1] The memory of a great forgiveness is not a barrier but a link.

> Thy sins are forgiven thee . . . Go in peace. (Luke vii. 48, 50.)
> Salvation is come to this house. (Luke xix. 9.)

These sayings must surely mean that the secret of personal religion had been granted through contact with Jesus. But apart from these stories, the glimpses which the Gospels give us into the mind of Christ prove that His problem, whether soon after the beginning of His ministry (Mark iv), or at the end, when He was going up to Jerusalem, was the minds of those who would not or could not repent. He falls back on a passage of Isaiah, full of brokenhearted irony (Mark iv. 12). He saw that men were making Him the instrument of their own hardening.

> For I say, this is death and the sole death
> When a man's loss comes to him from his gain,
> Darkness from light, from knowledge ignorance,
> And lack of love from love made manifest.

The remedy which Jesus adopted was the method of speaking to the crowds in parables. His parables carried God's truth to the mind without forcing a premature moral decision. They deferred the act of refusal. They gave men time.[2] The very imagery chosen implies that men were meant by Jesus to read God's meaning in the world He made, to see God at work in a 'mighty sum of things for ever speaking'. Thus we infer from the choice of this method for His popular teaching that for the mind of Jesus the Kingdom included the thought of direct personal communion of the individual hearer with God.

[1] Schlatter, *Geschichte des Christus* (1923), 200; Gloege, *Reich Gottes*, 115.
[2] Cf. W. R. Maltby, in *Manuals of Fellowship* (No. 8, on Mark iv).

Wellhausen finds other evidence for this in the term *Life* as used in the Synoptic Gospels.[1] In the world to come eternal life—that means 'an individualizing of religion'.

But we must go farther than Wellhausen has gone if we are to prove that the thought of personal communion with God in this life lies at the heart of the message of the Kingdom. In one sense it is strange that we cannot buttress this position by a strong array of *logia*.[2] The saying on solitary prayer is perhaps enough, though it is the only saying. But, like His interest in the ordinary concerns of human life, His passion for bringing individual men and women to know God needs no specific texts to prove it. It is implicit in all His teaching. Without it His life and death are inexplicable. The name for God which He taught us is enough to give us all the historical justification we require. Suppose it be granted, for the sake of argument, that He never used the great confession of Matt. xi. 25–30. Suppose that we only have left to us the Lord's Prayer. If God is Father, He must desire that His children shall have relations with Him. If the relationship is not recognized in the experience of His children, men are not saved. The consciousness of the relationship is not a secondary thing. It is an essential part of the relationship. If my mind was disordered so that I could not recognize my own father or my own children, it would be no comfort in that tragic situation to say that the relation is there all the same. Hence the very preaching of God as Father implies that communion with God is essential to the Kingdom, and can in some measure be enjoyed ἐν τῷ αἰῶνι τούτῳ. In the light of this conclusion we can interpret a characteristic *logion*:

οὕτως λαμψάτω τὸ φῶς ὑμῶν ἔμπροσθεν τῶν ἀνθρώπων, ὅπως ἴδωσιν ὑμῶν τὰ καλὰ ἔργα, καὶ δοξάσωσιν τὸν Πατέρα ὑμῶν τὸν ἐν τοῖς οὐρανοῖς. (Matt. v. 16.)

---

[1] *Einleitung*, 104. Cf. Holtzmann, i. 256. Cf. Mark x. 17; = Luke xviii. 18, Matt. xix. 17; Matt. xxv. 34, 46; Mark ix. 47; x. 23–5; Matt. vii. 14 equiv. to vii. 21 (find the way to life = enter the kingdom).

[2] Cf. Titius, i. 104, who frankly recognizes the absence of texts. C. A. Scott, *Christianity According to St. Paul*, 136–7.

The ideal for a follower of Jesus is that he should so live that by his conduct men should be drawn to thoughts of God. With such implicit meanings the words of Jesus show His concern for the communion of the believer with God, in this present age. In the age to come the vision of God is the ultimate goal.[1]

4. The Kingly Rule of God implies a society. The Ideal is never merely individual.

Jesus set the love and service of man in the centre of His ethical teaching; this fact alone makes it impossible to regard the individualism of His appeal as absolute and unqualified. Again, some of the figures used to describe the eschatological hope (e.g. the marriage feast, the eating and drinking in the Kingdom, the new temple) imply a perfected society.[2] Thirdly, Jesus gathered a community to be the missionaries of the Kingdom. This was His first act at the beginning of His Galilean ministry. To this little flock it was God's good pleasure to give the Kingdom. The limitation of the number of the Apostles to twelve is proof that Jesus regarded His earthly community as the new Israel, the remnant called to share His redeeming work. These three facts are knit together by the conception of God which Jesus taught.

In the last resort, the idea of fellowship springs from the fact that those who are being purified for the sake of God meet in Him; and since the dominating thought of God is not that of a peaceful happiness into which souls are gathered but that of a creative will, so those who are united in God must be inspired by the Will and the Spirit of God, and must actively fulfil the loving Will of God.[3]

5. The Kingly Rule of God allows for the idea of growth.

The presence of the parables of the seed, the mustard seed, and the leaven, in the teaching of Jesus (Matt. xiii. 31–3; Mark iv. 26–32; Luke xiii. 18–21) is a fact of extraordinary significance. Here the Kingdom comes only

[1] Windisch, *Bergpredigt*, 159.

[2] Matt. xxii. 1 ff.; viii. 11 = Luke xiii. 28, 29; xxii, 29, 30; Mark xiv. 58; cf. Klostermann, ad loc.; see Joachim Jeremias, *Jesus als Weltvollender*, 74–81.

[3] Troeltsch, *Social Teaching*, i. 56.

to its full manifestation after a process hidden from the eyes of men. The end is sudden, but the process is gradual. But both the process and the climax are the work of God. The seed grows, but the sower 'knoweth not how'.

The conception of progress is not that which is common to-day. The parables do not say that there is an inevitable tendency in history towards the perfect society, or that the perfect divine end to which creation moves can be evolved from within human civilization and human morality. Indeed, within human history is that other kingdom, hostile to God, whose nature is also being more clearly manifested (Matt. xiii. 25). The Rule of God itself does not evolve. But the chief significance of these parables is, firstly, that time is allowed for the full manifestation of the kingdom over human life. This does away with the 'disconcerting suddenness and discontinuity' which some have discovered in the Synoptic eschatological picture.[1] The final establishment of the kingdom will be no mere display of might. Redeeming love is at the heart of it, and love gives men time.

Secondly, since growth is a property of this order of space and time, these parables represent God's Rule as it operates in the present age, and therefore the implication must be drawn that no one can claim to have reached the goal until the next age. Even if the kingdom is in some sense present, its full manifestation is lacking. From this idea to the thought of progress within the individual religious life is an easy transition, and the step was swiftly taken (Phil. iii. 9–14; i. 25).

In the third place, 'the implied Old Testament references in the parable of the Mustard Seed (to the tree of Nebuchadnezzar's empire in Daniel and the Cedar-tree of Ezekiel) suggest that the life of a society is in view. The common application of the proverb "A little leaven leavens the lump" also suggests the thought of a community.'[2] The Kingly Rule of God creates a society through which He obtains fuller obedience in the world of men.

---

[1] v. Hügel, *Essays and Addresses*, i. 133.
[2] C. H. Dodd, in *Theology* (May 1927), 260.

It is also probable that the evangelist, at least, is thinking of the missionary work of the disciples in gathering out of the world those who expect the full manifestation of the Kingdom.[1] In this case it is surely just as likely that the same thought was in the mind of Jesus. If it was His supreme aim in this parable to make clear to anxious disciples that the divine consummation of the work already begun was certain, in spite of its apparent incompleteness in the present,[2] may he not be thinking of the evangelistic work of His own lifetime? The calling of the disciples cannot be separated from their mission to be fishers of men.[3]

6. The Kingly Rule of God is related to the Present World.

Jesus regarded the present order, or 'civilization', as coming to an end in catastrophe. But He did not therefore believe in its annihilation. There was good as well as evil in it, and the good would be preserved and fulfilled.

His own ethical teaching was no provisional asceticism, of value only in view of the imminence of the end. All His moral injunctions He saw as part of the eternal will of God. He repudiated customs with no inner meaning or life in them. He appeals even from the Mosaic law to the primeval will of God. *From the beginning it was not so* (Matt. xix. 8, expanding Mark x. 6.) From this we see, first, that His positive teaching was given because He saw divine meaning and value in what He Himself enjoined; and, second, that He looked backward to an original purpose of God for man and woman before the beauty of marriage had been marred by sin.

Similarly the Parables prove that His teaching must have been not a denial but an affirmation of the value of this present life. The contrast made in the similitude of the children in the market-place proves the distinction between the stern asceticism of John the Baptist and the glad freedom and joy in life with which Jesus walked

---

[1] Cf. J. Weiss, *Die Schriften*, on Mark iv. 29; Strack-Billerbeck, i. 182, who points out that Hellenistic Judaism still believed in its world-mission.

[2] Jülicher, *Gleichnisreden*, ii. 581.

[3] Schlatter, *Geschichte d. Christus* (1923), 127–8.

among men. The other contrast made by His critics between
His disciples and the disciples of John the Baptist and the
Pharisees gave rise to one of the most lyrical of all His *logia*.

> Can the sons of the bridechamber fast
> While the Bridegroom is with them?

But these two sayings are only striking examples of an
attitude and habit of mind which finds expression in all
His parables.

Nietzsche makes Zarathustra greet the world with
laughter, and finds Jesus void of this joy in life. Swin-
burne sets into the mouth of Julian the cry that the world
has grown grey with the breath of the pale Galilean. How
remote is this phantasy from the One who in the Galilean springtime likens Himself to the Bridegroom, whose
daring unconventionality startles the joyless worshippers
of a joyless God! In His speech Jesus does not set the
axe at the root of the trees. He has no fan in His hand
wherewith He may thoroughly purge the floor. These
fierce metaphors may suffice to clothe His action on the
day when He drove the money-changers out of the Temple,
when His was the white wrath of the Lamb. But the
imagery which comes so congenially to the mind of His
ascetic predecessor is not the natural talk of Jesus. He
saw God behind the flowers. The little dead bird spoke
to Him of the Father. The tree was no mere excrescence
to be hewn down but a habitation for the birds of the
heaven, a fit symbol of the ideal whose advent in glory
He proclaimed. The Sun for Him was the great lamp of
reconciliation, and He tells us that if we look up we shall
see how God loves His enemies. The passion for redemption and the vision of natural beauty do not always go
together. But not even the Poverello of Assisi was more
friendly to the sights and sounds of Nature than Jesus
Himself.[1] Alice Meynell sings to the daisy:

> Slight as thou art, thou art enough to hide
> Like all created things, secrets from me.

---

[1] See on this point Grandmaison, *Jésus Christ*, ii. 111 (E. tr. 225);
Weinel, *Die Bildersprache Jesu in ihre Bedeutung für die Erforschung
seines inneren Lebens* (1900), 10.

It was Jesus who saw that the ultimate reality of the universe could be expressed in parables drawn from the slightest things in Nature. Indeed we may say that the holiness of *things* was not clearly seen until Jesus saw it.

The attempt has recently been made to draw a sharp distinction between the earlier and the later periods of the life of Jesus. It is from Wellhausen that this distinction derives. Take for example the treatment of the Apocalyptic element in the teaching of Jesus by the Baron von Hügel. He traces the distinction between the scenes and sayings which declare or imply a sunny, continuous, balanced temper, and the scenes and sayings which declare a stormy, abrupt, one-sided temper. The distinction is like that between Prophecy and Apocalyptic:

> There is a great difference of general temper between, on the one hand, the great plant parables, the appeal of the lilies and the birds in the Sermon on the Mount, the blessing of the children, and the sleeping in the storm-tossed ship; and, on the other hand, the parables of expectation, the urgent appeals to be ready for the Lord who comes as a thief in the night, and the vehement acts in the Temple, and the terrifying predictions on the Mount of Olives.[1]

The point of change from one set of sayings to the other is set at Caesarea Philippi. It is here that, after Peter recognized His Messianic dignity, Jesus first announces His coming Passion and introduces the Son of Man as coming to judge all the world upon the clouds of heaven.

The subtle change of atmosphere can hardly be denied. There is a new tension in the air; the disciples begin to dread something unknown and ominous. Jesus drives rapidly onward like some great commander in the day of battle, making an assault on the citadel of Judaism with a speed and overwhelming power which make us marvel still. But there is nothing in all this dramatic change of atmosphere to prove a change either in the ethical teaching of Jesus or in His attitude to Nature or to human life. For, in the first place, it is our contention that from the beginning the teaching of Jesus was eschatological. From the moment of His entrance into public life Jesus proclaimed

[1] *Essays and Addresses*, i. 121.

the nearness of the Kingdom of God. It does but make our appreciation of the 'sunny, continuous, balanced temper' more complete[1] when we realize that He who told men to consider the lilies and the birds of the air was charged with a fiery message of urgency. Somehow we must think the two facts together. The instancy was majestic, the speed deliberate.

Secondly, the very proclamation of the Kingdom implies an insistence on choice (Matt. viii. 22; Luke ix. 62).[2] The early conflict with the Scribes and Pharisees, and the sayings of Mark iii (How can Satan cast out Satan?—implying the organization and might of evil as an hostile power) prove that the first period had its storms.

Thirdly, we have even in the Synoptic tradition of the Last Supper a hint of joy. By this farewell meal Jesus is reminded of the Messianic feast in the Kingdom of God (Mark xiv. 25). He sees the old friendship transfigured, carried over into the New Age, transplanted into another world.[3]

Titius reminds us[4] that we may call another witness to the authenticity of this tradition (John xvi. 22).

> Now ye are sorrowful.
> But again I shall see you.
> And your heart shall rejoice.

These sayings sound authentic. They are harmonious with the experience of great saints as they have faced the last enemy. Socrates was not the only martyr who died reaffirming the joy of old friendship, in the expectation of a fuller life beyond.

Our conclusion must be that the two strands of teaching as to the relationship of disciples to those who are seeking the Rule of God are closely intertwined in the thought of our Lord. Both the joy in the goodness of the present

---

[1] Cf. the fine pages in H. Scott Holland, *The Real Problem of Eschatology* (1916); and the proof in Windisch, *Bergpredigt*, 17–18, that the two sets of *logia* are coherent.

[2] Cf. Bultmann, *Jesus*, 31–2.

[3] Cf. v. Dobschütz, *The Eschatology of the Gospels*, 119–20.

[4] i. 60, 61.

order and the self-sacrifice which renounces family ties
for the higher good are set within the eschatological
framework. They both belong to an *Interimsethik*, since all
Christian morality is ἐν τῷ αἰῶνι τούτῳ. Viewed from the
divine side the life of this world is an interim between
creation and consummation, between the beginning of
human history and the end of the temporal order. But in
this interpretation the original meaning of Schweitzer's
phrase,[1] as implying merely a 'world-negating' ethic, is
transcended. For the ethical teaching of Jesus has no other
purpose than that of making intelligible the good and
acceptable and perfect will of God for those who live in
time. And so it has a validity for all time.

7. The Kingly Rule of God is present in Jesus Himself.

In Mark's Gospel the connexion of the Kingdom with
the Person of Jesus is apparent from the very first verse.
The good news begins with the announcement of the nearness of the Kingdom by John the Baptist. And the Kingdom is near because Jesus is there.[2] Wernle thinks that
the strange saying of Mark ix. 1 can only be interpreted
in the light of the Transfiguration scene which follows.
The three trusted followers of Jesus have there, before
their death, seen the Kingdom of God come with power.
Whether this was the original meaning of the word as
spoken by Jesus need not be discussed. But that the
Evangelist so interpreted it is almost an inevitable conclusion.

So too in Q:

Whosoever therefore shall confess me before men, him will I too
confess before my Father in heaven. (Matt. x. 32.)

If thou art the Son of God . . . (Matt. iv. 3, 6.)

. . . A greater than Jonah is here. (Matt. xii. 41, 42.)

The Christologies of the two oldest sources are practically identical.

---

[1] *Das Messianitäts- und Leidensgeheimnis* (1901), 10; cp. *Quest*, 364,
400–1.

[2] See Wernle's criticism of Bousset in *Zeitschrift für Theologie und
Kirche* (18 März 1915). *Jesus und Paulus*, 5.

These facts may be admitted, and yet the historicity of the self-consciousness of Jesus revealed in these passages may be called in question.[1] Let us for the sake of argument grant that some of the *logia* which speak of the Son of Man originally referred to men generally rather than to Himself. Suppose that the rôle of World-Judge assigned to Him in the 'Parable of the Great Surprise'[2] is the product of later reflexion. Yield for the moment, if need be, the supreme word of Matt. xi. 27, 'No one knoweth the Father but the Son.' Still there remains the confession of Peter at Caesarea Philippi. Still we have to reckon with the facts that Jesus rode into Jerusalem with an implicit claim to be Messiah, and as Messiah was crucified under Pontius Pilate. Those facts can only mean that Jesus was aware that in the new order the highest place, next to that of God Himself, had been given to Him by God.

But from the evidence already assembled, we cannot but infer that in His own mind the Kingdom and His own Person were closely knit together. From the often-quoted *logion* about John the Baptist we can safely reason to the mind of Jesus. For Him John was the greatest figure in an age which was passing away. Jesus clearly, even if here only implicitly, claims to belong to the new age. The darkness is passing away; the day is at hand. He feels already the breath of the morning on His face. Well, then, what was His own place? A prophet of the Kingdom? Yes, but John the Baptist was already a prophet, and more than a prophet. A martyr? John the Baptist had sealed his testimony by a martyr's death. From the consciousness of possession of supernatural power, from His message of the presence of the Kingdom, from His discernment that His attitude to the suffering children of men transcended the ordinary piety of the day, He must have been forced sooner or later to the conviction of His own uniqueness in the Kingdom of God.

But the final argument remains to be stated. The secret of Jesus lies in His own awareness of God. Those

---

[1] Cf. the position of G. P. Wetter, *Der Sohn Gottes*, 137–53.
[2] Matt. xxv. 31–46.

critics who have given up their belief in the authenticity of the great word at the end of the eleventh chapter of Matthew have often based their rejection on the impossibility of ascribing to Jesus the claim to a 'metaphysical' sonship.[1] But the saying implies a unique knowledge of God, and the power to communicate it. Is this metaphysical? Both here and in the rest of the New Testament the term denotes a filial relationship. Those who deny the authenticity of this *logion* usually admit[2] that Jesus set the Fatherhood of God at the centre of His teaching. Does not this alone give us all the argument we need for deducing the authenticity of a saying which implies a unique religious relationship of Jesus to God?[3] If the offer of Jesus was essentially the message that God was Father, He must have been aware of God as His own Father, ere He could preach such a message with compelling power. The next step was the perception that sincerely religious people did not see God as Father with that same radiant clearness. And, if Jesus be the greatest religious teacher of all time, He must soon have seen that His consciousness of God was unshared save in so far as He could Himself communicate to others the overwhelming reality of the Fatherhood of God.

The question as to the exact moment when Jesus came to the conviction of His Messiahship can never be answered. It is as probable as any other theory that already at the Baptism, or even before, He had come to a consciousness of a unique call. A recent Roman Catholic work, beginning from the truth which was exaggerated in the work of Wrede, suggests that only by the theory of a reserve, an 'economy' of the truth, can we account for the disconcerting phenomena of the Synoptic story.[4] Jesus knew Himself to be Messiah at the Baptism. But

---

[1] Cf. Adolf Jülicher, in *Kultur der Gegenwart*, 56. See also Klostermann, *Das Matthäus-Evangelium*, 102–3.

[2] See Klostermann, *Das Matthäus-Evangelium* (1927), 56.

[3] Cf. Rawlinson, *The New Testament Doctrine of the Christ*, 252.

[4] Grandmaison, *Jésus Christ*, i. 338. Cf. Schniewind in *Theologische Rundschau*, ii (1930), p. 186: 'Die Synoptikerexegese bedeutet Entfaltung des Messiasgeheimnisses.'

He made no open claim because, by that very act, the
common misconceptions of the reign of God would have
been authorized, and indelibly imprinted on the minds of
men. 'Every one would have contemplated the Chosen of
the Most High through the prism of his own desires and
his own dreams.'[1]

Without adopting a phrase which has unfortunate
associations for English readers, we may make two modifications of this view of Père Grandmaison. In the first
place, He made no open claim to Messiahship because
His own ideal of Messiahship utterly transcended not only
all the current notions but also the Old Testament ideal.
To claim Messiahship from the beginning would not have
been a mere tactical mistake. As language is commonly
used, it would have been a falsehood. Only when His personality was as well known as in this world the personality
of any living man can be known to his contemporaries,
could Jesus claim the highest name they knew.

In the second place, Jesus Himself was not exempt from
His own law, that greatness consists in serving, that he
who loses himself alone can find himself, that only by the
cross can the soul win its true incoronation. A cult of His
Person was what He desired to avoid. He rebuked those
who would say Lord, Lord, and did not do what He said.
When called good, He straightway flung back His ques-
tioner on the thought of the unapproachable Perfection of
God. Even after His secret has been revealed, He says
that the seats of honour by His side in glory are not for
Him to give. How could He lay all the stress on His own
Person until the shadows across His life were lengthening
ominously, and all men could see the risks He ran in
exposing Himself to the hatred of His foes?

Just as the meanings and purposes of a great drama cannot be unified or discerned until the last act, and then are
gradually or suddenly revealed, so the full content of
His teaching on the Perfect Realm cannot be seen except
in the light of His Personality, and especially as that light
streams from the Cross. In that light the varied elements

[1] Grandmaison, i. 315; E. tr. ii. 20.

of His preaching are fused into one. The great words of Jülicher are verified when we seek to apprehend His teaching of the Ideal. 'In His Person, which belonged both to the Present and to the Future, the contradictions are reconciled.'[1] There is no understanding of the originality of any great poet unless this method of resolving contradictions be essayed. It has recently been said of Wordsworth that he 'had something in his own experience in which the whole process and meaning of the French Revolution were implicit. That is why, despite the many influences to which he submitted his mind, he is ultimately a spirit the most truly original. By which I mean, firstly, that more than other men he has his source in himself; and, secondly, in himself, at this source there was a well . . . of consciousness unique in its depth and clearness.'[2] In the same way we can say that there is that in the experience of Jesus in which the whole meaning of the Kingdom was implicit. He is the most truly original of all men because more than any other He has His source in Himself. And at that source there was a well of unique consciousness of God.

The only explanation of the absolute demands which Jesus made, conjoined with the divine grace which He offers, is that He was conscious of *being* the Kingdom. The phrase of Origen,[3] αὐτοβασιλεία, fits the facts. Jesus belongs both to the present, and to the future, Rule of God.

8. The Kingly Rule of God is manifested in the Cross.

The preceding argument has brought us to the last act of the drama. No ideal of perfection would be true either to the facts of life or to the mind of Jesus if it left out the Cross. To this statement humble believers would give immediate assent. Yet it is precisely this element in the ideal which some critics would exclude from the mind of

---

[1] *Die Kultur der Gegenwart*, 58.

[2] H. W. Garrod, *Wordsworth*, 95.

[3] In Migne, *Patr. Graeca*, xiii. 1197; *Comm. Matt.* xiv. 7. See Feine, *N.T. Theol.* (1919), 99; G. Kittel, *Spätjudentum u. Urchristentum* (1926), 130; Gloege, *Reich Gottes u. Kirche* (1929), 144–5.

Jesus until late in His ministry. It is this exclusion which I find most difficult to understand. Natural, indeed, is the reaction from the official dogmatic view which tended to make the life, from beginning to end, a mechanical fulfilment of prophecy. But the picture of a Jesus who had not reckoned with the probability of a violent and premature death is not only contradicted by our available evidence, it is contrary to all the realism of His mind. It would render the call of Jesus to His life work less rich in its insight into the facts of life than the story of the conversion of St. Paul. *I will show him how many things he must suffer.* It is credible that St. Paul had counted the cost, and saw dimly some of the suffering. Was the servant above His Lord? Could not Jesus have seen?

It is probable that the voice at the Baptism is a transcript of the inner experience of Jesus, whereby for the first time the idea of the triumphant Messianic King of the second Psalm was united with the picture of the Suffering Servant passages in Second Isaiah.[1] It is not necessary to maintain that Jesus foresaw that He would die by crucifixion, or that a violent end must be His at the last. But it is necessary to assume that He had already counted the cost at the time of His Baptism. His consciousness of vocation was firmly linked with His conviction of the inevitability of suffering in His chosen path of love. The next step is given in the account of the Temptation. His rejection of all lower, easier, more popular alternatives, is in effect a choice of the way of suffering love. The early resistance which His interpretation of the Kingdom met from the Pharisees (Mark ii) must have forced such thoughts upon His mind. We cannot lay stress on a *logion* like Luke xii. 50 (*I have a baptism to be baptized with*) as we cannot be sure of its date. But it is surely unlikely that One who was accustomed to the daily cost of love should never have counted the possible cost of His supreme mission long before Caesarea Philippi.

We say, then, that for Jesus, whether at His Baptism

[1] Rawlinson, *The N.T. Doctrine of the Christ,* 48, 49; *The Gospel according to St. Mark,* 251 ff.

or later, the ideal of the Kingdom included the Cross. But were the sufferings merely a *condition* of the coming of the Kingdom? This would seem to be the view with which Schweitzer is working, when he claims that Jesus went up to Jerusalem to force His death and so secure the Parousia. There is a certain externality about this view of suffering. A Stoicism which endures in order to attain is one of the most creditable characteristics of very ordinary men. Who would not endure a few days' pain, if that were the sole condition, in order to secure for the race the speedy advent of the greatest ideal ever dreamed by mortal man? Fortunately the power to lay down one's life for others, even for a delusive ideal, is a glorious commonplace of history. There is nothing original, little that is distinctive, in the mind of Jesus about His Cross if that were all He had to bear. But another view is possible. The word of perpetual service as the mission of the Son of Man is joined in the teaching of Jesus with the profound paradox:

> He that will save his life shall lose it.
> He that will lose his life for My sake shall find it.
>
> (Mark viii. 35.)

There is something almost perverse, strangely belittling to the mind of Jesus, in any attempt to explain this word as referring solely to the possible martyrdom of the disciples. Does not the very play upon words imply that, into that appeal for self-abandonment in face of the momentary peril, Jesus is flinging an eternal principle?[1] These sayings can be thought together. Together they must mean that wherever the Kingdom of Heaven is present and realized among men, there is the eternal paradox that 'death to self' is the law of the new order.

> Stirb und werde!
> Denn so lang du das nicht hast,
> Bist du nur ein trüber Gast
> Auf der dunkeln Erde.

[1] Klostermann, *Das Markusevangelium*, 95. 'Das Wortspeil ensteht dadurch dass *das Leben retten* und *verlieren* in doppelter Beziehung gebraucht wird, nämlich in bezug auf die irdische Gegenwart und auf das göttliche Endgericht.' But this need not refer to martyrdom alone.

If Goethe could have seen this, was it not possible for Jesus? Jesus had read Hosea, and penetrated to the innermost heart of the prophet.[1] 'No really sympathetic person ever desired to live sheltered by his own innocence apart from all the fellowship of sin and suffering, but Hosea stands out as a supreme prophetic figure, because he raised this to an understanding in principle of God's rule, and of our share in it, which we can call an atoning service, if by it we understand participation in God's task of reconciliation.'[2]

Wherever the Kingdom is, there is the Cross. The reverse is also true. Wherever the Cross is, there is the Kingdom. Whenever any one makes service to the uttermost and for the highest possible ideal, he knows the ultimate paradox of life; he knows love; and 'love *is* the consciousness of survival in the act of self-surrender, the consciousness of dying for another and thereby of becoming one with that other'.[3] Jesus must have been conscious that His ideal was as yet only partially shared by His intimate friends. And knowing how fruitful suffering is, He sees how His own obedience unto death would release new moral forces at present undreamed of. History bears its own witness to His prevision. There is a power not of this world in the preaching of the Gospel of the Kingdom. There is only one explanation of that fact. His ideal of the Kingdom was nailed to the Cross.

In the early centuries legends gathered round Golgotha, the place of a skull.[4] Here was Adam created, and here was he buried. Here was the centre of the world, and here earth's highest point. Here was the entrance to the underworld, and here the confluence of the hidden streams that feed Jerusalem's living spring. But the Christian instinct for the significance of the Cross rises to a sublimer height

---

[1] As the quotation of Hosea vi. 6 in Matt. ix. 13, xii. 7 proves, when contrasted with Matthew's own use of the Old Testament. See Burkitt, *Gospel History*, 202–3.

[2] John Oman, *The Natural and the Supernatural*, 456–7.

[3] Nettleship, *Philosophical Remains* (1901), 41.

[4] See Joachim Jeremias, *Golgotha* (1926), for a full discussion.

in the inscription in a niche of the Adam's chapel at the foot of the hill: Golgotha has become Paradise. τόπος κρανίου παράδεισος γέγονεν.

CONCLUSION

The apocalyptic language contained in the Synoptic gospels presents one supreme difficulty which so far we have not faced. Jesus seemed to expect His Second Coming suddenly and soon. The edge of this difficulty is removed when the other saying expressly disclaiming knowledge of the day and hour is taken into account. The Rule of God for the Jew, as we have seen, is eternal, and therefore traditional Christian theology has always asserted the simultaneity of God, Who is not confined within the time-process. The prophet who seeks to proclaim the offer of the Ideal Perfection to men can hardly avoid expressions which seem to foreshorten the time-process. 'The very suddenness springs from the need to express a junction between the Simultaneity of God and the Successiveness of man'.[1]   The real question is not so much whether Jesus was mistaken in the language which seems to imply a speedy consummation, but whether He was mistaken in choosing Apocalyptic thought-forms in which to cast His message.

We have seen how He used them in His own royal way, but we must also claim that there is an abiding value in the Apocalyptic forms, which may be summed up in a phrase of Dr. Edwyn Bevan.[2] It is 'worthy of God' that, even in this sphere—the history of Man on this planet— 'good should triumph' and we may draw a hope for the race upon this planet even from the expectation of a millennium. It may well be that just as a glimpse of final truth was given to the poet who wrote Isaiah liii, so there is such a measure of prescience in the chapters of Daniel

[1] Von Hügel, *Essays and Addresses*, i. 133-4. The same principle holds in descriptions of sudden conversions.

[2] I am indebted to his *Hellenism and Christianity* (1921), 201-25, for the thought of this paragraph. Other notable discussions in von Hügel quoted above, Oman (*The Churchman*, July 1932), and E. F. Scott, *The Kingdom of God* (1931), 115-28.

and Enoch dealing with the Son of Man, if the Son of Man works as Jesus worked, in the passion of reconciling love.

To sum up, therefore, we may claim that in the light of such a doctrine of the Ideal the main force of the difficulty is overcome. Jesus chose the apocalyptic message because in that form the profoundest truths of His message could be best conveyed. Better than any other thought-form it expresses 'the junction between the simultaneity of God, and the successiveness of man'. It teaches that the ultimate ideal of man is the pure gift of God; that, in the present age, forgiveness, communion with God, a life of love among men, a life lived on the level of miracle—all flow from the infinite love of the Father. It proclaims that Perfection is never merely individual, and that the ideal for the race must be a society knit together by communion with God. The ideal is inextricably bound up with the Person of Jesus and with the thought of His Cross. And, finally, it teaches that since this world is God's world, the history of man upon this planet will end worthily of Him Who made the world and guided its destiny. The final fulfilment of the divine purpose for man is set in the next life. Yet there is to be a consummation of the present age, and, since the Kingdom of God in this world is not builded by man, we are not to calculate the speed of its coming by the lingering processes, the delays and reverses which men's unbelief have interposed in the past. That past has been lived for the most part without conscious reference to the God whom Jesus revealed. But suppose a richer and more vivid sense of the presence of our Lord than is common among the Christians of to-day. Imagine a society in which that experience might be shared by all. Then it would be true to say that our Lord had indeed returned; that the heaven and the earth would be new; and that a new creation, too, would be the society of human beings who so knew their Lord.

CHAPTER II

ST. PAUL

'Η ἀγάπη οὐδέποτε πίπτει.

1 *Cor.* xiii. 8.

Hic nullus labor est, ruborque nullus;
Hoc iuvit, iuvat, et diu iuvabit;
Hoc non deficit, incipitque semper.

Petronius Arbiter.

WELLHAUSEN himself confessed that, when all is said, no man has understood Christ Himself so deeply and so thoroughly as Paul.[1] I hope to offer a further proof of this by outlining the teaching of St. Paul on the Ideal of the Christian life, and then by comparing it with the teaching of Jesus Christ.

That ideal was eschatologically conceived. There is something dramatically appropriate in the fact that the earliest writings in the New Testament are the letters to Thessalonica. Just as Jesus, following John the Baptist, had proclaimed the nearness of the Kingdom, so the first glimpse we have of the dealing of any Christian missionary with the Church he has founded shows them one in their expectation of the end of the age. Those letters give us, moreover, an overwhelming impression of the reality of God for the mind of writer and readers alike. In the first few verses of the first epistle a new note in Greek literature is sounded. This is a man whose whole being is centred in the living God. He lingers on the very word with joy. *You turned unto God from idols, to serve a living and true God.* 'The language of the heart was born again' with Paul of Tarsus, says Norden.[2] A new sense of God has visited the soul of man, and it is linked with a vast ideal, so near that it is now knocking at the doors.

It is true that in the other letters the expression of the eschatology is not so pronounced. There are obvious reasons for this. In the church of Thessalonica the

---

[1] *Isr. und Jüd. Geschichte*, 319.

[2] Norden, *Antike Kunstprosa*, ii. 459, quoted by Glover, *The Christian Tradition*, 107–8.

practical problem had been raised. Why carry on the
ordinary business of life when the End is so near? Paul's
answer accounts for the emphasis on eschatology in these
two letters. Seldom do we encounter the expression so often
used by Jesus: The Kingdom of God.[1] But it would be
a mistake to infer that the original idea of the Kingdom of
God has been quietly set aside.[2] Just because for Jesus
His Ideal was inseparably bound up with His own Person
and His death, Paul found a more natural and more fruitful method in his mission preaching to substitute for the
phrase The Kingdom of God, the more personal word,
Jesus Christ and Him Crucified. But the eschatological
foundation of his Gospel is nevertheless often uncovered
for us to see. Hope is set among the cardinal virtues
because Christ is not only a present possession but a future
goal.[3] Paul's own yearning is for that fuller life, where we
walk not by faith but in the blaze of beatific vision.[4] The
prelude will be the Judgement-seat of Christ,[5] which is
the supreme and future counterpart and consummation
of all that is included in justification by faith. Even the
Spirit is but a pledge and instalment of the life to come.[6]
Jesus Christ is the divine 'Yes' to all the promises of God.
It is because He is the 'Yes' that God has confirmed both
Paul and his hearers *in Christ*, and stamped them with His
seal and given them the Spirit, as an ἀρραβών in their
hearts.[7] It is in the chapter (Rom. viii) which outlines
most completely the Ideal of the Christian life that the
eschatological hope finds a full expression. Those who
have received this ἀπαρχή are all the more intent on its consummation, which will be the full redemption of their
personality.[8] In this chapter, as we shall see below, the

---

[1] This is possibly due to Paul's desire to avoid the danger that his Hellenistic converts might misconstrue the phrase in a political sense. Cf. Acts
xvii. 7. So Titius, ii. 33.

[2] Ritschl, ii. 297–300.   [3] 1 Cor. xiii. 13.

[4] 2 Cor. v. 7.

[5] 2 Cor. v. 10.   [6] 2 Cor. v. 5.   [7] 2 Cor. 1. 20–2.

[8] Rom. viii. 23. σῶμα is used for personality; cf. C. A. Scott, *Christianity
according to St. Paul*, 209. Johannes Weiss, *Der Erste Korintherbrief*, 163,
164, on 1 Cor. vi. 16.

vision of Paul is widened to embrace the universe. The whole creation moves to that glorious destiny awaiting us at the day of the unveiling, when the sons of God shall come to their own.[1]

It is clear that for Paul it is the thought of that vast drama of the future, that immense change and con-summation, that gives meaning and power to the present. Shelley could sing

> Life like a dome of many-coloured glass
> Stains the white radiance of eternity.

Paul would have said that it was the eternal world, the immeasurable future, that gave to this present life all its variegated colour. It is this sense of eternity that made Paul into the evangelist who swept through that Graeco-Roman world with a message that answered all its deepest need, 'yea, every bygone prayer'. When he spoke of salvation he set its beginning right back in the infinite spaces of the past. God 'ordained salvation for us before the foundation of the world'. But its full completion was at hand, near to that generation on whom the ends of all the aeons had come. Could any message bring eternity nearer, to colour with its dazzling light that old world which, as Mommsen said, 'not even the richly gifted genius of Caesar could make young again'?

In this setting of his message Paul was one with His Master. But inevitably there was one supreme difference. Jesus regarded the Kingdom as bound up with His own Person. He could look forward to His death as releasing new sources of power hitherto undreamed of. Paul, on the other hand, could point to the perfect life as already lived, to the Ideal as already realized in a Person, and supremely revealed in His Cross, His Resurrection, His gift of the Spirit of power.

I. THE NEW FACTS

(i) The Cross and the Resurrection.

When St. Paul cried out: *I have been crucified with*

---

[1] Rom. viii. 19.

*Christ; and yet I live. And yet it is not I, but Christ liveth
in me,* something new had come to pass in the history of
religion. The word *faith* is the key to unlock the door of
that mystery. The word is used in pre-Christian books
to mean a trust that the promises of God will be fulfilled
in the distant future.[1]   This sense is also found in the
Pauline letters. In various passages the word is used of
God, and is equivalent to fidelity, loyalty to a covenant.[2]
But in the characteristic Pauline sense the word faith has
broken free from all its Old Testament associations. It is
true that the full consummation of all that Christ brings is
still in the future. But faith here is present religious life,
and is definitely related to an historical Person of the
recent past, Whose love was as the love of God, and Who
died upon the Cross, and Whose love and death have a
personal reference to a man who is living now.

It is true that a Jew might have said: 'Our faith, too, has
a reference to the past and a meaning for the present. Is
not our literature full of allusions to the deliverance from
Egypt? And when we trust in God, do we not think of
One who has wrought salvation for us throughout our
history and guides us even now?' But such an answer
would not touch the distinction of the Pauline conception
of faith. Here in primitive Christianity we find the word
related for the first time to one particular Person of the
recent past, and especially to certain historical events.
From henceforth the word includes an acceptance of such
and such historical events as having really happened.

> If thou shalt confess with thy mouth that Jesus is Lord;
> And shalt believe in thy heart that God raised him from the dead,
> Thou shalt be saved. (Rom. x. 9.)

The context of this passage is dominated by the thought
of the presence of salvation here and now. 'The word is
nigh thee, in thy mouth, and in thy heart: that is, the word
of faith, which we preach.' So, too, faith in Gal. ii. 20

---

[1] 1 Macc. ii. 52; cp. 4 Macc. xvi. 20–2; Jubilees xvii. 15, 18; and see
Philo. *Quis. Rer. Div. Heres,* 90 ff.
[2] Rom. iii. 3; 1 Cor. i. 9; 2 Cor. i. 18; 1 Thess. v. 24.

includes a decisive reference to the present. 'The life that I now live, I live in faith.'

This faith is the primary function of the religious life. How much does it include? 'It includes renunciation of all past desire to earn salvation by his own merit, repentance for the past, confidence that God is really willing to forgive sin, the child-like trust, with which he places himself in the hands of God, the thankfulness towards Him 'who gave Himself for me', the love which seeks no longer anything for itself but all for Him, the obedience to all the claims that He may make, the resolve to live a new life in the service of God and of His Son.'[1] The criticism has been passed on this analysis of faith that it ascribes to faith what really belongs to the contents of the salvation which faith apprehends. But Dr. Anderson Scott answers his own criticism when he says[2] that 'this transformation of religious relationships and of ethical outlook was in all its parts ideally complete at the moment when faith had shot forth a hand to accept and to grasp. Practically, of course, the experience was a double one . . . Christians though really "spiritual" might still show many tokens of being unspiritual. But in essence the religious and ethical situation had been completely changed.'

So far the analysis of the single word faith has sufficed to prove our present contention. The ideal proclaimed by Jesus was also preached by Paul. But the death and resurrection of Jesus had made an inevitable difference. New sources of power had been released. The Ideal of a new life lived on a supernatural level was firmly rooted in history, and was offered to men as a present possession, here and now.

(ii) The Experience of the early Christian communities.

The next new fact to be reckoned with is the existence of various Christian communities in Palestine and Syria, with a new religious experience. In the minds of the early Christians, the Spirit was conceived as a supernatural power which lifted them to ecstasy, worked

---

[1] J. Weiss, *Das Urchristentum*, 142.
[2] *Christianity according to St. Paul*, 111.

miracles, revealed the secrets of the Most High. These supreme moments, which were not lacking in the lives of individual disciples, commonly came when the church was assembled together.[1] But while the minds of the rank and file, then as now, tended to linger on the unusual, the sensational, the ecstatic, there was at least one in those communities who possessed the power to discriminate, and who was able to see the supreme work of the Spirit in the grasping of the whole personality by God, and in the creation of a new moral life. I cannot agree with Bousset[2] that this setting of the Spirit at the centre of the whole religious life of the individual and of the community was a complete μετάβασις εἰς ἄλλο γένος. It is likely that there was a real antithesis between the naïve popular conceptions of many in those early communities and the conceptions of their spiritual leaders. There is hardly a minister of any little congregation, where there is a real religious life, who could not draw out a similar antithesis between the views of the many and the views of the few. But such an antithesis does not prove that the primitive conception of the Spirit which reigned in the church was unconnected with the higher conceptions which we meet in the epistles. The contrary is the case. Look at the very church where the antitheses of Bousset would be truest—the church of Corinth. When we are allowed a glimpse of the dealing of Paul with those poor dissolute creatures, who could only too easily fall back after a few days' forgetfulness into the old disastrous sins, we see that in their minds the Spirit is inalienably associated with the new moral life. 'Don't you know', he says[3] (1 Cor. vi. 19, 20), 'that your body is the shrine of the Holy Spirit?' The whole point is that the man does know. He has been lifted out of mire by the awareness of God which had come to him in Christ.

The book of Acts gives us evidence that in the interpretation of the work of the Spirit there were ethical

---

[1] Acts iv. 31.

[2] *Kyrios Christos*, 112.

[3] Cf. the careful discussions in F. Büchsel, *Der Geist Gottes im Neuen Testament* (1926), 249–56; P. Feine, *Der Apostel Paulus* (1927), 290–6.

values included from the very beginning. (1) Boldness of
speech is considered to be the work of the Spirit, and this
is connected with Jesus.[1] Other moral virtues are mentioned, as the immediate result of being filled with the
Spirit—unity of spirit, and generosity in sharing their
goods with one another,[2] joy and singleness of heart in the
common ways of life[3] (μετελάμβανον τροφῆς ἐν ἀγαλλιάσει
καὶ ἀφελότητι καρδίας). Evangelistic power is always connected with the Spirit.[4] (2) Whenever they seek for an
explanation of the strange power that has come to them
their minds immediately refer it to its source in Jesus[5]
(Acts ii. 22–36; iii. 13; iv. 7–12, 30; v. 29–32, 40–2).
This habit could not have been without its moral effect.
The Spirit of power was connected in their minds with
their ideal of Perfection. (3) To them the revelation of
God in the earthly life of Jesus, in His risen life, in His
gift of the Spirit, forms a coherent and intelligible whole.
Their minds can piece the different phenomena together,
and to them it all makes sense. Thus it would be false
to say that they associate the work of the Spirit exclusively
with ecstatic and extraordinary phenomena. Again, the
relation of Paul with Barnabas (Acts xi. 22–6), and
through him with the Twelve, forbids the supposition that
there was any conscious gap in religious experience between Paul and the early Christian community. When
Paul appeals to Peter it is on the common ground of the
supreme value of faith.[6] As Wernle says: 'Faith, and
not the cultus, is the token of early Christianity.'[7] On the
sole ground of faith, the gifts of the Spirit had been poured
out on those primitive communities.

Our conclusion is that the diffusion of that religious
experience known in the New Testament as the gift of the
Spirit will be likely to influence St. Paul's presentation of

---

[1] Acts iv. 8, 13, 29–31; v. 29, 40–2; vi. 10; vii. 55–60.
[2] Acts iv. 32–4.
[3] Acts ii. 46.   [4] Acts ii. 47; v. 14.
[5] F. Büchsel, 256.
[6] Gal. ii. 16. Cf. Acts xv. 7–12, 24–6.
[7] *Zeitschrift f. Theologie u. Kirche* (18 März 1915),64.

the ideal. If he emphasizes freedom from sin, his doctrine can only be understood in the light of that which had actually happened in the communities which he knew.

(iii) The Experience of St. Paul.

The third new fact is St. Paul's own experience. It is now almost universally admitted that the formula, ἐν Χριστῷ, which occurs 164 times in the Pauline epistles, is of decisive importance in any discussion of the religion of St. Paul.[1] Even if some of the examples which Deissmann has interpreted in the mystical sense are capable of another exegesis, there remain enough to prove that in the idea ἐν Χριστῷ we have something entirely new, and supremely characteristic of Paul. It is singular that if he speaks so often of εἶναι ἐν Χριστῷ he speaks rarely of εἶναι ἐν θεῷ.[2] He avoids precisely that element in the Hermetic mysticism which was dangerous, while he takes up and emphasizes that element in the Christian religious tradition which was unique.

And it is to be noticed that in the most spontaneous of all his religious confessions (Gal. ii. 20) after he has said: *I live no longer but Christ lives in me*, he immediately goes on to speak of *the life I now live in the body*. This life, he says, I live by faith. There is no thought of complete absorption. As Johannes Weiss[3] has said, the whole confession is quite compatible with a 'Thou and I' religion.

Life, with all the riches of its content, life in God and to God, had moved forward from the far horizon which it has occupied for Jewish hope—moved forward and enveloped him as an atmosphere, penetrated him as the fabric of a new personality. All that he had been taught to expect as the contents of a distant salvation was already his—peace with God, freedom from the dominion of sin, the gift of the Spirit—righteousness and peace and joy in the Holy Spirit. Of this Paul could have no doubt. It was witnessed by every day's experience.[4]

---

[1] See Johannes Weiss *Das Urchristentum*, 360; Anderson Scott, *Christianity according to Paul*, 151–4; Bricka, *Le Fondement Christologique de la Morale Paulinienne* (1923), 41–2.

[2] Bousset, 119; Schweitzer, *Mysticism of Paul* (E. tr. 1931), 3–5.

[3] *Das Urchristentum*, 361.

[4] C. A. Anderson Scott, op. cit., 137–8.

Here, in the Christ-mysticism of Paul, is another influence tending to root the idea of the Kingdom of God more firmly in this present world. The βασιλεία τοῦ θεοῦ is the κυριότης Χριστοῦ. Paul never gives up his dominant conviction that the full consummation of the message he preaches is beyond this present age, in the age that is to come. But he renders more explicit the last two characteristic marks of the kingdom which we have already noted in the teaching of Jesus, and which could only be brought into the Christian consciousness, as vital elements in religion, after the experiences of Calvary and Pentecost.

A second main category in Paul's religious experience is Spirit. I have already suggested that the contrast between the view of the Spirit given in the early chapters of Acts and the view of Paul has been over-pressed. Can we accept the further contention that Paul borrowed from current Hellenistic dualism his contrast between flesh and spirit? Did he believe that the flesh was inherently evil,[1] or that the Spirit-Christ is conceived as a quasi-material atmosphere or fluid, into which the Christian enters, thus undergoing a hidden or mystical change of nature?

The question whether Paul regards the body as inherently evil is vital, not only for our present purpose, but for any interpretation of the Pauline Gospel. On this view there can be no genuine salvation except through the release of the soul from the body, though possibly a transient and fleeting freedom from evil could be attained by ecstasy or some incomprehensible magical change.

The most exact and exhaustive study (so far as I know) of the meaning of the words is the book of Professor Burton, *Spirit, Soul, and Flesh* (1918). His conclusions would seem to have settled the question.[2] The first is that nowhere in Hellenistic thought up to this time is there any evidence of a definitely formulated doctrine of an ultimate

---

[1] E. F. Scott, *Spirit in N.T.* (1923), 128–35; W. Morgan, *Religion and Theology of Paul* (1917), 16 ff., 27; Reitzenstein, *Hellenistische Mysterienreligionen* (3rd ed. 1926); Bousset, *Kyrios Christos* (1921), 129–34; *Religion des Judentums* (1926), 405.

[2] Reitzenstein takes no account of them, even in the 1926 edition.

ethical dualism of spirit and matter. The Gnostics held it
later. There is a tendency to dualism in Plato's thought,
and he sometimes disparages the body as a hindrance to
philosophical thought. 'There was an intellectual soil out
of which there might easily spring up the doctrine that
embodied man is *ipso facto* a sinful man. But apparently
it had not yet sprung up.'[1] Second, the New Testament
usage is not simple but highly developed. The 'flesh' can
even mean at last the whole complex of life's relationships
into which one enters by being born; it can do much, but
only the spirit can produce the true, the perfect (Phil. iii.
3 ff.). Again it has an ethical connotation including the
impulses to evil which, like the good but inadequate things,
seem to be born in us (Gal. v. 16–25). Paul does not
ascribe compelling power to 'flesh' in this sense, because
faith and the resultant fellowship with God can overcome
it (Rom. vi. 1–2; Gal. v. 16, 22, 23), and he retains his
Hebrew belief that the soul could not be wholly happy
without a body (1 Cor. xv; 2 Cor. v).

Burton concludes: 'The body is inferior to the spirit
and the occasion of temptation. But embodied man may,
by the power of the Spirit, triumph over all evil tendencies.'

Reitzenstein has sought[2] to explain all the Pauline references to πνεῦμα as derived from pagan ideas. But in not a
single case has he attempted to connect the ethical fruits
of the Spirit, the love, joy, and peace which meant so much
to Paul, with any pagan parallels. The reason for his
omission is simple. The pagan parallels are not there.[3]

Can it be said that[4] the Spirit effects a deification of
human nature? The case rests on 2 Cor. iii. 18: *We all,
with unveiled face gazing as in a mirror at the glory of the
Lord, are being transfigured into the same likeness, passing from
one glory to another; for this comes from the Spirit of the Lord.*[5]

---

[1] Burton, 193.

[2] Op. cit., 308 ff. General criticism of Reitzenstein and Bousset in
Schweitzer, *Mysticism of Paul*, 26–33; Karl Holl, *Ges. Aufsätze*, ii. 18–27.

[3] Cf. Karl Holl, 25.   [4] Reitzenstein, 357–61.

[5] Kurt Deissner, *Paulus u. die Mystik seiner Zeit* (1921), 111–14, shows
how distinct from the Hellenistic conception is the idea of Paul here.

Amid the swift darting hither and thither of Paul's
mind in this passage we can see certain leading ideas.

I can use freedom of speech with you. You and I share the same
religious privilege which the Jews have forfeited. The veil which
Moses wore in his intercourse with them is now really lying on their
own hearts when they hear Moses read. There is truth in this old
story—that a human being (Moses) once saw God without a veil.
You remember the words used: *Whenever [Moses] shall turn to
the Lord, the veil is taken away.* The Lord here means the Spirit.
You and I know the Spirit's power. All of us with unveiled face can
gaze on the glory of God, mirrored in Christ, and by gazing on him
we are all transformed.[1]

The metaphor of the mirror is used in another passage
(1 Cor. xiii. 12) on the goal of the Christian life. There
the stress is on the inadequacy of our present vision,
here on its glory. But there is a hint here that the full
vision is reserved for the world to come. The 'meta-
morphosis' (the word used for the Transfiguration in
Mark) is interpreted by yet another Pauline passage; it is
by 'the renewing of our mind'. The Spirit creates us anew,
and refashions us in Christ's likeness ($\epsilon i\kappa \omega \nu$), the word used
in Genesis LXX for God's creation of man in His own
likeness. There is no suggestion that human nature is
'deified'. The transformation is into 'the same image as
that which is reflected in the mirror, the image of the perfection that is manifest in Christ.'[2] These considerations
bring us to the conclusion that Paul was one with his
Master in proclaiming an ideal life of communion with
God which was at once the ultimate goal, and fragmentarily, but yet actually, could be lived in the world. The
vision was in a mirror, but it was a real knowledge of One
who would some day be seen face to face.

[1] The above interpretation of $\kappa \acute{\nu} \rho \iota o\varsigma$ in this passage as referring to
Yahweh in the Old Testament quotation seems justified. I owe it to my
colleague, Dr. H. M. Hughes, art. in *Expository Times*, Feb. 1934,
pp. 235–6. See Rawlinson, *New Testament Doctrine of the Christ*, 155.

[2] Plummer, *C.G.T.*, ad loc.

II. THE DOCTRINE OF THE IDEAL

Let us now attempt a summary statement of St. Paul's doctrine of the goal of the Christian life, so far as it can be put in a systematic form.

1. In the first place, he distinguished between absolute perfection, which was reserved for the future (1 Cor. xiii. 10; Phil. iii. 12–14), and a relative perfection which he regarded as realizable by himself and his converts. Indeed, that relative perfection was the goal of apostolic work (Col. i. 28; iii. 14; iv. 12; 1 Cor. ii. 6; Eph. iv. 12–13).

2. The absolute perfection, the final destiny of believers, is described as the face-to-face vision of God. It is contrasted with the obscurer vision to which believers now attain (1 Cor. xiii. 12). We may identify this final destiny with 'the prize of the high calling of God in Christ Jesus', and the resurrection from the dead, to which St. Paul hoped to attain (Phil. iii. 14 and 11).

Such a description of absolute perfection should preserve us from the error into which many scholars have fallen, of assuming that St. Paul's admission that he has not attained the final goal is equivalent to an admission that the whole course of the Christian life in this world must be marked by sin.[1]

3. The relative perfection attainable in this life is a progress towards the goal of the final destiny. It is tempting to interpret St. Paul, as many do,[2] as saying that the essence of this relative perfection is the striving after absolute perfection, and to leave it at that. But such a description would be inadequate. There is a positive gift of God to the believing soul.[3] The Christian walks by the Spirit, and so can fulfil the law of Christ (Gal. vi. 2). The positive marks of the Christian experience will be set down later. For the moment we note that St. Paul's doctrine of perfection is essentially a doctrine of growth. This is proved by his thanksgivings and his intercessions, his hopes for his converts, his warnings, and the unstudied utterances of

[1] e.g. Warfield, *Perfectionism*, i. 180, quoting Clemen.
[2] e.g. Juncker, *Die Ethik des Apostels Paulus* (1904), i. 202, 221.
[3] Cp. E. Cremer, *Das vollkommene gegenwärtige Heil in Christo*, 112.

his desires. He prays that he may perfect that which is lacking in the faith of the Thessalonians that they may increase and abound in love, that their desires and deeds may be brought to fulfilment (1. iii. 10–11.; 2. i. 11). He speaks of a transformation from one glory to another, a renewal of the mind, a daily renewal of the inward man (2 Cor. iii. 18; iv. 16; Rom. xii. 2). But in these passages he does not draw the conclusion that the increase in love or faith implies that they had been living in sin before that increase was given.

4. Is the sinlessness of the Christian part of the Pauline doctrine of perfection? Does he attribute sinlessness to his converts? This issue was raised in 1897 in an immature and one-sided book by a brilliant young Swiss theologian.[1] Wernle subsequently modified or abandoned his earlier views. The resultant discussion has been described and reviewed by the Calvinistic theologian Benjamin Warfield, who is, of course, uncompromising in his opposition to any doctrine of perfection. The chief result of the discussion was the great work of H. Windisch, *Baptism and Sin in the Oldest Christianity up to Origen*, published in 1908. His main contention is that according to the doctrine of the primitive Church, Christians are in their real nature sinless men, and are expected to live in this world without sin. It would be a mistake for the English reader to conclude that the vigorous polemical writings of Warfield have completely refuted Windisch. It would be truer to say that the problem thus raised has not yet been solved.

A few conclusions may be set down here, to modify the extreme position taken by Windisch or other writers.

(*a*) St. Paul fully recognized that there were sins in the lives of Christians. To say, as Wernle originally said,[2] 'Paul does not wish to see the problem of sin in the life of Christians; therefore it has no existence (*also ist es nicht da*)' is absurd. It would have been impossible for Paul to

---

[1] Wernle, *Der Christ und die Sünde bei Paulus*. See the summary of his views in B. B. Warfield, *Perfectionism* (1931), i. 151–76.

[2] p. 105.

say: A Christian does not sin. One passage alone is enough: 'I fear . . . lest when I come again, my God should humble me before you, and I should mourn for many of them that have sinned hitherto, and repented not of the uncleanness and fornication and lasciviousness which they committed.'[1]

(b) St. Paul does not speak of himself as sinless after conversion. The passages adduced as proving a claim to sinlessness (1 Thess. ii, 10; 1 Cor. iv. 3) are unconvincing. The evidence of Acts xxiv. 16–21 may prove that he was willing to admit wrong-doing ($\dot{a}\delta i\kappa\eta\mu a$), or at all events that he is not regarded as entirely blameless even by the author of the Acts (xv. 39) to whom he is a hero. But it is a striking fact that in his epistles we meet no heartfelt utterances of deep contrition for present sin such as are common in Evangelical piety, under the influence of the Reformation. Titius[2] can only find two passages (1 Cor. xi. 31, 32; Rom. xiii. 12) which even remotely hint at a consciousness of sin in St. Paul's Christian experience. But these passages are very dubious evidence. It seems certain that the famous description of the divided mind in Rom. vii must refer to his experience before conversion.[3] St. Paul is speaking there of the position 'under the law'. But the law has been brought to an end by Christ.

(c) The passages which speak of the continuance of struggle in the Christian life[4] do not hint that defeat is the inevitable end of struggle. His reference to his own self-discipline (1 Cor. ix. 24–7) does not imply a consciousness of sin,[5] but rather the severity and exhilaration of racing for the heavenly wreath.

---

[1] 2 Cor. xii. 20–1. Windisch, 151, is in difficulties over this passage. See Warfield, i. 260–2. Other passages are Romans xiii. 14, where Warfield (254–6) is less fortunate in his criticism of Windisch (191–2); Gal. v. 25–6; vi. 1.

[2] *Die N.T. Lehre von der Seligkeit*, ii. 83. Juncker (222) adds 2 Cor. vii. 1.

[3] Cf. C. H. Dodd, *Romans* (1932), 104–8. The attempt of Kümmel, *Römer Sieben und die Bekehrung des Paulus* (1929), to show that there is no autobiographical reference is not proven.

[4] As against Windisch, 172. Cp. Warfield, 251.

[5] As Titius, ii. 81, maintains.

(*d*) Indeed, it is one of these cries of struggle that must be classed among the utterances which create our problem. Paul promises complete victory.

'Walk by the Spirit and you will certainly not fulfil (οὐ μὴ τελέσητε) the desire of the lower nature. For the desire of the lower nature is against that of the Spirit, and the desire of the Spirit is against that of the lower nature; for these are opposed to each other, that you may not do whatever you will' (Gal. v. 16–17). There is a third way, he says, distinct from that of legal obedience, distinct from that of yielding to the impulses of the lower nature.[1] *If you are led by the Spirit, you are not under law* (v. 18). It is the way of faith and love, it is life under the control of the Spirit.[2]

It is for such a life as this that Paul directs his intercessions to God. For the Thessalonians (1. iii. 13) he prays that God may 'fix' or establish their 'hearts in holiness, so that they are blameless in the sight of God at the Parousia'.

The word στηρίξαι implies that the moral cleansing which is now proceeding will simply be confirmed by the Parousia. The use of the word 'heart', which in Hebrew psychology is the seat of the thoughts, implies that Paul has in mind a complete inward cleansing of the source whence the evil might proceed.[3] He recognizes that growth in love is possible, even when the divinely taught love is already in their lives (1. iv. 9–10).

A new distinction[4] meets us in the Corinthian letters, forced on Paul by the facts—that between σαρκικοί and πνευματικοί (1. ii. 6, 14–16; iii. 1–4). There is a development from the lower stage to the higher. But both classes know the reality of the gift of the Spirit. The danger to the soul from any continuing in sin is more forcibly expressed than ever before (1. iii. 16, 17). The calling of the com-

---

[1] The passage, of course, is proof that Paul knew well enough that some of his readers were still falling into sin. So Kurt Deissner, *Paulus u. die Mystik* (1921), 38, as against Windisch, op. cit., 123.

[2] So Burton (in *I.C.C.* ad loc.), 302.

[3] Windisch, 107.

[4] Windisch, 123–4.

munity to be sinless is set forth clearly (1. i. 2–9). The
very remedies he proposes (clear out the old leaven, 1. v.
6–7) prove that his faith in his ideal is unshaken. The
words which follow show how near he believes the ideal
to be, even to the sinning Corinthians. 'Because Christ
has been sacrificed for us, *let us keep the feast.*' He is not
thinking of a distant future but of the present. He
expects of men as sinful as the Corinthians had been
(1. vi. 9–11) that they shall display gifts of spiritual wisdom because they have known the Spirit of God (1. vi. 19,
20; xii. 8). The task of walking in the new way demands
all the powers of the personality.

In the second letter the testimony of his own conscience
is set forth again in unmistakable language (2. i. 12–14).
The demands which he made to secure the purification of
the community have been met. The sinlessness expected
of the Christian is now put in its true setting. εἴ τις ἐν Χριστῷ
καινὴ κτίσις· τὰ ἀρχαῖα παρῆλθεν, ἰδοὺ γέγονεν καινά. τὰ δὲ
πάντα ἐκ τοῦ θεοῦ . . . (2. v. 17, 18). The Christian is the
new creation which was expected in the Messianic time.[1]
There is jubilation in the air. St. Paul knows that the new
age is beginning, but it has not fully come.[2]

The Corinthian Church was far from the ideal; but the
ideal itself remains unshaken and inviolable in the mind
of Paul. Perhaps the surest proof of this is the way in
which he deals with erring individuals. He assumes that
each of them knows the reality of the power of the Spirit;
knows enough of the Spirit to be sure in his inmost heart
that sin and an experience like that were utterly incompatible. 'Don't you know?' Paul asks (1. vi. 19; 1. iii.
16). He says it to those who a short time ago had been
living in sins like those mentioned in 1. vi. 9–11. The
whole point of his question is that such an one does know.
So we can conclude, with Windisch, that the thoughts of
Paul on sinlessness rest on experiences of Paul himself and
of other Christians.

It is the Epistle to the Romans which gives us the most

---

[1] Cf. Windisch, *Taufe und Sünde*, 34–45; 146–7.
[2] Cf. Wernle, *Der Christ und die Sünde bei Paulus* (1897), 19.

explicit statements of the freedom from sin possible for the believer.

'We who died to sin, how shall we any longer live therein. . . .

'The old man was crucified with him, that the body of sin might be done away, that so we should no longer be in bondage to sin. . . .

'Even so reckon ye also yourselves to be dead unto sin but alive unto God in Christ Jesus.

'Sin shall not have dominion over you; for ye are not under law but under grace.

'Now, being made free from sin, and become servants to God, ye have your fruit unto sanctification, and the end eternal life.'   vi. 2, 6, 11, 14, 22.

These statements are strong enough. They need not be exaggerated[1] to mean that the Christian *cannot* sin. Let us attempt an interpretation which shall sit closely to the actual data of the Pauline declarations. The objection with which St. Paul is grappling in the chapter is not that which modern critics would be inclined to bring—that the new life in Christ is a process, and that elimination of moral evil must be gradual. His adversary is that prior misunderstanding which has often attended the preaching of the free grace of God.[2] 'Shall we remain on in sin, so that there may be all the more grace?' He answers by demonstrating how incompatible the evangelical experience is with continuance in sin. We must therefore be on our guard against hardening the arguments of this chapter into proofs that Christians 'cannot' fall into sin. But his dominant thought is that the Christian knows what it is to have fellowship with Christ crucified. Both sacraments set forth and strengthen this communion. St. Paul chooses Baptism as a symbol to bring home to his readers the truth that fellowship with Christ involves the death of sin. To the dominant thought of fellowship

---

[1] As by Windisch, 181. I cannot agree with Joh. Weiss, *Das Urchristentum*, 400, that Rom. viii. 5–9 denies the possibility of sin for Christians.

[2] Dodd, 84, 85.

with Christ he adds a second conviction, that the new
Messianic age heralded by the prophets is already here,
that the believer may live in it by his fellowship with the
risen Christ. He has a keen sense of 'the inter-penetration
of two worlds, the deathless order being already present
in moral experience'.[1]

Windisch[2] goes farther, and adds a third conviction
which he discovers in this passage: that in the sacrament
of Baptism an objective change is made in the personality;
in the rite the sinful organism is destroyed. There is no
such statement in the passage. The 'conviction' has to be
imported from without. The parallels produced[3] from the
mystery-cults are unconvincing. Paul does not use the
idea of rebirth, but of resurrection. Life in Christ is a new
creation. Mr. A. D. Nock regards this simple fact as a
proof of Paul's 'unfamiliarity with the mysteries'.[4] The
chief argument against the view that *ex opere operato*
Baptism itself effected a change in the substance of the
soul is the unvarying Pauline emphasis on faith. In the
fifth chapter he has shown how faith has linked the believer with Christ, has brought him into a new realm of
grace and hope and love, the gift of the Spirit of God. Is
it credible that faith which has had the pre-eminent place
hitherto, on the human side, should suddenly abdicate, and
yield to a ritual act the power of changing the moral life?
In another passage where Baptism is linked with Christ-
mysticism (Col. ii. 11–12) the Christian rite is used as
a parallel to circumcision. 'Paul cannot be thought to hold
that baptism in "the flesh made with hands" would have
any more virtue than circumcision with the like limitations.'[5] There are other passages which speak of dying and
rising with Christ where there is no mention of Baptism.[6]

[1] Dodd, 126.

[2] 171–2. He appeals to Heitmüller, who is followed by Lake, *Earlier
Epp.* (1914), 385–91; art. in *E.R.E.* ii. 381–2.

[3] As by Lietzmann, *Römerbrief* on Rom. vi. 3, 4.

[4] *Essays on Trinity and Incarnation* (1928), 116; cf. Burkitt, *Christian
Beginnings*, 109.

[5] Dodd, on Colossians in Abingdon Commentary, 1258.

[6] Gal. ii. 20; vi. 14–15; 2 Cor. v. See Büchsel, *Der Geist Gottes im N.T.*

The conclusion to which these considerations are leading us is that St. Paul is not so much in bondage to
the popular conceptions of his time as some scholars
would have us believe. He does not want his readers to
believe that at Baptism they experienced a mysterious
change in the substance of the soul, so that now they
cannot sin. But he does say, in effect: 'You need not sin.'
The statement does not rest on any blindly optimistic
views of human nature, but on the immeasurable resources
of God and the actual gift of freedom from habits of sinning already experienced by Christians. He shows, from
the nature of the evangelical experience itself, that it is
irrational to suppose that any one who has saving faith
should continue in sin. It is not impossible (as he knows
very well) for any one to step down from the lofty level
of life in the Spirit to the fetters and filth of the old life.
But it is unnecessary. And the same grace of God which
set the prisoner free can clothe him in the lovely raiment
of compassion, kindness, humility, meekness, longsuffer-
ing. Perhaps it is correct from one point of view to interpret St. Paul's imperatives as meaning: *Werde was du bist.*
Become what you are.[1] Work out ethically all that is involved in being *in Christ*. But that does not do full justice
to the images used. *Put on*, he says—as if the heavenly
garments were already there, woven by the hand of
Another, awaiting only the grasp of faith. *Consider yourselves dead to sin*. As if mere considering might not be
delusion! But, then, he knows, and the Christian knows,
that it is not delusion. *What is old is gone, the new has come,
it is all the doing of God*. To consider ourselves dead to
sin is the only rational attitude when we remember the
facts on which that consideration is based. In order that
St. Paul's thought may be fully expounded we must look
at those supreme facts as he regarded them, of the divine

(1926), 296 f.; Clemen, *Primitive Christianity and its Non-Jewish Sources*,
225; J. S. Bezzant, 'Sacraments in Acts and the Pauline Epp.' in *The
Modern Churchman*, Oct. 1926; Kurt Deissner, *Paulus u. die Mystik seiner
Zeit* (1921), 35, 36.
    [1] Lietzmann.

order; first, the Christian experience of God, and, second, the ideal love which was the natural issue of that experience.

A. THE NORMAL CHRISTIAN EXPERIENCE OF GOD

The Eighth of Romans is the *locus classicus* of the Pauline doctrine of the perfection attainable in this world. In it the question of sinlessness takes its due place. He does not linger on it. He nowhere admits that sin must persist in the life of the believer. He proclaims the Gospel from the Godward side 'as though on behalf of Christ'. The Christian has been set free from the law (or habit) of sin, with all its soul-destroying consequences. But this statement is set in the context of a description of the Christian life as a life controlled by the indwelling Spirit of God. This chapter may not answer to the life of the 'average' Christian. It is intended to answer to the life of a normal Christian. If we dismiss St. Paul's description as 'ideal' because we know no lives like it, that may be no condemnation of St. Paul, but rather of ourselves. It may be that we have been content habitually to live far below the level of life as God intended it to be lived in this world. At all events the man who understood Christ as no other who has ever lived, intends this chapter as normative, as a standard. It is no esoteric teaching for a few, for elect souls who purpose treading the Mystic Way. It contains an offer, not a mere demand. It describes a level of life which every man who had despaired about himself, and known the agony of the divided mind, might reasonably expect here and now. As the late Dean of Carlisle has said: In St. Paul, 'belief in Christ, submission to his influence, reception into the Church and all the new spiritual influences and experiences which followed upon that reception did have these transforming effects. The effects . . . were so overwhelming in his own case and in that of whole masses of other Christians, that it was natural enough for him to assume that the same effects would follow in the case of all Christians.'[1]

[1] H. Rashdall, *The Idea of Atonement in Christian Theology* (1919),

1. The Passing away of the sense of guilt. *So then the old sense of being in the wrong with God has gone, and God has not one word of condemnation now for those who are united with Christ Jesus.* If St. Paul uses the language of the law-court, so did Jesus when He said to the adulteress: *Neither do I condemn thee.* One may hazard the conjecture that St. Paul had this story or something like it at the back of his mind. There, as here, the experience of acquittal is joined to the experience of release.

2. Freedom from the Habit of sin (ver. 2). The word is used in varying senses in the first three verses. The law of sin is the principle, the system, the compulsion, almost the habit of sin. The law of the Spirit is a paradox. *Where the Spirit of the Lord is, there is liberty.* A new habit or rule has been set up in the mind, to take the place of the former rule. The new freedom is conceived partly in the current Stoic sense,[1] as power to be oneself, to do the right. But it is more.[2] The moral freedom of a Christian rests on his religious transformation. It is the Spirit who sets him free.

3. The New Freedom to fulfil the law of Love is God's gift through Christ Crucified (vv. 3–4). Two ideas are introduced here. The first is that the ideal experience includes a consciousness of debt to the act of God in the Cross. The early Christians connected their forgiveness with the death of Christ, and here that forgiveness is interpreted as including freedom not to sin. *God sent his own Son in a nature like ours, save that ours is always sinful— sent him to deal with that same sin. Thus he condemned sin in our human nature, and made an end of its hold over us.* The second idea is that now the requirements of the Law (cf. Gal. v. 14) may be fulfilled in our lives.[3] Judaism held

116. In the following analysis I am permitted to make free use of Dr. W. R. Maltby's paraphrase *The Eighth of Romans* (1929).

[1] J. Weiss, *Urchristentum,* 400 n. Troeltsch, *Die Soziallehren,* 163 n. (E. tr., 194–5).

[2] Otto Schmitz, *Der Freiheitsgedanke bei Epiktet u. das Freiheitszeugnis des Paulus,* 36.

[3] Lietzmann comments: 'd.h. damit uns Christen die Möglichkeit zum sündlosen Leben gegeben würde.'

that because the law was given to be obeyed, it could be fulfilled. 'That man is capable of choosing between right and wrong and of carrying the decision into action was not questioned.'[1] At the same time, universal sinfulness was admitted.[2] Here Paul says that the Law gave no power to enable us to fulfil it, but now power is given. The Law's requirements 'are summed up in brotherly love, for he does not imply that the redeemed man . . . goes back to carry out the old law in its ceremonial or even in its ethical details'.[3] The distinction already drawn by Jesus between the outward form and inner content of the Jewish law is presupposed.

4. Awareness of the indwelling Spirit of God (vv. 5–9). There are two opposing principles, each of which makes its own world. To live κατὰ σάρκα means to live in a world where self is the centre, to live the life of those whose interests are in lower aims. To live κατὰ πνεῦμα means that the Spirit of God dwells within, we are aware of His presence, and by Him we can be led into newness of life.

It is a mistake to distinguish, as Deissmann does,[4] between the passages referring to the exaltation of Christ at the right hand of God, and the passages which use the more intimate language of indwelling, as though the one were Jewish and the other Hellenistic. In Paul's religious experience the two are inseparable. The Spirit who dwells within is the Spirit of One who is transcendent. Between the pantheistic mysticism of the time and the religion of Paul there is a great gulf fixed. He uses the language of the Spirit dwelling in us, or of Christ living in him, because only by these metaphors can he describe the unutterable inwardness of the change experienced and the communion given. But it is always a communion, never an identification or a deification. 'Jesus is mine, and I am His, and He knows my heart.' Such was the baptismal testimony of the first convert of the Irish Presbyterian

---

[1] G. F. Moore, *Judaism*, i. 454. It was probably admitted, even in the first century, that *all* nations were offered the law at Sinai, i. 277.

[2] Op. cit. i. 467–8.   [3] Moffatt, *Grace in N.T.*, 235.

[4] *Paul* (E. tr. 1926), 137–40, criticized by Kurt Deissner, op. cit., 117.

Mission in Gujarat. The phrase may stand for a description of Paul's 'Christ-mysticism', and he clearly believes that such an experience is within the reach of all.

5. The Spirit gives Life (vv. 10–13). 'The more closely we examine his religious outlook, the more distinctly we shall find that it is dominated by the conception of life.'[1] The foundation of his thought is the fact of the Resurrection, which for Paul formed an integral part of God's redeeming work.[2] The risen Christ is for him the pledge of perfected being. Therefore life is used as a synonym for perfection. It is true that there are other senses in which the word is used in the Pauline epistles.[3] But the two senses in which it is used of the supernatural life of believers, the eschatological sense and the ethical sense, are both intermingled in Paul's mind. In 2 Cor. iv. 10–v. 5 he says that he always bears about with him in his body the dying of Jesus, ἵνα καὶ ἡ ζωὴ τοῦ Ἰησοῦ ἐν τῷ σώματι ἡμῶν φανερωθῇ. But this eschatological sense immediately runs into the idea of present ethical renewal. 'The inward man is renewed day by day.' He knows that the life of Christ will in the future have its perfect work in him, even in his body (2 Cor. v. 4). The Spirit is the present pledge of that future perfecting (2 Cor. v. 5).

That passage elucidates the meaning here. The ζωή is not merely future. It is not an acquirement added on after the death of the body, or at the Parousia. It is a present possession of the believer.[4] It is a partaking of the life of God Himself. It is God's original design for man (cf. Rom. vii. 10, ἡ ἐντολὴ ἡ εἰς ζωήν—the commandment which was intended to give life). On the human side, ζωή includes the physical life (as we have seen from 2 Cor. iv) as well as the ethical and religious. It is 'the totality of the believer's energies. It cannot be divided up into provinces of which one may be contrasted with another. Its only

---

[1] H. A. A. Kennedy, *St. Paul's Conceptions of the Last Things* (1904), 137; Holtzmann, ii. 54.
[2] Cf. H. A. A. Kennedy, *The Theology of the Epistles* (1919), 70 ff.
[3] Bauer, *Wörterbuch zu den Schriften des N.T.* (1928), 531.
[4] Anderson Scott, op. cit., 140.

contrast lies in Death. Death for the apostle means the ruin of the whole personality. Life means its triumphant continuance in the power of the Spirit beyond the barriers of earth and time, in conformity with the nature of the glorified Christ, who is the image of the invisible God.'[1]

6. The Sense of Sonship (vv. 14–17a). The Spirit it is who inspires this sense of sonship. The Spirit is the cause, not the effect. So too in Galatians (iv. 6).

The 'concurrent witness' is Paul's way of preserving the distinction of the Spirit of God from the spirit of man. All human attempts to distinguish clearly the limits of one from the other in religious experience break down at last. But Paul does here assert that, by the Spirit's power, every believer may know that conscious communion with God as a child knows a father. Here Paul was true to the teaching of Jesus concerning the Fatherhood of God. But, as in Gal. iv. 7, he draws out the implications of this sonship. *If children then heirs.* The inheritance is the δόξα of Christ. Here the predominant meaning is eschatological.[2] But can we say that the consciousness of sonship is a gift only to be enjoyed in the future? On the strength of Rom. viii. 23 Johannes Weiss has maintained this.[3] It is difficult to see how this interpretation can stand, in view of the past tense used here and the meaning of the word 'adoption'. You received the Spirit which made you sons. Adoption is admission into the family of God. Paul is continually insisting that justification places men on a new footing in relation to God. The love of God is shed abroad within them by the Holy Spirit. The sense of sonship (cf. Gal. iv. 7) is the gift of the Spirit here and now.[4] Therefore the consciousness of the relationship is an essential part of the relationship.

7. The acceptance of suffering in the life of present

---

[1] Kennedy, *St. Paul's Conceptions of the Last Things*, 157; cf. Dodd, *Romans*, 125–6.

[2] Cf. Col. i. 12; Eph. 1. 18.   [3] *Das Urchristentum*, 390.

[4] See Kennedy's excellent treatment of the identity between the message of Jesus and that of Paul as to the filial relationship; *The Theology of the Epistles*, 137–9.

communion with God (vv. 17 b–26). The ideal is expressed in the eschatological language of the time. The ματαιότης to which the creation is subject is referred to in 4 Ezra vii. 11, 12. The thought of a new heaven and a new earth is found in Isa. lxv. 17; lxvi. 22; and Jub. i. 29. But the old language carries a new ideal. Jesus had already linked the Kingdom with the Cross. Paul now draws out the meaning for the individual life. First, suffering is transformed, because it is suffering with Christ. Paul has his own way of expressing this revolutionary message. 'He lets the thought of suffering merge into that of dying.'[1] Schweitzer points out that in First Peter there is found more about suffering than in all the Pauline epistles put together, but the idea of dying with Christ does not occur. However, both writers find a divine meaning in suffering in the present life. Paul strikes a note which we shall hear continually in Christian spirituality. We may leave it with the comment of Canon A. L. Lilley: 'Above all, [the most careful Christian teaching] has most consistently taught that the true attitude of prayer always includes a simple and even joyful acceptance of all the unavoidable pains and disabilities of our lives, as, if so accepted, richly ministrant and contributory to our spiritual growth. In other words, it has planted the cross at the centre of the prayer-life.'[2]

Second, we notice that the suffering of man is joined with the sufferings of Nature. Both are pointing from the present to the future. It would be a mistake to label Paul's view of Nature as pessimistic.[3] Jesus, whose vision of the outward world was undimmed and friendly, speaks of the Palingenesia (Matt. xix. 28; cf. xxvi. 29), when all things shall be made new, and sees, too, that

---

[1] Schweitzer, *The Mysticism of Paul* (1931), 142. The evidence is set out in 141–3.

[2] *Prayer in Christian Theology*, 8.

[3] As Weinel does, *Die Bildersprache Jesu in ihrer Bedeutung für die Erforschung seines inneren Lebens* (1900), 9. Otto Schmitz, *Das Lebensgefühl d. Paulus* (1922), 85, 130, quotes Ganzenmüller's book on the 'Feeling for Nature in the Middle Ages.' Paul had 'ein tiefes Mitgefühl für die gesamte Natur'.

there are tares as well as wheat. So Paul hears a voice
crying in Nature, harmonizing with the music of humanity,
which is neither so still nor so sad as in the poetry of
Wordsworth, and both blend with the sighs of the Spirit
which pass beyond the reach of words. All are making one
symphony of yearning for the great consummation of all
things in the age to come.

The third noticeable mark of this acceptance of suffering is that Hope is set among the cardinal virtues. This
results from the incompleteness both of Nature and of
man. Hope is a gift of the Spirit (Gal. v. 5). Those without hope are the heathen (1 Thess. iv. 13). By hope
are Christians saved (Rom. viii. 24; cf. Col. iii. 3, 4).
Perhaps the chief differentiation of Paul from the men and
women of to-day is in the high place he assigns to hope.
If we were making a list for ourselves, it would hardly
occur to any of us to include this quality in it. For us,
as for Watts, Hope is a blinded figure holding a shattered
lyre and listening for the music of the one remaining
string. For the New Testament, Hope is the Winged
Victory of Samothrace, 'as she stands there, in the Louvre,
on the prow of the rushing galley. Her great white wings
are spread above her, every fibre instinct with energy, and
she is in act to fleet away across the blue waters to bring to
some waiting city by the Aegean sea the news of Mara-
thon or Salamis.'[1] So Hope for Paul is an unshakable
certainty of the coming victory, and rests on the possession
of the Spirit in the present age.[2]

8. The Spirit takes up the task of Prayer (vv. 26–7).
This is our 'deepest glimpse into Paul's praying'.[3] He
assumes that all Christians are like himself and do not
know how to pray as they ought. There are times when
they can offer nothing to God but an inarticulate yearning.
But Paul declares that these yearnings that pass beyond
the reach of words are inspired by the Spirit and are accept-

---

[1] D. S. Cairns, *The Reasonableness of the Christian Faith* (1918), 123.

[2] See the fine exposition of Büchsel, *Der Geist Gottes im N.T.*, 315–18;
cf. W. Weber, *Christusmystik* (1924), 82.

[3] Büchsel, op. cit., 320.

able to God. *The Searcher of Hearts recognizes the mind of His own Spirit, because the Spirit pleads for the saints according to God's own mind.*

Again we recognize a mark of true communion with God which has distinguished Christian spirituality throughout the ages. Mere man cannot pray at all. It is God within us who prays. There is no quotation from Scripture more often on the lips of saints and doctors of the Church when they expound the prayer-life than this word, *We know not how to pray as we ought.*[1]

9. God co-operates with us in all things for good (ver. 28). The familiar English rendering is inaccurate. 'It would not occur to Paul to look for "things" to work together for the salvation of man. What he does look for, and find, is God's co-operation with us, *in* things, even things which are hostile to us.'[2] This faith integrates life for us. It is based upon a conception of God who is active will, and whose deeds may be recognized in human history. The phrase 'to those who love God'[3] is a summary of the Christian life. *Pietatis summam sub dilectione Dei complexus est* is Calvin's comment on this verse.[4]

10. The consciousness of belonging to an eternal purpose (vv. 29–30). The relationship of God with the believing soul is initiated by God Himself. This conviction inevitably results in some kind of belief in a decree of grace before history came to be. So far from being a new fatalism, such a belief was in Paul's day an escape from fatalism. 'What determines our lot is not the planet under which we were born, much less the fact that we were born either inside or outside the Law, but the unconditioned goodwill of the living God. This must have been a relief for many in that superstitious age.'[5] The believer is able to trace his deliverance backward to

---

[1] See Archdeacon Lilley, op. cit., 8, 9, 67, 68, 118, 119.

[2] Dodd, *Romans*, 138. See the full exposition, 137–9.

[3] There are only five specific references in Paul to the Christian's love for God (1 Cor. ii. 9; viii. 3; xvi. 22; Eph. vi. 24; Rom. viii. 28).

[4] Moffatt, *Love in N.T.*, 160.

[5] Moffatt, *Grace in N.T.*, 256.

eternity and also forward to eternity. 'In due time He gave
the "call", and when we came He justified us, yes and
"glorified" us too, for we may count it as good as done.'[1]
The glorification is to share the likeness of Christ (viii. 17;
cf. 2 Cor. iv. 6). This is, indeed, an individualizing of
religion. The distinction of the sense of eternity which
we find in St. Paul may be brought out by a comparison.
Seneca has painted an eschatological picture. Borrowing
his colours from the older teaching of the Stoics, he depicts
a dissolution of the world in fervent heat, but he is uncer-
tain whether the soul will maintain any individual existence.
Far different is the picture of St. Paul; there we see on
the horizon of world history One supreme Person appearing
in triumph bringing this age to an end, conquering by
almighty love all that is opposed to God, and yet carrying
with Him a personal redemption for each individual soul.[2]

11. The consciousness that in the religious life everything is given (vv. 31–4). In itself this saying is a complete proof of the harmony of the teaching of Paul with
that of his Master on the ultimate conviction of the
religious life. But the fact lies patent on every page of
the Epistles. He will scarcely allow himself to use the
words which imply man's activity in the work of salvation
unless he guards them by the thought of the initiative,
prevenience, and deeper working of God Himself.[3]

12. The consciousness of victory in the present world
through God's love (vv. 33–9). First, there is a consciousness of triumph over the accusing voices. There is no
escape from our Judge but in His heart. And we are
there. Paul does not recommend a sense of sin, but rather
of victory. The Judge has become our advocate. 'Christ
who is Himself the Ideal we fail to reach, pleads our cause.
We are thus freed from the negativity of the sense of
failure and set towards positive attainment.'[4] Second,
the Christian experience includes dominion over the world

---

[1] W. R. Maltby's paraphrase.
[2] Cf. Kurt Deissner, *Paulus und Seneca* (1917), 9–13.
[3] e.g. Gal. iv. 9; 2 Cor. v. 18; Phil. ii. 12, 13.
[4] Dodd, *Romans*, 145.

(vv. 35–7). Third, the love of God is recognized as the ultimate reality of the universe (ver. 38).

B. THE IDEAL LOVE

Such convictions point us forward to a description of the human love that will answer God's love, a love which bears Christ's stamp upon it. The Hymn of God's love in Rom. viii is thus the presupposition of the Hymn of human love in 1 Cor. xiii.

1. Love is a gift of the Spirit (Gal. v. 22). The Hymn of Love is set amid the discussion of spiritual gifts. When Paul asks Christians unknown to him to intercede for his mission, he invokes the love which the Spirit inspires (Rom. xv. 30), and he knows that the Thessalonians (1. iv. 9) are taught by God to love one another. 'Love is something divine in men, not the ideally human.'[1] For Paul this is part of his own experience. His own love knows no barrier of nationality or status. He is debtor to Greek and Barbarian, Jew and Gentile, bond and free. He feels a fatherly love for the most wayward of his converts (2 Cor. xii. 14, 15). *I seek not yours, but you; for the children ought not to lay up for the parents, but the parents for the children. And I will most gladly spend and be spent for your souls. If I love you more abundantly, am I loved the less?* Like the pain in the love of a mother is his sorrow for their wandering (Gal. iv. 19). But he is fully aware that love with such constraining power in it (2 Cor. v. 13 ff.) is supernatural. Perhaps the most exquisite expression of it is in Phil. i. 8. *God is my witness how I long for you all with a love that is not mine but Christ loving in me.*[2] At the heart of it, love of this divine quality is love towards God.[3] 'Paul could not, while speaking all through the hymn about love for one's neighbour, have brought in faith and hope at the end, if love had not been for him inseparably bound up with the love of God, and an indissoluble unity with it.

[1] Büchsel, op. cit., 312. 'Liebe ist etwas Göttliches im Menschen, nicht das ideal Menschliche.'

[2] W. R. Maltby, *Philippians* (1916), 7.

[3] Cf. Moffatt, *Love in N.T.*, 183.

This view, prepared in the Old Testament, can be traced back to Jesus Himself.'[1]

2. Love is the summary of the moral law (Gal. v. 14; Rom. xiii. 8). In this Paul is true to the mind of his Master.[2] He does not mean, of course, that the individual has freedom to follow his own impulses. Nor did St. Augustine in the most memorable and most misquoted of epigrams, *Love, and do what you like*. Paul means (Rom. xiii. 8) that love will lead a Christian to the fulfilment of all his obligations as a citizen. But after he has thus discharged the recognized duties, there is another debt which he can never discharge. 'The debt of love abides for us, and never ceases; for it is good for us both to pay it every day and yet always to owe it.'[3]

3. Love implies a society. *Above all put on love, for love gives cohesion to the perfect life* (σύνδεσμος τῆς τελειότητος). The meaning here (Col. iii. 14) is probably the perfect fellowship that ought to exist among Christian men.[4] Love is the bond that unites them in a common service.

Throughout the music of the Hymn of Love there is moving a passionate and creative imagination, which sees what church life even at Corinth might be, if love ruled. *Love is not glad when others go wrong, but is gladdened when they obey the truth.*[5] . . . *Love is always hopeful* for the offender. The very love demanded in community life is imagination. 'Love, as we define it, would be that outreaching power of the imagination by which we grasp and make real to ourselves the being of others.'[6] 'Love is that will which aims at the enrichment of another's existence . . . which accepts the task of advancing the end of other personal beings of like nature with oneself.'[7] Add

---

[1] Harnack, *The Apostle's Hymn of Love* (E. tr. in *Expositor*, 1912), 498. Cf. J. Weiss on 1 Cor., 312.

[2] See Anderson Scott, *N.T. Ethics* (1930), 76, 77; Moffatt, op. cit., 166–8; Dodd, *Romans*, 206–7.

[3] Origen (quoted by Sanday-Headlam); Lommatzsch, vii. 335.

[4] So E. F. Scott, *Colossians and Ephesians* (1930), 73; Moffatt, op. cit., 191.   [5] Moffatt and J. Weiss.

[6] Paul Elmer More, *The Christ of the New Testament* (1924), 123.

[7] Ritschl, *Justification and Reconciliation* (E. tr. 1900), 277, 381.

these two definitions together; if active will and out-reaching imagination are both of the very essence of love, if love of this quality is indeed a gift which the Spirit gives, then we surely have in the Christian message the incomparable instrument for social reform.

At this point we expect, and find, a doctrine of an ideal earthly community. This was present before the Epistle to the Ephesians had been penned. In the first Corinthian letter the Stoic conception of the human body-politic becomes one with the ideal of the people of God.

It has here attained the greatest possible elasticity, tenderness and vitality. For an all-embracing self-conscious Spirit—the Spirit of one who loved, and immolated Himself, wholly and to the end—is here the link and medium by and in which all human spirits, in pro-portion to their awakeness and acceptance, are bound and fitted together. And further the conception presupposes throughout, not the self-sufficingness of the individual spirit, but the utter pressing need, for each human spirit of all the others, and for the totality of human spirits of the Christ, the Spirit, God—of His initiation, puri-fication, sustainment, and crowning of it all.[1]

4. Love is linked with the Cross (Rom. v. 8; viii. 32, 35; Eph. v. 2; iv. 32). In nothing is Paul more original than in his insight in interpreting the ideal for human love in the light of Christ Crucified. He had received the common tradition that *Christ died for our sins, according to the Scriptures*; he had received, too, that command of love which Jesus made central in His ethical teaching. Paul fused these two facts into one, and founded all Christian love on the love revealed in the supreme sacrifice of Christ.[2] Love becomes giving, not the desire to possess. Love pours itself out, even to the uttermost. *Love never breaks down* (1 Cor. xiii. 8). This love is one with the passion of the shepherd who goes after the lost sheep, *until he find it.*

5. Love abides (1 Cor. xiii. 13). The last verse of the Hymn of Love has caused difficulty.[3] Why are faith and hope suddenly introduced? How can faith and hope endure in the next life, when the vision will be face to

[1] von Hügel, *Eternal Life*, 71.   [2] Cf. A. Nygren, *Agape and Eros*, 84–98.
[3] J. Weiss, and Lietzmann, ad loc.

face? If faith is interpreted here as the human response to the offer of God, instead of being contrasted (as in 2 Cor. v. 7) with 'sight', it will be the eternal attitude of the soul. Similarly, since love admits of growth, there may be perpetual progress in the life beyond. Thus hope will abide. In any case the supremacy of love will be manifested. Whether in this present age alone, or in both this age and the age to come, faith receives love and hope expects love as the gift of the hands of God.

If we now compare the teaching of Paul with that of Jesus, we see the correspondence of the ideal of love with the main characteristics of the Rule of God as Jesus proclaimed it. (1) The final victory of God is the victory of love with a supernatural quality in it, miraculous as the raising of Jesus from the dead (Rom. viii. 11; 1 Cor. xv. 57; Eph. i. 19). (2) The love shed abroad in human hearts is God's gift. (3) It is communion with God. (4) It points forward to a perfected society. (5) It admits of infinite progress, and yet it is a life that can be lived in Corinth or Thessalonica in the first century because it is God's will and God's gift. (6) It accepts all the goodness that there is in human nature and is glad in it; and it is not blind to the life and work of the present world. (7) Love is a life founded on the personality of Jesus Himself; indeed the love wherewith one Christian loves another can be called the love of Christ Himself. (8) Love is linked with the cross. These eight affirmations prove the fidelity of the disciple to the mind of the Master. He knew an ideal which spanned both worlds. He had been translated, even in this life, to the kingdom of the Son of God's love.

> No weariness is here, no shamefastness,
> Here is, was, shall be, all delightsomeness.
> And here no end shall be,
> But a beginning everlastingly.[1]

[1] Helen Waddell's translation of Petronius Arbiter, *Mediaeval Latin Lyrics* (1929), 15.

> Hic nullus labor est, ruborque nullus:
> Hoc iuvit, iuvat, et diu iuvabit;
> Hoc non deficit, incipitque semper.

CHAPTER III

THE EPISTLE TO THE HEBREWS

ὅθεν καὶ σώζειν εἰς τὸ παντελὲς δύναται τοὺς προσερχομένους δι' αὐτοῦ τῷ Θεῷ.

Heb. vii. 25.

προσεληλύθατε Σιὼν ὄρει καὶ πόλει Θεοῦ ζῶντος.

Heb. xii. 22.

WE turn now to the literary masterpiece which holds a place altogether unique in the New Testament writings. The Epistle to the Hebrews is evidence that there was at least one teacher of genius in the early Church who was scarcely influenced by the Pauline presentation of Christianity.[1] His conception of the Gospel is independent and original. At first sight it may seem to promise little for our present purpose. Those who have written on the doctrine of perfection have usually recognized that the allusions in the Epistle to the term do not carry us far.[2] Though Wesley preached a sermon[3] from the text (vi. 1): *Let us go on unto perfection*, he makes no attempt at exposition of the context. Indeed it is evident that τελειότης here means maturity, and in particular the mature mental grasp of the truth about Christ. The writer tells his readers that it is high time to awake out of their dogmatic slumbers: let them make an intellectual effort. It would be idle for him to traverse the elementary ground of repentance and forgiveness yet again, because in the case of wilful sin a second repentance is impossible. 'More often than we know, the failure of religion, as a moral power, is due to intellectual sloth.'[4] Let them therefore claim the privilege of adults. But this meaning for the word τέλειοι, as contrasted with νήπιοι, does not give us a doctrine of perfection, though it provides us with a hint that the author has his own standards of attainment for the members of the Christian Church. Similarly the other great text in

[1] Cf. E. F. Scott, *Ep. to Hebrews*, 49, 50.
[2] e.g. W. B. Pope, iii. 57, on Hebrews vi. 1 and x. 14.
[3] *Works*, ii. 388–401, Sermon LXXVI.
[4] E. F. Scott, 44.

Hebrews (x. 14) with our word in it: *By one offering he hath perfected for ever them that are sanctified*, does not give us our point that perfection on earth is a promised goal. It is rather an assertion of the never-failing efficacy of the supreme deed of Christ. The distinctive phrase in this verse is εἰς τὸ διηνεκές, which means 'in perpetuity'.[1] The thought is that to all time the perfect offering once made by Christ will have its full effect on those who successively are called to faith in Him. Not only is the guilt of sin removed by the sacrifice of the Cross, but everything is given in the perfection of that act to bring believers in Christ to their promised goal.[2] It is the just expression of the truth in Cowper's familiar quatrain.

> O Lamb of God, Thy precious blood
> Shall never lose its power,
> Till all the ransomed church of God
> Be saved to sin no more.

But both Cowper's last line and the phrase εἰς τὸ διηνεκές warn us that a doctrine of perfection is bound up with their explanations of the death of Jesus Christ. 'As there is one divine will, and all wills freed in it, so there is one achieved perfection, and each successive perfecting of men is by partaking in that one.'[3]

Both passages suggest the real aim and pastoral interest of the writer. Faced with the threatened defection of a community which he loves, he knows no more certain remedy than this of portraying in all its splendour the uniqueness and finality of the Christian ideal. His method is to use the one religion of antiquity which could worthily be compared with the new faith, and by a comparison of its central ritual with the supreme act of the Christian revelation, to prove that Christ in His dying achieved the aim which the *cultus* of Judaism missed. The real danger[4]

---

[1] See Nairne, *The Epistle of Priesthood*, 200–1. 'It is not the eternity of the sacrifice itself that is meant, but its effect for the future.'

[2] I follow here the clear exposition of Riehm, *Hebräerbrief* (1867), 581.

[3] Nairne in *C.G.T.*, 100.

[4] The view of the Epistle presupposed in this chapter is that the writer is addressing Christians and knows no distinction between the two branches

of the readers of this Epistle is that which is the subtle and incessant enemy of the church in every age, to take their religion for granted, to lose their sense of God, to drift into a merely nominal faith. What is the way of renewal? The writer preaches perfection and he reminds them of their past experience of God.

What, then, is the nature of this perfecting? Our answer must take us to the dominant ideas of the Epistle.

The structure of the thought reminds us of a medieval cathedral. Just as the cathedral of Ely, let us say, bears the impress of three great moments or architectural ideas —the Norman period in its nave, the Early English in its choir, and the genius of the Decorated period, taking visible form in the exquisite Lantern Tower, and dominating the whole—so there are three decisive structural ideas in the theology of this Epistle. The ground plan is laid down for the author by the human life and perfect death of Jesus Christ. This shrine is most certainly cruciform. Secondly, we have the idea of priesthood, taken over from Judaism and transformed by the method of Alexandrian exegesis. And, in the third place, crowning and dominating the whole, is the Platonic doctrine of the two worlds. Only recently has the decisive influence of this doctrine upon the thought of the author been recognized,[1] and it is precisely at this point that we shall find his doctrine of perfection.

I. Perfection is 'the world to come'.

The writer defines his subject as the world to come. He has fresh phrases for his idea. Christians are those who

of the early Church; the title is a misnomer; and the readers were not in danger of any relapse into Judaism. The commentaries of Moffatt (*I.C.C.* 1924), H. T. Andrews (*Abingdon Commentary*, 1929), E. F. Scott, *The Epistle to the Hebrews* (1922), should be consulted for a fuller justification than can be given here.

[1] See Holtzmann, ii. 329 ff., especially 331. Pfleiderer, *Prim. Christianity*, iii. 272–99; Moffatt's Commentary (*I.C.C.*, 1924), Kennedy, *Theology of the Epistles* (1923), 190 ff.; E. F. Scott, *Ep. to the Hebrews* (1922), 50 ff.; Nairne, *Epistle of Priesthood* (1913), 36, 38, and *passim*; Peake (in Century Bible); H. T. Andrews, in *Abingdon Commentary*, 1929). On the other side see Gayford in *A New Commentary*; Schlatter, *Die Theologie der Apostel* (1922), 473–8; Feine, *Die Theologie des N. T.*, 493.

have tasted the power of the age to come (vi. 5). We have received a kingdom which cannot be shaken (xii. 28). Our search is for the city which is to come (xiii. 14). There the people of God have their *sabbatismos*, their sabbatic rest (iv. 9). It is a city which has fixed foundations, in contrast to the restless nomadic life of this world; and the maker and designer of the city is God (xi. 10). The heavenly city, the world to come, is the heavenly reality of which this age possesses only the earthly shadows and copies (x. 1). It has existed from all eternity. It is not called μέλλουσα because it is in the future, but only because it has not yet been fully realized in time. 'The seeming confusion of past, present, and future is removed by his Platonic conception of eternity as reality, not length of time.'[1]

In the Timaeus (28, 29) Plato says that the universe is a copy (εἰκών) and not an original or pattern (παράδειγμα). The visible universe which is material and imperfect must have been constructed after the pattern of the unchangeable and eternal. Philo's account of the Divine plan in creation reflects the argument of Plato.

Since God in virtue of his Deity realized beforehand that a beautiful copy (μίμημα) could not come into being apart from a beautiful pattern (παράδειγμα) and that none of the things perceived by sense could be flawless which was not made after the image of an Archetype and a spiritual (νοητήν) Idea, when he designed to create this visible world, he first formed the ideal world, so that he might produce the bodily by the use of an incorporeal and most Godlike pattern, the later modelled on the earlier, and intended to contain as many classes of things apprehensible by the senses as there were ideas in the archetypal world.[2]

There are thus two orders of things existing side by side, a higher and a lower, Idea and Appearance, Eternal and Temporal, Heavenly reality and earthly universe, original pattern and the derived copy. The *Auctor ad Hebraeos* shares this primary conviction with Philo, but it is only in the sphere of religion that he works out the contrast, and even there he employs most frequently the last category mentioned—that of original and copy. Christ

[1] Nairne, *C.G.T.*, 41.   [2] *De Opificio Mundi*, 16.

is described (viii. 2) as the High Priest who has entered the heavenly sphere and who officiates in the sanctuary, the real tabernacle (τῆς σκηνῆς τῆς ἀληθινῆς), which the Lord erected, not man. The Aaronic priests serve a mere pattern (παραδείγματι) and shadow of the heavenly, 'as Moses was instructed when he was about to execute the building of the tabernacle. See, said God, that thou makest everything according to the model (τύπον) shown thee on the mountain' (viii. 5). Later on (ix. 11) our author says: 'When Christ arrived as the high priest of the bliss that was to be, he passed through the greater and more perfect tabernacle not made with hands, that is, not belonging to the present order.'

Those who, like Feine, deny the presence of the Platonic doctrine of ideas in this Epistle are hard put to it to explain away such passages as these. But Feine is surely right when he says[1] that the chief interest in the writer's mind is not the exposition of any philosophic dualism, but rather the description of the process of development of the history of salvation from the imperfect to the perfect. We may go further and say that the author uses the Platonic doctrine as an instrument. If it dominates his mind, it does not master his religion. And it is of supreme value because it expresses a doctrine of perfection, realizable in this world. He says to those whom he wants to stir to fresh adventure in their religious life:

See what the best religion of the olden times could do. The rites of the old covenant were only the earthly shadows of the heavenly realities. In the New covenant the heavenly realities themselves have broken through into the world of time and space. Because of that one act of perfect obedience, Christ opened up for us a path into the eternal world, where is no σκιά, no εἰκών, but the παράδειγμα itself. We may live in that realm with Him, here and now.

On this view the most significant passage in the Epistle is the beginning of the practical exhortation in the tenth chapter.

Brothers, since we have confidence to enter the holy Presence in virtue of the blood of Jesus, by the fresh living way which he has

[1] *Theol. des N.T.*, 493.

inaugurated for us through the veil, that is, through his flesh, and since we have a great Priest over the house of God, let us draw near with a true heart, in absolute assurance of faith.

The death of Jesus has this eternal efficacy, that as the consummation of His life-long obedience it has power for all time to bring believers into the Presence of God. The Law is a mere shadow of the bliss to come and it can never perfect those who draw near with their annual sacrifices. That perfection is to stand in the eternal world, in the presence of God.

This, then, is the first mark of our writer's doctrine: 'Perfection is communion with God.' It is true that he never uses the word κοινωνία in this sense.[1] But his picture of the central fact of religion is access to the divine Presence. Such access cannot be secured without forgiveness, and Christianity is the absolute religion, first, because of the perfect act on which this forgiveness is based, and second, because it secures the access to God. The High Priesthood of Christ introduced the 'better hope by means of which we can draw near to God' (vii. 19). As Professor Milligan points out,[2] the text of the whole Epistle may be found in the twice-quoted prophecy of Jeremiah which promises to the house of Israel the forgiveness of sins and direct immediate knowledge of God. To this better hope the soul is anchored, safe and sure, 'as it enters the inner Presence behind the veil.'

II. In the second place, this perfection rests upon the perfect life and perfect achievement of Jesus Christ. For our present purpose it is unnecessary to expound in detail the Christology of the Epistle. But we must notice how the ideal life, now realizable in space and time for sinful men, depends on the historical person and work of Jesus Himself.

1. This is shown in the conception of Faith. It was Jesus who was the Pioneer and the Perfecter of Faith (xii. 1). He was the Pioneer because He Himself exercised such faith (xii. 2; see also ii. 13) in enduring the

---

[1] In xiii. 16 it means charity.
[2] *Theology of the Epistle to the Hebrews*, 57; Jeremiah xxxi. 31 ff.

cross and despising shame. In some of the senses in which the writer uses the word,[1] faith would seem to be a rudimentary belief that God exists, and that He does reward those who seek Him (xi. 6). In some aspects it is indistinguishable from hope (xi. 1). The splendid eleventh chapter, with its roll-call of the heroes and martyrs of faith, is continually equating hope and faith. Faith meant for the patriarchs a confident trust in the promises; but those promises were not all fulfilled in this life. They greeted them from afar. Their aspiration was towards a better land in heaven, and with patience (vi. 12; x. 36; xii. 1) they waited for it. But there is a difference between these and another meaning of the word which emerges in the course of the argument. Faith is a conviction of the reality of what we do not see. It is almost 'seeing the invisible' (xi. 3, 27). It is singular that the writer does not actually say so. What we miss in this chapter is a statement of faith as the power of realizing the eternal world here and now.[2] The writer is probably hampered by the necessity of drawing his illustrations from the Old Testament. He is aware (xi. 40) that Jesus has made a difference between the primitive faith of the heroes of old and the faith of those who are living after the revelation in Jesus; but his examples and his sweeping eloquence obscure that distinction. If this chapter may be called the Westminster Abbey of the Bible, those who

---

[1] See the excellent excursus in Windisch, *Hebräerbrief*, 97–9; E. F. Scott, 169–92.

[2] Professor E. F. Scott says (p. 170) that faith is described as that attitude of soul to which future and unseen things are so sure that they become actual—more truly so than if they were apprehended by the senses. It is true that this is the meaning of faith which we should like to find, but the chapter does not go so far. In ver. 27 the phrase ὡς ὁρῶν is ambiguous. Of the two meanings, 'as though he saw' or 'inasmuch as he saw', the second is usually chosen (as by Westcott, 373). Moses 'spoke with God face to face' (Exod. xxxiii; Num. xii. 7, 8). Therefore because of this 'peculiar gift of Moses', ὡς ὁρῶν can only be interpreted as meaning that he actually saw God the invisible. But the passages adduced from Philo do not say this. According to Philo, Moses had never seen God himself. (See Windisch, *Die Frömmigkeit Philos*, 42 ff.) And the ambiguity could have been avoided if the ὡς had been omitted.

read it are often like the wondering tourists whose eyes are often holden by the magnificence of the historical symbols, so that they forget the purpose of the shrine.

We are left to deduce the distinction of Christian faith from the whole tenor of the argument and from one or two significant phrases. First comes the phrase in xi. 40. What is this 'better thing' without which the saints of old could not attain their promised goal? As Professor A. B. Davidson saw,[1] 'it is the perfection referred to in the end of the verse, which is the full removing of sins, and introduction into a condition of true covenant fellowship with God. This better thing, carrying with it the full realizing of the promise (v. 39), God has provided for us.' The promise is that of the Messianic age in the 'better country'. This therefore means that 'we' Christians have the privilege now of entering into the heavenly world. Second, the following verses, at the opening of the twelfth chapter, give us the reference to Jesus Christ which is the distinguishing mark of Christian perfection. The phrase ἀφορῶντες εἰς τὸν τῆς πίστεως ἀρχηγὸν καὶ τελειωτὴν Ἰησοῦν, is one of the most decisive utterances of this Epistle. It carries with it both the idea of continual gazing on the person and work of Jesus which is so vital for Christian devotion and also the suggestion that only by gazing upon Jesus can faith reach its goal. We are told that Jesus has sat down on the right hand of the throne of God. He is there within the veil. Surely the inference must be that we also can enter within and dwell in the realm of eternal realities. The word τελειωτήν is emphatic. Faith when perfected by Jesus, faith in its full Christian sense, is a consciousness of dwelling in the ideal world, in the heavenly sanctuary.

2. The ideal life depends on the humanity of Jesus.

The stress laid upon the human experience of Jesus is particularly congenial to men of the twentieth century. We would not willingly let die those impassioned words[2] which glory in every detail of the real humanity of our Lord too often only grudgingly conceded by the teachers of the later church:

---

[1] *Hebrews*, 231.   [2] iv. 15, v. 7.

Who in the days of his flesh . . . though he was a Son, yet learned obedience through the things he suffered, and having been made perfect, he became unto all them that obey him the author of eternal salvation.

But it should be noted that the author does not begin where the moderns begin. His view of Jesus is never merely humanist. He assumes that his readers will never question the eternal divine Sonship. 'He uses the category of the Son quite frankly in order to express the absolute value of the revelation in Jesus; it is his sheer sense of the reality of the incarnate life which prompts him to employ the transcendental ideas.'[1] His argument is that Christ could not be high priest unless His experience had been human. 'Jesus became man because He was Son. He is High priest because once He was man.'[2]

The meaning of the humanity of our Lord for the author's doctrine of perfection is, first, that the perfection must be wrought out by struggle in the time process; second, that His achievement in the time process carries with it the promise of our own. The goal is not reached at a single bound.

'It is by no breath,
Turn of eye, wave of hand, that salvation joins issue with death.'

The perfection is costly. It entails a process in time. How this series of events in time comes to assume an eternal significance is a question not completely answered by the author. But at all events he does boldly grapple with the problem. He is not content with an unrelieved dualism, an unbridgeable gap between the world of eternal ideas and the world of time and space. He affirms that in the humanity of our Lord the gulf is surmounted and the two worlds meet. The inference from his language (e.g. in ii. 10–13) is that the perfection which Christ came to inaugurate in His brethren is the perfection achieved in this earthly life and consummated in His death when He offered Himself through eternal spirit (ix. 14) to God. The constant prominence given to Christ as the pattern, rather than as the

---

[1] Moffatt, *I.C.C.*, Intro. vi, p. l.   [2] Moffatt, loc. cit.

object of faith, can only mean that this Christ-like perfection is possible for us in time.[1] But the starting-point
and the centre of the Christology, as of everything else
in the epistle, is the purification achieved by the death upon
the Cross.[2]

3. Christ's teaching of the Kingdom is accepted, but
transformed. The epistle has not abandoned the primitive apocalyptic hope. The evidence on this point is
convincing.[3] The terrors of judgement are mentioned
more than once (vi. 2; ix. 27; x. 27; xiii. 4). This visible
world will be annihilated or transformed (xii. 26–8).
Evidently the eschatology is not spiritualized, as always
in the thought of Philo.[4] But a change has come over the
primitive hope. The soul's vision of spiritual realities is
supplanting the bodily vision of the Messiah for which
the earliest Christians were waiting.[5] The true home of the
saints is in the divine realm of spiritual realities. There,
within the veil, is the unshaken kingdom, the heavenly
Jerusalem.[6]

It has been claimed[7] that the apocalyptic doctrine is
really superfluous to the thought of the epistle and that
the Platonic conception of the earthly and the heavenly
world leaves no room for the Messianic expectations of the
primitive church.

This view overlooks the distinction between the full

---

[1] Du Bose, 116.

[2] Cf. Denney, *Christian Doctrine of Reconciliation*, 172–4.

[3] i. 2 (see Moffatt and Windisch, ad loc.); ii. 8; iii. 13; ix. 26, 28; x.
25, 37.

[4] Cf. Kennedy, *Philo's Contribution to Religion*, 134 ff. The whole of
Philo's conception of the future is different. See Bréhier, *Philon*, 240–2.

[5] The use of the words for 'seeing', ἀφοράω in Heb. xii. 2 and ἀποβλέπω xi.
26, is instructive here. They do not occur elsewhere in the New Testament
or in the LXX. Both have the sense (so Westcott, 373–4, 394–5) of looking away from the things of earth. Compare Arrian, *Epict*. ii. 19, 29 εἰς τὸν
θεὸν ἀφορῶντες ἐν παντὶ μικρῷ καὶ μεγάλῳ, Philo, *De Mundi Opif*. 18, ἀποβλέπων
εἰς τὸ παράδειγμα. Moulton-Milligan, *Vocab*. i. 59, quote an inscription of
Ephesus, second century A.D., ἀποβλέπων εἰς τὴν εὐσέβειαν τοῦ θεοῦ. Both
ὁράω and βλέπω in ii. 8 and 9 are used of spiritual vision.

[6] See Windisch, *Hebräerbrief*, 81, 82.

[7] E. F. Scott, *Ep. to Hebrews*, 109–121.

consummation of the work of Christ and the 'relative perfection' to which Christians may attain in the present age.
If the view be correct that the letter is written with the
practical aim of spurring on the readers to win the ideal,
there is a deep religious value in the hope of the Parousia.
At present they are partakers in the process of τελείωσις.
Then the process will be complete.[1]

III. The third mark of the teaching of perfection is
the Cross. The appeal of the last chapter is characteristic
of the whole letter. *Let us go to him outside the camp,
sharing the insults directed against him.*[2] The Pioneer of
our salvation is made perfect through suffering (ii. 10) and
therefore that is the only way for His followers. *Although
he was God's Son, yet he learned obedience from the sufferings
which he endured, and so, having been made perfect he became
. . . the author of eternal salvation* (v. 8–9). Perhaps the
thought (in ii. 9) is more daring still. *We see Jesus made for
a short time lower than the angels because of the suffering of
death crowned with glory and honour that by the grace of God he
might taste death for every man.* The best interpretation of
this difficult verse seems to be that the glory of Jesus
was His humiliation on the Cross, that the reference is
not to any subsequent exaltation wherein Christ receives
the reward of His voluntary endurance of suffering, but
rather to an honour and glory contemporaneous with the
humiliation on the Cross, in fact, just the other side of the
same experience. God crowns Him with glory and honour
not because He has suffered but in order that He, by the

---

[1] We shall meet the same distinction in the discussion of the doctrine of
St. Thomas Aquinas. It is vital for any theory of Christian perfection.

[2] xiii. 13. Even Holtzmann thinks that this must be interpreted as an
exhortation to break with Judaism, but I cannot see that this meaning is
involved in the symbolism. The 'camp' does not necessarily symbolize
Judaism. It may symbolize worldliness. Passages from Philo can be
adduced to prove this: *De Gig.* 54; *Quod. det. pot.* 160. In *De Ebr.* 99
he says that ἐν τῷ στρατοπέδῳ means ἐν τῷ μετὰ σώματος βίῳ, the material
interests of the earthly life. These must be forsaken if the soul is to see God.
I am happy to find myself in agreement with the exposition of Professor
H. T. Andrews (*Abingdon Commentary,* ad loc.) although the majority of
modern commentators take the older view.

grace of God, might taste death for every man.[1] 'While it is a humiliation to die, it is glorious to taste death for others.'[2] The vocation to suffering, then, will be an element in our author's doctrine of the ideal life on earth. He would have set his seal to that word of St. Paul: 'Unto you it has been granted as a favour (ἐχαρίσθη) not only to believe in Him, but also to suffer for His sake.'

What is fresh and distinctive in the conception of cross-bearing is the call to an act of will. Or rather should we say that the writer sets forth plainly what he conceives to be the will of God for his readers in the crisis which presses, and urges them to embrace that will gladly, even though to embrace it is hard for flesh and blood. That such moments of choice come to every man is an axiom for the experienced director of souls. It is the merit of our author that he so clearly expounded the principle and linked it up, on the one hand, with the joyful choice of the Cross on the part of our Lord, and, on the other hand, with the entrance into that peace which is the soul's home.[3]

IV. The fourth mark of the ideal is that it is a society of souls, no mere individual blessing. It can be said of all true Christian believers (xii. 22–3) that they are already come 'to Mount Zion and to the city of the Living God, the heavenly Jerusalem, to myriads of angels in festal gathering, to the assembly of the first-born registered in heaven, to the God of all as judge, to the spirits of just men made perfect, and to Jesus'. The heavenly Jerusalem is an idea of Jewish origin.[4] The translation of the apocalyptic idea of the kingdom into the Greek word city, so frequent at the end of this epistle,[5] inevitably carries

---

[1] See Bruce, *The Epistle to the Hebrews*, 79–87, where he defends this view against the scorn of A. B. Davidson (*Hebrews*, 59). So Hofmann and Rendall; also, with considerable modifications, Dods. The interpretation is warmly welcomed and finely drawn out by Professor Nairne; see *E.P.*, ch. iii, esp. 67, 117.

[2] Bruce, *Humiliation of Christ* (1876), 39.

[3] See Nairne, *E.P.*, 180; *C.G.T.*, civ, cv.

[4] See *Excursus* of Windisch; *Hebräerbrief*, 103.

[5] See xi. 10, 16; xii. 22; xiii. 14.

with it fresh associations for Greek readers reared in the traditions of the Greek city-state. 'The solemn troops and sweet societies' of the redeemed, the festal assembly[1] of the angels—such are the inhabitants of the heavenly places with whom we may mingle even now. But this does not imply conscious fellowship with the spirits of the departed. The first-born are the Old Testament saints. We are told that we are encompassed about with them as with a great cloud of witnesses, and that they are waiting for that full communion with Christian believers on which their own perfection depends.

Philo, whose thought is crowned rather by the ecstatic vision of God than by the communion of saints, has a beautiful passage which is not without its own relevance for our present purpose:

There is another expression in the Psalms: The course of the river makes glad the city of God. What city? For the holy city which exists now . . . is far from any sea or river, so that it is clear that the writer speaks figuratively, of some other city than the visible city. For in good truth the continual stream of the divine word, being borne on incessantly with rapidity and regularity, is diffused universally over everything, giving joy to all. And in one sense he calls the world the city of God, as having received the whole cup of the divine draught, and it is gladdened thereby, so as to have derived from it an imperishable joy of which it cannot be deprived for ever.'[2]

Such is the bliss of the saints. But it will be observed that the idea of the communion of saints is altogether foreign to Philo's mind. He goes on to say that the city of God is the soul of the wise man in which God walks as in a city. There is nothing in common between the individual communion with God, which is Philo's interpretation of the word 'city', and the mingling of the vast assembly of the saints in Mount Zion, save the joy which flows from the presence of God.[3]

---

[1] In the word πανήγυρις the idea of joy is paramount; cf. Philo in Flacc., 118. ἱλαρᾶς ἐπιθυμίας ἦν πανήγυρις ἐπιζητεῖ. A papyrus of the fifth century A.D. (Moulton-Milligan, 476) uses the word of a birthday festival.

[2] *De Somn*. ii. 246-8 (Yonge's tr., altered).

[3] The contrast between Philo and Ep. Hebrews is well brought out by Riehm, *Lehrbegriff des Hebräerbriefes*, 252-5.

V. The last and greatest difficulty, like Plato's wave, awaits us. The ideal must imply moral perfection. How far is moral perfection possible in this life?

It has been maintained[1] that all the terms used in this epistle for describing the effect of Christ's work in man do not primarily refer to ethical change at all. The word to cleanse or purify (καθαρίζειν, ix. 14) describes the inward efficacy of the New Testament sacrifice. But the result is that man is put in a position to offer religious service (λατρεύειν) to a living God. In some way it neutralizes or annuls sin, so that religious approach to God is possible in spite of it. The word to sanctify (ἁγιάζειν) is not to be taken in the sense of Protestant theology. The people were sanctified, not when they were raised to moral perfection, but when their sin had been so neutralized or annulled that they had access to God. On this view ἁγιάζειν would correspond to the Pauline δικαιοῦν. Again, the word to perfect, as we have seen, means to achieve their end, to reach the ideal. 'The word *He hath perfected for ever those who are being sanctified* cannot mean', says Dr. Denney, 'that He has made them sinless, in the sense of having freed them from all the power of sin, from every trace of its presence; it means obviously that He has put them in the ideal religious relation to God.'[2]

In the foregoing pages we have already recognized the main truth contained in this view. But the distinction between religious and ethical is over-pressed by Principal Denney in a way that does injustice to the thought of the epistle. Granted that the primary sense of words such as καθαρίζειν, ἁγιάζειν, τελειοῦν is not moral change but a change in religious attitude, yet the words hold inalienably the conception of moral cleansing in their context here. The exhortation to pursue holiness (διώκετε . . . ἁγιασμόν) occurs in a context where ethical considerations are strongly evident. The readers are to make common cause with their fellow Christians to seek the bliss and security

---

[1] See Denney, *The Death of Christ*, 221; Milligan, *Theol. of Epistle*, 80–2, 159–60.

[2] Denney's *The Death of Christ*, 223.

of a life under God's control (εἰρήνην διώκετε μετὰ πάντων).
They are to avoid any root of bitterness springing up
which may result in the defilement of the community.
The illustration of Esau and the mention of fornication
make it plain that the writer is thinking of people who
prefer the immediate gratification of their wishes to any
higher end in life. This gives an ethical content to
ἁγίασμος at once. Similarly the ἡγιασμένοι of New Testament times are those who have God's laws written on their
hearts (viii. 10). There is no doubt that this must include
moral purification.

But we must go farther still. There are two stern
passages in the epistle which will serve as our starting-
point. It is indisputable that for certain sins the writer
denies the possibility of a second repentance.

In the case of people who have been once enlightened, . . . and
then fell away—it is impossible (ἀδύνατον) to make them repent
afresh (vi. 4–6, Moffatt's tr.).

Here apostasy is the sin after which there can be no
repentance, no renewal. Thus early in the apostolic age
do we meet a rigorism with which later periods have made
us familiar. But the actual form of the teaching here
merits further study. The repentance which cannot be
repeated is defined as repentance from dead works. These
ἔργα νεκρά are sins that lead to death.

The one thing clear about the phrase is that these ἔργα νεκρά were
not habitual sins of Christians; they were moral offences from which
a man had to break away, in order to become a Christian at all.
They denote . . . occupations, interests, and pleasures, which lay
within the sphere of moral death.[1]

The author implies two facts—first, that these sins have
been forgiven and that for the future they are finished
with, done away. The imperfection of the Jewish sacrifices lay in the necessity for the repetition of the offering
every year (ix. 7 and 25) and in their merely external
efficacy (ix. 13), whereas the perfection of the sacrifice of

---

[1] Moffatt, *Hebrews*, 74.

Christ lies in the single offering ἐφάπαξ and in the cleansing
of the conscience from dead works (ix. 14) and the taking
away of sin.[1] It is noticeable, too, that the self-sacrifice
of Christ has taken place at the end of the world (ix. 26—
ἐπὶ συντελείᾳ τῶν αἰώνων), while the second coming will be
χωρὶς ἁμαρτίας (ix. 28)—apart from sin, not to deal with sin.
Evidently the doctrine of Jewish Apocalyptic that sinlessness will be one of the blessings of the Messianic age[2] has
helped to mould our writer's thought at this point. When
he speaks of Christians as those who have tasted the
powers of the age to come, he includes freedom from
ἔργα νεκρά as a gift of God which is already theirs. Τελειότης,
therefore, does inherently imply a certain freedom from
sin. In a sense the future age is already here. But the full
consummation is yet to come.

A distinction between sins for which there is no repentance and sins of inadvertence is discernible from the
second 'severe section' of the epistle (x. 26–31).

For if we sin deliberately, after receiving the knowledge of the
truth, there is no longer any sacrifice for sins left, nothing but an
awful outlook of doom. . . . Any one who has rejected the law of
Moses dies without mercy. . . . How much heavier do you suppose
will be the punishment assigned to him who has spurned the Son of
God, who has profaned the covenant-blood with which he was
sanctified, who has insulted the Spirit of grace? (cf. the reference to
the sin of Esau, xii. 15–17).

The distinction between the two kinds of sin is well-
marked in the Old Testament and is taken over by the
writer from the Pentateuch.[3] In the New Covenant the
distinguishing mark of one who sins deliberately is that
he insults the Spirit of Grace. This implies that the Spirit
cannot dwell in a man who deliberately sins.[4] The recog-

---

[1] εἰς ἀθέτησιν τῆς ἁμαρτίας, ix. 26, which must be interpreted in the
light of ἀφαιρεῖν ἁμαρτίας (x. 4).

[2] *Jubilees*, i. 29; v. 12; xxiii. 29; *Life of Adam and Eve*, xiii, xxix. 8;
Slav. Enoch 65, 8. See Windisch, *Taufe und Sünde*, 37–45.

[3] Lev. iv. 2; v. 15; iv. 13; xxii. 14; Num. xv. 24; Deut. xvii. 6.

[4] What were the deliberate sins which endangered a man's salvation?
Apostasy (xii. 25), sexual vice (xii. 16; xiii. 4). Farther than that we
cannot go.

nized normal position which the writer assumes is that the man in whom the Spirit dwells does not sin. But he knows that there are sins of inadvertence.[1] The most winsome and appealing passages in the epistle are those which speak of the compassion of our High Priest. He had to become like his brothers in every respect, in order to prove a merciful and faithful High Priest in things divine, to expiate the sins of the people. It is as He suffered by His temptations that He is able 'to help the tempted' (ii. 17, 18). 'The tempted' must mean those who are already Christian. But even here the author does not say that Christ's sacrifice avails for the sins that may follow on temptations. His meaning is rather that the succour is available to prevent them from falling into sin. So, too, in another passage (iv. 16): *Let us approach the throne of grace with confidence, that we may receive mercy and find grace to help us in the time of need.* It is expressly said in the preceding verse that the temptations of Jesus were χωρὶς ἁμαρτίας. 'The time of need' must mean the time of temptation.[2] In the next few verses we have the clearest statement of the mercy of Christ for those who sin through ignorance and the weakness of nature (v. 2, μετριοπαθεῖν δυνάμενος τοῖς ἀγνοοῦσιν καὶ πλανωμένοις).

The author's thought does not finally rest in this distinction between heinous and venial sins. The mature (τέλειοι), he says (v. 14), have their faculties trained by exercise to distinguish good and evil (πρὸς διάκρισιν καλοῦ τε καὶ κακοῦ). His readers are called to this task of moral discrimination. The putting away even of these sins of ignorance and weakness should lie in the normal development of the Christian life.[3]

[1] Windisch, *Taufe u. Sünde*, 302, points out that according to the author there must be a sin-offering for such sins. The sacrifice of Christ must have a perpetual efficacy for these. But the writer never actually says this.

[2] See Milligan, 80.

[3] Windisch points out (*Taufe u. Sünde*, 306, 307) that the writer bases his proposed advance from elementary truths to such teaching of moral discrimination on the permission of God (καὶ τοῦτο ποιήσομεν ἐάνπερ ἐπιτρέπῃ ὁ θεός). He is certain that some sins admit of no repentance. But here

That conclusion is the result of the practical logic of the epistle throughout. It is expressed in the exhortation which follows on the thought of the great cloud of witnesses—ὄγκον ἀποθέμενοι πάντα καὶ τὴν εὐπερίστατον ἁμαρτίαν. It may well be that the thought here is of the smaller sins that so easily impede our course.[1] But whether the distinction with which he has hitherto worked is present to his mind or whether he simply means here 'sin' in general, he has no doubt that the goal at which the Christian aims in this life is freedom from sin. His last prayer is for their perfection—that God may furnish them with everything for the doing of His will and may create in their lives through Jesus Christ what is well-pleasing in His sight (xiii. 21).[2]

The nature of the τελειότης contemplated has now been sketched in this chapter. The broad result is that far more is assigned to the salvation attainable in this life than was recognized, for example, in the massive work of Riehm.[3] And this result is due to the recognition of the Platonic influences at work on the mind of our author. According to the older interpretation 'the world to come' was purely future. Now we see that the phrase means the heavenly realm of spiritual realities. Hence the seeming paradox that 'the world to come' is really present. This holds good even of the conception of the sabbath rest, which at first sight seems to be set in the future. But the stress is really on the *To-day*. Owing to disobedience Israel failed to enter into that rest. The whole stress of the

---

[1] he shows that he believes the commission of sins of weakness is something contrary to the true development of the Christian life as intended by God. Windisch, *Hebräerbrief*, 99.

[2] It is doubtful whether we can give assent to the thesis so ably advocated by Windisch (*Taufe u. Sünde*, 312) that the τέλειοι are the baptized. This is unlikely (Feine, 501). Probably the word was used in the Pauline churches in the sense in which in certain evangelical churches to-day the minister will speak of a minority of those under his care as 'spiritually-minded'. No fixed or organized group is intended. But he knows the few on whose spiritual instincts and religious maturity he can rely. Such men—τέλειοι—the *Auctor ad Hebraeos* thinks his readers ought to be.

[3] See, for example, the description of τελείωσις in Riehm's *Lehrbegriff*, 794 ff. Contrast E. F. Scott, 109–15.

passage is on the idea that the rest of God has always existed, and that God desires to share it now with His sons.[1]

But at the same time we must recognize that the full and final perfection is set beyond the grave (cf. vi. 2). It is the vision of God (xii. 14). It is the establishment of a realm that cannot be shaken, after the anguish and catastrophe of the present age (xii. 26–9). The references to the Parousia are few, but unmistakable. And more evident is the forward look, the pervasive hope, which characterizes the epistle.[2] 'We are not the men to shrink back and be lost, but to have faith and so win our souls.' And the end of that faith, the crown of that achievement, the inheritance of the blessed, will be granted to those who are 'looking for' their Lord. Then the vision will be face to face.

[1] Riehm's discussion (798–808) is admirable.
[2] x. 39; ix. 28; cf. Nairne, *E.P.*, 293.

CHAPTER IV

THE JOHANNINE THEOLOGY

τετελείωται ἡ ἀγάπη μεθ᾽ ἡμῶν.

1 *John* iv. 17.

That is τετελειωμένον which has reached its τέλος, has achieved its end, has run its full course. And the end of God's Love to us is attained in our loving one another. . . . Then Love's circuit is complete, from God to us, from us to our brother, and through our brother back to God.—*R. Law.*

IN writing a slender tract destined to be so intimately intertwined with Christian devotion in all ages, the Evangelist has achieved a miracle. They still show to visitors at Bonn the poor little piano which belonged to Beethoven. The contrast between the instrument and the Sonatas is almost overwhelming. So in the Fourth Gospel, the writer's instruments of thought are unpretentious. With all the riches of an unsurpassed language before him, he uses only the simplest possible words. He plays only on a few ideas. He has the wealth of the synoptists for his use; he selects, rearranges, corrects, adapts; but he does not attempt to convey all their treasures through the medium of his art. It is possible that like Luke he may not have had the advantage of personal knowledge of Jesus in the days of His flesh. But with all his limitations, what a marvellous symphony he has composed! With this gospel a Church predominantly Hebraic in tradition and in temper was able to offer Christ to the Gentiles of that Hellenistic world. With this gospel the Church absorbed them. When we next meet a great Greek Christian teacher at the end of the second century, he is still predominantly Hebraic in the temper of his mind. Clement has learnt from this 'spiritual gospel' how the message of Jesus, without suffering a complete transformation into something 'rich and strange', can be presented to the Greeks.

In the discussion of Johannine theology, the method pursued often determines the conclusions. For Evangelical piety, any discussion of St. John's teaching on Christian

Perfection would have begun with the exegesis of the difficult texts in the first Epistle.

Everyone who abideth in him doth not sin. (1. iii. 6; see also iii. 9 and v. 18.)

But any such method begins by concentrating attention on sinlessness; and Christian Perfection is greater even than sinlessness. Further, the Fourth Gospel falls to be considered together with the First Epistle. Any difficult saying must be judged in reference to its context. In this case the context is the whole of the Gospel and the Epistles of John.

We must set in the supreme place the conception of eternal life, which in this Gospel has taken the place of the Kingdom of Heaven. But in order to draw out the meaning of 'Eternal life' we shall have recourse to the First Epistle, to discover, if possible, its main structure, and to trace out the ideas which bind its aphorisms into an architectural unity.

The justification for this method lies, first, in the close relation in which the two writings admittedly stand; second, in the fact that the writer of both is essentially a pastor with the one supreme aim of edifying his flock. In the letter, more easily than in the Gospel, we can trace the motives which move his mind.[1] In the third place we know that the difficulties which confronted the Church at the end of the first century were such as have hardly ever been paralleled in any age. If we can find that John's reasons for writing were in close touch with the menacing facts, we may be able more readily to assign the true interpretation to many concepts of the Fourth Gospel about which controversy still persists.

Fortunately, among the various analyses of the First Epistle there is one of outstanding excellence.

---

[1] See the excellent remarks in A. E. Brooke, *I.C.C.* viii. Singularly enough R. Bultmann (*Die Analyse des ersten Johannes-Brief*), in his attempt to find a written source which the writer of the letter has utilized, strikes out the passages which are homiletical and edifying, and *therefore* are not so original!

Haering[1] finds in the letter a triple presentation and two leading ideas—an Ethical thesis, and a Christological thesis. These two are intertwined, but they give us convenient divisions for our discussion. The first section will be an exposition of the Ideal of Eternal Life; the second, the meaning of the Christological thesis for the Ideal of Eternal Life; and, third, the meaning of the Ethical thesis for the Ideal of Eternal Life.

I. THE CONCEPT OF ETERNAL LIFE

Of all the ideas in the Johannine teaching the central unifying thought is life. The aim of the Fourth Gospel is expressly stated to be the impartation of life in Jesus through belief that Jesus is the Christ. With this ζωή is salvation given, and ἀπώλεια is its opposite.

So far there is no difference between the Johannine writings and the rest of the New Testament. But the next step carries us into a new realm of thought. As we have seen, eternal life in the Synoptic Gospels was used as an individualizing of religion. But it is always eschatologically conceived. In the Fourth Gospel eternal life is conceived as essentially present.

He who believes in the Son has eternal life, but he who disobeys the Son shall not see life. (iii. 36; cf. v. 24, vi. 47; 1. iii. 14, 1. v. 13.)

The phrase 'eternal life' is used in the Fourth Gospel as synonymous with life, and both refer to life in the present (e.g. v. 39; vi. 53).

In some passages a future meaning is possible. The most noticeable is xii. 25: *He that loveth his life destroyeth it, and he that hateth his life in this world shall keep it unto life eternal.* The saying reads like a quotation from the synoptists which has not been completely rewritten to harmonize with the thought of the Fourth Evangelist. Eternal life is here clearly thought of as the future life.

[1] In *Theologische Abhandlungen Carl von Weissacker Gewidmet* (1892) 171–200. Gedankengang und Grundgedanke des ersten Johannesbriefs. The complete analysis is translated by Professor A. E. Brooke, *The Johannine Epistles* (*I.C.C.* 1912), xxxiv–xxxvi.

There are a few other passages of which the exposition is more doubtful.

In his commentary B. Weiss has expounded a number of passages in the eschatological sense.[1]

So must the Son of Man be lifted up, in order that every one who believes on him may not perish but have life eternal. (iii. 15.)

But here the present ἔχῃ proves that the permanent possession of life is meant, as opposed to the definite moment of death implied in the aorist ἀπόληται, which is used in the next verse.[2]

He that disobeyeth the Son shall not see life, but the wrath of God abideth on him. (iii. 36.)

Does the future ὄψεται compel us to accept an eschatological meaning? Surely the meaning is rather that from the present onwards into the next world, the disobedient man is denied the possession of life. The phrase which precedes in this very verse (He that believeth on the Son hath eternal life) makes it impossible to regard the eschatological meaning as primary here.

The reaper is receiving his wages and harvesting for eternal life. (iv. 36.)

There is here an ambiguity, perhaps designed. *For eternal life* may mean *resulting in the eternal life of the Samaritans.* Or the phrase may mean that the real wages of the reaper are the souls saved by his preaching, those who will be his reason for rejoicing when the future life comes.

Labour not for the food which perishes, but for the food which remains to life eternal. (vi. 27.)

The water which I shall give him will become in him a well of water springing up to life eternal. (iv. 14.)

These two examples may be taken together. They are both cited by Bernard[3] as illustrations for the eschatological use of the phrase 'eternal life'. But this interpretation

---

[1] His views are set forth consecutively in *Der Johanneische Lehrbegriff* (1862), 2–5.

[2] Hence I cannot agree with Bernard (*I.C.C.*), i. 116.

[3] *I.C.C.* i. 142, 191.

ignores the close connexion between the spiritual food and drink and the idea of life eternal. Again the preposition εἰς need not mean 'until'. It may mean 'resulting in'. The food of life and the water are communion with God. The word ἁλλομένου in iv. 14 is applied in the LXX to the Spirit of God falling violently on Samson, Saul, and David.[1] It would seem that once again present communion with God and eternal life are closely joined in the thought of the evangelist.[2]

So far, then, we find only one exception to the rule that eternal life is regarded in the Fourth Gospel as a present possession. But at the same time we have references to the last day. The writer evidently shares to some extent the eschatology of his time.

My little children, it is the last hour. (1. ii. 18; cf. 1. ii. 28.)

The Spirit of Antichrist is already in the world (1. iv. 3). There will be a resurrection on the Last Day (vi. 38, 40, 44, 54; xi. 24). On the Last Day, too, there will be the Judgement (xii. 28), even if the judgement is already spoken by the word of Jesus in the present.

Are these references to the future life to be regarded as a desertion of the distinctive point of view of the Fourth Gospel? Professor E. F. Scott finds here one of those apparent contradictions so characteristic of the Gospel. 'John with all his originality of thought was still partly bound to the past. Along with his own conception he strove to make room for the belief that had impressed itself upon the Church at large, of which he was a member.'[3]

It is unnecessary to see any contradiction here. The conception of eternal life forms a *continuum* in the mind

---

[1] Abbott, *Diatessarica*, 2315. Dr. Bernard admits that εἰς will express 'the purpose of this spiritual torrent of grace'. But he does not correlate the meaning of the Spirit here with the idea of eternal life. Cf. vi. 63: *It is the Spirit who gives life*.

[2] Cf. E. von Schrenck, *Die johanneische Anschauung vom Leben* (1898), 73, 74.

[3] *The Fourth Gospel*, 216. Cf. Macgregor, *The Gospel of John* (1928), 146, 147.

of the writer. The 'last day' marks the definite close of the process which has been going on in this world.[1] Whether in the present age or in the world to come, eternal life is found in Christ alone.

The eschatology of the First Epistle does not read like a message which is dominating the writer's mind. When John speaks of Antichrist he refers (καθὼς ἠκούσατε) to the general apostolic teaching. But he 'refers to a popular tradition only to spiritualize it'. All we can say is that in the epistle the expectation of the Parousia is 'more clearly stated and more obviously felt than in the gospel'.[2] There is no necessary inconsistency between the belief that the world is near its end, and the belief of eternal life as already realized and present.

The particular phrase which is used for the Parousia is 'manifestation'. He uses the word both for the Parousia and for the earthly life of the Lord. 'For him the "Presence" is no sudden unveiling. . . . It is the consummation of a process. . . . It is the final manifestation of the things that are, and therefore the passing away of all that is phenomenal.'[3]

But this eschatology does not dominate the thought of the writer. There is one clear statement of the perfection which may be looked for at the Parousia.

> We are children of God now, beloved. What we are to be is not apparent yet, but we do know that when He appears, we are to be like Him, for we are to see Him as He is. (1 John iii. 2.)

Even here the eschatology is only used as an exhortation to purity in the present. 'He that has this hope set on him purifies himself, even as he is pure' (1 John iii. 3).

In the thought of the Gospel there is a similar stress on the present, and the perfection of the future finds scanty expression. Nowhere is the change of emphasis more marked than in the High-Priestly prayer of Christ. From

---

[1] See Holtzmann-Bauer, *Evangelium des Johannes* (Tübingen, 1908), 91, 127; Bernard, i. clxi.

[2] A. E. Brooke, 52 and 37.

[3] Ibid., 37.

the beginning to the end the prayer is governed by the idea of δοξάζειν. But the δόξα is not the eschatological 'glory' of the Synoptic Gospels. The Son has already glorified the Father by accomplishing the work given to Him to do. His prayer is that He may be glorified by the Father in order that He may give eternal life to all those whom the Father has given Him. This glorification is therefore a present glorification; the glory given even now is the eternal glory enjoyed by the Son with the Father before the world began. Their mutual unity is both the proof and purpose of the gift. The Son is to be in them as the Father is in Him, and His disciples are to be perfectly one because of this union, in order that the world may know that Christ has been sent by God. Here again the stress is on the glory to be manifested in the present age by mystical fellowship with Christ and brotherly love to one another.

In the story of the raising of Lazarus there is an explicit displacement of the primitive eschatology of the Church.

Jesus said, Your brother will rise again. I know, said Martha, he will rise at the resurrection on the last day. Jesus said to her, I am myself resurrection and life.

This can only mean that all that the older eschatology promised as a future good is now in Jesus a present possession.[1]

Another illustration of the same deliberate intention is to be found in a saying which Holtzmann calls 'the great now already'.

Verily I say to you, the time is coming, it has come already, when the dead will listen to the voice of the son of God, and those who listen will live. (v. 25.)

Eternal life then is present; it is the goal of mankind, it is the nature of God.[2] In vi. 57 God is described as ὁ ζῶν πατήρ. The life of Jesus is διὰ τὸν πατέρα. So 'he who eateth me shall live also δι' ἐμέ.' Life is to share in what

[1] Cf. E. F. Scott, 304.
[2] Cf. Feine, Die Theologie des N.T. (3rd ed. 1919), 449, 451.

God is. At the end of the First Epistle Jesus is described as the true God and eternal life (1. v. 20; cf. xi. 25; xiv. 6). Everything that is good is bound up with eternal life, that is, with Jesus Himself. Jesus calls Himself the Bread of Life, and draws out the spiritual meaning of His picture by saying that whoso comes to Him shall never hunger, and whoso believes in Him shall never thirst (vi. 35).

Various marks of the possession of eternal life are given both in the Gospel and in the Epistle.[1] The first is *Joy*. The fulfilment of the joy brought by fellowship with the Father and the Son is the motive for writing the letter. Jesus promises perfect joy to His disciples (xv. 11). It is His own joy, and through His intercession and ascent to the Father His perfect joy will be given to them (xvii. 13). This joy endures. It comes from the vision of Christ, and cannot be taken away by man (xvi. 22; cf. xx. 20). In prayer all things are given to them. *Ask and ye shall receive, that your joy may be perfected* (xvi. 24). Just as Abraham rejoices at the day of the appearance of Christ (viii. 56), just as the Baptist is glad when he hears the Bridegroom's voice and knows that the promised Messianic reign is beginning (iii. 29), so believers find an inexhaustible source of joy in the presence of their Lord. The reason for this is their perfect obedience to His supreme command of love; by remaining thus within His love and God's love, their joy will be perfect (xv. 10–11).

Another mark is *Peace*. This is the gift of Jesus to His own (xiv. 27). His presence fills the old familiar greeting with a new content (xx. 19, 20, 26). This peace is a harmony of the soul which is not disturbed by trouble; it is due to His conquest of the evil forces of the world (xvi. 33). Peace implies the absence of any mental perturbation (xiv. 1) and is given in answer to prayer (xii. 27). It is freedom from the world, a sublime recollectedness wherein the soul puts all its trust in God.[2]

---

[1] The inclusiveness of the idea of eternal life is well brought out by Titius, *Die Johanneische Anschauung unter dem Gesichtspunkt der Seligkeit* (1900), 21–30.

[2] Cf. H. Fuchs, *Augustin u. der antike Friedensgedanke*, 41.

A third mark is the παρρησία whereby the soul draws near to God and enjoys intimate communion with Him (1. v. 13, 14). There will be confidence at the Day of Judgement because the soul is already in this world abiding in God (1. ii. 24, 25, 28; 1. iv. 17). Our heart does not condemn us and so *we have confidence in approaching God and we get from him whatever we wish, because we obey His commands and do what is well pleasing in His sight* (1. iii. 21, 22).

We have briefly sketched the main characteristics of eternal life. But how are we to define eternal life? This question is the focus of all the difficulties in the interpretation of the Johannine writings.

The answer might seem simple. We have a definition in the High-Priestly prayer of Jesus.

This is life eternal, that they may know thee, the only true God, and him whom thou hast sent, even Jesus Christ. (xvii. 3.)

On the strength of this passage we can come to the conclusion that eternal life is the knowledge of God in the face of Jesus Christ.[1]

But objections have been brought against this identification.[2] The first is that the definition comes in an unsuitable place. It is too late in the book to define a term which is presupposed as already well known to his readers. And it is unsuitable in a prayer.

But the Fourth Gospel is not a formal treatise. The writer is putting into words a religious experience. He is transcribing into new thought-forms the ideal of an earlier age. Is it not likely that he will give to his readers the key to his meaning in this supreme chapter wherein he unveils the heart of his Lord?

It has been urged[3] that the form of the sentence αὕτη δέ

---

[1] B. Weiss has worked out this view in his *Biblical Theology of the New Testament* (E. tr. 2 vols. 1883). Also in *Der Johanneische Lehrbegriff* (1862). Cf. *Feine Theol. der N.T.* 451.

[2] The chief monograph on eternal life is that of E. von Schrenck, *Die Johanneische Anschauung vom Leben* (Leipzig 1898). I have followed his objections one by one and tried to answer them in the text.

[3] E. von Schrenck, 134, following Huther.

ἐστιν ἡ αἰώνιος ζωή, ἵνα ... does not convey the impression of an identification of the ideas of 'eternal life' and 'knowledge of God'. But the author of the Fourth Gospel has his own syntactical constructions. This particular expression is not unusual with him.[1]

A third objection is that the identification of eternal life and knowledge of God cannot be carried through. 'Let any one try to read the fifth and sixth chapters of the Gospel, substituting the "knowledge of God" for "life" and he will soon find that the conception is narrowed in a way unlike St. John.'[2]

Let us take the one passage which is said to prove this objection.

> ... *He that eateth this bread shall live for ever.*

Is it any narrowing of the thought to transpose this sentence so that it reads: *He that eateth this bread shall know his Father for ever.* The communion with God which the soul enjoys in this life has about it the mark of everlastingness, of that which abides.

> This savours not of death:
> This hath a relish of eternity.

As we have seen above, the life beyond the grave is regarded by the Fourth Evangelist as the continuation and completion of the communion with God which is already given here.

The only passage where the identification cannot be carried through is v. 26.

> *As the Father hath life in himself, so he has given the Son to have life in himself.*

The idea of 'life' in the Fourth Gospel varies. Sometimes it is a state of being. Sometimes it is a power. Here, when seen from the Godward side, it is the power of giving life—a thoroughly Hebraic conception.[3] Here the author's point is that Jesus has the power which belongs to God. He can communicate the highest good to men

[1] Cf. 1 John iii. 11; v. 3; xv. 12.
[2] v. Schrenck, *Die Johanneische Anschauung vom Leben* (1898), 135.
[3] Bernard, i. 243.

because He is the Son of God. The highest good may well be the knowledge of God, through Jesus Christ.

The only valid objection remaining would be an allusion to any spiritual blessing which could not be included in the knowledge of God. As we have seen immortality belongs to the very idea of knowledge of God.[1] Can it be said that the idea of blessedness, of spiritual fulfilment, is distinct from the knowledge of God?[2] Eternal life is the good which quenches all thirst, and satisfies all hunger (iv. 13, 14; vi. 35). *I am the door: by me if any man enter in he shall be saved, and he shall come in and go out and find pasture* (x. 9). The last passage gives us the secret of this life. It is the knowledge of Jesus Who is the door to it, Who is that life itself.

We conclude, therefore, that the meaning of the eternal life, which is the privilege of believers, is fully given in the High-Priestly prayer. It is the knowledge of God in the face of Jesus Christ. The knowledge of God is the Johannine term for fellowship with God. It is not a mere intellectual possession; it is not only 'a realm of thought which is grounded in Jesus'.[3] The believer who knows God has received the gift of God which is love; there is an inner binding of the believer who knows God and God Who is known. By our knowledge of God we are actually in the heart of God.[4]

We know that the son of God has come and has given us understanding that we should know Him that is true and we are in Him that is true, in His son Jesus Christ. (1. v. 20.)

To know God is not a momentary experience. It is an 'abiding in God'. So eternal life is used as equivalent to abiding in Christ.[5] Compare the two verses:

He who eats my flesh and drinks my blood has eternal life.

[1] Cf. A. B. Davidson *The Theology of the Old Testament* (1904), 402–532.   [2] So E. von Schrenck, 143, 144.

[3] Holtzmann-Bauer, *Hand-Commentar*, 308.

[4] The second ἀληθινός must refer to God, not to Jesus Christ. Holtzmann (*Hand-Commentar*, ad. loc.) is right here as against Bernhard Weiss.

[5] The only passage which could be quoted against this conclusion is 1. ii. 24, 25, which looks at first sight as if the life were given to those who abide in the Son and in the Father.

He who eats my flesh and drinks my blood abides in me and I in him. (vi. 54 and 56.)

II. THE CHRISTOLOGICAL THESIS AND ITS MEANING FOR THE IDEAL OF ETERNAL LIFE

Hereby know ye the Spirit of God:
Every spirit which confesseth Jesus Christ has come in the flesh is of God. (1. iv. 2).

In the development of this thesis the writer lays all the stress on the fact that Jesus is the Son of God (see especially 1. v. 5–12). That the thesis is pre-eminent in the Fourth Gospel is proved by the avowed intent of the writer (xx. 31).

It is a tempting path that wanders through the maze of religious syncretism at the end of the first century. The very stress on the title the 'Son of God' is inviting. Could not this be explained by parallels from contemporary cults?

But the temptation must be resisted. The fact of over-whelming significance is that the writer regarded Jesus as the Messiah of Jewish hope.[1] John the Baptist (i. 34; iii. 27–36) denies that he himself is the Christ, and on the next day greets Jesus as the One Who was to be manifested to Israel, as the One Who was to baptize with the Holy Ghost (i. 15, 20, 29–34; cf v. 33). The earliest disciples greet Him by the Jewish name, *Rabbi*, which is explained to the Greeks as meaning teacher, and after half a day with Him acknowledge Him by the Jewish name of *Messiah, which is being interpreted Christ*. Philip goes to Nathanael and says *We have found Him of whom Moses in the law and the prophets wrote*. Nathanael greets Him in the words of Jewish expectation which prove that the writer of the Fourth Gospel interpreted the words Son of God from the Messianic title of the king in the second psalm: *Rabbi thou art the son of God, thou art the King of Israel* (i. 38, 41, 45, 49). It is in the light of Messiahship that we must interpret the later confession of the twelve (*we have*

[1] Cf. the valuable monograph of Fr. Büchsel, *Johannes u. der hellenistische Syncretismus* (1928).

believed and known that thou art the Holy One of God, vi. 69),
and of Martha (*I have believed that thou art the Christ, the
Son of God, who is coming into the world*, xi. 27).

The question of Messiahship is the battle-ground for
the Jewish opponents of Jesus. (*If thou art the Christ, tell
us plainly*, x. 24.) Jesus enters Jerusalem as Messiah, and
is greeted as the King of Israel, and after the Resurrection
the disciples are said to have remembered this fact and its
connexion with Jewish prophecy (xii. 13–16). As the
King of the Jews Jesus is delivered to Pilate, and as the
King of the Jews He is crucified (xviii. 33–40; xix. 3,
12–15, 19–22).

I have set out the evidence in detail, because of the
temptation which besets the modern student to find Greek
ideas everywhere in the thought of the Fourth Evangelist.
But, with his own elusive way of statement, he has clearly
told us that the predominant idea in his mind when he
speaks of Jesus Christ, the Son of God, is that of Messiahship. If he borrows stones from Greek quarries, all is
built on a solid Jewish foundation. It is, of course,
Christianized. This Messiah is not confined in His
mission to the Jewish race. He is no political king.[1] But
He it is who awakens the dead, and brings the abundant
gift of eternal life.[2] He abdicates the old Messianic
function of Judgement, but only because judgement is in
the present, and not on the distant horizon. And the
present judgement is inseparable from Himself (iii. 18–19).

The second title used for Jesus is *Son of God*, or Son.
This occurs more frequently than any other in the Fourth
Gospel. It is not a superfluous title of honour. It must go
beyond the meaning of the Jewish word 'Messiah'. The
writer says expressly that when Jesus calls Himself Son it
meant to make Himself equal with God.[3] In the controversy with the Jews the use of the title Son of God is the
cause of their bitterness against Him (x. 33–6).

It was because of this blasphemy that they delivered
Him up to death (xix. 7). For the author of the Fourth

[1] xviii. 36, 37; cf. xix. 19.   [2] v. 21–9; x. 10.
[3] v. 18.

Gospel this was no tragic misunderstanding of the words of Jesus; it was a statement of the simple fact that Jesus was one with the Father (x. 30).

The value of this thesis for personal religion was seen and emphasized by the evangelist.

He that seeth (ὁ θεωρῶν) me, seeth him that sent me. (xii. 45.)

He that hath seen me (ὁ ἑωρακὼς) hath seen the Father. (xiv. 9.)

The conception of Messiahship has been placed on a surer foundation when it is thus explained in terms of Sonship.[1] Because Jesus is Son of God He is loved by the Father, and this love means that God has committed all things to His hands (v. 20). The perfect communion of Father and Son conditions all the work of Jesus (v. 19). *My meat is to do the will of him who sent me, and to bring his work to perfection* (iv. 34). This saying is usually interpreted[2] in connexion with xvii. 4—I have finished (perfected) the work thou didst give me to do. In this case it means the work of the earthly life of the Messiah. But in xvii. 4 the work is a definite task committed to Jesus by His Father during His earthly life. In iv. 34 the ἔργον is the work of God, without any such restriction. There is a special allusion to the work of bringing the Samaritans to the knowledge of eternal life. In view of the expressed desire of the Fourth Evangelist to break down the distinction between the earthly Jesus and the exalted Christ, may we not find in this saying a hint that it is God's will that Christians should live in this world in complete communion with Himself? It is always and everywhere the function of Christ to bring the work of the Father to its completion; He is in virtue of this function the Saviour of the world (iv. 42).

The result of our survey of these two titles for our present purpose is becoming clear. Eternal life, the ideal of present perfection, is the gift of Jesus Christ who is united with God. So far we have found no necessity to explain any of the categories of the Gospel by the invasion

---

[1] Cf. Schlatter, *Theologie der Apostel*, 157–8.

[2] e.g. Holtzmann-Bauer, ad loc.

of Greek thought. The ground on which the author of the Johannine writings is building is the common experience of the early Christian Church. Just as on the day of Pentecost it was impossible for Peter to separate Jesus from God, just as for Paul, Jesus was on an equality with God (Phil. ii. 5), just as Mark could see in his Gospel the story of One who was no mere man but the Son of God Who was higher than the angels, to receive Whom was to receive God (i. 1; xiii. 32; ix. 37), so John sees in the historical Jesus God Himself, God in human flesh, God alive and active among men.[1]

It is almost impossible to over-estimate the significance of the fact that, at this particular crisis of the world's history when the religious beliefs of East and West were melting into one another, the profoundest ideal of personal religion was linked with the perfect life of an historical Person, and presented to the Greek world in a form that could be understood.[2] There is really no parallel in the other religions or cults of antiquity for such a proclamation. 'He who has seen me has seen the Father.' It sounds so familiar to the ears of the Christian. But nothing like it can be produced from the Hellenistic writings of that age.[3] In the cults the vision of God was associated with some ritual, or it is an ecstatic vision, or it is an intellectual glance. Here it is the knowledge of a Person who actually lived and died and came back to the hearts of His own.

The distinctiveness of the Johannine conception becomes clearer when we advance farther. The gift of eternal life which Jesus brings to men is fellowship of the same quality as already exists between the Father and the Son. It is love. The perfection of which human beings are capable is grounded on the love-relationship between Jesus and God Himself. It may not be altogether fanciful to see a parallel between the Only-begotten Son, Who lies upon the Father's breast, and the Beloved Disciple, who lay upon the breast of Jesus. The same intimate quality of

---

[1] μονογενής, i. 51; v. 20; iii. 13; xvii. 5, 24; xii. 45; xiv. 9.
[2] Cf. Schlatter, *Theologie der Apostel*, 211–12.
[3] See Fr. Büchsel, *Johannes und der hellenistische Syncretismus*, 26–7.

the divine communion is meant to be reproduced in the quality of the relationship between the disciple and the Lord. The ultimate ground for such an intimate relationship lies in the nature of God Himself. God is love (1. iv. 8). Love is goodness revealing itself, life communicating itself. 'The whole of Christianity may be, as in point of fact it is, by John (1. iv. 8–12) developed from this idea; God the eternal love, Christ the infinite divine proof of love, who is to constrain the heart of man to a responsive love to God and to his brethren for God's sake; that is everything.'[1]

The idea of fellowship with Christ is closely connected with the ascent of Jesus to His Father's side.[2] At that time the communion will be more intimate and illuminating (xvi. 25). After His glorification He will have the opportunity of granting eternal life to all men (xvii. 1, 2; xii. 32). The glorification is closely connected with the Cross (xii. 28–33). The link which binds them together is the thought of love. Only through His exaltation to the right hand of God can Jesus be set free from the limits of His earthly life, and thus be the appointed means of leading men into fellowship with God. And the highest proof of the love of God is the obedience of Christ into the death of the Cross. John here has entered into the inheritance of Pauline thought.[3] His Christ-Mysticism is fellowship, even through suffering, with God.

The thought of the Gospel thus forms an exquisitely wrought unity. Heitmüller has described the contrast between the first three Gospels and the fourth as that between the bright crowded streets of a city and the stillness of a lofty cathedral where the light is only poured through windows of stained glass.[4] If I may adapt his simile, I would add that as we linger in the cathedral we become aware that all the devotion of the building gathers round the altar. At the central shrine the passion of love is beating within this dimly-lit cathedral calm. *The blood of Jesus his son cleanseth us from all sin.* Is this sentence a mere homiletic note which the writer has added as an

---

[1] Beyschlag, *N.T. Theology*, ii. 431.   [2] Titius, 67, 68.
[3] Feine, 416–17.   [4] *Die Schriften des N.T.* (1908), ii. 685.

afterthought?[1] Or is it the transcript of a vivid experience, the offer of a salvation which the other religious cults could never promise to their devotees? Again our answer must not depend on the First Epistle alone, but on the coherence of the religious experience described both in the First Epistle and the Fourth Gospel.

The phrase 'the Saviour of the World' only occurs twice. But it means much for the mind of the writer.[2] It is the love of Jesus for His own that causes Him to lay down His life for them (x. 11; xiii. 1; xv. 13), and the purpose of the sacrifice is to bring them into the closest possible fellowship with God.[3] The purpose cannot be fulfilled so long as any mist of sin remains to blind the soul to the vision of light.

III. THE ETHICAL THESIS AND ITS MEANING FOR THE IDEAL OF ETERNAL LIFE

God is light, and in Him there is no darkness at all. (1. i. 5.)

> He appeared to take our sins away.
> In Him is no sin.
> Anyone who remains in Him does not sin. (1. iii. 5,6.)

The moral conduct of the believer is not a mere external preparation for eternal life. It is an integral part of it. The God with whom we may walk in light has in Him no darkness at all. There can be no communion of darkness with light.[4] Already we are aware that the metaphor ought not to lead us astray into imagining that we have here a metaphysical definition of God. The God who is Light is also Love. Where there is no love there is no knowledge of God.[5] Love to God and man is the fulfilling of all moral commandments. And therefore morality becomes religion.[6]

---

[1] So Bultmann in the *Jülicher Festgabe* (1927), 140.

[2] Cf. Büchsel, 44.

[3] Schlatter, *Die Theologie der Apostel*, 173, 174. 'Seine ganze Darstellung Jesu ist Kreuzeslehre.'

[4] Cf. 2 Cor. vi. 14.   [5] 1. iv. 8; 1. ii. 3, 4; 1. iii. 6.

[6] Cf. Titius, 58: 'Die neue Religion ist sittlich geartet, und die neue Sittlichkeit ist selbst Religion.'

The difficulty with which we have to deal in the exposition of this section may be seen in two contrasted sets of aphorisms of the First Epistle:

If we say 'We have no sin' we are deceiving ourselves and the truth is not in us. (1. i. 8.)

If we say 'We have not sinned' we make Him a liar and His word is not within us. (1. i. 10.)

He who says 'I know Him' but does not obey His commands, is a liar and the truth is not in him. (1. ii. 4.)

The dilemma would seem to be absolute. Either we make God into a liar or we are liars ourselves.

There is no way out of this difficulty except to expound the sentence *we have no sin* strictly in its context as the second of the three false claims of the opponents with whom John is dealing. The first is the claim of enjoying communion with God while living in sin. That is hypocrisy. The second is a general denial of sin in principle. *We have no sin.* The third is a particular denial of one's actual sins. We are not to understand the 'we' as a general statement about Christians. That may be the interpretation which comes naturally enough to Englishmen who constantly hear these words in their Liturgy, but it is at variance with the context. Again and again we are told that fellowship with God means freedom from sin. The thought of 1. i. 7, as Westcott says, 'is not of the forgiveness of sin only, but of the removal of sin'.[1]

The writer of the epistle, then, must be dealing with a specific claim put forward in the Church by some who would not admit that there was any sin in them at all. At the end of the first century when Gentiles with hardly any moral sensibility were finding themselves within the Church, such a claim must have been not infrequent.[2] There is only one way, says our writer. We must confess our sins. Then forgiveness is granted and a complete cleansing.

Once again we hear the austere note of absolute

---

[1] *The Epistles of St. John* (1892), 21.
[2] So Findlay, *Fellowship in the Life Eternal*, 106, 107.

freedom from sin as the mark of a believer. *I write to you
my little children, that you may not sin.* There may be a
fall from this ideal standard (1. ii. 1). But this is evidently
regarded as altogether exceptional. The possibility of
fulfilling the commands of God is set forth later in the
epistle (1. iii. 22).

So, too, in parallel passages in the Fourth Gospel (xv. 7,
8, 16) the fruit of the disciples is expected to 'remain'.
The Christian in this world is to be in life altogether like
his Lord.

> He that says he abides in Him (i.e. in God)
> Ought himself to walk even as He (ἐκεῖνος, i.e. Christ) walked.
> (1. ii. 6.)

The whole of the Fourth Gospel is the true exegesis of
this verse.

The excursus on the heretics who had gone out from
the Church (1. ii. 18–29) leads to the same conclusion.
Their heresy included a docetic Christology (1. ii. 22 and
1. v. 6), and probably a denial of the reality of the sufferings of the Cross (1. v. 6). It is likely that antinomianism
in their case, as often, went along with their disparagement
of the life of the flesh. They claimed that they walked in
the light, enjoyed full communion with God, and had no
sin. The writer of the epistle has proved their hypocrisy
from the facts of their lives (1. i. 6–10). He now exposes
the falsity of their claim to enjoy communion with God
from the unreality of their Christology. The argument
runs: (1) Jesus promised us eternal life, which is the
knowledge of God. (2) This life was given through Him,
so that anyone who has really seen Him has seen the
Father. (3) He who denies the earthly life of the Son of
God cuts away the ground of historic reality on which our
knowledge of God rests. (4) Therefore he who denies the
Son has not the Father. The whole argument depends on
the reality of the second assertion, that a χρῖσμα of the
Holy Spirit has been given by the Christ to those to whom
John writes. He proceeds to urge them to abide in that
experience. It is of the essence of that experience that

they should walk with a Person Who is perfectly righteous and they must be like Him (1. iii. 7; cf. 1. ii. 29).

So far we have seen how every avenue traversed in this letter leads to the same conclusion. Christ and sin have nothing whatever in common. Sinlessness is not only the end at which the Gospel aims. It is presupposed as the foundation of the Christian life.[1]

We have now come to the point when both the two main theses of the epistle, Christological and Ethical, are blended into one in the idea of the new birth from above, wrought by God through Christ.

> Everyone who practises righteousness is born of God.
> Born of God! See what a love the Father has for us,
> He allows us to be called children of God.
> That is what we are. (1. ii. 29; iii. 1.)

Just as Jesus, the Son of God, is ἁγνός, so must we, God's other children, be like Him. Jesus appeared to take away our sin. In Him there is no sin, and anyone who remains in Him does no sin. Even the smallest sin separates us from God.

> Anyone who is born of God does not commit sin,
> For the offspring of God remain in him,
> And they cannot sin because they are born of God. (1. iii. 9.)

The value of this reference of sinlessness of the Christian to its source in the new birth lies in the definite appeal to the experience of the Church. The writer knows that his readers will understand such an appeal. The new birth has meant for them a re-fashioning of the whole personality. Let us take the last of these astounding declarations, perhaps the most succinct and comprehensive of all:

> We know that everyone who is born of God does not sin,
> But he who was born of God preserves him,
> And the evil one has no hold upon him.

The usual explanations of the commentators do not really meet the situation. To say that the freedom from sin is given ideally and in principle, while the man himself still

---

[1] Cf. Windisch, 263.

goes on sinning, does no justice to the passion and the earnestness of the writer, nor to the assumption which underlies the whole letter that his readers will understand what he means. The only explanation that will meet the facts is that a considerable number in the community addressed have passed through the experience of deliverance from habits of sinning. A notable analogy would be the autobiographies of the early Methodists, examples of which are given later on. With such illustrations we may be able to detach ourselves from the assumption which, often unknown to ourselves, governs our modern interpretations, that the spiritual level of the communities of New Testament times was not very much higher than that of the Church of to-day. Many of the movements which have brought new illumination and power to the Church in after ages have proceeded on the opposite assumption. If that assumption is supported by a more coherent and less laboured exegesis than is commonly presented to us, we are justified in presuming that many of those early communities were living in an experience of God which involved astounding moral transformation as a credible and normal issue.[1]

It is possible that the metaphor of the new birth is affiliated to the idea of a new creation in the apocalyptic literature. The Apocalypse of Baruch and the Book of Jubilees lay especial stress on the changing of human nature in the Messianic age.

And he made for all his works a new and righteous nature, so that they should not sin in their whole nature for ever, but should be all righteous, each in his kind alway. (The Book of Jubilees, c. v. 12; Charles's translation.)[2]

It would be in keeping with the Johannine method to transform the old conception of Jewish apocalyptic so as to make it refer to the new creation of the Christian in Christ, of which Paul had spoken.

It is impossible to discuss the question fully. But such

[1] Cf. Windisch, 277.

[2] The reference is to the final judgement; so Charles and Box. Cf. Apoc. Baruch, 30, 49–51.

an origin would help to explain one of the perplexing features of the First Epistle of John—the drastic distinction between children of God and children of the devil. The picture of human life is in black and white; there are no neutral tints, no intermediate shades. From the creation of the world it has been the same. Cain was on one side of the line, Abel on the other (1. iii. 12). The Incarnation was the last decisive battle between good and evil (1. iii. 8), between God and the devil. The Church belongs to God; the whole world lies in the power of the Evil One (1. v. 18). We may spiritualize this as we please. But the drama was intensely real for the writer's mind. The same ethical dualism, and the like moral passion, are traceable in the Fourth Gospel. They may be explained by the author's belief that the new creation of the Messianic age has already come to pass.

As we might expect, there are in this epistle some recognitions of the frailty of human nature. What we do not expect is that any lapses are regarded as exceptional.

Thus it is that we may be sure we belong to the truth and reassure ourselves in his presence whenever our heart condemns us (καὶ ἔμπροσθεν αὐτοῦ πείσομεν τὴν καρδίαν ἡμῶν ὅτι ἐὰν καταγινώσκη ἡμῶν ἡ καρδία).

For God is greater than our heart and he knows all (1. iii. 19, 20).

The text here is not above suspicion. But we can find a coherent meaning in it as it stands. The Christian is visited by dark misgivings. Do they arise from his failures, his 'venial sins'? The author does not say. He deals only with that accusing heart, those inward tortures. And he dares to find reassurance in the thought of the all-knowing God. This thought would bring no reassurance at all to any man who had not known that intimate communion with a Father of love of which the epistle is full. But the point of the passage is that the readers know what it is to live in a rich communion with God. Rothe has caught the meaning here.[1]

John says: if we know from our sincere and active love to the brethren that there must really be in us, though only as a minimum,

[1] See Commentary, ad loc.

the true divine nature, then, when conscience accuses us, the thought of God's omniscience is a great support to us. For we say to ourselves: this beginning of the true, divine nature, which is well-nigh concealed from ourselves, is well known to God; and, therefore, notwithstanding all our trespasses, He will deal with us as being of the truth, and will consequently not reject us. . . . The natural man is interested in representing God as not too great; for this greatness fills him with fear. . . . But the Christian finds in the transcendent greatness of God and in it alone, the perfect stilling of his heart. . . . As a Christian, he can show his heart's core to anyone, for it belongs to God, it is full of love to God and the brethren. . . . Only if God is in the fullest sense of the word the searcher of hearts is real fellowship with Him possible. Every recess of our heart must be penetrated by God.'

Perhaps our author has in mind some whose tortured consciences condemn them because of their own failures. He reminds them of the love of God which is 'larger than the measure of man's mind'. He does not, like Faber, go on to say that

> The heart of the Eternal
> Is most wonderfully kind.

He hardly allows himself to express what he must mean— that forgiveness is for such tortured consciences as these. He swerves back again to the main line of his argument, but even there (1. iii. 21, 22) the full observance of the commands of God is presupposed as the condition of our confidence in approaching God.[1] The second concession to our frailty is made at the end of the letter, immediately before the final declaration of the sinlessness of the man who is born of God.

> If anyone sees his brother committing a sin which is not deadly
> He will ask and obtain life for him—
> For anyone who does not commit a deadly sin. (1. v. 16.)

Two points are noticeable here—first, the distinction between deadly and venial sins, and, second, the necessity of the intercession of a brother. Some sins cannot be atoned for. Their end is the soul's death. Already, in a parallel passage, we have noticed the expiation of the

[1] Windisch, *Taufe u. Sünde*, 269.

Intercessor (1. ii. 1, 2). Both these characteristic marks of John's treatment only prove how serious the problem of sin in believers was for his mind.

There remains for discussion one difficult passage in the Gospel. In the sacramental act of the Washing of the Disciples' Feet, Jesus says:

> He who is bathed needs only to wash his feet;
> He is altogether clean;
> And you are clean, but not all of you.
> He knew the traitor;
> That was why he said, You are not all clean. (xiii. 10, 11.)

It has been maintained that the 'bathing' contains an oblique reference to the cleansing waters of baptism; venial sins committed after baptism need the daily forgiveness, the daily cleansing. One objection to this is that it interrupts the thought. The act of Christ is the Sacrament of Homely Love. Why should the thought of another Sacrament be obtruded at this moment?

At the same time the cleansing must mean a moral cleansing. The reference to the sin of Judas makes that clear. Does the saying mean that those who have entered into the cleansing fellowship of Christ are washed free from sin, but that regularly they will need a lesser cleansing for the stains of every day? Is there a distinction between the Great Forgiveness and the Daily Forgiveness?

Probably some such thought lies in the writer's mind. But he cannot be said to have made it clear. It is as though he were afraid to minimize his high doctrine by any concession. In the twentieth chapter, Jesus gives to His disciples (who are 'clean') the power to remit or retain the sins of those in the community who fall. This passage would seem to point not to any recognition of the ecclesiastical leaders of the first-century communities as vicars of Christ, but rather to a practice which has its parallels to-day in mission churches. When a member of the Church has fallen into sin, the whole community meets to decide what is to be done with him. They pray for guidance; they are led by those whose wisdom and discretion are undoubted, and the penalty or reinstatement which they suggest is usually accepted by the European missionary.[1]

If this suggestion is correct, this passage (xx. 23) would provide for the practical *modus vivendi*. But the necessity for stating the truth by which the community lived—that a Christian need not sin—would be all the more imperative for the writer of the epistle.

We can now summarize our results.

The Johannine teaching of the ideal is one with the Pauline, save that in John there is no emphasis on growth in the spiritual life.[2] For both of them God is Love, and Love means Holy Love, a love that is all light, all righteousness. The ideal is inextricably intertwined with the historical Person of Jesus Christ. There is no way to the ideal save by union with the Crucified. Communion with God through Jesus Christ is looked upon as the privilege of all members of the Christian community. Such communion makes sinning unthinkable. The power and the desire to serve the will of God are His alone. For Paul and John alike the new life is to be lived on the level of miracle, because God is alive and active in His own world.

There are minor differences. It may be true, as Windisch has maintained, that the gaze of Paul is fixed on the Crucified Messiah, whereas John finds in the whole life and appearance of Jesus that which determined and transforms the Christian life. And it is certainly true that the framework of Paul's thought is that of Jewish apocalyptic, whereas the achievement of the Johannine writings was to set the Christian message in a new framework of thought for the Graeco-Roman world. Something of power and urgency has been lost in the process. The cathedral calm of the Fourth Gospel is not so tense with

[1] I owe this suggestion to Dr. Sydney Cave, of New College, Hampstead.

[2] The words for 'increase', 'grow', 'abound', hardly occur in the Johannine writings. The Stoic προκοπή and its kindred verb, used several times by Paul, are not to be found in John.

life as the open-air preaching of the first three. The shadow of a Stoic ἀπάθεια is already falling on the supreme figure. For Him there is no Gethsemane. He goes out of the Upper Room to face no desolation. There are no words in the Fourth Gospel with the horror of ἐκθαμβεῖσθαι καὶ ἀδημονεῖν (Mark xiv. 33) crying in them. Even if Jesus weeps, the story of the tears reads more like a refutation of Docetism than the sob of a wounded heart. Serene and confident, He has no unexpected problems to face. He knows no surprise, for He sees every step of the pathway in front of Him to the very end.

This impoverishment or blurring of some of the human traits in the face of Jesus Christ has not been without its effects on the history of the Christian ideal. We are hardly surprised to meet ἀπάθεια as a supreme characteristic of the perfect man in the writings of Clement of Alexandria, a century later. By the time of the great figures of monasticism, it is a dominant aspect of the ideal. There is a certain detached, intellectualist, abstractive tendency in the Fourth Gospel. 'The book has an outer protective shell of acutely polemical and exclusive moods and insistences, while certain splendid synoptic breadths and reconciliations are nowhere reached.'[1]

But as we have said, these criticisms do not touch the main features of the Christian ideal. So long as the inexhaustible riches of the first three Gospels have been drawn upon by believers, any slight impoverishment of the ideal in the Fourth Gospel was bound to be unnoticed.

[1] Baron v. Hügel, *Enc. Brit.* (11th ed., 1911), xv. 455.

CHAPTER V

THE EARLY CHURCH

Sans doute, il n'était pas impossible au baptisé de garder toute sa vie cette pureté baptismale. . . . En thèse, cette fidélité était normale.—Pierre Batiffol.

Vita hominis visio Dei.—S. Irenaeus.

THE study of the New Testament teaching on perfection has indicated several lines for our investigation.

In the first place we must trace the history of the idea of the Kingdom of God, until by Augustine that idea is re-set for the generations that came after him in a new and splendid framework of thought. Secondly, we must trace the history of the ideal that the Christian need not sin. And a third question will be considered as we investigate the other two. Granted that the New Testament ideals have suffered transformation or eclipse, what vestiges are traceable? Does the ideal remain, even if attenuated, a ghost of its former self? Do the Fathers of the second and third centuries teach any communion of the soul with God that is comparable to the evangelical offer of the New Testament? Such a communion would surely hold within itself the promise of a relative attainment in this life.

The natural term for this study will be the rise of Monasticism, for with Monasticism the Church is embarked on a fresh voyage and the heavenly treasure is sought over uncharted seas.

I. THE IDEA OF THE KINGDOM OF GOD IN THE POST-APOSTOLIC CHURCH

By the Johannine writings we have been prepared for a transmutation of eschatology, and therefore for a change in the conception of the Kingdom of God. Something of strength and urgency has been lost in the subordination of the apocalyptic idea. But whatever changes we may trace in the faith of the church of the second century cannot be traced to any weakening of the conviction of the imminence of the End. The Judge is even now at the doors.[1] St. Clement says:

Truly His will shall be quickly and suddenly accomplished, as the Scripture also bears witness that 'He shall come suddenly and shall not tarry'.[2]

God has shortened our time of waiting says Barnabas. τὸ τέλειον σκάνδαλον ἤγγικεν.[3] 'These are the last times' says Ignatius.[4] Hermas unites with Barnabas in the belief that the great Tribulation is at hand. 'Is the end near?' he asks. And the Church cried out with a great voice, saying, 'Foolish man, do you not see the tower still being built? Whenever therefore the building of the tower has been finished, the end comes. But it will quickly be built up. Ask me nothing more.'[5] 'The time that is left to you', says Justin Martyr,[6] 'is short.' If these post-apostolic writings fall far short of the New Testament in religious enthusiasm and creative power, we must not explain the higher tension of the apostles merely by their conviction that they stood by the bedside of a dying world. Even so late as the fourth century, Eusebius justifies the ideal of virginity by the claim that the end of the world is nigh, and that this is no time to be begetting children.[7]

At the same time there is no doubt that the Kingdom of Heaven has lost much of the content that the idea held for Jesus and His followers. (1) The Kingdom is conceived as lying wholly in the future. Chiliastic dreams are bound up with the primitive expectation; schemes of the order in which the last things will occur are displacing the more distinctively religious and ethical ideas hitherto connected with the Kingdom; stress is laid on the life of the world to come.[8] (2) In their conception of God, the

---

[1] See Knopf, *Das nach-apostolische Zeitalter* 397–8.
[2] 1 Clem. xxiii. 5.   [3] iv. 9; iv. 3; xxi. 3.
[4] Ignatius, *ad Eph.* xi. 1.
[5] Vis. iii. 8. 9; cf. Vis. ii. 2. 7; 3. 3 f.   [6] *Dial.* 28, 2.
[7] Epideixis, 29, 31, Ferrar's translation, i. 48, 50.
[8] 1 Clem. xxvi. 3; xxxv. 2; 2 Clem. vii. 5; xiv. 5; xx. 5. Ignatius *passim*. Barnabas xv. and the Excursus of Windisch, *Barnabasbrief*, 385,

Apostolic Fathers do not move on the same high level as most of the writers in the New Testament. God is to them primarily the Almighty Creator, who works in Nature and in history.[1] To Gentiles in that Hellenistic world this conception was overwhelming and revolutionary, and it is not surprising that their minds were held captive by it. The idea of the Fatherhood of God is secondary. Even the word πατήρ when it is used no longer expresses a personal, but rather a cosmological relationship.[2] Faith in God is especially connected with the thought of His omnipotence.[3]

(3) Christianity becomes a new Law. The teaching of St. Paul is not understood,[4] although the person of the apostle is surrounded by great reverence and affection. The righteousness which is of the law comes back as the goal of man's striving and with it comes a tendency to distinguish between degrees of good works. Christ becomes the great Law-giver and Judge.

(4) The idea of the Church is clothing itself in forms which were inconceivable in the earlier days. Already the Church has become a heavenly aeon, almost a pre-existent personality.[5] As the bride of Christ she is elevated to the rank of an original pattern (resembling a Platonic 'idea') of the earthly church, and so is pictured as a community of saints, without stain of sin.[6] So the idea of the Church in the Second Epistle of Clement is parallel

386. Frick, *Die Geschichte des Reich-Gottes-Gedankens in der alten Kirche*, notes how the tone of Active moral striving which is bound up in the Synoptists with the preaching of the kingdom, disappears in the Apostolic Fathers. It is characteristic that in 2 Clem. v. 5, the idea of ἀνάπαυσις, rest, is the content of the idea of the kingdom.

[1] See 1 Clem. inscr.; ii. 3; viii. 5; xxxii. 4; lxi. 2; Hermas, *Sim.* v. 7. 4; *Pol.* inscr. *Mart. Pol.* xiv. 1. The best summary of the doctrine of God in the Apostolic Fathers is given by Seeberg, *Lehrbuch der Dogmengeschichte* (1908), i. 88–90.

[2] 1 Clem. xix. 2; xxxv. 3.

[3] xxvii. See Ritschl, *Die Entstehung der Altkatholischen Kirche*, 282.

[4] Loofs, *Leitfaden*, 89–90.

[5] Hermas, *Vis.* ii. 4. 1; cf. i. 3. 4; i. 1. 6. See Dibelius, *Der Hirt des Hermas*, 459; Knopf, *N.T. Studien für Heinrici*, 216 ff.

[6] 2 Clem. xiv.

to the Kingdom of God in the New Testament. The Didache distinguishes the church from the kingdom. But in Hermas (*Sim*. ix. 12. 3) the door of the church is practically equivalent to the door of the kingdom. Here on earth we are citizens of the heavenly city. 'Your city is far from this city'[1] said the Angel to Hermas, meaning that the interests of the *civitas dei* were far other than the interests of the *civitas terrena*, and thus identifying the ideal church and the actual church.

History is often written with an unconsciously deterministic bias, as though the processes traceable from age to age were normal and inevitable. It is difficult to see anything inevitable in this elimination from the New Testament idea of the Kingdom of God of many of its finest characteristics. Somehow the sense of God has grown dim, the consciousness of present communion is not so joyful and convincing; an excellent and worthy moralism is usurping the place of that splendid awareness of the perpetual activity of Christ which still makes the New Testament the most interesting and the most influential book in the world.

The same processes are visible in the apologists. In Justin, God is primarily creator, though His creative work is conceived not under the forms of Old Testament thought but in the categories of Greek philosophy.[2] The perfection of God is that He is incomprehensible and self-sufficient.[3] Because He is described by negatives, communion with Him is not insisted upon. The relationship between man and God is an impersonal kinship, a natural affinity. The work of the Redeemer-Logos is to communicate the new Law, and the gifts of grace are especially incorruption, immortality, freedom from passion ($\mathring{\alpha}\pi\acute{\alpha}\theta\epsilon\iota\alpha$).

What was God's original purpose for mankind? The position of man in Paradise before sin had entered into the world becomes a significant indication of the ideas of perfection at this period. There are various views which

---

[1] *Sim*. i. 1.
[2] Engelhardt, *Das Christentum Justins*, 136.
[3] Athenagoras, c. 10 and c. 16.

can be traced in the Greek Fathers. The first is that of Justin Martyr.

> We have been taught that God in His goodness made all things out of shapeless matter for the sake of men, and if men show themselves by their works worthy of this his design they are deemed worthy of reigning with Him; they will be delivered from suffering and corruption.[1]

Adam and Eve were made ἀπαθεῖς καὶ ἀθάνατοι and yet worked out death for themselves.[2] All men have acted like Adam and Eve. This original state of mankind is identified with the goal of the Christian life.[3] Perfection, which includes ἀφθαρσία and ἀπάθεια, is set beyond the grave.

> Impelled by the desire of the eternal and the pure life we seek the abode which is with God. . . . This then to speak shortly is what we have learnt from Christ and teach.

Christianity becomes the natural fulfilment of the original destiny of mankind. Here Justin claims to be speaking for the Church in his day.

A second view is put forth by Tatian. Man was given a special divine power at the creation, and owing to the Fall this power has been lost. He distinguishes between ψυχή and πνεῦμα. The soul is not in itself immortal.[4] But at the beginning the Spirit was a constant companion of the soul, but forsook it because it was not willing to follow. To the Spirit it was due that the first man was an image and likeness of God (εἰκὼν καὶ ὁμοίωσις) and that he had the capacity of immortality.[5] The loss of the Spirit at the Fall means that now the Spirit of God 'is not with all, but takes up its abode with those who live justly, and intimately combining with the soul, by prophecies it announced hidden things to other souls'.[6]

On this view Christian perfection is communion with the Spirit of God. 'We must seek for what we once had but have lost, to unite the soul with the Holy Spirit and to strive after union with God.'[7]

---

[1] *Apol.* i. 10.　　　　[2] *Dial.* 124.　　　　[3] *Apol.* i. 8
[4] c. 13.　　[5] c. 12, and c. 7.　　[6] c. 13.　　[7] c. 15.

The view of Justin was that in Christianity man was destined to the immortality which God gave him at the beginning; the view of Tatian was that in Christianity man attained to the original endowment with the Spirit of God. Irenaeus unites the two lines of thought. Man is not created perfect, because the very idea of being created involves imperfection, and because it was God's will that man should grow and develop as a child is first fed with milk and only afterwards is able to eat meat.[1] What is wanted for perfection is the possession of the divine Spirit which has been lost.[2]

On the whole there is little room in the schemes of the second-century apologists for the ideal of the Kingdom of God. Eschatology they have, and it is varied. Chiliasm is there, in the thought of some apologists, and the resurrection of the body is prominent in others. The end is near, thinks Justin. But the Kingdom is set in the next age, or in paradise. And the new life is described as perfect knowledge and perfect Being.[3] It is a Greek picture. And Greek eyes must have rested on it with pleasure. The artists knew their contemporaries, and did their own work. But it must be said that in their attempts to explain their faith, the gospel is reduced.

It is often said in extenuation that the power of Christianity in this age lay not in its teaching but in its spirit and practical life.[4] That is true enough. But in the long run the power of the Christian Church is in its message. The life will suffer, and the enthusiasm will die down, if there be no convincing experience of God large enough to be explained and communicated by man to man. There are some fine touches in Justin's picture of the future. 'We shall reign with Him, we shall be delivered from corruption and suffering. That is why we do not fear when men cut us off.'[5] But even here the Kingdom is purely

---

[1] iv. 38. 1, 2; cf. iv. 38. 3; Harvey, ii. 293.
[2] Wendt, *Die christliche Lehre von der menschlichen Vollkommenheit* (1882), has provided a thorough study of these views.
[3] *Dial.* 28. 2; *Theoph.* ii. 26; Justin, *Dial.* 3, 4.
[4] Frick, 40. [5] *Apol.* i. 10, 2; i. 11.

future, and therefore something of the power and urgency of the idea has disappeared.

Irenaeus is the most representative personality of the second-century Church. He had the gift of uniting in his thought tendencies so various that recently Bousset has aptly called him the Schleiermacher of his time.[1] We may trace the secret to his rare personal piety. He had a deep sense of the greatness of God, and though he did not really understand the message of St. Paul, he is steeped in the New Testament writings.

The conception of the Kingdom of God plays a great part in his eschatology.[2] In general it may be said that the term is used in opposition to this world. The reference is purely to the future, but he believes that all the prophecies have reference to the millennial kingdom to be established on this earth after the resurrection of the saints. He will not have this hope allegorized away (v. 35), interpreted of celestial blessings. Like the simpler believers of every age, he appealed[3] to the Apocalypse of John. The New Jerusalem shall descend upon the new earth. There shall be various mansions for the saints, according to the merit of each individual. Some who produce a hundredfold will be taken up into the heavens, and those who produce sixtyfold will dwell in paradise, and those who produce thirtyfold will dwell in the city. The world shall not be annihilated, but renewed. When the present order has passed away, and man has been renewed, there shall be the new heaven and the new earth in which the new man shall abide always holding fresh converse with God.

Nothing in Irenaeus is quite so simple as at first sight it may appear. Vivid and simple, a piece of coloured tapestry to hang on cottage walls—so this description may seem. But it is woven into the pattern of his thought with consummate skill. Three modifications of this popular millennarianism should be added. In the first place

[1] *Kyrios Christos*, 334.
[2] The term occurs thirty times in his biblical citations. Frick, 60.
[3] *Adv. Haer.* v. 35.

Irenaeus is working with the idea of development. For the first time in Christian theology history is considered as a process, from stage to stage, from period to period. The old apocalyptic views are thus completely modified. He does not expect a sudden overwhelming catastrophe, but rather a fulfilment of the development which is already proceeding.

But Irenaeus believes that we are now living in the last stage of this development. There have been four supreme moments in the history of mankind; the first three are associated with the covenants granted to Adam, Noah, Moses. The last which completes the process is the renewing covenant of Christ, which 'lifts men up and bears them on its wings into the heavenly kingdom'. The essential fact in this new stage of man's development is the outpouring of the Spirit. Only those, he says,[1] are 'perfect' in the sense of complete, who have received the Spirit of God. 'The perfect man consists in the commingling and the union of the soul which receives the Spirit of the Father, and the admixture of that fleshly nature which was moulded after the image of God.' So since Christ appeared the lordship of the Spirit of God among men has been growing. Growing, too, has been the power of evil in the world. When the power of Antichrist shall have come to its height his ruin is at hand.[2] The advent of Christ means the downfall of Antichrist. The idea of a development in history is thus combined with the traditional Christian eschatology, and both are pressed into the service of a doctrine of perfection upon the earth.

Secondly, the thought of Irenaeus is always dominated by his strong conviction of a present communion of the soul with God. He knows well that this is what is meant by 'receiving the Spirit'.[3] The recently discovered Armenian text of '*The Demonstration of the Apostolic Preaching*' shows that this thought was vital for Irenaeus.[4] The purpose of the Incarnation was 'to abolish death, and

---

[1] v. 6. 1; Harvey, ii. 333.   [2] v. 25–30.
[3] v. 9. 3.
[4] c. 6 (E. tr. J. A. Robinson, 75); cf. 31, p. 97 and c. 40, p. 105.

show forth life and produce a community of union between God and man'. When the divine kingdom shall
be established on earth the supreme felicity will be communion with God. In this they will grow; and they will
learn more of the glory of God the Father just because
they are gazing on the Face of Christ.[1] It is here, in a
single phrase, that we stumble on the secret of the personal
piety of Irenaeus. His eyes are held by the wonder of the
Face of Christ.

Just as those who behold the light[2] are within the light, and
participate in its splendour, so those who behold God are in God,
and participate in the splendour of God.

And, for Irenaeus, to behold God is to look upon the God-
Logos Who has appeared in the flesh.[3] We cannot know
God by thinking of His greatness. He cannot be measured.
No one is able, either in Heaven or on earth, to open the
Book of the Father and behold Him, save the Lamb which
was slain.[4] And this Lamb, this Jesus, is the Love of God
whereby we too can come to know Him. It is His will
that all things, through the Word, should see Him,
through the Light of the Father which rests upon the
resplendent human nature of the Son. When Irenaeus
speaks of life, of incorruption, of immortality, he does not
think primarily of the future. 'God bestows life on those
who see Him. It is not possible to live apart from life,
and the means of life is found in fellowship with God; and
fellowship with God is to know God, and to enjoy His
goodness.'[5]

In the third place, the doctrine of recapitulation is
closely connected with the ideal of perfection in the
thought of Irenaeus. We have already seen how the
Incarnate Lord 'narrates' God, as it were; declares God
from the beginning;[6] and that apart from the sight of
Jesus man could not attain the end of his being and live
in fellowship with God. But the doctrine of Irenaeus is

---

[1] *Adv. Haer.* v. 35. 1.　　　　　　　　　[2] iv. 20. 5.
[3] Cf. Bousset, *Kyrios Christos,* 338–40.
[4] iv. 20. 2.　　　　[5] iv. 20. 5.　　　　[6] iv. 20, 7.

still bolder. All things are to be summed up in Christ.[1]
It is well known that Irenaeus borrowing the idea of
ἀνακεφαλαίωσις from St. Paul (Eph. i. 10; Col. i. 19), and
combining it with the Johannine ideal of the unity of the
disciples in Christ (John xvii. 21–3), interprets thus the
greatness of Christ as the centre of all history and the goal
of its final development.[2] For our present purpose it is
enough to point out that, seen from another side, the idea
of ἀνακεφαλαίωσις is inherently a doctrine of perfection,
and that it is at the heart of the theology of Irenaeus. That
is the goal of our being—to be in Christ, and having
received the Spirit, living in communion with God, we
are well on the way to that goal.

It is difficult to assent to the view of Bousset that the
goal is deification, and that the whole conception is a
product of the surrounding Hellenistic polytheism.[3] The
theology of Irenaeus was wrought out under the menace
of, and in opposition to, a semi-polytheistic gnosticism.
As we have seen, he is steeped in the New Testament
writings. His personal religion is rooted and grounded in
the historic fact of Jesus Christ. It is at least unlikely that
a thinker with these presuppositions should have yielded
the central pass of his thought to his opponents at the
very moment when he fondly imagines he is achieving
victory. But the exposition of perfection already quoted
proves that 'deification' is no accurate description of the
goal of man. The complete man is compounded of body,
soul, and spirit. Irenaeus actually finds difficulty in
expounding that word of Paul, so misused by his gnostic
opponents, that 'flesh and blood shall not inherit the
kingdom of God'. He explains that the real sense is that
the flesh of itself, when destitute of the Spirit of God,
cannot inherit the promised kingdom, and that it would be
more strictly true to say that *the flesh is inherited by* the Spirit
of God when it is translated into the Kingdom of Heaven.[4]

---

[1] iv. 20. 7.

[2] Cf. Bethune Baker, *Intro. to Hist. of Christian Doctrine*, 131, 132;
Seeberg, *Lehrbuch*, I. 325–30.

[3] *Kyrios Christos*, 342, 343.   [4] *Adv. Haer.* v. 9. 3 and 4.

The summing up of all things in Christ, therefore, does not mean an equation of men with God, or an identification of men with God. It does not involve a loss of human personality in the divine. Rather it is defined in terms of the benefits which God the Giver bestows on man the recipient, when man is brought in Christ to the presence and fellowship of God. The Kingdom is the Sabbath of God. Man shall then enjoy peace, and share in the table of God.[1] There is freedom in God's presence.[2] There is love, which will be shown in the unity and concord among men when the Kingdom shall be established.[3] But rarely indeed does Irenaeus venture beyond the biblical language, and in his own summary of the ideal he says simply that 'the Son of God appeared on earth and was conversant with men: that man might be after the image and likeness of God'.[4]

With Tertullian we return to more ordinary views of the Kingdom of God. He holds to the millennarian hope. It is only just and worthy of God that His servants should have their joy in the place where they have suffered affliction for the sake of His name.[5] He looks forward to the day when the saints shall reign in the *nova civitas*, the kingdom of the just. But his millennarianism has little meaning for his thought.[6] All his expectation is centred on the kingdom on the other side of the grave, not on earth but in heaven. This, he tells us, is the theme of his work (which is not extant) *De Spe Fidelium*. While the servants of God were permitted to announce the earthly glory, it was reserved for Christ alone to announce the glory of the heavenly future.[7]

The popular piety of the second century affords us hardly any traces of a living hope of the Kingdom of God on earth. Frick has collected the evidence of early

---

[1] *Adv. Haer.* iv. 16. 1.   [2] Cf. iv. 34. 1.

[3] *Demonstration*, c. 61 (J. A. Robinson, p. 124).

[4] *Demonstration*, c. 97 (149–50).   [5] *Adv. Marc.* iii. 24.

[6] See R. E. Roberts, *The Theology of Tertullian*, c. xi, for a full discussion.

[7] *Adv. Marc.* iii. 24.

Christian art and early inscriptions. It is singular that in the catacombs and on the sepulchral monuments there is no interest discernible in the fate of the body, only in the further history of the soul after death. Had the popular piety expected the resurrection of the body to be followed by a millennarian kingdom on this earth, some trace of such a hope would surely be found.[1]

Where the conception of judgement finds any pictorial expression, it is not the judgement of the world, but only the judgement on the individual soul immediately after death. The soul then goes forthwith to Paradise. Paradise, or the heavenly kingdom, is conceived as the other side of the grave. It is the reward for the righteous after death.[2]

In the theology of the Latin Fathers we find a double process at work. On the one hand, the idea of the visible Church is taking the place of the Kingdom of God on earth. For Cyprian the Church is the bride of Christ, uncorrupted and pure. 'It is she who preserves us for God. She it is who appoints the sons whom she has borne for the kingdom. He can no longer have God for his father who has not the church for his mother.'[3] So Ambrose saluted the Church as the heavenly Jerusalem,[4] and sets the Kingdom of God in the future.[5] Tyconius, from whom Augustine learnt much for his own conception of the Church,[6] distinguishes between the true Church, the *communio sanctorum*, and the great Church. It is the severest trial for the true Church that they must live as brothers with those who are in reality members of the Beast from the Abyss.[7] But this time of suffering is a good training in humility and patience. In the Catholic Church the righteous and the hypocrites are living side by side; it is only the *communio sanctorum* that is the invisible heavenly Church. On earth this exists among those who

---

[1] See Sybel, *Christl. Antike*, i. 269.
[2] Sybel, op. cit. i. 135. [3] *De unitate ecclesiae*, c. 6.
[4] *Apol. David.* i. 17.
[5] Cf. *De spir. sancto*. iii. 20. 157. See below, pp. 189–92.
[6] See Seeberg, *Lehrbuch*, ii. 421.
[7] Traugott Hahn, *Tyconius-studien*, 52.

are pure in heart.[1] The reality transcends earth, for Paradise is simply the Church.[2] At the same time Tyconius holds to another idea, that the visible Church on the earth is the Body of Christ, and he uses the formula *corpus bipartitum* to cover the problem of the good and evil so inextricably mingled in the *permixta ecclesia*.[3]

On the other hand, the older eschatological expectations are fading into the background. When the idea of the Church takes the place of the idea of the Kingdom, such a postponement of the great hope to the life beyond is almost inevitable. The Church is too evidently *permixta* for any hope of speedy purification in this life. The idea of development which wrought on the mind of Irenaeus, Clement, and Origen, gave the Church a divinely-ordered place in human history. The stage is set for the appearance of Augustine, who was to combine the hope of a *civitas Dei* on earth with a profound conviction that only in the next world could the true blessedness of the Christian be attained.[4]

Meantime the forms of the early eschatological ideas remained; the inner spirit had departed.[5] As we have seen, the apocalyptic conception of the Kingdom in the New Testament is bound up with a certain conviction about the character of God. This bond was sundered in the thought of the third and fourth centuries. In St. Paul the longing for the Kingdom is ἀποκαραδοκία, a passionate yearning which is essentially an element in his communion with God. In the later thought which we are now studying, the teaching of the end is a piece of Church doctrine; phantasy runs riot as faith grows faint. Thus Hippolytus deduces the events of the future from the Old Testament prophets. Heaven becomes a place of reward, and Hell is punishment.[6] Cyprian sees the Kingdom as future reward,

---

[1] *Beatus*, 56; Traugott Hahn, *Tyconius-Studien*, 64.
[2] *Beatus*, 148; Traugott Hahn, *Tyconius-Studien*, 64.
[3] Seeberg, *Lehrbuch* (1910), ii. 420, shows how St. Augustine took over this conception of Tyconius.
[4] Harnack, *History of Dogma*, v. 91–3.
[5] Cf. Harnack, iii. 189.   [6] See *Christ and Antichrist, passim*.

inconceivably greater than our deserts, but none the less as reward.[1] For him the end is nearer than it is for Hippolytus,[2] and he fears it. The Last Judgement will be more terrible than the sufferings of the present time.[3] Lactantius[4] teaches a purgatory after death for Christians, and an immediate hell for the wicked. At the second coming of Christ the Resurrection and Judgement take place. These are for Christians only: the non-Christians are already judged. The millennarian reign is taught merely as a piece of Church tradition.[5]

In Tyconius we meet with a spiritualizing of the old eschatology. He interprets it in terms of historical process. Like Irenaeus he divides the course of time into periods. The first is the period of natural religion and natural morality. The hero of this period is Abraham. Second comes the period of Law, with Moses as its Lawgiver, and third, the time since the appearance of Christ. But Tyconius identifies the third period with the millennium.[6] The length of this period is only 350 years, for Tyconius interprets the number 1000 as a parable, and finds the key to it in Rev. xii. 6. He is expecting the end speedily. His real interest, however, is not in painting any pictures of the future, but in the conflict which he sees raging in the present, between the *civitas dei* and the *civitas diaboli*.[7]

II. THE PROBLEM OF SINLESSNESS

The second historical question we must now attempt to answer. What answer do the leaders of the Church make to the challenge of the New Testament, that the believer need not sin?

St. Clement writes on behalf of the Church of Rome to the Church of Corinth. There is a division among them,

---

[1] *de hab. virg.* 21.
[2] *Ad Fortunat.* Praef. 2; *de un. eccl.* c. 16; *de bono pat.* c. 4.
[3] *Ad Demetr.* c. 22, c. 24.
[4] *Inst.* vii. 21.   [5] Epit. 72.
[6] *Beatus*, 412. 2 ff.; cf. 423. 11–27; *Tyconius-Studien*, 79, 87, 88.
[7] 533. 24 to 536. 21; *Tyconius-Studien*, 28–9.

stirred up by a few. And though he recognizes to the full
their following of the ideal in the past he has no doubt of
their sad declension in the present. He diagnoses their
malady with insight. He sees that jealousy, which brings
in its train innumerable other sins, is the cause of their
sickness. As a practical shepherd of souls he prescribes his
remedy.[1] But on the whole we must give assent to the view
of Windisch,[2] that in this letter, for the first time in any
Christian writing, we find a teacher assuming that a condition of sinfulness is permanently to be expected in the
Christian Church. There is no failure in ethical earnestness; Christians will strive passionately against sin; they
will repent and find the promised forgiveness. But the
liturgical prayer at the end of the epistle by giving a fixed
form to the confession of sin, assumes not that sin is
intolerable in Christians, but on the contrary, quite likely.[3]
On the other hand, it must be pointed out that as a
petition for deliverance from all sin quickly follows the
confession, the Church expects a perfect cleansing from
sin. The confession and the ideal lie side by side. Unfortunately the whole attitude of Clement, and the advice which
he gives, show that some commanding elements in the
teaching of St. Paul have been forgotten. The gift of God
is not so much the removal of the barrier of guilt, nor a
redemption from the bondage of sin, but rather an educa-
tion of those who were alienated from God and sitting in
heathen darkness, so that now they are conscious of their
privilege as the sanctified people of God (c. 36. 2; 59. 2
and 4). When he speaks of the greatness of the divine
promises (c. 24; c. 26; c. 35) he means especially the hope
of the Resurrection. Once indeed Clement exhorts them
to look upon the Cross of Jesus Christ.[4] But even here our
author has no more in mind than that a τόπος μετανοίας is
provided for those who turn to our Master (ὁ δεσπότης).
And in his strategy in dealing with the fallen there is
lacking that sure reminder, which is Paul's final court of

---

[1] c. 30.   [2] 321, 328.   [3] Windisch, 322.
[4] c. 7. 4. See R. S. Franks, *History of the Doctrine of the Work of Christ*,
i. 16, 17.

appeal, that his readers know the reality of personal relationship with God.[1]

'In Hermas and in the second epistle of Clement', says Harnack,[2] 'the consciousness of being under grace, even after baptism, almost completely disappears behind the attempt to fulfil the tasks which baptism imposes.' There can be no doubt as to the moral earnestness of the author of 2 Clement. Heaven, hell, judgement, are realities to him. But the writer's idea of grace can be summed up in the word 'Let us repent'.[3] The exhortation occurs repeatedly.[4] This means moral struggle, with eternal life as the reward for victory.[5] Among the exercises recommended is almsgiving,[6] which 'lifts off the burden of sin'; lowest in the scale is prayer, which yet avails to deliver from death. There is apparently no such religious experience of release and communion to which the homilist can appeal. He describes himself[7] as an utter sinner (πανθ-αμαρτωλός), still in the midst of the engines of the devil, struggling to come near to righteousness at least, and fearing the judgement to come. This is not to be classed with the cries of penitence which we hear from the lips of the great saints. The homilist is still struggling.

There is striving in St. Paul (Phil. iii. 8–9), but it is the striving of one who has already won a victory and received the peace of God. The homilist has his theory of the ideal. In baptism he was regenerated. But now the problem is to keep the baptism undefiled. The theory has broken down. As Windisch bluntly says: 'Er hat nichts Gewaltsames erlebt.'[8] He has not experienced the might of God's grace.

The Shepherd of Hermas makes a new attempt to reconcile the ideal of sinlessness with the reality of sin in the Church. The aim of the book is that he who has sinned may sin no more. 'Because Christendom is a

[1] The view of Pfleiderer (*Primitive Christianity*, E. tr. iv. 347–58) misses the main point of the Pauline message.
[2] i. 173. [3] 2 Clem. ii. 4–7; Harnack, i. 171 n.
[4] See viii. 1, 2; ix. 8; xiii. 1; xvi. 1; xvii. 1; xix. 1.
[5] vii. 1–6; viii. 4–7; xi. 5–7; xiv. 1; xv. 1; xix. 3.
[6] xvi. 4. [7] xviii. 2. [8] *Taufe u. Sünde*, 338.

community of saints which has in its midst the sure salvation, all its members—this is the necessary inference—must live a sinless life.'[1] Hermas, like Justin Martyr, presupposes the idea that serious sins committed after baptism should not, and could not (except under special circumstances), be forgiven. The revelation announced in the Shepherd may have been an attempt to 'break the iron ring of despair'.[2] 'No second repentance' said the Epistle to the Hebrews. But the Angel of Penitence announces that God is willing now to forgive all who earnestly repent, and to receive them into His Kingdom, but there is great need for haste. From the time of this second repentance onwards, sinlessness will be required.[3] Hermas has no doubt that this is possible[4] and that the truly religious man can do more than that which is commanded.[5] An example of the higher service recommended is almsgiving with the money saved by the obligatory fast.[6] The idea of works of supererogation has already entered into the Church.

We shall expect to find in the apologists what the Church could offer to those that were without. Was it deliverance from sin?

Aristides tells Antoninus Pius that Christians carry the behests of their Lord Jesus Christ engraved on their hearts, and live as God commanded them. All sins are far from them, and perfect purity is to be found among them.[7] How does this come to pass? Christians pray for their unbelieving neighbours, and strive to win them from their error. When a man turns to God, he is ashamed; he confesses to God, saying, 'In ignorance I did these things', and his sins are forgiven; his heart is cleansed.[8] Any reader of this Apology would understand that after acceptance in the community he was expected not to sin.

---

[1] Harnack, i. 173.
[2] Mitchell in *D.A.C.* i. 561. See Mand. iv. 3.
[3] Windisch, 375, 376, as against Seeberg, *Lehrbuch,* i. 128.
[4] *Sim.* ix. 24.   [5] *Sim.* v. 2.
[6] *Sim.* v. 3. See Bigg, *Origins,* 81.
[7] c. 15.   [8] c. 17.

But Aristides says that sometimes a member of the Church dies in his iniquity. This is a cause of bitter grief to the Christian. But when a child dies they 'praise God mightily, as for one who has passed through the world without sin'.[1]

Athenagoras quotes the Sermon on the Mount to Marcus Aurelius, and claims that artisans and uneducated people and old women are able to love their enemies and pray for those who persecute them.[2] 'Pure from all wrongdoing',[3] declining to entertain the thought of the slightest sin, they know that God is witness to what they think and say both by night and by day.[4] Even the least defilement of thought 'excludes us from eternal life'.[5] He concludes that 'those who are persuaded that nothing will escape the scrutiny of God . . . are not likely to commit even the slightest sin'.[6] The sinlessness of the Christian is linked with the thought of the Judgement Day.

Theophilus, Bishop of Antioch, claims for Christians that among them unrighteousness is exterminated and sin rooted up. They are not allowed to dwell upon sin even in thought.[7] The purpose of God throughout His revelation is that men may sin no more.[8] The new birth is connected with the water of baptism.[9] When the eyes of the soul are purified from sin they can see God.[10]

Justin Martyr is equally uncompromising. The word of Christ is the power of God,[11] and Christians are able to fulfil the strict word of Christ on abstaining from evil desire.[12] There is a profound difference between Christians before their conversion and after. Justin exults in the saying of Christ: 'I came not to call the righteous but sinners to repentance.' Christians pledge themselves to do no wickedness.[13] They are made new by Christ in the waters of baptism,[14] but genuine repentance must precede

---

[1] c. 15. Rendel Harris translation, *Texts and Studies*, i. 50.
[2] c. 11.   [3] c. 12.   [4] c. 31.
[5] c. 32. This is quoted as a saying of the Logos Himself.
[6] c. 36.   [7] *Ad. Autol.* iii. 13 and 15.   [8] iii. 11.
[9] ii. 16.   [10] i. 2, 7.   [11] *Apol.* i. 14.   [12] *Apol.* i. 15.
[13] *Apol.* i. 15, 16.   [14] *Apol.* i. 61.

remission of sins.[1] After that they must live sinless lives.[2] The goodness and loving-kindness of God and His immeasurable riches hold as righteous and sinless the man who repents of sins.[3]

The author of the *Epistle to Diognetus* can proudly say that the lives of Christians surpass the demands of the laws which they obey; there is no explanation save the power of God.[4]

The testimony of the apologists is altogether at variance with the situation contemplated by the author of 2 Clement. We may not admit the explanation 'that the Apologists were merely intending to exclude the heinous sins from the church. . . . We must admit that they are convinced that the Christians of their day are actually striving after the ideal of sinlessness. Certainly they were not of the opinion that the ideal was for most Christians and permanently in the unattainable distance. They saw light and power all around them, a picture in which shadows and impotence were melting away.'[5]

Irenaeus says expressly that the achievement of Christ was that He did away with disobedience utterly; He gave salvation to His creatures by destroying sin.[6] He has loosed our fetters.[7] Those who belong to Christ will abstain not only from evil deeds but from evil desires.[8] The power to fulfil the law rests on the freedom wherewith the Logos has set the soul free.[9] Love is the mark of Christians, and 'the love of God is far from all sin, and love to the neighbour worketh no ill to the neighbour'.[10]

The view of Irenaeus is that at conversion and baptism the Holy Spirit is received.[11] Christians are *pneumatici* because they have put aside the lusts of the flesh and received the Holy Spirit.[12] The man who so receives the Spirit changes the quality of his works and receives another name, showing that he is changed for the better. He is now not merely flesh and blood but a spiritual man.[13]

---

[1] *Dial. Trypho.* 14.   [2] *Dial.* 44.   [3] *Dial.* 47.   [4] v. 10; vii. 9.
[5] Windisch, 397.   [6] iii. 18. 6.   [7] *Apost. Preaching*, 38.
[8] iv. 13. 1.   [9] iv. 13. 2.   [10] *Apost. Preaching*, 95.
[11] *Apost. Preaching*, 3.   [12] v. 12. 3.   [13] v. 10. 2.

The lusts of the flesh are cut away.[1] The natural weakness of the flesh will be absorbed by the power of the Spirit.[2] 'Those, then, are the perfect who have had the Spirit of God remaining in them, and have preserved their souls and bodies blameless, holding fast the faith of God, that is, the faith which is set upon God, and maintaining just relationships with their neighbours.'[3]

How is this purification from sin wrought in the Christian? Irenaeus hesitates between two answers. Sometimes he says that it is the gift of the Spirit which effects the purification.[4] Sometimes he speaks of the purification as a condition to be fulfilled before the Spirit can be received.[5] A similar ambiguity lurks in his use of the word 'perfect'. Usually the perfect are the spiritual men; the disciples who by receiving of the Spirit were made perfect.[6] But Irenaeus also speaks of the educative work of the Spirit, while man gradually makes progress, and ascends towards the perfect.[7]

In this sense perfection is the goal of the human development, the beatific vision when man is finally fit to look upon the face of God.[8] Here, perhaps, we may interpret him as not referring to ethical imperfection; he means rather that physical corruption has not yet been overcome. The bodies of men are a hindrance in the attainment of the vision of God.

[1] v. 10. 3.   [2] v. 9. 2.   [3] v. 6. 1.   [4] v. 8. 1.
[5] iv. 38. 2.   [6] iii. 12. 5.   [7] iv. 38. 3.
[8] iv. 38. 3; cf. v. 8. 1.

CHAPTER VI

THE CHRISTIAN PLATONISTS

CLEMENT OF ALEXANDRIA

ὅρα τὸ ᾆσμα τὸ καινὸν ὅσον ἴσχυσεν.
Protrepticus.

He drew me, and I followed on,
Charmed to confess the voice divine.
Doddridge.

To realize in himself the perfect Christian of Clemens Alexandrinus was
the object of his heart.
Alexander Knox on John Wesley.

THE goal of life is described as assimilation to God.
Clement has passed in survey the various views of
the chief end of man, as set forth by Cynics, Epicureans,
and Stoics. It is not till he comes to Plato's words in the
Theaetetus that he lets down his anchor. 'Evils make the
circuit of mortal nature', said Plato. 'Wherefore we must
try to flee hence as soon as may be. For flight is likeness to
God, as far as possible, and likeness is to become holy and
just with wisdom.'[1] And then he sets Plato hand in hand
with Paul as his leaders on the heavenly pathway. 'Assimilation as far as possible in accordance with right
reason is the end, and restoration to perfect adoption by
the Son. . . .' The apostle precisely describes the end in
the Epistle to the Romans: 'But now, being made free
from sin and become servants to God, ye have your fruit
unto holiness and the end eternal life.' In another place[2]
Clement says that the ideal is to be as perfect as the Father
wishes us to be.

Those who strive after perfection must approve themselves not
to men but to God.

It is our study with perfect concord here to agree with the will
of God, and press towards the restoration of the perfect nobleness
and true relationship with God, which is the fullness of Christ.[3]

[1] *Strom.* ii. 22: *Theaet.* 176 A and B.   [2] *Strom.* vii. 14. 88.
[3] *Strom.* iv. 21.

1. THE TRANSFIGURATION OF THIS EARTHLY LIFE

The immediate effect of such an aim should be the hallowing of what is still called the secular work of life. There are few of the Christian writers of that age, or indeed of any age, who see with such clearness as Clement that the gift of communion with God brings with it not only a reinforcement of heavenly virtues, but also a transfiguration of the common task. Clement is depicting as an ideal a life that can be lived in Alexandria, near the Serapeum, amid a busy, commercial, pleasure-loving, and excitable population. And he can show that there is a Christian way of life, a grace and dignity of behaviour, that come as the natural fruit of the new relationship with God. This new way of life is apparent throughout the pages of the *Paedagogus*, or *Instructor*, the second of his great treatises. But rarely has the transformation of the work of life been sung more harmoniously than in the famous passage of the *Protrepticus* (ch. x). He says of the man who has now heard the message:

It is his nature, as man, to be in close fellowship with God. As then we do not force the horse to plough, nor the bull to hunt, but lead each animal to its natural work; for the very same reason we call upon man, who was made for the contemplation of heaven, and is in truth a heavenly plant, to come to the knowledge of God. Having laid hold of that which is personal, special, and peculiar in his nature, that wherein he surpasses the other animals, we counsel him to equip himself with godliness, as a sufficient provision for his journey through eternity. Till the ground, we say, if you are a husbandman; but recognize God in your husbandry. Sail the sea, you who love seafaring; but ever call upon the heavenly pilot. Were you a soldier on campaign when the knowledge of God laid hold of you? Then listen to the commander who signals righteousness.

Clement knows that we are living in God's world, and that it is God's will that we should have God with us in it. 'Have you found God? You have life.'[1]

[1] *Protr.* x (tr. Butterworth).

II. FAITH AND KNOWLEDGE AS CONJOINED IN THE IDEAL LIFE

The ideal life is defined as γνῶσις, and the meaning of this term must now be examined. At first sight it seems that Clement's doctrine of the two lives, which he draws from Philo, rests on a difference between faith and knowledge; and that the lower life of the ordinary believer is a life of faith, while the higher life, that of the Christian Gnostic, is a life of knowledge. Dr. Bigg has given the weight of his authority to this interpretation.[1] But there are reasons for questioning this view.

The practical problem which lay before Clement must first be stated. Crowds were pressing into the Christian Church; the level of moral attainment was low, and their faith elementary. They were bringing with them many pagan prejudices, and the moral taint of the past still lingered about them. Such believers needed discipline and instruction. Clement has essayed that task in his *Paedagogus*. But in addition to these, and perhaps even among them, there were other enquirers after truth, who could not be content with spiritual mediocrity, and who hungered after a richer experience of God. Every minister of a church who understands his people knows that such a group exists, and often he has words which he speaks to them alone. To such an inner circle Clement addressed his *Stromateis*. 'From the premises of his own intellectual mysticism, the greater knowledge of God to which they aspired involved not only a better comprehension, but also a more complete assimilation of the divine life, so that these gnostics in achieving their goal would become a kind of divine aristocracy.'[2]

But before the mind of Clement there was the fear of gnosticism, which had made its appeal to the latent pride of those who thought themselves fit for esoteric teaching.[3] He had developed a theory of the equality of salvation.

---

[1] *Christian Platonists* (2nd edn. 1913), 121, 124, 126.
[2] Casey, *Harvard Theol. Review*, xviii. 71.
[3] See, e.g., *Paed.* i. 6. 128, 129.

How could there be a group who possessed a spiritual knowledge superior to that of their fellow Christians? If faith is the gift of God, is not God ultimately responsible for this difference between the quality of the faith of the ordinary believer and the faith of the Christian gnostic?

This difficulty is a real one for any doctrine of perfection. Casey calls it insuperable from Clement's premises, and declares that it is merely evaded, though evaded with such skill that the system betrays hardly a sign of the danger to which it had been exposed.[1] In the *Stromateis* Clement teaches believers to go on unto perfection. In the *Paedagogus* he says that all Christians are in reality perfected in the sight of God.[2] 'When we were re-born we received straightway that perfect thing (τὸ τέλειον) for which we were striving. For we were enlightened—and that is to know God (ἐπιγνῶναι τὸν θεόν); he cannot therefore be imperfect who has known that which is perfect.' Perfection is here regarded from the side of God Who is known. But the expression is more justifiable than would at first sight appear. It is the essential characteristic of religion as contrasted with morality that it changes aspiration into fruition, anticipation into realization. It does not leave man in the interminable pursuit of a vanishing ideal, but makes him the actual partaker of a divine or infinite life. Principal Caird once pointed out[3] that 'in the sphere of devotion all prayer for spiritual improvement, for growth in grace, is already efficacious, just because of the deeper conviction on which it rests—the conviction that we are already perfect even as our Father in Heaven is perfect'.

The perfection, then, contemplated by the *Paedagogus* is the perfection of all genuine religious experience, when the soul meets God. The perfection to which believers are called by the *Stromateis* is θεωρία, a full unification of the powers of the soul. There is knowledge in it, but there is also love,[4] complete harmony of purpose and desire. The first kind of perfection leads naturally to the

---

[1] Op. cit. 71. [2] i. 6.
[3] *Intro. to Philosophy of Religion*, 288–9. See the whole chapter.
[4] Cf. *Strom*. vii. 11. 68.

second because the second is already given and implicit in the first.

A second reason for refusing to acquiesce in any strict severance of the two lives is the meaning of the word faith. Bigg dismisses Clement's use of the word as a sheer misunderstanding of the Pauline word.[1] But faith is used in many senses by Clement.[2] Faith is not a vain and barbarous thing, as the Greeks calumniate it. It is a voluntary preconception, the assent of piety. 'We can learn nothing without a preconceived idea of what we are aiming at. Faith is such preconception (πρόληψις).[3] It is also defined as the assent of the intellect to an unseen object; as the beginning of action. It is thus an activity of the reason as well as of the religious soul, and is sometimes actually called γνῶσις by Clement.[4]

So too the γνῶσις of which Clement speaks as the characteristic of the Christian gnostic is never 'merely' intellectual. He says[5] that the word is used commonly in two senses, but he himself uses it in a third. 'It is a kind of perfection of man as man, harmonious and consistent with itself and with the divine Word, being completed both as to the disposition and the manner of life and speech, by the science of divine things. For it is by insight that faith is made perfect.'[6] The general principle is that faith and knowledge are indissolubly related. 'Neither is knowledge without faith, nor faith without knowledge.'[7]

Clement is working with an idea of God which is essentially Hebraic and not merely nor even predominantly Hellenic. To him God is not pure Being, self-sufficient in His own blessedness; His goodness is deed; He is living and working; He is creative Will.[8]

It follows that the γνῶσις at which the seeker aims

---

[1] *Christian Platonists*, 120, 121.
[2] See the excellent summary by Patrick, *Clement*, 151–3.
[3] *Strom.* ii. 4. 17.   [4] *Strom.* vii. 10.   [5] *Strom.* vi. 1.
[6] *Strom.* vii. 10 (tr. Mayor).   [7] *Strom.* v. 1.
[8] Cf. Frick, *Die Geschichte des Reich-Gottes-Gedankens*, 83. See *Strom.* vi. 12. 104, *ad fin.*

involves not only intellectual insight but ethical perfection. No one in the century after the apostolic age has fathomed the moral grandeur of the Gospel so deeply as Clement. Christianity has certainly given him a new sensibility to sin, 'a pain to feel it near'.[1] More than this, he continually emphasizes the strenuousness of the Christian life.[2]

The final statement of γνῶσις in the seventh book of the *Stromateis* makes it clear that Clement is in harmony with St. Paul in regarding love as the goal of the moral life. This love is first of all to God,[3] but it is also love for his fellow men.[4] Clement lays stress on the disinterestedness of perfect love. Not from fear, not from any hope of reward does the gnostic do his good and love His Maker, but only the doing of good out of love and for the sake of his own excellence is his choice; only so as to pass his life after the image and likeness of his Lord. The Gospel tells us not to do our good deeds so as to be seen of men; the gnostic himself who shows mercy ought not to know that he shows mercy! Such virtue will be a habit (ἕξις), a disposition (διάθεσις), and this lovely freedom from self-consciousness is the soul's ideal.[5]

III. COMMUNION WITH GOD

The prize of the Christian life is not to be won without dust and heat. Clement knows that the attainment of insight into the Divine Will is God's own free gift, and yet that the reception of the gift is costly for the soul. The price to be paid is prayer, and Clement's exposition of prayer is a proof of his own knowledge of God. From the earliest days the teachers of Christianity have taught a doctrine of prayer far removed from the pagan conceptions which still prevail and are popular in Christian countries. The least possible stress is laid by Clement on petition for earthly goods. In the search after perfection

---

[1] See, e.g., the handling of the views of Valentinus in *Strom.* ii. 20.
[2] *Strom.* ii. 19; iii. 6.
[3] *Strom.* vii. 10. 56; vii. 11. 67; cf. *Protr.* xii. 244.
[4] *Strom.* vii. 11. 62.
[5] *Strom.* iv. 22. 135–8.

the Christian is right in not seeking after any of the necessary conveniences of life. God knows all things, and will
supply whatever is expedient to the good even without
their asking. He that aspires to true insight will ask for
the perfection of love. He prays that 'the power of contemplation may grow and abide with him, just as the
ordinary man prays for a continuance of health'.

But apart from his discrimination in the things for
which he prays, the true Christian regards all moral discipline and all intellectual struggles after the Truth as part
of the exercise of prayer. 'Doing the Will we come to
Insight', says Clement. And this doing is costly. 'We
may not be lifted up and transported to our journey's end.
We must travel there on foot, passing over all the distance
of the narrow way.' The most valuable, and perhaps the
most neglected, truth in Clement's doctrine of prayer is
his emphasis on the pursuit of knowledge as a religious
duty. The ignorant and helpless babes in Christ may be
granted a knowledge of God which is denied to the wise
and understanding who trust in human intellect. But,
nevertheless, the ignorant beginners must go on to perfection, and there is no attainment of any quest for them
if they are not willing to learn. All scientific knowledge is
spiritual, according to Clement. The clearness of mind
won by pursuing knowledge is infinitely valuable in aiding
the Christian to attain to uninterrupted contemplation of
God. The mental discipline, therefore, which is the duty
of the Christian, is a part of prayer.

Clement knows the absolute necessity of setting apart
certain times of the day for thanksgiving and communion
and certain periods for public worship. But the seeker
after holiness must learn

to pray in every place, not however publicly or for all to see; but in
every sort of way his prayer ascends, whether he is walking or in
company or at rest or reading, or engaged in good works; and though
it only be a thought in the secret chamber of the heart, while he
calls on the Father in groanings which cannot be uttered, yet the
Father is nigh at hand, even before he has done speaking.[1]

[1] *Strom.* vii. 7. 49 (tr. Mayor).

Pray without ceasing! There is not one of the early Fathers who so enters into and understands the mind of St. Paul at this point. Clement knows that the Christian life was meant to be a close and unbroken converse, a wondrous great familiarity with God. Such colloquy with the ever present Friend would increasingly impress on the life a supernatural character. This would not be the result of any human effort, but the gift of the grace of God.

If the presence of some good man always moulds for the better one who converses with him, owing to the respect and reverence which he inspires, with much more reason must he, who is always in the uninterrupted presence of God, by means of his knowledge and his life and his thankful spirit, be raised above himself on every occasion, both in regard to his actions and his words and his temper.[1]

Prayer then, to speak somewhat boldly, is converse with God. Even if we address Him in a whisper, without opening our lips or uttering a sound, still we cry to Him in our heart. For God never ceases to listen to the inward converse of the heart.[2]

IV. THE BEATIFIC VISION OF GOD

By this time certain characteristics of the final stage of the soul's attainment will be evident to the reader of Clement. He looks for an unbroken and abiding contemplation of God. The experience of divine grace granted to most of us is fragmentary; our communion is fluctuating and incomplete. Clement points us to a vision that is permanent and clear. He will have it that these aspirations of ours after an uninterrupted intercourse with our Father are destined to perfect satisfaction. That which now we know only in our purest and highest moments will become a constant possession. This, then, is the first mark of the Beatific Vision—it abides. Secondly, the Vision is the soul's peace. Clement follows Plato here, where Plato is most certainly at one with the writers of the New Testament, and with the promise of rest for the heavy-laden given to us by our Lord. Only in the contemplation of the Eternal Beauty shall we find rest unto our souls. And that

---

[1] *Strom.* vii. 7. 35 (tr. Mayor).   [2] *Strom.* vii. 7. 39.

which is lovely has the power to draw into this serenity every one who gives himself to the contemplation of God. In the very passage in which Clement speaks of this poise of soul which is given by the vision of God to the pure in heart, he seems forced, by his intuitions of this experience, to deny that the soul is merely static and quiescent when lifted up by grace so to gaze upon God. Those who look upon Him are so carried away by the magnificence of the vision that 'they keep on always moving to higher and yet higher regions'. There is unbroken development and yet the soul is at peace. In the third place, the power that so draws the soul into knowledge of the Divine Beauty is Love, and this love assimilates the soul of the consecrated man to the pure likeness of God. 'He is united to the Spirit through the love that knows no bounds.'[1] The marks of this marvellous union are virtues that may be known and read of all men. Clement singles out especially 'gentleness, kindness, and a noble devoutness'. These are the canons, or standards, by which we can test the attainment of the soul.

But we must let Clement describe the goal of life in his own words.

This takes place whenever anyone hangs upon the Lord Jesus Christ by means of faith and insight and love, and ascends up with Him to the presence of the God and Guardian of our faith and love. He is the ultimate source from which insight is imparted to those who are fitted and approved for it.

This insight easily transplants a man to that divine and holy state which is akin to the soul, and by a light of its own carries him through the mystic stages till it restores him to the crowning abode of rest, having taught the pure in heart to look upon God face to face, with understanding and absolute certainty. For herein lies the perfection of the soul that knows, that having transcended all

---

[1] If this union is sometimes described as deification (see *Strom*. iv. 23. 149–55; vii. 10. 56; 13. 82; 16. 95) it must be noted what a gap Clement sees between the most perfect of men and God. The soul is προσεχῶς ὑποτεταγμένη (vii. 10. 57). If we speak of a perfect gnostic, 'none of his perfections, to whatever height it may attain, is regarded as coming into comparison with God' (vii. 15. 88). Cf. the view of Harnack, *History of Dogma*, ii. 338, n. 1.

ceremonial purifications and modes of ritual, *it should be with the Lord*, where He is, in immediate obedience to Him.[1]

There is a restraint and delicacy in Clement's treatment of the goal of the spiritual quest by which we recognize the authentic word of the seer. He is not describing an experience from outside or at second-hand. Temperamentally our humanist is somewhat discursive, and he can rarely resist the luxury of a Greek quotation. But in his descriptions of the discoveries that await the seeker in the realms unseen, he treads with a controlled certainty, a slow sureness of step, as if held in awe by a vision that passes beyond the reach of words. So, too, St. Paul had spoken of the sighs going beyond all power of utterance, that mark the presence of the Spirit of God interceding for the human soul wherein He works. And Plotinus was soon to despair of transcribing, even into the most flexible of all languages, the wonder unveiled in the Holy Mount. 'He who has seen it knows what I mean.' And with the same reticence Clement falls back, almost helplessly, on a word of Aeschylus spoken at the outset of the tremendous drama of the *Agamemnon*, by one who knows far more than he can ever tell;—*For the rest I keep silence;* but he significantly adds to his quotation his own phrase, *giving glory to God.* Here is another who can sing with a confidence and gladness the lyrical cry dear to the hearts of humbler and less learned believers; he knows

> The o'erwhelming power of saving grace,
> The sight that veils the seraph's face;
> The speechless awe that dares not move,
> And all the silent heaven of love.

V. SINLESSNESS

In the light of the foregoing discussion we can set the problem that remains. Did Clement teach that sinlessness was possible in this world?

In the *Protrepticus* he says that Christians are the first-born sons of God (Col. i. 15, 18; Heb. i. 6) who have been the first of all mankind to know God, the first to be torn

[1] *Strom.* vii. 10. 56, 57 (tr. Mayor).

away from our sins.¹ The ideal of the Greek philosophers
is now for the first time realized among the Christians.
'The entire life of men who have come to know Christ is
good.'² This regeneration is connected with baptism.³ But
the passage (*Paed.* i. 6) on which Windisch⁴ chiefly relies
to prove that Clement teaches sinlessness does not in fact
go so far. 'Being baptized, we are illuminated, illuminated
we become sons; being made sons, we are made perfect;
being made perfect, we are made immortal.' Another
passage in the same chapter expressly leaves the time of
the cleansing vague. 'We are washed from all our sins,
and are no longer entangled in evil. This is the one grace
of illumination that our characters are not the same as
before our washing. *You cannot tell the time.*'⁵ At the end
of the same chapter Clement expounds the perfection to
which Paul had attained (Phil. iv. 15) as renunciation of
sin and being born again into the faith of the only perfect
One, and having forgotten the sins that lay behind. The
language here is careful.

But when we advance to the *Stromateis* we find that
repentance is regarded as involving complete abandon-
ment of sin.⁶ By a fine phrase he expands St. Paul's
meaning ὥστε εἴ τις ἐν Χριστῷ καινὴ κτίσις, οὐκέτι ἁμαρτητική.⁷
The gnostics who tread in the footsteps of the apostles
ought to be sinless, and out of love for the Lord to love
also their brother.⁸

VI. THE PREVENIENCE OF GOD

Many of the usual criticisms passed on the teaching of
Clement have been answered, at least in part, by the foregoing exposition of his ideal. But it is impossible to acquit
him of the old charge of disparaging the sweet human
affections and the common joys of men. Thus marriage
is said to be superior to celibacy merely because it offers
so many more temptations to surmount.⁹ The gnostic

---

¹ ix. 69.   ² xii, *ad fin.*   ³ *Protr.* x. 79; cf. *Paed.* i. 6.
⁴ *Taufe und Sünde*, 445.   ⁵ *Paed.* i. 6, 116.
⁶ ii. 6. 443.   ⁷ iii. 8.   ⁸ iv. 9.
⁹ *Strom.* vii. 12. 70; cf. *Strom.* vi. 12. 100–1.

does not love any one with the ordinary affection but he loves the Creator in the creatures.[1] Grace is seen here supplanting nature; whereas in the true Christian view, as von Hügel loved to say, Grace is never the cuckoo driving the other bird out of the nest.

Here again, most unhappily, says Bigg, Stoicism comes in and casts the chill shadow of Apathy over the sweetest and simplest of Christian motives. Platonism also helped to mislead. For though the Alexandrines held that Matter is the work of God, they could not wholly divest their minds of the old scholastic dislike of the brute mass and the emotions connected with it. . . . Clement could not bear to think that the rose of Sharon could blossom on common soil.[2]

The human life of Jesus is emptied of the emotions of courage, fear, anger, zeal, joy, desire. 'It would be ridiculous' to suppose that the body of Christ demanded bodily aids for its continuance. 'He was entirely impassible;—inaccessible to any movement of feeling, either pleasure or pain.'[3]

These failures in Clement's delineation of the ideal are due ultimately to a defect in his conception of God. It is tempting to connect them with his transcendentalism whereby he affirms that God is $\dot{a}\sigma\dot{\omega}\mu\alpha\tau\sigma\varsigma$, beyond the One and above the Monad.[4] But here we can only point out that side by side with such views of the Apathy of God there is another, more personal, and Hebraic conception of God as prevenient, active, forthgoing, infinitely persevering in His love for His children. In the exposition of the work of the Logos in the *Protrepticus* we see this

[1] *Strom.* vi. 9. 71.

[2] *Christian Platonists*, 126.

[3] *Strom.* vi. 9. 71. The history of the idea of Christ's humanity is treated in Schulte, *Die Entwicklung der Lehre vom menschlichen Wissen Christi* (Paderborn, 1914). See p. 20 for a treatment of Clement. Cf. also the fragment of the Hypotyposeis in Stählin, iii. 197. The $\sigma\acute{\alpha}\rho\xi$ which is crucified in Gal. v. 24 is our body, and also the $\pi\acute{\alpha}\theta\eta$ connected with it. Other passages dealing with $\dot{\alpha}\pi\acute{\alpha}\theta\epsilon\iota\alpha$ are *Strom.* iv. 6. 30; 18. 111; 22. 135–46; vi. 16. 138.

[4] *Paed.* i. 8. 71; *Strom.* v. 11. 71. So Mozley, *The Impassibility of God*, 54–9; De Faye, *Clément*, 214–30; Bigg, 126; Casey, *Harvard Theol. Review* (1925), xviii. 74–90. Inge's view is not the same: *Plotinus*, ii. 111.

greater view breaking down the bonds of the purely
Greek category. He sees Christ perpetually active for the
salvation of men.[1] He sees Christ at work in the hearts
and minds of men before His day. He sees a God who
had spoken through Greek Philosophy, as well as through
the words of the Hebrew Lawgiver. He sees One who
spoke in the loveliest poetry of the past, whose word was
manifest in all the fragments of truth that had been given
to the world, whose reason illuminated the minds of all
seekers after reality. Christ had been from the beginning
of the world the great Lover of mankind. And thus
recognizing the activity of Christ in the history of the
world before the Incarnation, Clement had reached the
truth which the Baron von Hügel calls the ultimate mental
and spiritual conviction of religion, and yet finds to be
somehow rare, even among religious men. It is 'that
Religion begins and proceeds and ends with the Given—
with existences, realities which environ and penetrate us,
and which we have always anew to capture and combine,
to fathom and to apprehend.'[2] It is that the first doctrine
of the Church is the Catholic doctrine of Grace. It is the
doctrine of the prevenience of God. Wherever we look,
whithersoever we go, Christ has been there before us. In
the salvation of our souls God has taken the initiative. The
communion for which our souls were made, and without
which they must go hungry, owes nothing to our own
origination or desert, and everything to His prevenient,
pursuing, self-sacrificing Love.

This Clement knows, as St. Augustine knows it. Rarely
has human saintliness been defined with so much insight
and humility as in the seventh book of the *Stromateis*
(ch. vii. 42):

If prayer is thus an occasion for intercourse with God, no occasion
for our approach to God must be neglected. Certainly the holiness
of the gnostic, being bound up with the Divine Providence through
a voluntary acknowledgement on his part, shows the beneficence of

---

[1] *Protr.* i. 8; x *passim*. Cf. the view of Frick, *Die Geschichte des Reich-Gottes-Gedanken*, 83–4, and reff.

[2] *Essays and Addresses*, xiii–xv. See his works, *passim*.

God in perfection. For the holiness of the gnostic is, as it were, a return back on itself of Providence, and a responsive feeling of loyalty on the part of the friend of God.

A return back on itself of Providence! Could any description such as this awkward English phrase, which translates a single Greek word, bring out more clearly the ultimate truth that *all things are of God* in the life of the seeker after holiness? We are tied to this tremendous Lover of ours. It is in the same spirit that Clement recalls an old word from the myth in Plato's *Phaedrus*, about the destiny that governs human life and determines a man's career before he comes into the world.

This is the true Adrasteia, the law of destiny, owing to which we cannot escape from God.[1]

Elsewhere he interprets the destiny as the pursuing love of God. In one poignant evangelistic appeal he cries, not without a reminiscence of Homer:

Will you not escape to the pity that comes from heaven? For God of His great love still keeps hold of man, just as, when a nestling falls from the nest, the mother bird flutters above, and if perchance a serpent gapes for it, 'Flitting around with cries, the mother mourns for her offspring.' Now God is a Father, and seeks His creature, He provides a remedy for the falling away. He drives off the reptile. He restores the nestling to strength again. And He urges it to fly back to the nest.[2]

So it was that the first scholar-missionary, who broke down the barriers between the Christianity and the culture of his day, took his stand on the gospel of infinite and inescapable Love that will not let us go.

ORIGEN

καὶ γὰρ πᾶς ὁ τετελειωμένος ζῇ οὐκέτι, ἀλλ' ἐν αὐτῷ ζῇ Χριστός.

ὁ κεκαθαρμένος καὶ ὑπεραναβὰς πάντα ὑλικὰ νοῦς, ἵνα ἀκριβώσῃ τὴν θεωρίαν τοῦ θεοῦ ἐν οἷς θεωρεῖ θεοποιεῖται.

(*Comm. Joh.*).

In the teaching of Origen a fateful step is taken by Christian spirituality. The perfect Christian is one who at

[1] *Strom.* vii. 3. 20.   [2] *Protr.* x.

the summit of his progress has turned his back on the outward and visible world as well as on the emotions ($\pi\acute{a}\theta\eta$) of mankind. When he enters the secret chamber wherein is the treasure of wisdom and knowledge, without looking outside or troubling himself with things outside, he closes the door on all things perceived by the senses, that his senses may not lead him astray.[1] The true image of Christian piety is one who like Moses has ascended above all created things.[2]

Let us see how this result is reached. In his ideal Origen follows in the path marked out by Clement, but there are elements in his spirituality which Clement never knew. The most appealing is his vision of the Crucified. 'The Cross in all its wonder, its bounty, its power, is always before the eyes of Origen.'[3] In this fact there is an implicit modification of the ideal of Apathy, which he shares with Clement. He regards it as God's gift, but ranks love above it and, unlike the Stoics, he finds a divine meaning in suffering and disaster by which the soul is tried.[4] He was, as his pupil Gregory Thaumaturgus said, 'a wondrous hearkener to God'.[5] But with all Origen's devotion there were certain intractable elements in his intellectual heritage which his Christianity did not transform.

For those who desired to press on to perfection Origen's first advice was, Know Thyself.[6] The cause of the variety to which the creature is subjected is nothing else than the

---

[1] *De oratione*, xx. 2. So too the mind must transcend all material things to attain to accurate contemplation of God; Commentary on *John* (ed. A. E. Brooke, 1896, p. 201), xxxii. 27. See also *De princ.* i. i. 7, *ad fin.*

[2] *C. Cels.* i. 19.

[3] Bigg, *Christian Platonists*, 254. Cf. W. Völker, *Das Vollkommen- heitsideal des Origenes* (1931), 103. I must acknowledge a special debt to this thorough and learned monograph, which has set Origen's thought in a new light. Review by Van den Eynde in *Revue d'Histoire Ecclésiastique*, Juillet, 1932.

[4] Völker, 154–5; Fragment 30. ἐν χερσὶ κυρίου μένων ἀπαθής.

[5] Gregory Thaumaturgus, *Address to Origen*, c. xv. (S.P.C.K. ed. E. tr. Metcalfe, p. 81).

[6] Gregory, op. cit., c. xi; Harnack, *Hist. Dogma*, ii. 336–7. Other evidence in Völker, 23.

body.[1] The body is the fetter of the soul, and hinders it from attaining the knowledge of God. This conception is joined with a definition of sin as the absence of good (*bono carere*),[2] as darkness is the absence of light. But the stress laid in his homiletical writings on the freedom of the will, individual responsibility, and human guilt, bring Origen's view of sin nearer to that of the New Testament.[3] He says expressly[4] that there is a kingdom of sin which is irreconcilable with the Kingdom of God. There is a devil, who causes in us the loss of communion with God. There is a battle with the demons to be waged.[5] Hence the Christian is entangled in a ceaseless struggle, and can only win his victory therein by the weapons of asceticism. Paul's saying, *I buffet my body*, is interpreted in this sense. The words of Jesus (except ye . . . become as little children) means the mortifying of the lusts of mankind, because the child has not tasted sexual pleasure.[6] Origen taught his pupils to practise Plato's four cardinal virtues in order to rise above the things of the body and taste of the feast of contemplation in the Paradise of delight.[7] After six days (as Matthew says), Jesus took his disciples up into a high mountain, and was transfigured. Origen interprets the passing through those six days as meaning passing beyond created things, for the world was created in six days. If any one of us wishes to be deemed worthy of beholding the Transfiguration, let him pass beyond the six days, and no longer behold the things in the world. Then he will keep a new Sabbath and rejoice on the high mountain of God.[8] Origen has gone beyond Clement in thus introducing to his Santa Scala an asceticism that despises the world.[9]

The Ladder is a gradual ascent. There is no sudden break with sin. Conversion is only a conversion of the will. Redemption from sin only begins with baptism. He

---

[1] *De princ.* i. vii. 5.
[2] *De princ.* ii. ix. 2; *Comm. John*, ii. 13; Brooke, i. 75–6.
[3] Völker, 30–3.   [4] *De oratione*, xxv. 3.
[5] *Comm. Matt.* xiii. 17.   [6] Ibid. 16.
[7] Gregory, op. cit., cc. ix, xv, xvi.   [8] *Comm. Matt.* xii. 36.
[9] Contrast Clement, *Strom.* vii. 12. 70. Cf. Völker, 45.

distinguishes between *peccatorem esse* and *peccare*. The
son of God is not indeed the servant of sin; he sins but
he is not a sinner.[1] The Stoic theory of progress is applied
to the Christian conquest of moral evil,[2] and it is progress
to a definite goal.[3]

How does the Pauline message of grace fare in this
mingling of mysticism, asceticism, and the Stoic doctrine
of progress? An answer is not easily given. Origen is
clear that the good gift, perfect purity in celibacy and
chastity, is the gift of God, 'to those who ask Him with
the whole soul and with faith, and in prayers without
ceasing'.[4] The perfect spiritual Gnosis is not in our power,
but comes by revelation of God.[5] But it is not certain
whether Origen sees the divine grace active at every stage
of the spiritual life,[6] or whether the beginning must be
made by man[7] and then is followed by supporting grace.
On the whole the latter view is to be adopted. 'A union
of grace and freedom takes place within the sphere of freedom, till the contemplative life is reached . . . in which the
Logos is the friend, associate, and bridegroom of the soul,
which now having become pure spirit and being herself
deified, clings in love to the Deity.'[8] However this ideal
may be valued, we cannot term it Pauline,[9] nor indeed any
teaching which states that Paul became a child of God by
keeping the commandments,[10] or that the martyrs by being
baptized in their own blood will have washed away all
sin.[11] The purely intellectual character of faith is made

---

[1] *Comm. Rom.* v. 5. Bigg's comment (250) is that 'Theology finally
triumphs over Ethics'. Windisch says (*Taufe u. Sünde*, 491): 'So hat
Origenes das Sündertum in der Kirche legitimiert.'

[2] Cf. Windisch, 492.   [3] *Comm. Rom.* v. 8; Lommatzsch, vi. 388.

[4] *Comm. Matt.* xiv. 25 *ad fin.*

[5] Ps. 43. Lommatzsch, xii. 320.   [6] So Bigg, 201–2.

[7] *Selecta in Psalm CXX.* Cf. M. J. Denis, *de la Philosophie d'Origène*
(1884), 276, and the whole discussion, 266–82.

[8] Harnack, *Hist. Dogma*, ii. 376.

[9] So Völker, 40. Ritschl has stated this view uncompromisingly;
Entstehung d. altkath. Kirche (1857), 324–5; cf. 318. For progress to
perfection from faith to hope, and from hope to love, see *Comm. Rom.* iv.
6; Lommatzsch, vi. 271.   [10] *Comm. Joh.* xx. 17; Brooke, ii. 59.

[11] *Protrept. Martyr*, xxxix; cf. xxx.

plain in a passage of the commentary on John (xxxii. 16) where perfect faith is portrayed.[1]

That a relative perfection is attainable in this life is part of Origen's thought. Does it include freedom from all moral defect? He hesitates between two views. 'I do not think that any one's heart can become so pure that thoughts of evil will never stain it.' The Jebusites (evil thoughts) still dwell with the sons of Judah in Jerusalem. We must endeavour to drive them out, but we cannot drive them all out at once.[2] On the other hand, he speaks of those who are pure and sin no more.[3] There are few of them,[4] and as Windisch says, Origen does not add 'auch unter uns'! He is careful not to describe as sinless any in Alexandria. But the prophets and the apostles attained to perfection in this life.[5] Especially does he hold up Paul, who shows that there are two kinds of perfection. One is the final perfection of the virtues—this he had not yet attained, the other, the perfection which forgets the things that are behind, the perfection of those who always carry about in their bodies the dying of Jesus. When Paul wrote the closing words of Romans viii he had attained to the height when he did not need further to fight against his body.[6] There still remains a struggle for the spiritual man who has gained this degree of perfection, but he is now promoted to the battle against demonic powers.[7] Together with the ceaseless struggle goes a mystic attainment of the Gnosis. Origen describes this as the act of the Logos, who transports the soul out of human things and intoxicates us with an intoxication which is not irrational but divine. At such times we may be wholly united with God,[8] or 'deified';[9] and this may come to pass even in the

---

[1] Brooke, ii. 177–9. E. tr. in Tollinton, *Selections from Origen* (1929), 249–52. Other evidence in Seeberg, *Lehrbuch D.G.* i. 445.

[2] *In Jesu Nave*, xxi.

[3] *C. Cels.* iii. 62.   [4] Ibid. 69.

[5] *Hom. Jer.* xvi. 5.

[6] *Comm. Rom., Praef.*; Lommatzsch vi. 2–5; 313 (*Comm. Rom.* iv. 12).

[7] *De princ.* iii. ii. 4.

[8] ἕνωσις is the word. *Comm. Joh.* xix. 4; Brooke, ii. 5.

[9] θεοποιεῖται is used in *Comm. Joh.* xxxii. 27; Brooke, ii. 201. See also

present life. The mystic ascent to divinity is harmoniously combined in Origen's doctrine with the practical duties of fighting evil, teaching the divine secrets to the ignorant, bearing the burdens of the weak.[1] His ideal finds expression in the treatise on Prayer.[2] Like Clement, he saw all life as one single prayer, a mingling of action with devotion. Every holy act is reckoned by God as prayer.[3] Never is the soul in this life absolved from its task of wrestling with evil, and martyrdom is the highest prize for the spiritual athlete because it is the swiftest way to follow our Lord.[4] Amid the life of action there will be the deep inward prayer without words that is the true θεωρία, the highest peak attainable in this life, the vision on the mount of God.

Origen is the precursor of Monasticism. This is the conclusion of our brief survey of his spirituality. He envied Mary sitting at the Saviour's feet; he envied John who 'departed into the desert where the air was purer, the sky more open, and God more intimately nigh'.[5]

NOTE. It is too much to say with von der Goltz, *Das Gebet in d. ältesten Christenheit* (1901), 278, that there has been no advance on Origen's doctrine of prayer. But his distinction and influence may be seen in the next century in a study of Gregory of Nyssa's teaching of the ideal life (*On Perfection* and *On Virginity*—both these treatises in Migne, *P.G.* 46). Gregory emphasizes the following of Christ, the ceaseless struggle, the mortification of the flesh. Perfection is never to stand still, never to set any limit to perfection. τὸ μηδέποτε στῆναι πρὸς τὸ κρεῖττον αὐξανόμενον, μηδέ τινι πέρατι περιορίσαι τὴν τελειότητα. *P.G.* 46. 285. It is freedom from the bodily affections, the mind must be completely detached from all ordinary human life (*De virg.* c. ii, c. vi; Migne, 324, 349). Marriage is the first thing to be left (c. xii), though it is not altogether

Hort-Mayor, *Seventh Book of Strom.* 203–4; Harnack, *Hist. Dogma*, iii. 164–5 and i. 119–20.

[1] Völker, 168–96, works this out in detail.

[2] Völker, 197–215.

[3] *Comm. Matt.* xvi. 22; Lommatzsch, iv. 65.

[4] *Protr. Mart.* xii. There is now a French translation of the treatises on Prayer and Martyrdom by G. Bardy (1932).

[5] *Hom. Luc.* xi; Lommatzsch, v. 124.

a stranger to God's blessing (c. viii), in spite of Gregory's terrifying picture of its evils (c. iii). Virginity is the actual representation in this life of the blessedness to come, and is indeed perfection (c. xiii).

In concrete form it is described in the *Vita S. Macrinae*, Migne, 46. 972. The ultimate goal is the vision of God (*De virg.* c. xxiv). The progress of monasticism has influenced Gregory's treatment, but the main elements of Origen's doctrine are unchanged.

CHAPTER VII

MONASTICISM

Abiit in deserta, ubi purior aër erat, et coelum apertius, et familiarior Deus.—Origen.

MONASTICISM[1] is the boldest organized attempt to attain to Christian perfection in all the long history of the Church. Henri Bremond calls it 'a second Pentecost'.[2] Historians have often doubted whether monasticism should be regarded as an indigenous Christian product; its seeds have been traced to distant Buddhist asceticism, to the hermit devotees of the Egyptian Serapis, or to Greek religious sects. But to-day these doubts may safely be set aside. Our primary document shows us with dramatic appropriateness a word of the Gospel piercing to the heart of the true Father of Monasticism at the decisive moment of his life. St. Antony was on his way to church (so St. Athanasius tells us) and was exercised in mind by the thought of his own unworthiness, as compared with the apostles, who had left all to follow their Lord. It chanced that the Gospel for the day was the word of Jesus to the Rich Young Ruler: *If thou wouldest be perfect . . .!* Antony's hour had come. He sold all, and with this great price obtained his freedom 'from the chains of this world'.

His aim was to attain inward perfection; he set himself to win the virtues which he had seen in others, and by ceaseless prayer to win fellowship with God. But his struggles made it clear to him that the enemy was not only in the thoughts of his own heart. Behind those thoughts was the unseen world of evil, Satan and his host of demons. He must win his victory over these if he was to have in-

---

[1] The chief sources are Athanasius, *Vita Antonii*; Sulpicius Severus, *Vita Martini*; *Historia Lausiaca Palladii* (ed. of Dom Cuthbert Butler, Cambridge 2 vols, 1898 and 1904; E. tr. by W. K. Lowther Clarke); the works of St. Basil, especially those translated by W. K. Lowther Clarke, *The Ascetic Works of St. Basil* (1925); the *Conferences* and *Institutes* of Cassian (ed. Petschenig, 2 vols., Vienna 1886); E. tr. *N.P.N.* libr.

[2] *Les Pères du Désert* (1927), xlvi.

ward peace. He went out into the solitude; 'He confirmed his purpose not to return to the abode of his fathers, nor to the remembrance of his kinsfolk; but to keep all his desire and energy for perfecting his discipline (ἄσκησις).'[1] He fought and won. There came a time when he gained inward certainty. One night after the usual struggle with evil thoughts he saw the Devil cowering at his feet like a black child. 'I have deceived many,' wailed the Spirit of iniquity, 'I have cast down many, but as in the case of many, so in thine, I have been worsted in the battle.'

There is no hint of non-Christian influence at work here. The soil for the plant of monachism may have been prepared by many movements of the mind, many spiritual inundations like those of Father Nile, but the seed itself is easily recognizable, and it is sown by those at work within the garden of the Church. And the recital proves to us that if St. Antony is typical, it is at Christian perfection that monasticism aims.[2]

The most authentic document for the history of Pachomius has nothing quite so revealing. But the author is explicit on the aim of Pachomius to reach perfection.[3] Similarly with St. Basil. He tells us how in the time of his penitence for the sins of his youth his difficulties were resolved and the light broke upon his soul. It was in reading the Gospels. Here he saw that 'the greatest incentive to perfection was to sell one's goods, to share them with the poor, to give up all care (ὅλως τὸ ἀφροντίστως ἔχειν τοῦ βίου τούτου) for this life, to refuse to let the soul have any sympathetic concern with things on earth'.[4] In the lives of the monks, he says, he met the Gospel ideal made manifest. They did in very deed bear about in their body the dying of Jesus. The things seen he took for proof of things unseen. So did he come himself to tread

[1] *Vit. Ant.* i. 3.
[2] Cf. Karl Holl, *Gesammelte Aufsätze*, ii (1928), 271, 272, who shows in his fourteenth study, *Über das griechische Mönchtum*, that the ideal of Greek monasticism develops, as though by some inner necessity, from this decisive experience of Antony. [3] Ladeuze, *Le cénobitisme pakhomien*, 159.
[4] *Ep.* 223. 2; Loeb ed. iii. 292.

the self-same way.[1] St. Benedict, horrified at the licentious-
ness prevailing in Rome, 'withdrew the foot he had just
placed in the entry to the world; he despised the pursuit
of letters, and abandoned his father's home and property,
and desiring to serve God alone determined to become
a monk'.[2] The motive that drove all the chief founders of
monasticism to forsake the world was the desire of perfection. In the Rule of St. Benedict the same ideal is kept
steadily in view.

In describing the content of the monastic ideal we are
met by an almost insuperable obstacle. Monasticism is
a living force in the Church of the present day, whether in
East or West. It is almost impossible for Protestant
writers to approach the subject without prejudice.[3] In
particular the German writers on whose fruitful historical
researches every student must rely are usually operating
with two or three presuppositions which continually find
expression. One is that asceticism, the flight from the
world, has no support in the genuine Gospel, and that its
presence in the Church is due to a non-Christian dualism
which conceives of matter as essentially evil. A second is
that the good life according to monasticism is essentially
a negation of the world and of human nature; it says 'No'
to life. And a third is that the Roman Catholic Church
maintains that the life of perfection is monasticism; that
in Harnack's words, 'the true and perfect Christian is the
monk'.[4]

Modern Roman Catholic writers deny these presuppositions, or seek to modify them.[5] At first sight it would
seem reasonable to allow Roman Catholic writers to expound what the Roman Catholic Church teaches! But

---

[1] *Ep.* 223. 3.   [2] Greg. Magn. *Dialog.* ii. Prol.
[3] The studies of Hannay, W. K. Lowther Clarke, and H. B. Workman
have achieved the miracle.   [4] *Monasticism*, 10.
[5] See for instance Karl Adam, *Das Wesen des Katholizismus* (1924),
and four subsequent edns. E. tr. *The Spirit of Catholicism* (1929), 203–7.
Garrigou-Lagrange, *Perfection chrétienne et Contemplation* (Saint Maximin,
Var, 1923), 18, 19. Delehaye, *Sanctus* (1927), 246–59 (the sanctity possible in this world is also found outside the R.C. Church). C. Baur,
Johannes Chrysostomus u. seine Zeit (1929), 88–91.

what did the spiritual leaders of monasticism think and
feel then? Antony, Athanasius (who though no monk was
the first church leader to perceive the greatness of the
monk), Pachomius, the Fathers of the Desert, Basil,
Cassian, Chrysostom, Benedict—these must recount their
own ideal. The very mention of these names leads us to
another of our 'warning notices' to Protestants. Not only
must monasticism, like Christianity, be judged by its ideal
rather than by its realization, but the ideal must not be
limited to its exposition in any one life, however saintly,
or by any one mind, however opulent and full. Antony
cannot give us the whole truth of the monastic doctrine of
perfection, nor yet Benedict. And certainly we ought not
to judge the movement by the rhetorical extravagances of
a Jerome. It may be that we shall find Jerome countered
by Benedict.[1] Hence the method adopted here is to select
the chief characteristics of the ideal as it is shown in the
monastic movement from the third century to the sixth.

I. COMMUNION WITH GOD

The sombre genius of Rembrandt once achieved a picture[2] which may serve as a parable of monastic piety. In
the dim light of the Easter morning we barely see the
trees, the flowers, the rich brown earth, the stone rolled
away, the open gateway of the tomb. But we do see two
figures, luminously self-evident; the Christ standing,
tender and yet commanding; and the beseeching adoring
form of Mary Magdalene. All else is in the dark shadow;
on these two shines the light. So for the monk there were
two realities, God and the soul, the soul and God. Attempts have been made to qualify the individualism of the
monastic ideal. But neither the coenobitism of the Pacomian
monasteries, nor the family feeling[3] inculcated by the Rule
of St. Benedict, can hide the truth of truths, the reality on
which all monachism rests, that religion is the communion

---

[1] Jerome certainly would have been critically handled by Palladius.
See *H.L.* 36. 6; 41. 1.

[2] In the gallery at Kassel.

[3] See Butler, *Benedictine Monachism*, 212, 238.

of the solitary soul with God.[1] *On mourra seul*, says Pascal. 'Life too is a lonely business', said the monk. 'It is best to take the swift way, to attend at once to the transaction that must take place between God and the soul.'

This individualism, this forgetfulness of the social element in the primitive Christian ideal of the Kingdom of God, is already apparent, as we have seen, in the system of Origen. We find the same spiritualizing of the early eschatology in the life of Antony. The pivot of his address to his disciples, as reported by Athanasius, is the word 'The kingdom of God is within you'.

The classical description of the spiritual life in John Cassian begins by defining the goal as the kingdom of heaven. The means to the goal is purity of heart.[2] In the way to perfection, one sovereign virtue is needed—discretion.[3] The monastic life is a life of renunciation,[4] and there are three degrees in it. There will be severe combat; the flesh will war against the spirit; the vices live within us and against them we must wage war to the death.[5] Some trials come from God, some from the demons.[6] But the summit of perfection is prayer, prayer without ceasing.[7]

The distinctive contribution of Cassian to our subject is to be found in his doctrine of prayer. There is a shrewdness and sagacity in the probing of motive, a wealth of observation, a knowledge of the pitfalls which beset the seeker after the highest life, and above all a personal experience of the heights and depth of grace such as we shall look for in vain in most of the other writings of the early Church. *Experientia magistra, experientia magistrante*—the phrases recur frequently in his writings, and in his experience of God he had verified the great message he has to tell.

The Kingdom of Heaven, or eternal bliss, is nothing

---

[1] See Cassian, *Coll.* ix, the source from which St. Benedict drew his teaching on prayer. Butler, *Benedictine Monachism*, 63. It is clear that Cassian always regarded the life of the anchorites as in itself more perfect than the coenobitic life. See the last seven Conferences, *passim*; especially xviii. 4, 6. St. Thomas Aquinas agrees with this, II. ii^{ae}, q. 188, a.8.

[2] *Coll.* i. 4.   [3] *Coll.* ii.   [4] *Coll.* iii.

[5] *Coll.* iv, v.   [6] *Coll.* vi, vii, viii.   [7] *Coll.* ix, x.

else than unceasing prayer. Other descriptions of the goal
are 'continual recollection of God',[1] ever to offer to God
a perfect and clean heart and to keep it free from all
disturbances.[2] Our perfect life will be the fulfilment of the
High Priestly prayer of our Lord, *that the love wherewith
thou lovedst Me may be in them, and they in us.*[3]

This will come to pass when God shall be all our love, and every
desire and wish and effort, and every thought of ours, and all our
life and words and breath . . . so that we may be joined to Him
with a lasting and inseparable affection. . . . This then ought to be
the destination of the solitary, this should be all his aim that it may
be vouchsafed to him to possess even in the body an image of future
bliss, and that he may begin in this world to have a foretaste of
a sort of earnest of that celestial life and glory.[4]

This means that the mind will forget created things.
To cling to God continually is impossible for a man while
he is still in this weak flesh of ours.[5] Germanus asks: 'who
can be so intent on this contemplation as never to think
about the arrival of a brother, or visiting the sick, or
manual labour, or at least about showing kindness to
strangers and visitors?'[6] The answer is that these things
belong to the *vita actualis, actualis conversatio.*[7] The *vita
actualis* in Cassian by no means can be translated *active
life*. It is the life of the coenobium, the life given to good
works in order to extirpate the vices in one's own soul and
to acquire the heavenly virtues. Only by practice of the
vita actualis is the soul fitted for the mysteries of contemplation in the anchorite's life. But every monk, whether
in the desert or in the coenobium, must aim at it.[8]

What then does this contemplation imply for Cassian?
It is the look of the soul towards God. The look is simple,
but it produces unbounded admiration and wondering
awe.[9] It is to give heed to the things of God as Mary did
at the feet of Christ.[10] Lest it be thought that the creation

---

[1] x. 10.   [2] i. 6.   [3] x. 10.
[4] x. 10. Gibson's translation *N.P.N.* 404.
[5] i. 13; xxiii. 5.   [6] i. 12.
[7] i. 13; xviii. 4. *Praef. ad. Coll.* i.   [8] ix. 2.
[9] i. 15; xxiii. 5.   [10] i. 8; xxiii. 3.

be considered evil or a mere illusion as in the oriental
dualistic systems, it should be said that the object of contemplation is God, not merely God in His incomprehensible essence, but God in His relation to created things.
We may see Him through the greatness of the world which
He made. We may contemplate with pure minds His
dealings with His saints in every generation. With
trembling heart we may admire His power and the vast-
ness of His knowledge, for he counts the sands and the
drops of rain; His patience in enduring countless sins;
His Incarnation for the saving of men.[1] Contemplation
must always include in this life the reading and understanding of the Holy Scripture. To this end we must
begin by the contemplation of a few saints, and soon by
God's help we shall get beyond the actions and services of
saints, and feed on the knowledge and beauty of God alone.[2]

Why does Cassian give the primacy to contemplation?
First because it *abides*. Secondly, because in itself it is
better to look on God in Himself rather than on good
works (even of the saints) which have God for their motive
and object. To do a kindness to the poor man is doubtless
to do a kindness to God. But the immediate object of the
deed is the poor man, and not God. In contemplation the
immediate object of our regard is God Himself. But the
goal cannot be gained without love.

In justice to the principle with which we are working,
it must here be pointed out that St. Basil's views as to the
respective merits of the two lives are in almost complete
disagreement with those of Cassian. St. Basil recounts
various practical advantages in the common life which the
solitary cannot enjoy, and then he digs deeper down into
the comparison and comes upon a principle.

The fashion of the love of Christ does not allow us to look each
at his own good. For 'love' we read 'seeketh not its own'. Now the
solitary life has one aim, the service of the needs of the individual.
But this is plainly in conflict with the law of love, which the
apostle fulfilled when he sought not his own advantage, but that
of the many, that they might be saved.

[1] *Coll.* i. 15.　　　　　[2] i. 8.

A second reason Basil finds is the comparative fruitlessness of the solitary life: 'Who would choose the idle and fruitless life, in preference to the fruitful life which is lived in accordance with the commandment of the Lord?' A third reason is found in the possession of spiritual gifts—it is the Pauline conception (1 Cor. xii. 8–10). The individual cannot have all gifts, but the community has them, and the private charisma of one is thus available for all.[1]

It is clearly impossible to reconcile the view of Basil with that of Cassian. Bousset has shown that the division of opinion in early monasticism as to the two ideals went deep. The *Apophthegmata Patrum* are always on the side of the anchorites, and contain many stories, some not without a pretty humour, which dismiss the coenobites as definitely a lower order.[2] The view of Cassian would seem to be an attempt to mediate between the opposing views, and through St. Thomas Aquinas the conception of the solitary ideal as ultimately superior has gained currency in Roman Catholicism.[3] But Chrysostom and Jerome followed the lead of Basil.[4]

Another mark of the doctrine of communion with God as enunciated by Cassian is that the highest kind of prayer involves a deadness to all created things.[5] In this (third) type of renunciation the soul 'no longer feels that it is prisoned in this fragile flesh and bodily form, but is caught up into such an ecstasy as not only to hear no words with the outward ear, or to busy itself with gazing in the forms of things present, but not even to see things close at hand,

---

[1] *Regulae fusius tractatae*, 7. Clarke's translation, 163–5. Compare the recommendation in *Ep.* 295 of the common life because it was the life of the apostles.

[2] Bousset, *Das Mönchtum der sketischen Wüste*; *Zeitschrift für Kirchengeschichte*, xlii (N.F. 5), 1923. See esp. p. 15.

[3] Even the Benedictine, Father Delatte, can speak of 'the anachoretical life as too perfect' to suit most souls. See his *Commentary on the Rule of St. Benedict* (E. tr., 1921), 29.

[4] Chrysostom, *In Matt. Hom.* 72; *P.G.* 58. 671–2; Jerome, *Ep.* 125. 9; *P.L.* 22. 1077.

[5] *Coll.* iii. 10. See the excellent exposition of this point by Dom A. Ménager, 'La Doctrine de Cassien', in *La Vie Spirituelle* (Saint Maximin, Var), viii. 2 (May 1923).

or large objects straight before the very eyes'.[1] The genuineness of this to the mind of Cassian is vouched for by the welcome sign-post—*magistra experientia*. The experience he calls *spiritus excessus*,[2] *mentis excessus*,[3] *excessus*.[4] But this experience can only come to the renunciants who are *vere mortui*,[5] who have laid aside all earthly care, all anger, all covetousness. At its best the idea contains one of the profoundest truths of the spiritual life —that 'the life of a Christian must be a permanent and increasingly perfect prayer, if genuine and worthy acts of prayer are to be offered. Prayers are not real, they do not rise to God, if they are but incidental and occasional acts of a life which is not itself a constant and uninterrupted effort towards harmony with the divine will'.[6] In the ninth conference Abbot Isaac puts the truth in a fine and original way:

The nature of the soul is not inaptly compared to a very fine feather or very light wing, which if it has not been damaged or affected by any moisture falling on it from without or entering into it is borne aloft almost naturally to the heights of heaven by the lightness of its nature and the aid of the slightest breath; but if it is weighted by any moisture falling on it and penetrating it, it will not only not be carried upwards by its own natural lightness, but will actually be borne down to the depths of the earth by the weight of the moisture it has received. So also our soul, if it is not weighted with faults that touch it, and the cares of this world, or damaged by the moisture of injurious lusts, will be raised, as it were, by the natural blessing of its own purity, and borne aloft to the heights by the light breath of spiritual meditation; and leaving things low and earthly will be transported to those that are heavenly and invisible.

Rarely has the truth been better stated that the outward life should be of such a quality that it naturally and spontaneously issues in prayer.

> O that all my life might be
> One looking up to Thee!

---

[1] *Coll.* iii. 7. Cf. the striking instances in Bousset, *Apophthegmata*, 85–6.
[2] iv. 5.   [3] vi. 10 (Petschenig i. 163, line 19).
[4] xix. 4 (Petschenig i. 537, line 17).   [5] *Praef. ad Coll.* i.
[6] A. L. Lilley, *Prayer in Christian Theology*, 38.

But at the same time we must recognize that something
visionary and abnormal is clinging to the ideal of Cassian.
St. Paul, like St. Teresa, reckoned ecstasy to be an extraordinary accompaniment and not an essential part of the
ideal Christian life. In Cassian's doctrine it becomes the
norm. The life of Pachomius gives us many stories of
his visions. Instances abound in the *Apophthegmata*, of
visions granted to the anchorites, and it is possible that this
ecstatic visionary element in the ideal is another vestige
of the claim of the original founders, who were laymen,
non-clerical 'enthusiasts', to extraordinary spiritual endow-
ments.[1] In any case, the teaching of abstraction from
ordinary interests, from any preoccupation with the things
of sense, must be pronounced a grave defect in any
doctrine of perfection.[2]

A third fact to be noticed in Cassian's doctrine of communion with God is that the reward of the monk's seeking
comes at the end of a long process. There are few indications of a divine forgiveness, an introduction to a new
personal relationship with God, a communion offered and
inaugurated at once, as the monk begins his stormy
voyage and goes sounding on his dim and perilous way.
The nearest approach to the Pauline teaching is found in
the third Conference. Faith itself, says the Abbot Paph-
nutius, must be given us by the Lord.[3] It is He who draws
us towards the way of salvation. It is His inspiration that
gives us the beginning of our goodwill.[4] The understanding by means of which we can recognize God's commands
and the performance of a good intention are both gifts
of God.[5] In itself this teaching is an offer, an announcement of God's presence and the possibility of life-long
communion with Him. But virtually the offer is limited
because it is so inextricably interwoven with the call to
the monastic life. When Cassian speaks of the 'way of

---

[1] See Bousset, *Apophthegmata*, 236–44.
[2] Cf. the wise letter of von Hügel published in *George Tyrrell's Letters*
(1920), 40–4. See below for a modification of this doctrine in the teaching
of St. Basil.
[3] iii. 16.   [4] iii. 19.   [5] iii. 15.

salvation' he means the 'monastic' life. To say that God is present when any one feels the call to that life is not the same thing as the New Testament offer of entrance into a new world where God is the centre, where sins fall away at His touch, wherein knowledge of Him and freedom from torturing remorse are immediate gifts from His hands. Compare with the New Testament this advice of Basil to his disciple Chilo, in a letter[1] where the saint unveils his heart.

It is better to advance a little at a time. Withdraw then by degrees from the pleasures of life, gradually destroying all your wonted habits, lest you bring on yourself a crowd of temptations by irritating all your passions at once.

Amid all the practical wisdom of this letter there is only one promise, like a phrase of solemn music always sounding: 'Leave the world, embrace the monastic life; there in the wilderness you will find Christ.'

II. THE CROSS

Another supreme mark of the monastic ideal is the Cross. *Except I see in His hands the print of the nails . . . I will not believe.* Thomas would have been left without excuse if he had been set down in the deserts of Egypt in the fourth century. Cassian's favourite name for monk is Renunciant.[2] But it is vital for the understanding of the monastic ideal to recognize that sufferings and austerities are not embraced for their own sake. They are means to an end.

This principle is abundantly illustrated by the *Vita Antonii.* The end was perfection. The *ascesis* to which he gave himself[3] with patient training was to cleanse himself from restless thoughts. After a discipline lasting twenty years, his soul was free from blemish, for it was neither contracted as if by grief, nor relaxed by pleasure, nor possessed by laughter or dejection, for he was not troubled

---

[1] No. 42. *N.P.N.* 143–6.
[2] Cf. Butler, *Benedictine Monachism,* 36–45; cf. Workman, *Evolution of Monastic Ideal,* 5.   [3] *Vit. Ant.* 3.

when he saw the crowd, nor overjoyed at being saluted by so many. This positive element in the *ascesis*, the control of the thoughts, is continually apparent in the later literature. The Conferences of Cassian abound in shrewd psychological observations which are the fruit of long years of mental asceticism.[1] Karl Holl comments on the modernity of Antony's advice to his followers to write down their thoughts. 'We must recognize that here a higher stage of the whole spiritual life has been reached.'[2]

The discipline was regarded as necessary not only to the full moral cleansing of the personality but also to the attainment of spiritual power. A steady advance in strength is discernible in the *Vita Antonii*.[3] He comes out from his retreat 'as from a shrine, as initiated in the mysteries'. To the mind of the author miraculous stories told of Antony are no mere marvels to adorn or heighten the impression of the uniqueness of his personality. They are direct proofs of spiritual maturity. Power over evil spirits[4] is granted to the spiritual athlete. He can see farther than the demons.[5] For such reasons as these asceticism is practised. St. Basil's attitude to renunciation is precisely the same as that of Antony, and is continually traced back to the New Testament. In the *Regulae* (after quoting Matt. xvi. 24, Luke xiv. 33, and 26) he says[6]:

Accordingly perfect renunciation consists in a man's attaining complete impassivity as regards actual living, and having 'the sentence of death', so as to put no confidence in himself. Whereas its beginnings consist of alienation from external things, such as possessions, vainglory, the common customs of life, or attachment to useless things. . . . So he who is seized by the vehement desire of following Christ can no longer care for anything to do with this life.

[1] See ix. 7 ff.; vii. 3 ff.
[2] *Ges. Aufsätze*, ii. 277. See also *Enthusiasmus und Bussgewalt*, 141–55.
[3] *Vit. Ant.* 14. Cf. the vision in c. 10.
[4] *Vit. Ant.* 38.   [5] *Vit. Ant.* 34.
[6] *Reg. fus. tract.* 8. 348 E, 349 A. ἡ μὲν τελεία ἀποταγή ἐστιν ἐν τῷ ἀπροσπαθὲς κατορθῶσαι κτλ. Compare *Sermo Ascet.* ii, which, though probably not the work of Basil, is good evidence for the monastic ideal of the time.

But even this quotation, for all its express mention of Christ, does not fairly represent the mind of Basil as to the true goal of asceticism. The chapter with its frequent illustrations from the Gospels makes it clear that the goal was Christ. Basil quotes, as one who understands, that word of Paul: *For whom I suffered the loss of all things and do count them to be dung, that I may gain Christ.* 'Greatest of all', says Basil, 'renunciation is the beginning of our being made like unto Christ'. The goal is 'love towards God, which both stirs us up to work the Lord's commandments and is in its turn preserved by them in permanence and security'.[1]

It is in the light of such an ideal that we must judge the austerities of the pillar-saints, or the competitions in self-torment which disfigure the records of the anchorites in the desert. Even in the naïve pages of Palladius we can see how the founders of monasticism regarded these austerities. Macarius of Alexandria, one of the 'record-breakers',[2] came to the monastery of Pachomius, and by deliberately outdoing all the monks in the coenobium caused a mutiny. For the forty days of Lent he only ate a few cabbage leaves.

All the ascetics, therefore, seeing this raised a revolt against the superior, saying: 'Where did you get this fleshless man from, to condemn us. Either drive him out, or know that we are all going.' Pachomius, therefore, having heard the details of his observance, prayed to God that the identity of the stranger might be revealed to him. And it was revealed; and he took him by the hand and led him to the house of prayer, where the altar was, and said to him: 'Here, good old man, you are Macarius and you hid it from me. For many years I have been longing to see you. I thank you for letting my children feel your fist, lest they should be proud of their ascetic achievements. Now go away to your own place, for you have edified us sufficiently. And pray for us.' Then he went away, as asked.[3]

The real hero of this story, as Henri Bremond observes, is not Macarius, but Pachomius. 'You have edified us

---

[1] *Reg. fus. tract.* 8. 350 D; 5. 342 C.
[2] See Butler, *Historia Lausiaca*, i. 237.
[3] Palladius, *H.L.* 18 (E. tr. W. K. L. Clarke).

sufficiently.' It is delightful. Pachomius evidently felt that the 'record-breaker' was a nuisance, but that he had had his uses. What was wrong in his own sons was not their failure to equal Macarius, but the jealousy and anger into which the austerities of their guest had plunged them. Macarius, though he wins no word of praise from Pachomius, is treated with such courtesy that he departs happy, and does not see that they are glad to be rid of him. For it was doubtless from his own lips that Palladius heard the story. The 'record-breakers' were not ashamed to expatiate on their own feats.[1]

Others of the leaders condemned such competition. 'It should be noted carefully that the monastic rules not only never prescribe such feats of strength but even condemn them.'[2] An excess of asceticism is fatal to any monastic rule.[3] This fault accounts for the failure of Schenoudi. St. Benedict deliberately discarded corporal austerities.[4] The types of asceticism which he recognized and regulated were: (1) the purely internal self-discipline and spiritual exercising carried out in mind and heart and soul, without becoming in any way external; (2) the great renunciations—Poverty, Obedience, and Chastity—which have at all times been recognized as the principal external asceticisms. It will be clear that at its best and truest monastic asceticism was but a means to an end. But the spiritual genius of a Basil could see in any sacrifice endured for the sake of likeness to Christ something more than a preliminary exercise for the attainment of perfection. The monk must show obedience (to his superior) unto death, remembering the Lord who 'became obedient unto death, even the death of the Cross'.[5] Cassian tells us

---

[1] See Butler, *H.L.* i. 237.

[2] F. Cabrol in *E.R.E.* viii. 783; see Leclercq in *Dict. Archéologie Chrétienne et de Liturgie*, ii². 3143 f.

[3] See Ladeuze, *Étude sur le cénobitisme pakhomien*, 216–17.

[4] Butler, *Benedictine Monachism*, 39–45; esp. p. 39, from which the above analysis is taken.

[5] *Reg. fus. tract.* 28; *Reg. brev. tract.* 116. Compare *Hom.* 20. 5, 6 (*P.G.* 31, cols. 533–7) on the value of meditation in the human life of Christ. Cf. Rivière, *Saint Basile*, 186, 187.

that monks are 'crucified daily to this world and made living martyrs'.[1]

But the best proof of the desire to enter into communion with Christ Crucified is the passion that breathes through the closing sections of the *Moralia*.[2] There is a spiritual insight and fervour shown even in the last selection of passages, describing what manner of men Scripture wishes men to be. And then come the quick impetuous sentences that speak the soul of a man.

What is the mark of a Christian? To be cleansed from all pollution of flesh and spirit, in the blood of Christ. . . .

What is the mark of those who eat the bread and drink the cup of the Lord? To keep in perpetual memory Him Who died for us, and rose again.

What is the mark of those that keep such a memory? To live unto themselves no longer, but unto Him Who died for them and rose again.

What is the mark of a Christian? That his righteousness should abound in everything, more than that of the Scribes and Pharisees, according to the measure of the teaching of the Lord in the Gospel.

What is the mark of a Christian? To love one another, even as Christ also loved us.

What is the mark of a Christian? To see the Lord always before him.

What is the mark of a Christian? To watch each night and day and in the perfection of pleasing God to be ready, knowing that the Lord cometh at an hour he thinketh not.

There is no doubt that Basil believed that the commandments of love could be kept and the heart could be in this life purified from all sin.[3]

In another writer this judgement might seem shallow. Coming from Basil, who had the tenderest of consciences and raised the devotional standard considerably, it is very remarkable. In this respect his spiritual outlook is Perfectionist. He believes intensely in sanctification. In and by the Spirit, the Christian living under the favourable conditions of a monastery, can avoid sin.[4]

[1] *Coll.* 18. 7.　　　　　　　[2] *Morals* lxx. 22; 318 B, C.
[3] *Reg. brev. tract.* 280, 296.
[4] W. K. Lowther Clarke, *The Ascetic Works of St. Basil*, 45; Karl Holl, *Enthusiasmus und Bussgewalt*, 165: 'Denn auch Basileios ist—er

III. COMPREHENSIVENESS

Can we assert comprehensiveness of an ideal which avowedly can only appeal to a minority of mankind? Not even a St. Jerome would assert that all men were called to the monastic life. But the mind cannot but be impressed with a certain comprehensiveness of outlook in the monastic schemes of St. Basil and St. Benedict.

The most striking characteristic of Basil's scheme is its comprehensiveness. . . . He investigates the doctrinal basis of the monastic ideal, and finds it to be scriptural both in origin and intention. He fixes the centre of the monastic life in the religious instinct, in the love of man for God and the desire of union with Him. The method for the attainment of such union is the ascetic way of renunciation and self-denial, involving also discipline and obedience, work and prayer. The best environment for the purpose is that of the community. The scope of the monastic life includes all classes, both sexes, and, in some degree, all ages. Its great obligations are not to be undertaken without a most sure conviction of vocation, while its principles extend to every department of life and conduct, even to small details of food and clothing. Finally, the monastic ideal is social in implication, and involves the exercise of both hospitality and charity.[1]

There is a widening of the area of life hallowed by the monastic ideal when we come to the Rule and the influence of St. Benedict. His ideal for each of his monasteries was that of a family. His order was perfectly adapted to be the handmaid of learning even if he himself did not dream of the use to which the child of his brain would be set. It was the Benedictines who became the missionaries of Europe.[2] His Rule wrought a revolution in men's conception of the place of toil. It was the Egyptian monks who had led the way. In the Roman world manual labour was the task of slaves. But Palladius tells us that the monasteries of Pachomius were organized on the basis

stimmt darin nicht bloss mit Symeon, sondern mit seiner ganzen Kirche überein—der Meinung, dass die Gebote erfüllt werden können'.

[1] E. F. Morison, *St. Basil and his Rule*, 131–2.

[2] See Workman's *Evolution of Monastic Ideal*, 172–8, for a convenient summary.

of trades.[1] 'They work at every kind of craft'—agriculture, gardening, carpentry, iron-work, dyeing, tanning, boot-making, weaving, baking, and the rest.[2] But for the most part the Egyptian monks had not encouraged the idea of manual labour.[3] 'Benedict accomplished that most difficult of all tasks, a revolution in the moral life of man.'[4] 'Idleness', he said, 'is the enemy of the soul. Therefore should the brethren be occupied at stated times in manual labour, and at other fixed times in sacred reading.'[5] These bare sentences are an epitome and a programme of the revolution which he wrought.

The monk was not blind to the beauty of the world. The reproach has been made against monasticism that the world grew grey with its breath, and that the feeling for the wonder of creation perished. Harnack has pointed out that, on the contrary, some monks discovered in solitude what they had never seen—Nature. 'Into her they gradually grow; her beauty they search out and extol; from hermits of the fourth century we have pictures of nature such as antiquity seldom produced.'[6] When Antony was asked whether he did not miss the comfort of his books, he made reply: 'My book is the nature of things that are made, and it is present whenever I wish to read the words of God.'[7] Basil's love for nature was passionate. The famous fourteenth Epistle is proof enough. In his *De judicio* he draws an analogy from the bees, and the *Hexaemeron*, which consists of sermons apparently delivered to working men, is full of interest in the things that are seen.

But there is a limit to the comprehensiveness of the monastic ideal. In its suspicion of the temptations of sex, monasticism slighted human love. The married man, says Basil, will as a concession be granted pardon for his love

[1] *H.L.* 32. 7.
[2] Butler, *H.L.* 1, 235–6.
[3] See Cassian, *Coll.* xxiv. 3, 4.
[4] Workman, op. cit., 154–6.
[5] *Reg. Ben.* 48. See commentary of Delatte, 312–13.
[6] *Monasticism* (E. tr. 1913), 50.
[7] Socrates, *H.E.* iv. 23. See Sozomen, *H.E.* i. 12.

for his wife.[1] It is true that elsewhere Basil can speak with
another voice:

Husbands love your wives. . . . May this natural link, this yoke
imposed by the blessing, reunite those who are divided. However
hard or fierce a husband may be, the wife ought to bear with him,
and not wish to find any pretext for breaking the union. He strikes
you but he is your husband. He is a drunkard, but he is united to
you by nature. He is brutal and cross, but he is henceforth one of
your members, and the most precious of all.

What Basil means by 'nature' we can discover from his
more theological treatises. Holiness is not the driving out
of nature but its completion;[2] and the perfect goal of mankind is the perfect development of his natural powers.[3]

If the foregoing quotation be taken as proof that our
aim is not to overstate the case here against the monastic
disparagement of marriage, we may go on to state the
supreme difficulty here of any acceptance of the monastic
ideal as it is expounded in those early days. St. Martin
says that marriage belongs to those things which are
excused (*ad veniam*) but virginity points to glory.[4] One
virgin who always avoided men, refused to see even
Martin himself, and Martin praises her for her refusal.[5]
Martin only allowed a woman to touch him once; and then
it was a queen who flung herself at his feet and insisted on
waiting on him.[6] Cassian tells us approvingly of the action
of a monk who, after fifteen years of discipline, had received a huge packet of letters from his father and mother
and many friends in Pontus.

He turned over the matter in his mind for some time. 'What
thoughts will the reading of these suggest to me, which will incite
me either to senseless joy or useless sadness! For how many days
will they draw off the attention of my heart from the contemplation
I have set before me!' . . . So he threw it [unopened] into the fire

---

[1] *Sermo de Renuntiatione Saeculi*, 230 c (*The Ascetic Works of St. Basil*,
61). Cp. Rivière, *Saint Basile*, 208 ff.

[2] *De sp. sancto*, xix. 48.

[3] Scholl, *Die Lehre des heiligen Basilius von der Gnade* (Freiburg,
1881), 16.   [4] *Sulp. Sev. Dial.* ii. 10 (6).

[5] Ibid. ii. 12.   [6] Ibid. ii. 6, 7.

to be burnt, all tied up just as he had received it, crying, 'Away, O ye thoughts of my home, be ye burnt up and try no further to recall me to those things from which I have fled.'[1]

Even in the Rules of Basil the brethren are forbidden to receive relations whose lives are worldly and 'who set at nought the work of godliness'.[2] If relatives do visit the monastery, they must be received as no longer any nearer to us than any one is who does the will of God.[3] The brethren must not cherish any greater attachment for them than for any one else.[4]

It is clear that we have to do with the Stoic ideal of ἀπάθεια. St. Basil who always appeals to the Scriptures is more influenced by the Stoics than he knows.[5] But the monastic attitude to human affection merges into another and even larger question. What is the monastic attitude to all other Christians who are living in the world? The difficulty is acute. If monasticism is the full Christian ideal, if its appeal to the Gospel counsels of perfection is legitimate, then surely it is only the monks who can be called Christians in the genuine sense of the word. Karl Holl observes[6] that the fact that the *Vita Antonii* does not see any problem at all only proves that Christendom by this time was quite accustomed to the non-fulfilment of Christian duty, and that the Greek Church has never really escaped from the contradiction which underlies this question.

There is only one way out. If monasticism be regarded as a legitimate vocation for a few, and if the few regard their vocation as no mere self-fulfilment, but divinely ordered for the salvation of the many, then the appeal to the Gospels could be allowed. The Old Testament doctrine of the Remnant would be the monastic answer to the reproach of spiritual selfishness. There are a few indications

---

[1] Cassian, *Inst.* v. 32. I owe this reference and two previous examples to Dr. Workman's book, 59–60.

[2] *Reg. fus. tract.* 32.

[3] *Reg. brev. tract.* 188. Matt. xii. 47 is quoted as justifying this attitude.

[4] *Reg. brev. tract.* 190.   [5] *Ep.* 4.

[6] *Enthusiasmus und Bussgewalt,* 147.

that this was seen. Thus Macarius of Alexandria was once asked by Palladius: 'Father, what shall I do? Since my thoughts afflict me saying, "You are making no progress, go away from here." ' And he said to me: 'Tell them "For Christ's sake I am guarding the walls." '[1] The *Historia Monachorum* explains that 'there is no village or city in Egypt and the Thebaid which is not surrounded by monasteries as if by walls, and the inhabitants are supported by their prayers as if resting on God.'

Had this ideal mission of the monks as a remnant to aid in the task of purifying the church and evangelizing the world been clearly seen, we should have expected a Church leader like Basil to have drawn the monastery and the Church close together in indissoluble bonds. But he did not do this. The monastic community is not thought of as dependent on the life of the Church. It forms a self-sufficing whole. It needs no nourishment from without. It possesses within itself all needful spiritual gifts. The rules are so drawn up as to protect the purity of the community from defilement from without.[2] He despairs of the spiritual assemblies of the great Church.[3] On the other hand, he does not consider it part of the duty of his monks to influence the Church.[4] The brotherly love which he recommends is love for the other monks, not love for them that are without.[5]

The future of monasticism depended on finding the way of escape from this contradiction of the ideal of Christian love. The problem was not insoluble. Even in the New Testament, the Johannine Epistles betray a similar limitation of outlook. It would not be fair to condemn the early monastic ideal on this ground. Already there are indications in the days of eremitic monachism that a wider view was possible. Athanasius tells us of the activity of Antony in the cure of souls. 'It was as if a physician had been

[1] *H.L.* 18.
[2] *Reg. fus. tract.* 32.   [3] *Ep.* 42.
[4] Compare the modern Benedictine attitude as set forth persuasively by Abbot Delatte, *Commentary on the Rule of St. Benedict*, 340–2.
[5] Cf. Holl, *Enthusiasmus und Bussgewalt*, 169.

given by God to Egypt.'[1] And a naïve, unstudied story
from the pages of Palladius proves that men could see even
in those days of retreat and solitude that God could be
found in service. Two rich brothers became monks. The
one gave away everything at once, learned a trade by
which to earn his bread, and applied himself to asceticism
and prayer. The other gave nothing away immediately,
but spent his money in works of charity.

He made himself a monastery, and getting together a few brethren
welcomed every stranger, every invalid, every poor man. . . .

When the two were dead various eulogies were pronounced over
them, as if both had reached perfection. . . . But a contention
having arisen in the brotherhood over their praises, they went to the
blessed Pambo and referred the decision to him, imploring that they
might learn which was the better method. But he said to them:
'Both are perfect; for one shewed the works of an Abraham, the
other those of an Elijah'. And one party said: 'By your feet we
ask, how can they possibly be equal?' and preferred the ascetic,
and said, 'He performed an evangelical work, selling all and giving
to the poor, and every hour both by day and night bearing the cross,
and following the Saviour and his prayers.' But the other side
contended with them, and said: 'Our man showed such great mercy
to the needy that he even sat on the roads and collected the afflicted.
And not only did he refresh his own soul but the souls of many
others, treating their diseases and helping them.' Then blessed
Pambo said to them: 'Once again I tell you they are both equal. . . .
But wait until I receive a revelation from God, and after that come
and you shall learn.' So they came a few days after and he said to
them: 'I saw both standing in Paradise as it were in the presence
of God.'[2]

[1] *Vit. Ant.* 87.   [2] *H.L.* 14. 4.

CHAPTER VIII

THE HOMILIES OF MACARIUS
THE EGYPTIAN

I read Macarius and sang.

*Diary of John Wesley, during
a stormy voyage.*

IN 1921 Dr. A. J. Mason published an English translation of the *Fifty Spiritual Homilies of St. Macarius the
Egyptian*.[1] It is surprising that this masterpiece of the
devotional life should be so little known. But the work
has had its own influence in the history of spirituality.
William Law admired it greatly, and warmly commended
the book to his friend Byrom in 1737.[2] John Wesley published extracts from the work in the first volume of the
'Christian Library', a series designed to nourish the souls
of his followers on the finest products of the saints.
Macarius has never been without his readers in the
Roman Church. His writings have always been especially
treasured at Mount Athos; and his influence may have
radiated thence, especially in the fourteenth century.[3] He

---

[1] *P.G.* 34.

[2] Overton, *William Law*, 76. An English translation was published by
Thomas Haywood in 1721 under the title of *Primitive Morality*. See also
A. Knox, *Remains* (1834), i. 318–20.

[3] Cf. Stoffels, *Die Mystische Theologie Makarius des Aegypters und die
ältesten Ansätze christlicher Mystik* (Bonn, 1908), 173. See also the article
in *Dictionnaire de Théol. Catholique*; 'Macarii Anecdota' (1918) in *Harvard Theological Studies* (1907). Articles in *J.T.S.* viii. 85–90 (Gore);
January, 1920; April, 1921; July 1922 (Marriott); and Pourrat, *Histoire
de la Spiritualité chrétienne*, i. 172–5.

No notice has been taken of the recent theory (accepted by Marriott,
J.T.S., April 1921, and Menager, *La Vie Spirituelle*, December 1923)
that these Homilies are a manual of the Euchites. The provenance of the
book is irrelevant to our present purpose. Its doctrine of the goal of the
Christian life can be accepted as representative of monasticism.

I do not think the thesis of Stoffels is proved, that the essential characteristics of the thought of Macarius are due to Stoic influence. That the
ideal of ἀπάθεια had been evolved under that influence we have already
seen, but it is unlikely that the idea of κρᾶσις δι' ὅλων had influenced the

must be numbered with those who have fit audience found, though few.

1. The first pronounced characteristic of the doctrine of Macarius is its individualism. Immense stress is laid on the worth of the solitary human soul. That Christianity brought with it a deepening of the sense of human personality has long been a theme of historians. That monasticism intensified this tendency could be proved by many a quotation from Macarius.

The immortal soul is a precious vessel. See how great the heaven and the earth are, and God was not satisfied with them, but only with thee. Consider thy dignity and thy nobility, that to thy succour the Lord came in person, not by the medium of angels, to recall thee who wert lost, thee who wert wounded, and to restore to thee the primal fashioning of the pure Adam.[1]

The vision of the first chapter of Ezekiel is interpreted of the soul that was to receive her lord, and to become a throne of glory for Him.[2] His principle of exegesis is that everything in the Old Testament has reference to the individual soul, made in the image of God and fallen under the kingdom of darkness.[3] The dignity of the soul is greater than that of the ministering spirits.[4]

Behold then thy dignity, and of how great value thou art, that God hath made thee above angels because for thy help He came upon earth Himself in person. . . . The Immortal chose to be crucified for thee.[5]

The reason for this intense concentration on individual salvation is that God made the human soul in His own image.[6] The life of the soul does not come from its own nature but from the Godhead, from God's own Spirit.[7] Macarius uses the Logos-doctrine to explain the original perfection of man. 'So long as the Word of God was with

mind of Macarius. The examples given (Stoffels, 61–6) are unconvincing. The following discussion will, I hope, prove how thoroughly Christian are the chief ideas of Macarius.

[1] *Hom.* 26. 1.   [2] *Hom.* 1. 2.   [3] *Hom.* 47. 16.   [4] *Hom.* 15. 22.
[5] *Hom.* 15. 43, 44; cf. 11. 5; 26. 1; 30. 7.
[6] *Hom.* 15. 22.   [7] *Hom.* 1. 10.

him and the commandment, everything was his.'[1] He was clothed with the glory of God as with a garment.[2] That glory is now given inwardly to the saints; some day it shall cover and clothe their naked bodies and catch them into heaven.[3] After the Fall the soul was widowed and desolate, but at last returned to her kindred. 'For there is no tie of blood or suitableness like that between the soul and God, and between God and the soul.'[4]

The individualism leads to a disparagement of the ordinary human relationships. After a man has renounced the world his heart should not be tied to the charm of parents.[5] He devotes some space to the brotherly love that should exist in a monastic community, but he is 'not much concerned with what man owes to man'.[6] For him there is hardly any other way of following Christ save that of the monk.[7]

Another and even more startling sign of the solitariness of the Christian ideal is that the piety of Macarius seems to be independent of the cultus of the Church.[8] He is at war with the primitive doctrine that after baptism a Christian does not sin.[9] He insists that the Christian should have the remembrance of God with him when walking, or eating, or talking, as much as in the house of prayer.[10]

2. A second mark is that the true life of the soul is God-given. The characteristic notes of the Christian ideal are sounded here. The expectation of the monk is to be born from on high;[11] he looks for promises higher and greater than the first man had, that 'God should please to give him the presence of the Lord'.[12] It is the Incarnation which is the ground of the confidence of Macarius. His mysticism is a Christ-mysticism.[13] Because God in Christ

---

[1] *Hom.* 12. 6.   [2] *Hom.* 12. 8.
[3] *Hom.* 5. 11; Mason, 54.
[4] *Hom.* 45. 5; cf. 28. 5.   [5] *Hom.* 43. 3.
[6] Mason, xxxix. See *Hom.* 3. 1–3; Stoffels, 141–3.
[7] *Hom.* 11. 6, 7; cf. 38. 1.
[8] Stoffels, 171; Mason, xxii–xxiv.   [9] *Hom.* 15. 14.
[10] *Hom.* 43. 3.   [11] Cf. Stoffels, 122.
[12] *Hom.* 48. 6.   [13] Cf. Stoffels, 87, 121.

has drawn wondrously near, there is no region of the soul's progress where it does not find Christ.

The soul is surnamed the temple and habitation of God, for the Scripture says, *I will dwell in them and walk in them.* So it pleased God; because He came down from holy heavens and embraced thy reasonable nature, the flesh, which is of the earth, and mingled it with His divine Spirit, in order that thou, the earthy, mightest receive the heavenly soul. And when thy soul has communion with the Spirit and the heavenly soul enters into thy soul, then art thou a perfect man in God, and an heir, and a son.[1]

Macarius lays great stress on the freedom of man's will. He is no creature of necessity. He cannot be saved against his will.[2] But he knows the secret of the prevenient grace of God. 'Never think that you have been beforehand with the Lord in your virtue, according to him who says, *It is He that worketh in you both to will and to do of His good pleasure.*[3] The Christian life is one long looking to Christ, who prints his own resemblance in the heart.

As a portrait painter keeps an eye on the king's face and draws, and when the king's face is toward him he draws the portrait easily and well, . . . in like manner Christ, the good artist, for those who believe Him and gaze continually at Him, straightway portrays after His own image a heavenly man. . . . We must therefore gaze upon Him, believing and loving Him, throwing away all else and attending to Him, in order that He may paint His own heavenly image and send it into our souls, and thus wearing Christ, we may receive eternal life, and even here may have full assurance and be at rest.[4]

3. Macarius has his doctrine of progress in the Christian life. This is due in the first place to his strong insistence on moral purification. The truth must needs be persecuted, and those who suffer bear the marks of their Lord.[5] Experience of struggle against sin makes the

---

[1] *Hom.* 32. 6.   [2] *Hom.* 37. 10; 15. 23, 40; 26. 6.

[3] *Hom.* 37. 9.

[4] *Hom.* 30. 4; cf. 16. 7. Compare John Newton:

> As the image in the glass
> Answers the beholder's face,
> Thus unto my heart appear:
> Print Thine own resemblance there.

[5] *Hom.* 15. 12.

warriors firmer and wiser.[1] It is dangerous for any man
to affirm that a particular temptation no longer assails
him.[2] If they are tried they ought to take pleasure in
poverty and dishonour.[3] 'It is only gradually that a man
grows and comes to *a perfect man, to the measure of the
stature,* not, as some say, "Off with one coat and on with
another".'[4] There are some in this life who are like the
pearl divers who go down naked into the deep of the sea
into the watery death, and find there pearls fit for a royal
crown. So some saints who embrace the solitary life go
naked out of the world and into the gulf of darkness, that
from those depths they may bring up precious stones
suitable for the crown of Christ.[5] But such victories, the
great 'measures of perfection', are not won without toil and
suffering,[6] and only by the aid of God.[7] There are many
stages and measures of the Spirit; 'the mischief is strained
out and refined off bit by bit, and not all at once'.[8] The
moral transformation comes at the beginning of the new
life.[9] The ethical virtues are stages in the soul's development. A man must force himself to acquire these, as well
as give himself to prayer. Prayer alone, without a violence
which the man lays on himself to succeed in humility and
charity, will leave the character unchanged.[10] So the perfect
life will consist in a mixture of the moral virtues in order
that no one virtue may become hurtful to the soul. 'A man
must be well tempered together in all directions, kindness
with severity, wisdom with discretion, word with deed, in
everything to trust in the Lord, not in himself. For virtue
is seasoned with many different spices.'[11] After such effort,
the grace of God works the transformation in the man.
The new virtues are given to him, as the fruit of the Spirit,
and they become a second nature in the man.

---

[1] *Hom.* 15. 19.   [2] *Hom.* 15. 21.
[3] *Hom.* 15. 29. According to the story of Palladius, the saint had
practised what he preached.
[4] *Hom.* 15. 41; cf. 42, 43.   [5] *Hom.* 15. 51.
[6] *Hom.* 15. 53; cf. 5. 4; also Mason, pp. 43 and 51.
[7] *Hom.* 2. 3; 3. 4.   [8] *Hom.* 15. 7.
[9] *Hom.* 44. 1; 19. 1, 2.   [10] *Hom.* 19. 4.
[11] *Hom.* 16. 9.

It is difficult by any mere summary to do justice to the moral insight of Macarius. The wisdom of the desert, the 'discretion' which St. Antony praised as the most necessary virtue of the ascetic life, was his in full measure. He knows the deceitfulness of sin. Do not think, he cries, that there is any easy path to sanctity.

Mere abstention from evil is not perfection—only if thou hast entered into thy ruined mind, and hast slain the serpent that lies under the mind beneath the surface of the thoughts, and burrows into what we call the secret chambers and storehouses of the soul and murders thee—for the heart is a deep gulf. . . . Purity of heart can be gained in no other way than through Him who was crucified.[1]

Again, the goal is love, and there can be progress in love. The more souls that love God perceive in themselves a spiritual advance, the more hungry and thirsty they are for the participation and increase of grace. The richer they are spiritually, the more they esteem themselves to be poor. They are insatiable in the longing for the heavenly Bridegroom as the scripture says (Ecclus. xxiv. 21), *They that eat Me shall yet be hungry, and they that drink Me shall yet be thirsty.*[2] Macarius knows that eternal paradox of the religious life. And probably the frequent passages that speak of the perpetual quest of God in this earthly life are to be understood in this sense.[3] It is not as if Macarius promises no attainment in this life. But the soul that has attained is rewarded by a passion for higher attainment. 'If the heart at all times desires God, He is the Lord of that heart.'[4]

Those who are aflame with the heavenly longing for Christ hold all things else contemptible by reason of the fire of the love of Christ, which holds them fast and inflames them and burns them with a Godward disposition. This is the love of which Paul testified, when he said, *Who shall separate us from the love of Christ.*[5]

4. The Measures of Perfection. We have now reached

[1] *Hom.* 17. 15.
[2] *Hom.* 10. 1; cf. 10. 4.
[3] See, e.g. *Hom.* 9. 13.
[4] *Hom.* 43. 3.
[5] *Hom.* 9. 9.

the threshold of that love which for Macarius is the ultimate beatitude. What are the marks of the highest stages
of the Christian life in this world? We have seen that the
highest measure is love. 'If any man reaches the perfect
love, that man is from henceforth fast bound, and is the
captive of grace.'[1] But what manner of love does Macarius
mean? There seems to be no doubt that the primary
mark of it is ecstasy. He often warns the monks against
self-deception in the claim to attainment. Illustrations are
given of those who walked with God and yet afterwards
fell into abominable sin. But one who really 'arrives at
charity is bound and intoxicated; he is drowned, and
carried captive to another world, as if he had no consciousness of his own nature'.[2] The Eighth Homily is devoted
to this subject of 'the perfect measure'. He seems to
promise us a description of the various stages, but he only
gives us the last two. 'There are twelve steps, we might
say, which a man has to pass before he reaches perfection.
For a season that measure has been attained, and perfection
entered upon; and then grace gives in, and he comes
down by one step, and stands upon the eleventh. Here
and there one man rich in grace has stood always, night
and day, in perfect measures, at liberty and in purity,
always captive and aloft.' In the light of the previous
quotation this last phrase can only mean a rapture above
the things of sense. This is confirmed by the subsequent
comment of Macarius. If a man were always to dwell at
that height, he says, he would be unable to undertake the
dispensation of the word. He could not endure to listen
to any ordinary thing.

He could only sit in a corner, aloft and intoxicated. So the perfect
measure has not been given, in order that he may be free to take
an interest in his brethren and in the ministry of the word. Nevertheless the *middle wall of partition* has been *broken* through, and
death is overcome.[3]

So the final stage of attainment is constant ecstasy. As
Karshish says of Lazarus: 'His heart and brain move
there, his feet stay here.'

[1] *Hom.* 26. 16; cf. 27. 14.　　[2] *Hom.* 27. 16.　　[3] *Hom.* 8. 4.

And the last stage but one is that wherein a man has already been caught up into the third heaven, but has descended thence in order to preach again and 'to take an interest in his brethren'. We should call this a loftier attainment than the other. But then the monk had another ideal. The second mark of it is ἀπάθεια.[1] The soul must be disengaged from all affection of the world.[2] The third description is union with God, and this must be further explained.

Like all mystics, Macarius uses the metaphors of union[3] so that sometimes the reader wonders whether the soul is not altogether absorbed in God,

> Plunged in the Godhead's utmost sea
> And lost in Thine immensity

But in reality his religion is always an 'I and Thou' communion. The metaphors of fire and light are freely used. The fire is especially used of burning up the evil of the soul.[4] The light is used primarily of revelation.[5] Macarius does not go beyond the language of Paul when he speaks of reflecting with unveiled face the glory of God. And for two reasons, Macarius is kept free from any reproach of Pantheism. In the first place he insists on the vast difference between God and the soul. 'Listen. He is God; the soul is not God. He is the Lord; it is a servant. He is Creator; it is a creature. He is the maker; it is the thing made.'[6] But in His condescension He dwells within the soul. This is the rest of the soul, the mystical, ineffable fellowship of the heavenly King.[7] In the second place, the mysticism of Macarius is Christ-mysticism throughout. All the benefits described under these various metaphors— knowledge of the mysteries of the world invisible, freedom

---

[1] *Hom.* 17. 11, where ἀπάθεια is equated with perfection.

[2] *Hom.* 4. 14; cf. 10. 2. See Stoffels, 150.

[3] The most questionable is that of κρᾶσις, *Hom.* 9. 12. But this is only the result of a quotation from St. Paul. Cf. *Hom.* 12. 16; 32. 6, 7; 46. 3–6. In each case the ambiguous expressions are due to some quotation from Scripture.

[4] *Hom.* 4. 14; 25. 10.

[5] *Hom.* 7. 5; 46. 5; 5. 10.

[6] *Hom.* 49. 4. See Stoffels, 163.

[7] *Hom.* 4. 15.

from sin, communion with God, moral renewal—all are given in the personal relationship with Christ.[1] Christ is all in all to the soul. He gives true prayer, prayer in the Spirit. He it is who gives 'true charity, which is Himself in thee made all things—paradise, tree of life, pearl, crown, builder, husbandman, sufferer, incapable of suffering, man, God, wine and living water, lamb, bridegroom, warrior, armour, Christ all in all'.[2] Wherever this personal relationship with Christ is found, there is no real Pantheism. The historical personality of our Lord saves us from merging all distinctions of human personality in the divine life.

It would have been well if later mysticism had followed the way of Macarius rather than that of Augustine. His best descriptions of the ideal do not suffer by comparison with the *Confessions*, and his devotion has always, for its centre, Christ. There is variety in the spiritual life.[3] There is inexhaustible promise and wonder. There is the mark on his writing of one who knows, and who dwells in the secret place of the Most High. 'Tell us, if thou wilt,' says one of his disciples, 'what measures thou art in?' The answer[4] of Macarius must be quoted: as Dr. Mason says, it can only be read with awe:

After the sign of the cross, grace now acts thus. It calms all the members and the heart, so that the soul, for much joy, appears like an innocent child, and the man no longer condemns Greek or Jew, sinner or worldling. The inner man regards all men with a pure eye, and the man rejoices over all the world, and desires that all should worship and love, Greeks and Jews. At another moment, like the king's son, he is as bold in the Son of God as in a father, and doors are opened to him, and he enters within to many mansions, and the farther he goes in, doors are again opened in progression, a hundred mansions leading to a hundred beyond, and he is rich, and the richer he is, other new wonders are again disclosed to him, and he is entrusted as a son and an heir, with things that cannot be told by mankind, or put into syllables by mouth and tongue. Glory to God. Amen.

[1] Compare Karl Holl, *Enthusiasmus u. Bussgewalt*, 70, 71, where he says the same of Symeon, the New Theologian.

[2] *Hom.* 31. 4.   [3] *Hom.* 18. 7–11.   [4] *Hom.* 8. 6.

From the description of the ideal as essentially ecstasy, it follows that Macarius did not expect full attainment in this life. 'A perfect Christian man, one completely free, I have not yet seen. . . . Sin is still present within.'[1] As for the defects of his ideal, they have been touched on in the foregoing exposition. The excessive individualism of the monastic ideal, the stress on apathy, the divorce between Nature and Grace, the retreat from much that is good, as well as from all that is evil in the life of this world, the lack of any ideal for the masses of mankind—these defects are patent in Macarius. Had he trusted some of his own intuitions which he has confided to us, he would have transcended the ideal of his own century. As it is, in some respects he falls short of the broad-mindedness of Basil. He does not follow the lead of Clement in trusting the revelation given by the Logos to the Greeks. 'The wise men of the world, Aristotle, or Plato or Sophocles, . . . were like great cities, but they were made waste by enemies, because the Spirit of God was not in them.'[2]

But these Homilies are valuable evidence that, at its best, the genius of monasticism lay in the attempt to recover the apostolic experience of Christ. Macarius unveils his longings when he speaks of the Apostles, and especially of Paul.[3] 'The apostles could not sin, because they could not choose to sin, being in light and in such grace. . . . Grace permits even perfect spiritual persons to have the use of their will.' In an exposition[4] of the prayer of St. Paul in Eph. iii. 18, 19 (*That ye may be able to comprehend with all the saints what is the breadth and length and height and depth*) the heavenly habitation of the soul is described as by one who had often mounted there. The soul may be at times 'perfectly delivered from the passions of shame and be made pure through grace, and serve the Lord wholly in heaven in the spirit and serve Him wholly in the body'.

[1] *Hom.* 8. 5.   [2] *Hom.* 42. 1.
[3] I have counted nearly two hundred references to the Pauline Epp. (not including Hebrews) in the *Fifty Homilies*.
[4] *Hom.* 46. 3–6.

CHAPTER IX

ST. AMBROSE

Regnum meum Christus est.
> *St. Ambrose, Expos. in Luc.* v. 115.

> Qui corde Christum suscipit
> Innoxium sensum gerit:
> Votisque perstat sedulis
> Sanctum mereri spiritum.
> > *Hymn of St. Ambrose.*

IT is through the teaching of Ambrose that the transition may readily be made from the ideals of Eastern monasticism to the ideals of St. Augustine. For in the person of St. Ambrose are met together the chief tendencies of East and West. He is the true legatee of the *gravitas* of ancient Rome, the fearless representative of the Church, and at the same time a saint with a deep interior life. On the other hand he has been influenced by the thought of the Alexandrines, and is in close touch with the leaders of the East; his praises of virginity are as incessant as those of Basil or Gregory of Nyssa. Nothing less than this mingling of many qualities can account for the extraordinary influence he exerted in the crisis of the life of Augustine.

1. His conception of the Church. The idea of the Kingdom of God is approximating to the idea of the Church. He is no mere ecclesiastic, but he throws an aureole round the Church to which he has dedicated his life. To him the Church is the bride of Christ; espoused to Him in Paradise, heralded through the law, and in the sufferings of Christ wedded to Him for all eternity.[1] The Church is the Mother of the faithful. She is built upon Christ as the cornerstone.[2] She is the heavenly Jerusalem, whose walls are the churches dispersed through all the

---

[1] *Expos. in Psalmi* 118, *Serm.* 1. 4; Migne, 15. 1201. *Expos. Ps.* 118, *Serm.* 1. 16; Migne, 15. 1206–7.
[2] *Expos. in Luc.* 2. 86 (Migne, 16. 1585).

world and whose stones are the living souls of men.[1] Believers are anointed in baptism to be priests, and heirs of the Kingdom.[2] It is owing to the presence of the Holy Spirit in their hearts that they already share in the inheritance of the kingdom of God.[3]

2. The Spiritualizing of the Primitive Eschatology. Ambrose distinguishes the *primum regnum*, into which the righteous enter immediately after death, from the *secundum regnum* when they reign with Christ after the resurrection of the dead. But the fullness of the Kingdom is only the consummation of the reign which Christ has already enjoyed in the hearts of believers in this life. Ambrose loved to dwell upon the thought of Christ's reign and presence within. 'We are the kingdom, for it was said to us: *The Kingdom of God is within you.* And we are the kingdom, first of Christ and then of the Father, as it is written, No man cometh to the Father but by me. When I am on the way, I am Christ's; when I have passed through, I am the Father's; but everywhere through Christ, and everywhere under Him.'[4] Like Irenaeus, Ambrose has grasped the idea of development. 'The kingdom grows.'[5] It grows from the moment when we accept the grace of God in Christ.[6] It spreads as the Church spreads.[7] At the same time we may trace in Ambrose the idea of the conflict of the Kingdom of Christ with the Kingdom of Antichrist. He sees this conflict already proceeding in world-history. The final blow to the power of evil will be given at the second coming of Christ.[8]

3. The Ethical Ideal. Although his great ethical treatise is founded on the *De Officiis* of Cicero, the thought of Ambrose is dominated by the Christian ideal. The ideal

---

[1] *Apol. David*, i. 17. 83 (Migne, 14. 883).

[2] *De mysteriis*, 6. 30; Migne, 16. 398.

[3] *De sp. sancto*, iii. 20. 156, 157; Migne, 16. 812.

[4] *De fide*, v. 12. 149; cf. 150, 151, 152.

[5] Ibid. v. 12. 149. Cf. the summary of Niederhuber, *Die Eschatologie des hl. Ambrosius* (Paderborn, 1907), 89; *Expos. in Ps.* 118, *Serm.* 5. 35.

[6] *De sacram.* v. 4. 22; Migne, 16. 451.

[7] *Ennar. in Ps.* 40. 37; Migne, 14. 1085.

[8] Niederhuber, 149, 150 ff.

is the Kingdom. It is taken by force; and the force is the power of faith.[1] The Kingdom is Christ Himself.[2]

When we ask how far the ideal is attainable in this life, we meet the distinction between the precepts and the counsels. 'Every duty is either ordinary or perfect.'[3] This is proved by Matt. xix. 17–21. Mercy towards the poor and love of enemies are the marks of perfection.[4] Virginity is not a matter of precept, but it is a most powerful aid in the pursuit of perfection.[5] The distinction between precepts and counsels is modified altogether by identifying the precepts with the law, and the counsels with grace.[6] So the highest standard is for all those who are under grace, and the lower for those under law.

Ambrose does not identify perfection with either poverty or virginity. Paul and David attained to that relative perfection wherein they could bless when they were reviled.[7] But they sought a higher perfection.[8] This further perfection is the fulfilment of the promises of God, the end when the Kingdom is delivered up to God. But the mark of a Christian is to be striving for perfection and for truth.

Here is the shadow, here the image; there the truth. The shadow is in the law, the image in the Gospel, the truth in Heaven. In old time a lamb or a calf was offered; now Christ is offered. But he is offered as man and as enduring suffering. And He offers Himself as a priest, to take away our sins, here in an image, there in truth, where with the Father He intercedes for us as our Advocate. Here then we walk in an image, we see in an image; there face to face, where is full perfection. For all perfection rests in the truth.[9]

It would seem as if Ambrose believed that by virginity the loftier perfection of eternity was in some measure

---

[1] *Expos. in Luc.* v. 111 ff., 114–17; Migne, 15. 1667.

[2] Ibid. 115. Regnum meum Christus est; cf. *Sermo II de natali Domini veniente.*

[3] *De officiis*, i. 11. 36.   [4] Ibid. 37.   [5] *De virg.* i. 5. 23.

[6] Scullard, *Early Christian Ethics in the West*, 233–8, provides a much-needed corrective to the view which sees in the ethical teaching of Ambrose more of Cicero than of Christ.   [7] *De officiis*, i. 48. 244, 245.

[8] Ibid. 247 (of David). So in *De officiis*, iii. 2. 11.

[9] Ibid. i. 48. 248.

brought down to earth, and was realizable in time. Compare the two following passages:

The first is addressed to Virgins:[1]

That which is promised to us is already present with you, and the object of your prayers is with you. You are in this world, and yet not of this world.

The second is in his moral treatise:[2]

There is a twofold form of perfection, the one having but ordinary, the other the highest worth; the one availing here, the other hereafter; the one in accordance with human powers, the other with the perfection of the world to come. But God is first through all, wise above all, perfect in all.

It is hardly fair to Ambrose to suggest that his ethical teaching is one of merit and reward, and that he believes that a treasury of merit is laid up by those who in this life practise virginity and follow the evangelical counsels. The thought of Ambrose is too strongly dominated by his own communion with God to be contained within the categories of punishment and reward. Of God he says:[3] *ipse est utique merces perfecta virtutum.* But at the same time he had no considered ideal for those living in the normal relationships of life. The perfection attainable in this life was for the few, and therefore he does not give so much space to the doctrine as we should have expected.

[1] *De virg.* i. 9. 52; cf. 48.   [2] *De officiis,* iii. 2. 11.
[3] *Expos. Ps.* 118, *Serm.* 8. 11 (Petschenig, 156. 1).

NOTE. It is not possible from the evidence to conclude, with Niederhuber, that Ambrose identifies the Kingdom of God on earth with the Church. His thought is not clear at this point. See Niederhuber, *Die Lehre des hl. Ambrosius vom Reiche Gottes auf Erden* (1904), 84; the evidence is collected in this monograph.

CHAPTER X

ST. AUGUSTINE[1]

Ipse finis erit desideriorum nostrorum qui sine fine videbitur . . .
Nam quis alius noster est finis nisi pervenire ad regnum cuius nullus est
finis?

De civitate Dei, xxii. 30.

A MODERN literary historian has said that St. Augustine brought the sense of infinity into Latin prose. 'Suddenly in the midst of this lacquered correspondence, this pleasant Chinese game of painted ivories, of flowers and characters and dragons and seasons, the great wind blows.'[2]

No such wind blows upon the soul of man without bringing an ideal, as yet undreamed of by the uninitiated, to disturb the settled ways and confound the old securities wherein men slumbered. And the ideal which finds voice and challenge in Augustine is again that of a perfection attainable in its fullness only in eternity, yet also to be enjoyed in time, a home even now for the seeking spirit. Some have questioned whether Augustine can be ranked with the teachers of perfection just because in the stress of the conflict with Pelagianism he seems to deny the possibility of sinlessness in this life. Only Jesus and His Mother, among all those named in Holy Writ, says he, were without sin.[3] But once we are released from a negative definition of the word, we may see that his whole theology is essentially perfectionist, because his leading

---

[1] The primary sources are the *Confessions*, the *De civitate Dei*, the *De Trinitate*, *De doctrina Christiana*, and the earlier works (*De quantitate animae*, *De beata vita*, *Soliloquia*).

[2] Helen Waddell, *The Wandering Scholars* (1927), chap. i.

[3] *De natura et gratia*, 41, 42. Cf. 49. 'In truth I do not much care about expressing a definite opinion on the question whether in the present life there ever have been, or now are, or ever can be, any persons who have had, or are having, or are to have, the love of God so perfectly as to admit of no addition to it (for nothing short of this amounts to a most true, plenary, and perfect righteousness).' Cf. *De spir. et lit.*, c. 1 and c. 3.

idea is that of the *Summum Bonum*, which in some measure may be enjoyed and possessed in this world.

Such a statement as this brings us at once into the battle-line. The modern controversy over St. Augustine has centred round his ultimate ideal. Is he the Reformer of Church piety, the founder of Medieval Catholicism, perhaps even the begetter (though not the only begetter) of the Medieval Papacy? Or does he belong essentially to the old dying world of antiquity, one whose eyes are not holden by the existing ecclesiastical system, but perpetually gazing on an ideal which is not of this world? Such is the issue which since the publication of Hermann Reuter's *Augustinische Studien* (1887) has drawn the attention of some of the greatest theologians of our time.

A second, though a subordinate and more tractable problem, is that of the Neoplatonic influence upon his spirituality.[1] Is he essentially Christian in his mysticism, or does his picture of the ideal owe more than he himself recognizes to the second of the three influences—Manichaeism, Neoplatonism, Christianity—which, as he tells us in the *Confessions*, played upon his mind?

Here then are the main questions with which we must wrestle, if in the light of modern study we are to estimate the abiding contribution of Augustine to the doctrine of Christian Perfection.

I. THE POSITION OF ST. AUGUSTINE IN THE HISTORY OF THE CHURCH

Harnack has familiarized English readers with the idea that Augustine is the Reformer of Christian piety, the Church teacher whose synthesis of three great circles of thought dominated medieval theology, and the creator of the medieval Church.[2] The effect of this view is to transfer Augustine to the Middle Ages. So Dorner before him made Augustine the father of the Papacy. Ritschl in this

[1] Cf. Ritschl, *Rechtfertigung und Versöhnung*, iii. 467 (E. tr. 497), for the importance of this question.

[2] *History of Dogma*, v. 4 ff. Cf. *What is Christianity?* 260–5.

view, as in so much else, was the inspiration and the precursor of Harnack.[1]

On the other hand, Hermann Reuter pointed out that when St. Augustine speaks of the Church he does not mean the organized, hierarchically governed Church, in the medieval sense of the word, but rather that part of the communion of saints which is at the moment to be found on the earth.[2] The reaction against the prevalent view went farther still in the protest of Troeltsch,[3] which has not yet been fully answered. Troeltsch maintains that Augustine does not belong to the Middle Ages, but is essentially a child of the Christianity of the ancient world; that his ideas are in no sense a programme of a new epoch in the world's history;[4] that the conceptions both of Church and State envisaged in the *De civitate Dei* are totally different from those of the Middle Ages.[5] Whatever use later generations made of him is another matter.[6] His real significance is that he was the fashioner of a new *Ethik*.[7] His dominant idea was that of the *Summum Bonum*. It was he who blended Christian piety with that inheritance of Greek religious life which had come down from the Stoics, and passed through Neoplatonism into his own soul. It was he who christianized the political-social theory of the ancient *lex naturae*, and the Ciceronian philosophy of the state. 'All these diverse elements were linked together in a great ethical system of the *Summum Bonum* by the thought of Christian blessedness and the love of God.'[8]

It will be at once evident that if the main contention of

---

[1] *Gesammelte Aufsätze*, 147–69; *Jahrbücher für deutsche Theologie*, xvi. 191–214. Cf. *Rechtfertigung und Versöhnung*, iii. 271, 272; E. tr. 286.

[2] *Augustinische Studien*, 150.

[3] *Augustin, die christliche Antike und das Mittelalter* (1915). It is no answer to Troeltsch to say that the writings of St. Augustine were constantly quoted in the Middle Ages, or that many of his ideas were used by Church-leaders, theologians, and mystics. Troeltsch freely recognizes these facts (see *Augustin*, 158). Augustine's ideas were used like the Bible and like Aristotle; appealed to when appeal was convenient. The best criticism of Troeltsch is a supplement—e.g. that of Karl Bauer (*Zeitschrift für Kirchengeschichte*, 1923, N.F. 5, 223–43).   [4] *Augustin*, 154.

[5] Op. cit. 6–7; 25–6; for the chief differences, 26–47.

[6] Op. cit. 7.   [7] Op. cit. 172–3.   [8] Op. cit. 158–9.

Troeltsch is correct, the whole edifice of the thought of St. Augustine is built upon the idea of perfection.[1] Our previous discussion both of the New Testament writers, and of Clement of Alexandria, Origen, and Monasticism, will have prepared us for the coming of a great theologian whose essential task it will be to gather up into a system all that the early Church had learnt of the Christian ideal.[2]

What is the *Summum Bonum*, the final blessedness of man? The answer is never in doubt. It is God. Man can only find the complete satisfaction of his restless desires, and his manifold activity, in God. God is the good wherein the angels are blessed.[3] In the course of his spiritual development the content of the idea of the *Summum Bonum* increases. At the beginning of his Christian life the intellectual aspect of the ideal is set in the foreground. In God the reason finds its goal and completion. 'The inner admonition which so works upon us that we remember God, search for Him, thirst for Him (all aversion gone), comes to us from the very source of truth.'[4] To the end St. Augustine held to it that to know God in a communion which was conscious was the goal of life. In a letter[5] written in 417 he speaks of those who know God with a merely intellectual knowledge without having God dwelling within them, and of those in whom God dwells without their knowing it. 'But most blessed are they with whom God dwells and who know it. It is this knowledge that is the fullest, truest, happiest.'

To Augustine God is also the *aeterna pulchritudo*, the

---

[1] The modifications and corrections which Karl Bauer has made in the position of Troeltsch do not affect the main position; e.g. it is probable that Troeltsch does not allow sufficiently for the absorption in the New Testament which profoundly affected the development of St. Augustine after his conversion (see *Zeitschrift für Kirchengeschichte*, 1923, 232–7). This fact means that there is more 'philosophy of history' in the *De civ. Dei* than Troeltsch will allow; even in Romans v there is a rudimentary philosophy of history, which Augustine appropriated. See also Figgis, *The Political Aspects of St. Augustine's City of God*, 38–9. But as Bauer admits (241–2) Troeltsch seems to have proved his chief thesis.

[2] Bauer, loc. cit., 241.   [3] *De civ. Dei*, ix. 22.

[4] *De beata vita*, 35. Cf. *c. Acad.* i. 5; Mausbach, i. 52–4.

[5] *Ep.* 187. 21.

fullness of beauty, Who is revealed in the harmonious ordering of the world:[1]

Though the voices of the prophets were silent, the world itself by its well-ordered changes and movements, and by the fair appearance of all visible things, bears a testimony of its own, both that it has been created, and also that it could not have been created save by God, Whose greatness and beauty are unutterable and invisible.[2]

Later, the influence of St. Paul brings into prominence the ethical question. Sin is not the mere absence of goodness and beauty, but is a universal depravity of the will. Augustine never surrendered his belief that the evil could be overridden, and even used by God, and that the opposition between good and evil could be finally resolved.[3] But a more evangelical view of the sinfulness of sin took possession of his mind. 'I know of no catholic writer before him,' says Reuter,[4] 'who has set Law and Gospel over against one another—I will not say after the Pauline fashion, but certainly in a Paulinizing fashion—as Augustine does in the *liber de spiritu et litera*; no one who so unveils that which is specifically new in the Gospel, its Christian freedom.' This development was due partly to the stress of the Pelagian controversy, and still more to a deeper study of life in the light of the Pauline gospel.[5] He saw the impossibility of attaining to that love of God which is the crown and fulfilment of morality without the change of the will wrought by the grace of God.[6] The *Summum Bonum*, then, will be to enjoy the God Who writes His own law in the hearts of men, by Whose presence is shed abroad in our hearts the love which is the fulfilling of the law.[7] Real liberty is promised by the Deliverer.[8]

What is better than this blessing, what happier than this happiness,—to live to God, to live on God, with whom is the fountain of life, and in whose light we shall see light. Of this life the Lord

---

[1] *De civ. Dei*, ix. 22.   [2] Ibid. xi. 4; cf. xxii. 24.

[3] See *De civ. Dei*, xi. 18 (quoting Ecclus. xxxiii. 14); xvii. 11; Enchiridion, 10, 11, 100.   [4] *Augustinische Studien*, 493, 494.

[5] Enchiridion, 33; *De spir. et lit.*, c. 5, c. 16, c. 17; *Expositio epistolae ad Galatas*, 17.   [6] *De lib. arb.* 1. 30.

[7] *De spir. et lit.* 21.   [8] *De perf. iust. hom.* 9.

Himself speaks in these words: *This is life eternal, that they may know Thee, the only true God and Jesus Christ whom thou hast sent. . . . We shall be like Him. . . .* This likeness begins even now to be re-cast in us, while the inward man is being renewed from day to day, according to the image of Him that created Him.[1]

On such a passage as this one comment must be made. The God Who is known and Who renews the inward man is a God Who is perpetually active. He is creative Will. Unlike the Absolute of Plotinus,[2] who is 'beyond existence' God is living and working in the world He made. 'Were He to withdraw His effective power (*efficacem potentiam*) from things, they . . . would not continue in possession of that nature in which they were created.'[3] 'He that made all does not depart for that He hath no successor.'[4] It is vital for the understanding of Augustine to reach certainty here. If he entered the Church through Neoplatonism and retained many of the Neoplatonic doctrines, the character of his theology is ultimately determined by a profoundly Biblical and Hebraic conception of God.[5] He understood the meaning of that word, *My Father worketh hitherto, and I work.*[6]

It is an essential element in this conception of God that miracles should be used in His government of the world.[7] 'The miracles of Jesus Christ were wrought for the purpose of drawing the human mind from visible things to the task of understanding God.'[8] We notice how the motive of God's working, whether in the meanest flower that blows, or in the unwonted but not greater act of the Feeding of the Five Thousand, is to draw the minds of men to Himself. St. Augustine is faithful to his own central principle, that the knowledge of God is the goal of life.

---

[1] *De spir. et lit.* 22 (E. tr. ed. Dods, iv, p. 193).

[2] See Inge, *Plotinus*, ii. 109–15.

[3] *De civ. Dei*, xxii. 24. 2; cf. xii. 5.

[4] *Conf.* iv. 11; cf. *De civ. Dei*, xii. 25; *De Trin.* iii. 6; *De civ. Dei*, xxi. 8. 2; *De Gen. ad litt.* vi. 26. The point has been well worked out by Weinand, *Die Gottesidee der Grundzug der Weltanschauung des hl. Augustinus*, 73–84.   [5] See Seeberg, *Lehrbuch*, ii. 373, 376–8.

[6] See the exposition in *De Gen. ad litt.* iv. 23.

[7] See Lacey, *Nature, Miracle and Sin*, 71–91.

[8] *In Joan.* 24. 1; cf. *De Civ. Dei*, x. 12.

The activity of God is especially shown in the illumination of the human mind and the awakening of the human conscience. Here Augustine appropriates the Logos-doctrine as part of his own synthesis. In his earliest writings after his conversion he had spoken of the Light that is poured into our inward eyes.[1] He is the master light of all our seeing. *Deus autem est ipse qui illustrat.*[2] The knowledge of God which is supernaturally given, the saving knowledge which is due to God's grace, is also due to an inward illumination. *Illuminatio nostra participatio verbi est.*[3] This participation is an inward communion with God far more intimate than the acknowledgement that *He is not far from each one of us.* This might be understood of this corporeal world. We live in Him and have our being in Him even when we do not know Him. And therefore the word should be taken in a more excellent way (*excellentiore modo*).

All are not with Him in the way in which it is said to Him, I am continually with Thee. Nor is He with all in that way in which we say, *The Lord be with you.* And so it is the especial wretchedness of man not to be with Him, without Whom he cannot be. For beyond a doubt he is not without Him in Whom He is; and yet if he does not remember, and understand, and love Him, he is not with Him.[4]

This wretchedness is due to the sin of man.[5] And this barrier to 'participation in the Word' is removed by the inpouring of a new power, which is love (*caritas*). Love, therefore, is an essential element in the *Summum Bonum*. In a letter[6] to St. Jerome, written about A.D. 415, virtue is described as love which directs our love to that which is worthy to be loved. So long as man is on the earth, that love is capable of increase. In that sense perfection is never attained here below. That is why we must all pray for forgiveness in the words of the Lord's Prayer.

Elsewhere he says that it is God's will for us that while we are in this mortal flesh there should always be in us

---

[1] *De beata vita*, 35.   [2] *Solil.* i. 12.   [3] *De Trin.* iv. 2.
[4] *De Trin.* xiv. 12.   [5] *De Trin.* iv. 2.
[6] *Ep.* 167. 15.

some enemy against which the mind must fight.[1] Pride is
the last and most perilous of such enemies, and pride can
only be exorcised by love of the supreme and immutable
Good. The soul when it comes to itself, tired of the
pleasures of earth, says like the lost Son, I will arise and
go to my Father. The clearness with which the soul sees
God and recognizes His infinite perfection will kindle
the love that springs from the vision of Him, will
engender that happy and spontaneous goodness, that
incapacity to sin, which is the fulfilment and end of our
being.[2]

The possession of God and the supreme virtue of Love
are thus inalienably linked together in St. Augustine's
conception of the supreme good. 'This love, inspired by
the Holy Spirit, leads to the Son, that is to the wisdom of
God, by which the Father Himself is known. . . . When
wisdom is sought as it deserves to be, it cannot withdraw
or hide itself from its lovers. . . . It is love that asks, love
that seeks, love that knocks, love that reveals, love, too,
that gives continuance in that which is revealed.'[3] All the
cardinal virtues, taught by the sages of antiquity, are manifestations of love.[4] True self-love is only possible to one
who loves God.[5] And there is no surer step towards the
love of God than the love of man to man.[6] These quotations come from an early writing against the Manichaeans,
but Augustine never wavered in the central position
assigned to love in his ethical system.

The Social character of the *Summum Bonum*.

Since love is pre-eminently a social virtue, we should
expect a systematic thinker to find the ideal of perfection
in the society of the redeemed. It has been made a reproach
against Augustine that his ideal is individualist. Such a
view vanishes before his conception of the unity of the

---

[1] *c. Jul.* iv. 28.
[2] *De civ. Dei,* xxii. 30. 3; *c. Jul.* iv. 28; cf. *De Gen. ad litt.* xii. 54;
De perf. iust. hom. 9.   [3] *De mor. eccl. cath.* 31.
[4] Ibid. 25, 35–47.   [5] Ibid. 48.
[6] See Weinand, *Die Gottesidee als leitender Gedanke in der Entwicklung
Augustins,* 50–3.

three ideas of love of God, love of self, love of one's neighbour.[1]

You love yourself in a way that leads to salvation (*salubriter*) when you love God better than yourself. What then you aim at in yourself you must aim at in your neighbour, namely that he may love God with a perfect affection. For you do not love him as yourself unless you try to draw him to that good which you are yourself pursuing. For this is the one good which is not too narrow, even if all are pursuing it together with yourself. From this commandment are born the duties of human society.[2]

Rarely has any one sung with the passion of Augustine the marvel of that Good which is not lessened by being shared.[3] But the *reductio ad absurdum* of the claim that the piety of Augustine is purely individualist is found in his masterpiece, the *De civitate Dei*.

How could the city of God take a beginning or be developed, or attain its proper destiny, *si non esset socialis vita sanctorum*—if the life of the saints were not a social life?[4]

Even in the life beyond the grave there are grades and diversities, but there is no envy, no unrest, because God

shall be the end of our desires, Who shall be seen without end, loved without satiety, praised without weariness. This outgoing of affection, this employment, shall certainly be, like eternal life itself, common to all.[5]

But our inquiry is concerned with the relative perfection which is attainable here below. Is the Kingdom of God realizable on this earth?

In his earlier days Augustine held a form of Millennarianism. In a sermon preached on a first Sunday after Easter he explains the 'Octave' of the feast; the eighth day symbolizes the new life in heaven, and the seventh day signifies the millennial rest of the saints on earth (*septimus*

[1] See Troeltsch, *Augustin*, 90–1 against Scheel. Cf. Thimme, *Augustins geistige Entwickelung* (1908), 249, who shows that the conception belongs to the earliest stage in Augustine's Christian life.

[2] *De mor. eccl. cath.* 49.   [3] *De lib. arb.* ii. 37 and 38.

[4] *De civ. Dei*, xix. 5; cf. xix. 17 (*ad fin.*).

[5] *De civ. Dei*, xxii. 30; cf. v. 16.

quietem futuram sanctorum in hac terra).[1] At present we are
in the sixth day (*in sexto die sumus*) for five *millennia* have
already passed away. But he tells us that he changed his
views. He explains that the first resurrection means not
any bodily resurrection but the resurrection of souls from
the life of sin to faith in Christ; the binding of Satan means
the limitation of his power to the hearts of the wicked; the
thousand years is the interval between the first and second
Advent. During this time the true saints, even on earth,
reign with Christ.

The projection of the millennium into the present is the
basis of Augustine's famous identification of the Church
and the Kingdom of God. The only chapter where the
identification is explicit is susceptible of more than one
interpretation and in view of its significance for our purpose must be quoted at length (*De civ. Dei*, xx. 9).

While the devil is bound, the saints reign with Christ during the
same thousand years, understood in the same way, that is, of the
time of His first coming. For, leaving out of account that Kingdom
concerning which He shall say in the end, 'Come, ye blessed of my
Father' . . . the Church could not now be called His kingdom or
the kingdom of heaven, unless His saints to whom He says 'Lo
I am with you always' were even now reigning with Him, though
in another and far different way (*nisi alio aliquo modo, longe quidem
impari, iam nunc regnarent cum illo sancti eius, quibus ait, 'Ecce ego
vobiscum sum usque in consummationem saeculi': profecto non etiam
nunc diceretur Ecclesia regnum eius, regnumve coelorum*).

He then quotes the parable of the wheat and the tares,
and proceeds, saying of the tares: *de isto ergo regno eius,
quod est hic ecclesia, colligentur*. Later in the same chapter,
after quoting Matt. v. 19, 20, he continues:

Accordingly the kingdom of heaven is to be taken in two senses.
In one sense it contains both him who breaks what He (Christ)
teaches, and him who keeps it—the one is least and the other great
(in the kingdom). In the other sense there is the kingdom of heaven
into which only he enters who keeps the commandment. The
kingdom which contains both is the Church as it now is. The

[1] *Serm.* 259. 2. Extreme Chiliasm he characterizes as ridiculous (*De
civ. Dei*, xx. 7. 1).

other is the Church as it shall be, when no wicked man shall be in it. Therefore the Church even now is the kingdom of Christ, and the kingdom of heaven (*ergo ecclesia et nunc est regnum Christi, regnumque coelorum*). Accordingly His saints even now reign with Him, yet not indeed in the same way as they will reign then. The tares do not reign with Him, although they grow in the Church along with the wheat. For those reign with Him . . . whose conversation is in heaven. They reign with Him who are so in His Kingdom that they themselves are His kingdom.

The traditional view of this chapter is that Augustine roundly identifies the visible Church with the Kingdom of God.[1] A careful reading of the chapter gives us ground to hesitate before accepting such a swift conclusion. But there are two reasons for the traditional view which must first be examined.

The first is that later on in the same chapter Augustine interprets the passage in the Apocalypse (xx. 4) as referring to the present age.

And I saw seats and them that sat upon them, and judgment was given. It is not to be supposed that this refers to the last judgement but to the seats of the rulers and to the rulers themselves by whom the church is now governed. But no better interpretation of judgement being given can be produced than that which we have in the words: *What ye bind on earth shall be bound in heaven.*

This passage proves conclusively that Augustine is interpreting the prophecy of the millennial reign of the saints as coming to pass in the contemporary Church. The reference to the *praepositi*—the bishops—is to his mind just one more proof of his main thesis, that the men of his own day were living in the millennium. But this passage does not prove that he identified the Kingdom with the organized, hierarchically governed, visible Church. The modifications on the earlier part of the chapter, on which more must be said, still stand. Even when we grant that the *praepositi* are a direct allusion to the hierarchy, we notice that the *sedes* on which the *praepositi* sit are not connected with the thought of reigning.

[1] So, e.g. emphatically, an authoritative writer like Professor Karl Adam of Tübingen, *Das Wesen des Katholizismus* (1924; E. tr. 1929), ch. ii.

The second reason for assuming that Augustine identifies the Church and the Kingdom is that the identification had already been made by a theologian whom he greatly admired[1]—and by whose work he was greatly influenced[2]—the Donatist Tyconius.[3] But even in Tyconius the identification is not made. All that can be said is that Christian thought had been preparing for the identification for some time past and it is surprising that the final step had not yet been taken.[4]

In Augustine's statement the modifications are more striking than the sentence in which the identification is made. Tyconius betrays an anti-hierarchical bias. By the beast of the Abyss, he understands bishops and priests who live carnal lives inside the Church.[5] Augustine is not so outspoken as his predecessor. But he recognizes the tares within the field of the Church. He declines to identify the visible Church with the higher meaning of the Kingdom, but only with the lower sense of the term, in which it includes both good and bad. If the Kingdom is present it is only because of the saints who are reigning with Christ, and they are reigning only in virtue of their character. Again, it has been pointed out[6] that nowhere in this crucial chapter of the *De civitate* is the equation found *ecclesia = regnum Dei*; six times he says: *ecclesia = regnum Christi*. The saints are said to reign *cum Christo*. This distinction of the Kingdom of the Son of Man from the Kingdom of His Father is an echo of the Pauline distinction in 1 Cor. xv (cf. Matt. xiii; Col. i. 13). In the third place, the Church is spoken of by Augustine as the *regnum militiae*, in contrast with the *pacatissimum regnum*.

---

[1] Traugott Hahn, *Tyconius-Studien*, 1–3.

[2] See the passages set out in parallel columns in the commentary by Scholz on the *De civ. Dei, Glaube und Unglaube in der Weltgeschichte*, 114–17. It is likely that Tyconius was responsible for Augustine's change of opinion on the subject of the millennium.

[3] Traugott Hahn, *Tyconius-Studien*, 28. See Scholz, 120.

[4] See Robertson, *Regnum Dei*, 173–4.

[5] Traugott Hahn, 76.

[6] See Johannes Weiss, *Die Idee des Reiches Gottes in der Theologie* (Giessen, 1901), 23–4.

He never identifies the *ecclesia peregrinans* with the *civitas Dei*. The *ecclesia* is said to be the *peregrinans in hoc saeculo civitas Dei*.[1] There is a strong contrast between the imperfect Church which exists on earth and the *superna sanctorum civitas*,[2] of which the earthly city of God is but a hint,[3] a shadow, a fragment, a copy. Of his *De Baptismo* he says: 'Whenever in these books I have mentioned the Church as not having spot or wrinkle, it is not to be taken as now existing, but of the Church whose existence is being prepared.'[4]

The foregoing discussion will have made it clear that in the hands of Augustine the ideal of the Kingdom did not suffer moral loss. It is a social ideal; it is *communio*. But above all it is *communio sanctorum*. This is the essence of the ideal of the *De civitate*. *It is good to cleave to God*, he says, quoting a favourite text.

And those who have this good in common have both with Him to whom they draw near, and with one another, a holy fellowship, and form one city of God—His living sacrifice and His living temple.[5]

This ideal is realizable only in part and fragmentarily on this earth. Friendship is too often broken by calamities or bereavement for the good life to be possible here below.[6] It is singular that in his picture of the suffering caused by the death of friends, Augustine does not include that communion with Christ whereby the pain of love is transfigured.

The social character of the ideal is seen from its description as peace.[7] Every man desires peace. Even those who make war desire nothing but victory—desire, that is to say, to attain to peace with glory. Therefore we may say that it is with the desire for peace that wars are waged.[8] The all-inclusiveness of Augustine's ideal of Peace may

---

[1] xv. 26; cf. xix. 17.
[2] xv. 1. See the excellent comments of Scholz, 122.
[3] xv. 2.   [4] *Retractationes*, ii. 18.   [5] xii. 9.
[6] xix. 8.   [7] xix. 11.
[8] xix. 12. On these preliminary sections see Harald Fuchs, *Augustin und der antike Friedensgedanke* (Berlin, 1926), 16–36.

only be seen from his summary[1] which, like a great intellectual Ode, he prefixes to his discussion of the Peace of the City of God.

> The peace of the body, then, consists in the duly proportioned arrangement of its parts (*ordinata temperatura partium*);
>
> The peace of the irrational soul is the harmonious repose of the appetites (*ordinata requies appetitionum*);
>
> The peace of the rational soul is the harmony of knowledge and action (*ordinata cognitionis actionisque consensio*);
>
> The peace of body and soul is the harmonious life and health of the living creature (*ordinata vita et salus animantis*);
>
> Peace between man and God is the well-ordered obedience in faith, under eternal law (*ordinata in fide sub aeterna lege oboedientia*);
>
> Peace between man and man is well-ordered concord (*ordinata concordia*);
>
> Peace in the home is well-ordered concord between those of the family who rule and those who obey (*ordinata imperandi atque oboediendi concordia cohabitantium*);
>
> Peace in a political community is a well-ordered concord between those of the citizens who rule and those who obey;
>
> Peace in the celestial city is the perfectly ordered, perfectly harmonious fellowship of those who enjoy God and enjoy one another in God (*ordinatissima et concordissima societas fruendi Deo et invicem in Deo*);
>
> Peace in the universe is the tranquillity of order (*Pax omnium rerum tranquillitas ordinis*);
>
> Order is that disposition of things equal and things unequal which allots each to its own place.

Any exposition of this extraordinary passage would demand a volume.[2] But one or two comments are necessary. (1) First, Augustine is portraying the ideal towards which all creation, all civil society, all families, all human beings in their solitary conflicts, are consciously or unconsciously striving. It is the end to which the whole creation

---

[1] xix. 13.

[2] Fortunately the volume is already available in the fine work of Harald Fuchs already quoted. I must gratefully acknowledge the stimulus of this book.

moves. It is his aim to show that the ideal of peace is
implicit in the struggle of the present. (2) Second, he is
deliberately expounding an ideal which cannot be fulfilled
in this world but only in the future life beyond the grave.
His definition of peace at the close of the nineteenth book
makes this evident. Peace is perfect freedom from all
inward and outward resistances.[1]

> It will not be necessary that reason should rule vices which no
> longer exist, but God shall rule man, and the soul shall rule the body,
> with a sweetness and facility suitable to the felicity a life where
> bondage is no more.

The depth and length and breadth and height of the ideal
if but once seen by the mind will render it impossible for
men to seek their satisfaction in the visible world.

These two guiding thoughts are explained by the apolo-
getic aim of the *De civitate Dei*. Augustine is a shepherd
of souls. He knows no surer way to deepen the spiritual
life of the faithful, and to attract cultivated pagans who
are hesitating on the verge of Christianity, than such an
exposition of the fullness of the Christian ideal. It is his
answer to the longings of the natural life. He rests his
case on the facts of the world, of society, and of the human
heart.

Can the Ideal be attained in this life?

In the light of the two guiding thoughts just expounded
we may interpret the many passages which tell us that
the goal cannot be attained in this earthly life. On the one
hand the ideal of peace spans the two worlds—the world of
time and the world of eternity, this earthly existence, in
which the lot of man is war-service, and the final beatitude
which surpasses all the thoughts of man.[2] On the other
hand it is essential that the realization of any ideal which
is Christian should be set in the future life. In the last
resort the Gospel is other-worldly:

> Our blessedness, our being's heart and home
> Is with infinity and only there.

---

[1] xix. 27.

[2] Fuchs, *Augustin u. der antike Friedensgedanke*, 43. If the above

In the early treatise (A.D. 393) on the Sermon on the Mount, Augustine defined the peace-makers who are called the children of God, as those who carried that peace within themselves, in whose souls all things were harmonious (*ordinata*). The passions are subject to reason. That which is pre-eminent in man (i.e. *mens et ratio*) rules without resistance over the others (*ceteris non reluctantibus*). The reason itself is brought into subjection to something better still, to the truth itself, the only-begotten Son of God. This is the peace which is given on earth to men of goodwill. This is the life of one completely and perfectly wise.[1] 'These promises can be fulfilled in this life, just as we believe them to have been fulfilled in the case of the apostles.'[2]

At the end of his life Augustine modified some of his language. But the change of view is not so complete as Fuchs maintains.[3] In his *Retractations* he says:[4] 'No one in this life can be so privileged that there should not be in his members a law fighting against the law of his mind.' The struggle still remains. He has withdrawn the strong expression *ceteris non repugnantibus*. Of the remark about the apostles he says:

we do not think that the Apostles on this earth were exempt from the struggle of the flesh against the Spirit. But we believe that those promises can be fulfilled here just so far as they were fulfilled, according to our belief, in the Apostles, that is to say in the measure of human perfection in which perfection is possible in this life. . . . The measure is that of the perfection of which this life is capable, and not as those promises are to be fulfilled in that day of perfect peace when it shall be said: *Ubi est mors contentio tua?*

There is, then, a relative perfection possible in this life. The retractation of Augustine is carefully worded. Its purpose is plain from the last sentence. He does not wish by any idle word to assign to the present life any element in the ideal which can only lie in the life beyond the grave.

interpretation is correct, Fuchs is inclined to exaggerate the contrast between this life and the future life in the thought of Augustine. See p. 48.

[1] *De serm. Dom. in monte*, i. 2. 9.

[2] Ibid., i. 4. 12.   [3] Op. cit. 46.   [4] i. 19.

So we have statements elsewhere, apparently contradictory but which can now be explained in the light of his
retractation. No one is perfect in this life.[1] There is a
perfection in this life.[2] But this perfection is of those who
are pilgrims and strangers on the earth, not of those who
are perfectly in possession of their promised home.[3]

II. THE VISION OF GOD

Augustine is the first Christian theologian who gave to
the idea of the Beatific Vision of God, the *fruitio Dei*, the
culminating place in his thought.[4] He is deep in debt to
Plotinus, and the debt is not merely intellectual. Plotinus
is one of those whose experience must be shared if his
thought is to be understood. Augustine soon proved that
he had not only thought the thoughts of Plotinus after
him, but had climbed the same ascent to the beatific
vision. In the *De beata vita* (A.D. 386) Augustine places
the highest stage of happiness in the presence of God in
the human spirit, and describes it as enjoyment of God.
In the *De quantitate animae* (A.D. 388) the gradual climbing
of the soul to God is divided into seven stages. The last
and highest is the ineffable delight of the *visio et contem-
platio veritatis*, the *perfructio summi et veri boni*. But the
ideal is more fully described in his later writings, the
Confessions, the *De civitate Dei*, the *De Trinitate*, and the
De doctrina Christiana.

We may distinguish two sides to his thought. In the
first place there is an intellectual preparation for the vision
of God. In the second place there are moments of attainment of the ideal when the faculties of the mind are silenced
and the soul transcends itself, and touches ultimate reality.
The dialectical process is described in the *De doctrina*

---

[1] *In Psalm.* xxxviii. 13; *De doctr. Christ.* i. 38, 43.

[2] *Contra duas epist. Pelag.* iii. 15.

[3] *Sermo.* 169. 14, 18; *De gratia,* c. 53. See the full discussion of Reuter,
Augustinische Studien, 404–9.

[4] A short sketch of the previous history of the *fruitio Dei* in Scholz,
Glaube und Unglaube in der Weltgeschichte, 197 ff. But he strangely
neglects Clement of Alexandria. For Basil, see Holl, *Enthusiasmus u.
Bussgewalt,* 162; *Reg. fus. tract.* ii. 337 B, C.

Christiana. In the preface to that work he expressly dis-
courages those who imagine that they will attain, without
application of the mind, to an ecstatic experience such as
that described by St. Paul (2 Cor. xii. 2–4) and who therefore discourage the reading of the Scriptures and the
learning of truth from others. He begins his systematic
exposition with a distinction between things which are to
be enjoyed and things which are to be used. To enjoy
a thing is to rest with satisfaction in it for its own sake.[1]
To use is to employ whatever means are at one's disposal
to obtain what one desires, if it is a proper object of desire.
This world is meant to be used, not enjoyed, so that the
invisible things of God may be clearly seen, being understood by the things that are made.[2] The true object of
enjoyment is God.[3] This implies a judgement of value.[4]
The world may be used, but its use is limited.[5] Since it is
our duty fully to enjoy the truth which lives unchangeably,
the soul must be purified that it may have power to perceive that light and to rest in it when it is perceived.[6] The
goal of this human life is that love of God which is indissolubly linked with love of neighbour and true self-love,[7]
and which is perfect so far as is possible in this life.[8]
Christ is the first Way to God; the Holy Spirit binds, and
as it were seals us, so that we are able to rest permanently
on the supreme and unchangeable good. The fulfilment
and end of all Holy Scripture is the love of an object which
is to be enjoyed. So the Scriptures themselves are means
to an end. The end is love and love can only reach its
perfection with an object which is eternal.[9] A temporal
object is valued more before we possess it and begins to
prove worthless the moment we attain it because it does
not satisfy the soul. The soul has its only true and sure
resting-place in eternity. An eternal object is loved with

---

[1] *De doctr. Christ.* i. 3.   [2] i. 4.   [3] i. 5.
[4] Scholz, *Glaube u. Unglaube*, 210.
[5] *De civ. Dei.* i, 10. Cf. *De div.* 83, quaest. 30.
[6] *De doctr. Christ.* i. 10.
[7] Ibid. i. 27 (ch. 26).
[8] Ibid. i. 43 (ch. 39).   [9] Ibid. i. 39.

greater ardour when it is in possession than when it is still an object of desire.[1]

So far the end has been discussed without any hint of the silencing of the faculties of the mind. On the contrary the search for God demands the use of all the intellectual activity of which the mind is capable. First the outward and visible world must be interrogated. The earth, the heavenly bodies, his own body, are in turn surveyed. They answer: 'We are not the God whom thou seekest'. But they do make some response concerning God. They say: *ipse fecit nos.* 'My questioning with them was my thought; and their answer was their beauty.' This famous passage of the *Confessions*[2] is paralleled by another in his exposition of the Psalms.[3] It is noteworthy that this process was part of the Neoplatonist discipline.[4] He goes on to interrogate his own soul. 'I come into the fields and spacious palaces of memory, wherein are housed the treasures of innumerable forms brought into it from the things perceived by the senses.'[5] But God is not the mind, nor the thoughts in the mind. Augustine is at his most eloquent in describing the riches of memory. The description itself is part of his process of thought. After the mind has detailed all the marvels of memory the conclusion is reached. God is above even memory.[6] *Transibo ergo et memoriam, ut attingam Eum.* He is not there where multiplicity reigns. Only where unity reigns is He to be found.

Evidently the powers of the human mind are to be exercised in their highest form and severest tension for such a search as this. For it is not till the soul has reached this point that true contemplation begins. 'That I might attain unto Him I thought on these things, and poured

---

[1] Ibid. i. 42 (ch. 38).   [2] x. c. 6.
[3] *Enarr. in Psalm.* xli. 7, and C. Butler, *Western Mysticism*, 26–34.
[4] See Gibb and Montgomery, *Confessions* (2nd ed. 1927), 279.
[5] x, c. 8; cc. 25, 26. See Fulbert Cayré, *La Contemplation Augustinienne* (Paris, 1927), 203–5. Augustine regarded Memory as the fundamental characteristic of Mind conscious of itself. Anselm followed him in his *Monologion* (c. 48; c. 59; c. 67).
[6] x, c. 17.

out my soul above myself.'[1] In this phrase is summed up the 'Recollection' and the 'Introversion', which are in Dom Cuthbert Butler's phrase 'the proximate preparation' for the act of contemplation.

Recollection consists first in the effort to banish from the mind all images and thoughts of external things, all sense perceptions and thoughts of creatures; then the reasoning processes of the intellect are silenced and by this exercise of abstraction a solitude is produced wherein the soul may operate in its most spiritual faculties.[2]

Introversion is the concentration of the mind on its own highest, or deepest part. . . . It is the final step before the soul finds God.[3]

The Act of Contemplation, the third or final stage in the quest for God,[4] is described in the celebrated colloquy at Ostia with his mother Monica:

We touched It and hardly touched with the utmost leap of our heart (*attingimus eam modice toto ictu cordis*).[5]

Elsewhere in his writings a few revealing phrases fly out like sparks hammered from an anvil:

In the flash of a trembling glance my mind came to Ultimate Reality, That which is (*mens mea pervenit ad id quod est in ictu trepidantis aspectus*).[6]

I entered and beheld with the eye of my soul, above the same eye of my soul, above my mind, the Light Unchangeable.[7]

From that everlasting perpetual festivity there sounds in the ears of the heart a mysterious strain, melodious and severe, provided only the world do not drown the sounds.[8]

What is that which gleams through me and strikes my heart without hurting it: and I shudder and kindle? I shudder inasmuch as I am unlike it: I kindle inasmuch as I am like it. It is Wisdom, Wisdom's self, which gleameth through me.[9]

On this supreme act of contemplation we may observe: (1) It is not ecstasy or trance. The phenomena of these

---

[1] *Enarr. in Psalm.* xli. 8.   [2] *Western Mysticism*, 38.
[3] *Western Mysticism*, 39.
[4] So Professor Cayré distinguishes it in his clear analysis, *La Contemplation Augustinienne*, 206–9.
[5] *Conf.* ix. 10.   [6] *Conf.* vii. 17.   [7] *Conf.* vii. 10.
[8] *Enarr. in Psalm.* xli. 9.   [9] *Conf.* xi. 9.

states were familiar to Augustine.[1] That which distinguishes the experience which he describes from any such complete alienation from the senses, or from any quasi-hypnotic trance is the strenuousness and thoroughness of the intellectual process which precedes the vision of God.[2]

(2) The experience is in its main outlines Neoplatonic. I have already pointed out that Augustine is no slavish imitator of Plotinus. He thought the thoughts of Plotinus after him. He did more: he lived for himself the experiences of Plotinus, and in so doing he added that incommunicable gift of himself, so that the experience became that of Augustine and not merely that of Plotinus. Nevertheless, the resemblances even of language are too close to be accidental. Thus in the colloquy at Ostia, *toto ictu cordis* corresponds to ἐπιβολῇ ἀθρόᾳ—'*with a mighty leap* must the mind seize this which transcends the nature of mind.' 'If to any one the tumult of the flesh were silent' almost reproduces a passage in the Fifth Ennead:

Let there be silent unto it (i.e. the soul) not only the body, and the restless surge of the body (ὁ τοῦ σώματος κλύδων), but also all that is round about it; let the earth be silent and the sea and the air and even the unsullied heaven.

But the evidence which seems conclusive to the present writer, more conclusive indeed than any of the arguments usually adduced, is the reason which Augustine relies upon for rejecting the idea that God could be found in the spacious palaces of memory. The reason is that in memory we find a multiplicity, and God cannot be where multiplicity is. This is the final presupposition of the Neoplatonic system.[3] Its reappearance at a crucial point in the

---

[1] The evidence is set out and discussed by Dom C. Butler, *Western Mysticism*, 71–8.

[2] This *differentia* has been finely expounded by Mr. W. Montgomery in an unpublished paper which I am permitted to quote, *St. Augustine and Plotinus* (printed privately for the London Society for the Study of Religion). The paper has been used by Dom C. Butler, op. cit., Appendix on Ecstasy, 337–9.

[3] See Inge's exposition of the Absolute, *Plotinus II*, 104–62, especially 127–42.

development of the argument of Augustine shows how his spirituality was dominated by the genius of Plotinus.

Again, the mystical experiences described in the seventh book of the *Confessions* were admittedly pre-Christian or, as Dom Cuthbert Butler calls them, pre-Catholic.

(3) It follows that we cannot admit that his conception of the highest point of contemplation attainable in this life was fully Christian. In one sense any attainment of communion with God is Christian. Christianity at its best has always endorsed and crowned any genuine awareness of the divine. Again, Augustine's experience was mediated by Christians stirred by memories of Antony, nourished by a mother's prayers. But at this point we are not concerned to deny that Augustine was a Christian saint. The question for the moment is that supreme moment of attainment which is won by a Neoplatonic ἄσκησις, and which consists in the silencing of all the faculties of the mind and in turning away from all thoughts of this world. Is this the spirituality that is unveiled in the cries of Gethsemane, in the exultation of spirit that the mysteries hidden from the wise and prudent are now revealed to babes? Does Augustine understand the spirituality which relies rather on the power which was made perfect in weakness than on the vision of the third heaven? Or can it be contended that an experience of God wherein Christ is left out, is unnamed even in the most breathless attempts to force language and describe the indescribable, is as fully Christian as the attainment of one who can say: *For me to live is Christ and to die will be more Christ.* Or of another who can say: *This is eternal life to know Thee . . . and . . . Christ?*

Surely we must agree with Professor Arundel Chapman in his illuminating discussion of the piety of St. Augustine:[1] 'Magnificent, but not quite the Christian way.' Unlike Santa Teresa, St. Augustine forgets the humanity of Jesus Christ when he draws near to God. In the *De doctrina Christiana* (i. 38) he interprets the saying of St.

[1] *Eleven Christians* (1925), 49.

Paul, *we know Christ no longer after the flesh*, as meaning
that in our communion with God we think no longer of
Christ the Man. Such thoughts, says Augustine, belong
to the *things behind* (spoken of in Phil. iii. 13) which must
be forgotten. Even thoughts of the example of Christ and
of His sufferings are described as milk for babes![1]

It is the custom in Provence to fashion tiny plaster
figures, and to place them before the model of a stable;
inside the stable is the Christ-child lying in the manger.
And all those who are pressing into the stable carry a gift,
all save one. Some have a lamb, some have fruit or corn.
They offer their tokens of the common life of man. But
one of these tiny figures comes with empty hands. He
carries nothing save an air of wonder, and his eyes are full
of an unearthly rapture. That is why, in Provence, they
call him *Le Ravi*. Certainly there is a place in the innermost shrine of the Christian Church for *Le Ravi*, the
mystic of the Neoplatonic type, who at the supreme
moment of his adoration has turned his back on the common life of man, and offers nothing save his contemplation
to God. But even so, whether he sees it or not, it is the
glory of Christian devotion that, at the summit of attainment, we frail mortal creatures seek and find a human
Face in the Deity to welcome us.

A Man like to me

Thou shalt love and be loved by for ever: a hand like this hand
Shall throw open the gates of new life to thee! See the Christ stand!

NOTE. Nothing in the discussion of Mausbach, *Ethik*, i. 69–79
(*Die himmlische Gottschauung in ihrem Unterschiede von der neu-
platonischen*), seems to me to touch this vital question. The chapter
of Pourrat, in *La Spiritualité Chrétienne*, i. 354–75 (*Le Christ
dans la Spiritualité*), is true enough. The person of Christ is vital
for the religious life of St. Augustine and in his teaching. But not
at the supreme moment of contemplation. I do not in general
contend for the Ritschlian objection to mysticism. But in the
spirituality of Augustine the objection appears to be justified:

[1] *Tract. xcviii in Joan.*; cf. Cayré, *La Contemplation Augustinienne*,
155.

'According to Mysticism Christ leads the man who becomes His disciple up to the threshold of blessedness. But then the mystic steps across that threshold, and at the highest point of the inner life, he has no longer to do with Christ but with God, for when a man really finds God he finds himself alone with Him. . . . Christ must vanish from the soul along with all else that is external.' (Herrmann, *Communion with God*, E. tr. 30, 31.) Cf. Mozley, *Ritschlianism*, 162.

CHAPTER XI

AFTER AUGUSTINE

Felix qui meruit ad quartum gradum amoris usque pertingere, quatenus nec se ipsum diligat homo nisi propter Deum.

s. BERNARD, *De diligendo Deo*, x.

THE great writers of the West set forth an ideal of the Christian life which differs only in details from that of Augustine. That has been proved by Dom Cuthbert Butler in his study of St. Gregory the Great, and St. Bernard of Clairvaux.[1] It is, therefore, unnecessary to pass in review every mystical writer of this long period. Can it be shown that there is any striking variety of type in the conception of the ideal in the centuries that lie between St. Augustine and St. Thomas? The learned M. l'Abbé Pourrat divides the spirituality of the Middle Ages into three schools.[2] The first he calls practical and emotional. It is the piety of St. Bernard. The second is speculative; its supreme representatives are the Victorines, Hugh and Richard, and St. Thomas Aquinas. The third was inspired by Hugh of St. Victor and sought to unite the intellectual, speculative piety with that of the heart. The great name here is that of St. Bonaventura. Thus the three schools of piety would correspond to the three chief monastic orders—the Benedictines, the Dominicans (with whom must be grouped the Canons of St. Augustine) and the Franciscans. These Hegelian categories are unsatisfactory for our purpose. In the first place the affective practical piety of St. Bernard cannot be regarded as merely Benedictine. 'It was the mysticism of the Church in the West in those days, and Benedictines quite naturally adopted it.'[3] Secondly, the piety of St. Gregory, the Benedictine *par excellence*, was of the same type as that of

---

[1] *Western Mysticism.* The teaching of the three writers is summarized as (1) pre-Dionysian, (2) pre-scholastic, (3) free from visions, locutions, and revelations, (4) free from ecstasy or trance, (5) free from lesser psychophysical concomitants of mystic states, (6) without thought of the Devil.

[2] *La Spiritualité Chrétienne*, ii, Préface.

[3] Butler, *Western Mysticism*, 190.

St. Augustine, at least in its predominantly intellectual character. 'There is, in contemplation, a great effort of the mind.'[1] Gregory's teaching on recollection and introversion, both activities of the mind, is like that of Augustine. Thirdly, it would be possible to maintain that St. Bonaventura was far more allied in spirit to St. Bernard than to any speculative piety. As the Abbé Pourrat himself says: 'Il n'est donc pas un intellectualiste au sens strict; il cultive beaucoup plus la volonté que l'esprit'.[2] For all these reasons we must seek elsewhere some clue to guide us in the historical development of the doctrine of the ideal.

I. DIONYSIUS THE AREOPAGITE

Let us take the first hint of Dom Cuthbert Butler. The influence of the works of Dionysius,[3] the pseudo-Areopagite, was far-reaching. It was perhaps the more potent inasmuch as his thought was Neoplatonic in its origin, and therefore was well adapted to intensify and reinforce the ideas of St. Augustine.[4] God in his system is absolutely transcendent. He is the cause of all, but is literally beyond all qualities. 'His superessential and Supernatural Being altogether transcends the creatures whatever their nature and essence.'[5] 'He transcends both time and eternity.'[6] Man can have no absolute conception of God as the subject of thought, but he can be united with Him by ecstasy. 'We must be transported wholly out of ourselves, and given unto God. For 'tis better to belong unto God, and not unto ourselves, since thus will the Divine bounties be bestowed if we are united to God.' Perfection means for God that His Being 'possesseth in Itself and from Itself distinctive Uniformity of Its existence . . . and that in Its transcendence It is beyond Perfection.'[7] Therefore human

---

[1] *Hom. in Ezech.* ii. 2. 12. (Quoted Butler, *Benedictine Monachism*, 83.)
[2] ii. 266. [3] Quotations from the edition of C. E. Rolt (1920).
[4] Harnack, *History of Dogma*, iv. 337–9.
[5] *Divine Names*, xi. 6; Rolt, 180.
[6] Ibid. v. 10; Rolt, 143.
[7] Ibid. xiii. 1; Rolt, 184.

perfection is to soar upwards, and plunge into the Darkness which is above the intellect.[1] The true initiate is
plunged into the 'Darkness of Unknowing (ἀγνωσία)
wherein he renounces all the apprehensions of his understanding, and is enwrapped in that which is wholly intan-
gible and invisible, belonging wholly to Him that is
beyond all things and to none else (whether himself or
another) and being through the passive stillness of all his
reasoning powers united by his highest faculty to Him
that is wholly Unknowable, of whom thus by a rejection
of all knowledge he possesses a knowledge that exceeds his
understanding.'[2]

Westcott said of Dionysius that however devotedly he
studied Proclus or Damascius, he studied them as a
Christian. 'He starts always from the Bible and not from
Plato.'[3] Even this highly dubitable judgement is irrelevant.
The more significant question is: where did he end? And
the ideal of Dionysius is certainly not the Christian ideal.
Yet owing to the discipleship of Johannes Scotus Erigena
and through the commentaries of Hugh of St. Victor, of
Thomas Aquinas, of Albertus Magnus, his writings came
to a position of extraordinary influence, and his authority
is quoted by medieval writers as decisive.

II. THE JESUS-MYSTICISM OF ST. BERNARD
OF CLAIRVAUX

The second fresh influence which dominated the religious life of the Middle Ages was the life of St. Bernard.
Ritschl has said[4] that no one can win any understanding
of Catholicism without a knowledge of Bernard's sermons
on the Song of Songs. With the Bernardine mysticism
there entered into the piety of the Middle Ages a warmer,
more intimate, more personal note. It is interesting to
observe that thus religion recovered what it was in danger
of losing if the thought of Dionysius had been allowed to

---

[1] *Mystical Theology*, c. iii; Rolt, 198.   [2] Ibid. i. 3; Rolt, 194.
[3] *Religious Thought in the West*, 187.
[4] *Geschichte des Pietismus* (Bonn, 1880), i. 46.

prevail without any counter-balancing influence. In the
system of the pseudo-Areopagite there is virtually no place
for Christ. In the piety of St. Bernard (who, fortunately,
shows no traces of any knowledge of Dionysius[1]) Jesus
Himself returns to the devotion of His people. The way
had been prepared by some representatives of the new
races which had been streaming into the civilization of
Christendom. It was from St. Augustine that the new
writers drew their inspiration. Ratherius of Verona (died
974) shows an intense practical interest in personal religion.
He lays stress on the necessity of conversion; he trusts in
the grace of God, he doubts himself. In his works, says
Rudolf Seeberg, we see the individual soul coming to its
own.[2] Othloh of St. Emmeram (died about 1083) tells of
his own experiences like an early Methodist.[3] In his
temptations he has 'experienced'—the very word occurs—
the power and presence of God.[4] So too Ivo of Chartres
'experiences' the power of the Cross.[5] William of St.
Thierry says that 'the mind cannot grasp what experience
has not attained'.[6]

In St. Bernard we hear the note of attainment and certainty clearly sounded. In the contemplation of the Passion of our Lord, as also in the humility of His earthly life,
we can rest.[7] Here we can find the love of God and feel
our sins forgiven.

When I name Jesus I set before my mind a man meek and lowly
of heart, kind and collected, chaste and pitiful, conspicuous for all
goodness and sanctity and that very same Man I see as God
omnipotent Who shall heal me by His example and strengthen me
by His aid.[8]

There is nothing more powerful for healing the wounds
of conscience and for purging the mind than earnest

---

[1] Butler, *Western Mysticism*, 181. Cf. Seeberg, *Lehrbuch*, iii. 133,
note 1.
[2] *Lehrbuch der Dogmengeschichte*, iii. 120. See Migne, *P.L.* 136. 575.
[3] Migne, *P.L.* 146. 32, *Libellus de suis tentationibus*.
[4] Ibid. 38.   [5] Ibid. 162. 566.
[6] *Spec. fid.* Migne, 180. 396. Many other interesting examples of the
religious use of the word are given in the learned note of Seeberg, *Lehrbuch*,
iii. 122–3.   [7] *In cant. S.* 43. 3, 4; 20. 2; 11. 7; 61. 4.   [8] 15. 6.

meditation on the wounds of Christ.[1] The Imitation of
Christ as the way of Christian life is set out by St. Bernard.
His life moves us to imitate it.[2] While His wisdom
teaches us and His love moves us, we know He is near.[3]
It is the humility of Jesus which above all we must imitate.
This is the sum of the Christian life.

This actual imitation of the life of Jesus Christ is a
decisive influence in the doctrine of the ideal. Before
Bernard, Ivo of Chartres[4] had similarly expressed what the
Christian should do in this life. *Quid est deum portare?*
imaginem dei repraesentare, Christum imitari. But none had
preached the ideal with such passion, none had such concentrated energy of life whereby to bring the message
home to the hearts of men. Without any fear of the
reproach of insincerity he could say:

To meditate on [the life and suffering of Jesus Christ] I have
called wisdom; in these I have placed the perfection of righteousness
for me, the fullness of knowledge, the abundance of merits, the riches
of salvation. There is among them for me sometimes a draught of
salutary bitterness, sometimes again a sweet unction of consolation.
In adversities they raise me up, and in prosperity repress my
exuberant delight. . . .

It is for these reasons, that I have them frequently in my mouth,
as you know, and always in my heart, as God knoweth. . . .

In a word my philosophy is this, and it is the loftiest in the world,
to know Jesus and Him Crucified.[5]

Haec mea interim sublimior philosophia, scire Jesum, et Hunc
Crucifixum. The words are aptly engraved on the statue
which stands in his native village near Dijon. There are
few in the history of the Church who, for their passionate
devotion to the Cross, are worthier to be signed with this seal.

It is the more disappointing, therefore, to find that he
deserts the humanity of our Lord when he comes to
describe the higher and rarer levels of Christian attainment
in this life.

The love of the heart is in a certain sense carnal, in that it chiefly
moves the heart of man towards the flesh of Christ, and what Christ

[1] 62. 7.   [2] 15. 6; cf. 43. 4.   [3] 69. 2; cf. 84. 6, 7.
[4] Migne, 162. 576.   [5] *In cant. S.* 43. 4.

in the flesh did and said. The sacred image of the God-Man, either being born or suckled or teaching or dying or rising again, is present to one in prayer, and must needs stir up the soul to the love of virtue. ... But although such devotion to the flesh of Christ is a gift, and a great gift of the Holy Ghost, nevertheless I call it carnal in comparison with that love which does not regard the Word which is Flesh, as the Word which is Wisdom, Justice, Truth, Holiness.[1]

The goal for which Bernard deserts the human life of Christ is the knowledge of God in contemplation, and that knowledge as Augustine had expounded it.[2] The soul must slumber. It warms with the love of something conjectured rather than seen, momentarily (*non tam spectati quam coniectati, idque raptim*).[3] It is an *excessus purae mentis in deum*.[4] The soul must ascend above earthly phantasms.[5] The heaven is opened; new thoughts flow into the heart.[6] All relationship with the other world is suspended. *Tranquillus Deus tranquillat omnia.* 'The soul is not troubled by the needs of the senses, or by piercing care or remorse of conscience or—and this is more difficult—by the phantom of sensible images. This soul when it will return to us will be able to say: *The King brought me into his banqueting chamber.*'[7] This is no ecstasy; there are no visions or auditions. The knowledge of God is the result of the previous discipline and devotion. The effect is experienced in two ways. There is a double *excessus beatae contemplationis: in intellectu unus, et alter in affectu, unus in lumine, alter in fervore, unus in agnitione, alter in devotione.* Those who may thus ascend are only the *perfecti* who are prepared by purity of conscience.[8]

Ritschl[9] has criticized Bernard's statement as being self-centred. He quotes the passage in 69. 8: 'The soul which sees God sees Him as if no other soul were seen by God. In such trust doth the soul take this reciprocal relation between itself and God as that it cares for nothing besides itself and Him.'

But it should be pointed out that there are many other

---

[1] *In cant. S.* 20. 6, 8.   [2] Cf. Pourrat, ii. 104.   [3] *In cant. S.* 18. 6.
[4] 31. 6.   [5] 52. 5.   [6] 74. 5; cf. 69. 6.   [7] 23. 16; cf. 45.
[8] Cf. the description in 74. 5, 6.   [9] *Gesch. des Piet.* i. 59.

passages which insist on the duty of returning to the practical duties of life. The Church must leave the wine of
contemplation and must feed her children with the milk
of knowledge.[1]

Often enough we ask for one thing and get another—long for
the repose of contemplation and are given the laborious task of
preaching—long for the Bridegroom's presence and are given the
task of bringing forth and nourishing His children instead. . . . The
embrace of divine contemplation must often be interrupted in order
to give nourishment to the little ones, and none may live for himself
alone but for all.[2]

At the same time the emphasis on the super-earthly,
and on the emancipation from all mental images, the
retreat from the thought of others, the desertion of the
humanity of our Lord at the highest moment of communion—all these are symptoms of a serious defect in the
monastic ideal. It never reached a satisfactory doctrine of
this world and the good things in this world.

In his *De diligendo Deo* St. Bernard declares that the
highest kind of love is impossible in this life. He has outlined four degrees. The first is the natural love that a man
has for himself. The second is the love of God for the
benefits He gives. The third is to love God for His own
goodness, without excluding the thought of His goodness
towards us.

At this third degree one remains a long time. I do not know
whether any man has arrived perfectly at the fourth stage when one
only loves oneself for the sake of God. If there are any who have
experienced it, let them speak; for myself, I confess, it appears to
me impossible.[3]

St. Bernard's doctrine would not have satisfied St.
Augustine. There must be something defective in this
statement of the ideal, if perfect love can never be reached,
even for a single moment in this life, by the grace of God.
And partly owing to this scepticism, partly owing to his
forsaking of the thought of the earthly life of our Lord at

[1] *In cant. S.* 9. 7 and 8.   [2] 41. 5.   [3] 15. 39.

the climax of his attainment, the edifice of devotion reared by Bernard for the shelter of the faithful was not so homely and hospitable in its atmosphere as he would have wished. It is usually rarer, and as Ritschl observes it was rarer among the monks and nuns of the Middle Ages, to attain to true spiritual freedom than to remain in the lowlands of abasement and humiliation. Attainment need not have been so rare, if only Bernard had recognized that one who is in communion with a living Lord through meditation on His Passion is already in possession of the secret of victory over the world.

CHAPTER XII

ST. THOMAS AQUINAS

Ultima hominis felicitas non consistit nisi in contemplatione Dei.
Summa contra Gentiles, iii. 37.

OF all theologians St. Thomas is most dominated by the thought of the ultimate perfection of mankind. One of his primary convictions is that the very nature and constitution of man contain an implicit promise of the attainment of his true end. But the goal postulated by human nature cannot be attained without revelation.[1] It is therefore in the Natural Theology of St. Thomas, as distinct from the Theology of Revelation, that we must look first of all, in order to discover the regulative influence of the idea of perfection upon his mind.

For reasons into which we need not now enter, Aquinas appropriated Aristotle's conception of God. God is the unmoved source of motion. 'On this principle', said Aristotle himself, 'all heaven and nature hang.'[2] It is indeed a principle not without its meaning for to-day in the light of the problems presented by modern science.[3] But in the thought of Aristotle the principle means far less than in the system of Aquinas. Aristotle defines the pure actuality which is God as νόησις νοήσεως.[4] God is at once subject and object of thought. He therefore thinks only Himself. In Him no other activity is possible, and in this ceaseless self-contemplation lies the divine pleasure which, says Aristotle, is 'always one, that is, simple'.[5] To think anything other than Himself would be to lower Himself. 'He would abdicate His essential changelessness.'[6]

---

[1] Compare the excellent treatment of Professor C. C. J. Webb, *Studies in the History of Natural Theology* (Oxford, Clarendon Press, 1915), especially 276–80. The whole essay on St. Thomas (233–91) is masterly.

[2] *Metaphysica*, xi, cap. 7 (1072*b*, 13, 14). Cf. Dante, *Par.* xxiv. 130 ff.

[3] See Wicksteed, *Reactions*, 232–4.

[4] *Metaph.* xi. cap. 9, 1074*b*.

[5] *Nic. Eth.* vii. 4, 1154*b*.

[6] R. Downey, in *St. Thomas Aquinas* (Cambridge, 1924), 77.

But Aquinas does not set God in this splendid remoteness from the affairs of men. In the *Summa contra Gentiles*, with amazing penetration and dialectical power he devotes all his mind to remoulding his Aristotelian principle till it becomes the Christian idea of God.[1] God has knowledge even of the most trivial things, and such knowledge does not diminish, or derogate from, the nobility of God. Rather does it belong unto His perfection.[2] God is not only the remote final cause towards which all things move. He is through His knowledge the efficient cause of all movement. 'Since God is the cause of things by His knowledge, His knowledge is extended as far as His causality extends. As the active power of God extends itself not only to forms, which are the source of universality, but to matter, the knowledge of God must extend itself to singular things, which are individualized by matter.'[3] And so it is that the God Who is Form without matter, pure actuality, absolute perfection, can take note of the sparrow's fall and care for His wandering children.[4]

For our present purpose it is enough to show that in appropriating to his own purposes Aristotle's conception of God as unmoved source of motion, Aquinas is led to assert the determining fact of the nature of man. In the third book of his most important treatise, the *Summa contra Gentiles*, he shows that *omne agens agit propter finem*. Every creature is directed by God to the attainment of its end, and that end is its 'good'.[5] The *summum bonum* is the end to which all things by their very nature and constitution must tend.[6] This end is God. All things tend to become like God (*ultimus rerum finis sit Deo assimilari,*

---

[1] *Summa contra Gentiles*, Book I, cc. l–liv and lxiii–lxxi. On the greatness of this achievement see Seeberg, *Lehrbuch der Dogmengeschichte*, iii. 369–70.

[2] *Summa contra Gentiles*, Book I, c. lxx.

[3] *Summa Theol.* I, q. xiv, a. 11; cf. a. 8.

[4] In the *De veritate*, q. ii, a. v, when handling the same question, Aquinas appeals to the experience of St. Paul who had said: 'Then shall I know, even as also I have been known.'

[5] *Summa contra Gentiles*, Book III, cc. ii and iii.

[6] Ibid., Book III, c. xvii.

c. xix). This means like the goodness of God. It is impossible that created things could ever be like God in His inmost essence. God is the only One of whom it can be said that to be, and to be good, are precisely the same. Created things have being. But to attain their perfection, they must be improved in the various and manifold respects in which they fall short of the ideal (c. xx).

In the second place, the ultimate perfection of mankind is deduced from the Christian idea of God as Love. 'In hoc vero quod aliquis amat alium, vult bonum illi; et sic utitur eo tanquam se ipso, referens bonum ad illum sicut ad se ipsum.'[1] This love is behind all the ordering of the world, and wills the supreme good of the creatures loved.[2]

In the third place, the dominant influence of the idea of perfection on the theology of St. Thomas is proved by his description of the age of innocence, the original harmony from which Adam fell. Dr. Wicksteed, the famous Unitarian scholar, has said:[3] 'I find it hard to conceive that any one can read Aquinas on the state of innocence and the Fall without having his vision cleared and his aspirations quickened, or without feeling that he has for a moment drawn a breath of the air of the homeland to which he inalienably belongs, even should it be the fact that neither he nor any other has ever yet dwelt there.'

What was the true state of unfallen man? To-day we dare not attempt an answer to this question. For us the myth of Eden is a very lovely child-story from the morning of the human race. We read it as a spiritual parable. But the story itself no longer is a part of our creed. Aquinas himself thought that it was imperative to investigate the nature of unfallen man, and that he had data to proceed upon. God's original purpose for man was traceable in Eden. Adam knew everything, without having learned anything. But his knowledge was natural, and not supernatural. His wisdom was typical and normal, but owing

---

[1] *S.T.* I, q. xx, a. 1, ad 3.
[2] Cf. Seeberg, *Lehrbuch der Dogmengeschichte*, 364–5.
[3] *Reactions*, 536.

to sin no one has ever attained to it since. The knowledge
was miraculously infused, but though miraculous it was
natural, because it was within the range of human
faculties.[1]

Adam was innocent. Innocence means that the 'passions' of the soul, such as love and joy, were free from any
taint of evil. The evil passions of fear and pain did not
beset him. The surging tide of avarice did not beat upon
his soul. Hope was there, and aspiration. But even the
finer emotions which we feel within ourselves are not quite
the same as they were in the state of man's innocency. For
in us there has been an inevitable modification of the inner
life, wrought by the very fact of sin. The *appetitus sen-
sualis*, from which come the passions, is not subject to the
reason. But in the time of innocence all the appetites and
desires were governed by reason.[2]

Reason (*ratio*) which is proper to man, in Aquinas[3]
means less than *intellectus*, which is the characteristic of
angels, and also is shared by men. *Intellectus* is perfect,
ratio imperfect. But *ratio* means more than the ratio-
cinative faculty (*ratiocinatio*). Wicksteed[4] has defined it in
somewhat modern terms as 'the whole range of faculties
that lead us to the recognition of the good, the beautiful,
and the true'. This definition at all events points to the
harmony and balance involved in St. Thomas's doctrine of
human innocence. Dante's spiritual penetration is well
shown when at the entrance to the Earthly Paradise Virgil
says:[5]

> Libero, dritto e sano e tuo arbitrio,
> e fallo fora non fare a suo senno.

> (Free upright and whole is thy will, and 'twere
> a fault not to act according to its prompting.)

Dante needs no external guide henceforward. In Eden the
wise man can follow his own pleasure, sure that the

---

[1] *S.T.* I, q. xciv, a. 3; q. xcv. Cf. Wicksteed, *Reactions*, 533.
[2] *S.T.* I, q. xcv, a. 2; q. xcviii, a. 2, ad 3.
[3] II. II, q. lxxxiii, a. 10, ad. 2. See the discussion of Rousselot, *L'Intel-
lectualisme de Saint Thomas* (Paris, 1924), 56–8.
[4] *Reactions*, 534.   [5] *Purgatorio*, xxvii. 140–1.

unworthy impulse will be resisted. The sweet fruit of divine communion grows on so many boughs that the harmony of man's nature will guide him always aright.[1]

From this picture in the mind of St. Thomas we may infer the influence of the idea of perfection on his theological system. In two ways we see the true perfection of man's nature. In the first place it is a certain original harmony of the human faculties and desires which is to be restored. Secondly, perfection will include in the world to come perfect intellection, a knowledge of the complete range of truth, a knowledge like the knowledge of the holy angels.[2]

From all that has been said it is evident that a profound belief in the action of the intellect, the survey of divine truth, is the most characteristic feature of the theology of Aquinas. This has been called the intellectualism of St. Thomas. Intellectualism does not mean rationalism. On the contrary the two terms are completely opposed.[3] But intellectualism does mean that an intellectual act is the final end of the universe, and that to knowledge is attributed the preponderating part in the formation of the religious life.

The explanation of this intellectualism takes us far back into the past. As early as Clement of Alexandria, the conviction entered the Christian Church that the mind was the only element in man's complex nature which was capable of apprehending or getting into any kind of touch with the divine nature. So too for St. Thomas, following this tradition, there is no communication or fellowship in this life between us and God or the angels. But there is fellowship between us and God in this life in respect of man's mind (*secundum mentem*). This fellowship is imperfect in this life (cf. Philippians iii. 20) but our conversation

---

[1] Cf. *Life of Mandell Creighton*, i. 115. It should be added that to Aquinas the sin of Adam was the desire to possess at once, and contrary to the Divine purpose, the insight of the angels which he was destined some day to enjoy. Adam fell through pride.

[2] Adam did not see God *per essentiam*, when in the garden. *De veritate*, q. xviii, a. 1.   [3] Rousselot, 224.

with God will be perfected in heaven. This fellowship *secundum mentem* includes *caritas* between ourselves and God.[1]

The comprehensiveness of the teaching of St. Thomas Aquinas may be seen by a study of four theses, all of which are essential to his exposition of the Christian ideal. First, the Contemplative Life is superior to the Active Life. Second, Christian perfection consists in Love, and may be attained in this life. Third, God must be loved for His own sake. Fourth, the full perfection of the soul can only be attained in the life beyond the grave.

I. *The Contemplative is superior to the Active Life.* Hardly any truth in the traditional Christian ideal is so liable to be misunderstood, so popularly denied, as this which seems to disparage the active virtues. The saying of Jesus, to which the saints and doctors of the Church continually appeal, *Mary hath chosen the good part*, is not believed, is indeed criticized, by Christians who pride themselves on their orthodoxy. The supremacy (perhaps only temporary) of Western civilization in the modern world, and the persistence of Protestant prejudice are causes deep enough to prevent most Christians from giving any sympathy to the ideal of the contemplative life. Yet, without such sympathy, there can be no appreciation of the genius either of Roman Catholicism or of St. Thomas. Let us begin with two Christian postulates. (1) The life of prayer, of inward communion with God, is the mainspring of the activities of the saints. Ask those who astonish us by their pre-eminence in active missionary or social service: 'How did you do it?' They all give the same answer. From St. Paul to David Livingstone, from the Blessed Elizabeth of Marburg to Elizabeth Fry and Mary Slessor, the secret of exterior action is ascribed to that which is not exterior action. They explain it by an inward communion, by an intercourse with God. (2) This world is transient: 'Passing away saith the world, passing away.' The busy tribes of flesh and blood disappear. Their

[1] See *S.T.* II. ii, q. xxiii, a. 1.

activities are lost in the vast Silence.[1] The great globe itself shall fade away and leave not a wrack behind. But the life of communion with God is not affected by the passing of time nor even by the accident of physical death. These commonplaces of the preacher are the presuppositions of dogma. We may assent to them without really believing them. But taken together the two postulates are enough to bear the weight of the first thesis in the thought of St. Thomas.

It would be unfair to say that St. Thomas disparages the active life. Great are the merits of the active life, he says, quoting Gregory.[2] To the active life pertain all the actions of the moral virtues. By such actions we may do good to our neighbour,[3] and show something of the love divine.[4] Without this love we cannot have perfection, and therefore the active life in some measure is essential for the attainment of perfect love. It is a useful preparation for the life of contemplation.

Those who are more fitted to pursue the active life can thereby be prepared for the contemplative; none the less those who are more fitted for the contemplative life can undergo the discipline (*exercitia*) of the active life in order that thereby they may be rendered still more prepared for contemplation.[5]

The thought of St. Thomas goes farther in welcoming the active life than even these words would indicate. At a later point in the *Summa* he discusses the relative excellence of the various religious orders. He finds a distinction in their active work. One kind of active work flows out from the fullness of contemplation as a river from the lake which is its source. Examples are teaching and preaching. The other kind of active work—almsgiving, hospitality, and the like—consists entirely in outward occupation. Such acts in exceptional cases of necessity may be preferred to contemplation in our scale of values, but normally they are not so excellent. Now it is noteworthy that St. Thomas, a true Dominican, a devoted member and

---

[1] Cf. Greg. *Hom.* xiv *in Ezech.* quoted by Thomas, *S.T.* II. ii, q. clxxxi, a. 4.   [2] *S.T.* II. ii, q. clxxxii, a. 2.   [3] II. ii, q. clxxxi, a. 1.
[4] q. clxxxii, a. 2.   [5] II. ii. q. clxxxii, a. 4 *ad fin.*; E. tr. 144.

brother of the Preaching Friars, gives the highest place to those religious orders which are directed to preaching and teaching. 'This work is more excellent than that of simple contemplation, he says. For even as it is a greater thing to give illumination than merely to shine, so it is a greater thing to pass on to others the fruits of contemplation (*contemplata* = what we have found in our contemplation) than merely to be engaged in contemplation.'[1] So the final 'order of merit' is, first, those orders which are devoted to preaching and teaching, second, those which are directed to contemplation, and third, those which are occupied with external actions.

There is thus a double movement in the ideal life as it may be lived here on earth. The mind ascends to contemplation and then passes back to the active life to communicate the fruit of the knowledge of God.

Contemplation is defined as *simplex intuitus veritatis*. If all truth were unveiled to man in this life, contemplation would be but a single act.[2] Pseudo-Dionysius had taught that herein was the difference between man and angel.[3] An angel perceives the truth by simple apprehension, whereas man arrives at the perception of a simple truth by a process from several premises. To see all truth in a single act, a *simplex intuitus*, would thus be the goal of the contemplative life. So might a geographer arrive at that point of knowledge when he can look at the map and in a single act contemplate all the geographical facts in their coherence, their mutual relation, and their diversity. But many acts would be necessary ere he arrived at that topmost pinnacle of knowledge. So too the contemplative life has many acts whereby it arrives at the final act.[4] 'Some of these relate to the reception of principles from which it goes on to contemplate the truth; others are concerned with deducing from the principles till the mind arrives at

---

[1] *S.T.*, II. ii. q. clxxxviii, a. 6. [2] q. clxxx, a. 3 and a. 6.
[3] *De Div. Nom.* vii. 2; Rolt, 148.
[4] *S.T.* II. ii, q. xlv, a. 3, ad. 3. See other passages in Durantel, *Le Retour à Dieu par l'Intelligence et la Volonté dans la Philosophie de S. Thomas* (Paris 1918), 272.

the truth of which knowledge is sought. The last act, consummating the whole, is the contemplation of the truth' (q. clxxx, a. 3).

The very illustration—that of the geographer—which I have used to elucidate the meaning of St. Thomas, reminds us that on its purely intellectual side, contemplation is akin to all knowledge. But as we shall see, contemplation is never 'merely intellectual', in the modern sense of the word. There is always a passion of love in it. In speaking of the Divine Indwelling, St. Thomas admits that there is a sense in which God is in all things. His essence, His power, His presence pervade the universe, as the operative cause of all effects which participate in the Divine goodness. But beyond this way of indwelling God is present in man in the special way which befits a rational being. It is by knowing and loving that a rational being reaches out to (*attingit*) God. And in one to whom God is thus an object known and loved God may be said not only to be (*esse*) but to dwell (*habitare*).

In one of his most moving articles (*S.T.* II. ii, q. clxxx, a. 7) St. Thomas asks whether there is delight in contemplation. The answer is that there may be delight in any particular contemplation in two ways. First each individual is so made that he takes delight in doing that which befits his nature and habit. Since contemplation of the truth befits a man according to his nature as a rational animal, all men will have delight in the knowledge of truth. Farther, those for whom contemplation has become a habit, so that they contemplate without struggle and difficulty, will find still greater delight. But in the second place 'contemplation may be delightful on the part of its object, in so far as one contemplates that which one loves, even as bodily vision gives pleasure, not only because to see is pleasurable in itself, but because one sees a person whom one loves. Since then, the contemplative life consists chiefly in the contemplation of God, of which love (*caritas*) is the motive, it follows that there is delight in the contemplative life, not only by reason of the contemplation itself, but also by reason of the Divine Love.' When we see one whom we

love, we are so aflame as to love him more. So says St.
Gregory the Great, whom St. Thomas feelingly quotes.
And then he sums up his result by saying: 'This is the
ultimate perfection of the contemplative life, that the
Divine truth be not only seen but also loved.'

II. Our second main thesis is that *Christian perfection
consists in love*. But this statement goes beyond any statement yet quoted from St. Thomas. He has been careful
to say that love is the motive of the contemplative life. He
is careful not to confuse love with the contemplation of
truth. In the former articles of the same *Quaestio* (II. 11.
clxxx) he sets the essence of the contemplation of truth in
the intellect, but the motive of the action is in the will.
The moral virtues, love of God and love of neighbour, do
not pertain to the essence of the contemplative life. The
reason for this is that the moral virtues are directed to
external actions. But the contemplative life involves rest
from external actions. Therefore, the moral actions do not
pertain to the contemplative life.[1] Their function is to
curb the impetuosity of the passions which withdraw the
soul's attention from truth to things seen. The love of
God and our neighbour is requisite to the contemplative
life as a motive cause. But motive causes do not enter into
the essence of a thing. They dispose and perfect it.

Aquinas proceeds to say that the perfection of the
Christian life consists chiefly in love. This is the theme of
Quaestio 184. It is love that unites us to God, Who is the
last end of the human mind. Similarly in his discussion of
the virtues (I. 11, q. lxvi, a. 6) he says *in his quae sunt supra
hominem nobilior est dilectio quam cognitio*. There is more
than a verbal contradiction in his thought at this point.
The discrepancy may arise from his deeply felt distinction
between the perfection possible in this life and the final
beatitude of heaven. He introduces his interesting doctrine of the *Status Perfectionis*, and points out that there are
three states or stages in the spiritual life, culminating in
the state of perfection whereunto the other states are
directed. Is it possible that he looks upon a love which

[1] Art. 2.

issues in external action as the perfection which is possible
here below, but the contemplative life motived by love as
the supreme perfection possible to us in the eternal world?
It would probably be more satisfactory to trace our difficulty to its source in that other problem in the study of
St. Thomas, the relation between the intelligence and the
will. As M. Durantel has pointed out,[1] it is possible to
adduce many passages decisively proving the primacy of
the intelligence, and then again other passages equally
decisive in proving the primacy of the will. But his mind
is constantly at work to show how will and intelligence
co-operate in the return to God which is the goal and home
of the human soul. The ultimate act of mankind is an act
of the intellect. To the will is assigned the motive and
tendency towards the end, by which the soul desires the
attainment of the end, and finally the resting in the will of
God, the silencing of itself, when the end shall have been
attained.[2]

Love is the bond of perfection (Col. iii. 14) because it
binds the other virtues together in perfect unity.[3] We are
never far away from the great medieval ideal of the perfect
and harmonious co-operation of all the faculties of man.
But the love of which Aquinas speaks is always a theological virtue. Love is given by God. Love means love for
God and for one's neighbours in God. *Caritas* is primarily
and specifically *amor Dei*. God communicates His own
beatitude to man, and a certain friendship is founded on
that fact. This is nothing else than Love. So we may call
love a friendship of man with God. This friendship does
not belong to the natural order. It is the gift of God. It
is due to the infusion of the Holy Spirit. The Spirit who
indwells the Christian community is the Spirit whereby
the Father loves the Son and the Son the Father.[4]

Is Perfection possible in this life? Aquinas[5] meets the

---

[1] *Le Retour à Dieu par l'Intelligence et la Volonté dans la Philosophie de
S. Thomas* (Paris, 1918), 376.
[2] Durantel, 385.   [3] *S.T.* II. ii, q. clxxxiv, a. 1.
[4] *S.T.* II. ii, q. xxiii, a. 1; II. ii, q. xxiv, a. 2.
[5] II. ii, q. clxxxiv, a. 2.

same objections as have always been levelled against any teaching of perfection. He meets them first by an appeal and then by some distinctions. The appeal is to the precept of our Lord (Matt. v. 48). The Divine Law, he says, does not prescribe the impossible. What is the meaning of the word perfection? Perfection always implies a certain universality, a totality from which nothing is lacking. And perfection may be threefold. First comes absolute perfection which is to be found in God alone. Another perfection answers to an absolute totality on the part of the lover; in this perfection the soul loves God as much as it possibly can. Nothing is lacking to the love that can ever be there. But all the possibilities of the soul cannot be developed in this life, and therefore this kind of perfection is not for us so long as we are on the way. We shall have it in heaven.

The third perfection refers to the removal of obstacles to the movement of love towards God. . . . Such perfection may be had in this life, and in two ways. First by the removal from man's affections of all that is contrary to love, such as mortal sin; and there can be no love apart from this perfection, and therefore it is necessary for salvation. Secondly, by the removal from man's affections, not only of whatever is contrary to love, but also of whatever hinders the mind's affections from tending wholly to God. Love is possible apart from this perfection, for instance in those who are beginners, and in those who are proficient.

The article just quoted gives us the fullest account of the idea of perfection, in so far as it is possible in this world, which is to be found in the *Summa Theologica*. But we are fortunate in possessing another work from the pen of St. Thomas, which is at once less systematic and more detailed and popular. This is the *De perfectione*. Here perfection is understood as the love of God and love of our neighbour. It is in love (*caritas*) that perfection principally depends. After the same division of perfection as that given in the *Summa*, he defines the perfection of divine love which is possible in this life, and necessary to salvation (c. v). We so love God if there is nothing in us which is wanting to divine love, that is, if there is nothing which we do not actually or habitually refer to God. All our

actions are directed to God. Our understanding is subjected to Him. All our affections are referred to the love
of Him. All our words and works are established in the
divine love (c. v). So far perfection is a matter of precept,
and is incumbent upon all of us.

But there are various counsels of perfection; the renunciation of earthly possessions, the renunciation of earthly
ties and of matrimony, and the abnegation of our own will.
And these three counsels are followed pre-eminently by
those who belong to the religious orders, and have taken
upon themselves the three vows of poverty, chastity, and
obedience.

On this exposition of the idea of perfection two criticisms
remain to be stated. First, the influence of the Platonic
inheritance of St. Augustine on the mind of St. Thomas is
deeper than was formerly recognized, deeper indeed than
was realized by St. Thomas himself. Indeed some of the
chief modern students of Aquinas are coming to see his
work as 'a masterly synthesis of both Plato and Aristotle
with one another and with St. Augustine, effected by
original insight of the first order'.[1] The Platonist is so
interested in the other world of the eternal and unseen
ideas that he often regards this world with its desires and
struggles as a bad dream, or a mere passing shadow. This
tendency is certainly carried far by St. Augustine. And it
is noteworthy that in the central passage of his description
of perfection, when he is describing the possibility of
the banishment of evil things from the soul, St. Thomas
appeals to St. Augustine. *Venenum caritatis est cupiditas;
perfectio nulla cupiditas.* But it is not in bodily desires that
the evil of human nature consists; nor is it in the denial of
them that perfection consists.[2]

Secondly, the whole description of perfection is confused and marred both in the *Summa* and in the *De perfectione* with discussions of the relative merits of those who

[1] Professor A. E. Taylor, *St. Thomas Aquinas as a Philosopher* (Oxford,
1924), 24.
[2] *S.T.* II. ii. q. clxxxiii, a. 2 *Carnal desire* is the translation given to
cupiditas by the Dominican Fathers. Cf. *De Perfectione*, c. ix.

are in religious orders, bishops, and other ecclesiastics. St. Thomas attempts to prove that bishops are in 'the state of perfection' because their office gives them the power of conferring grace and enlightenment on others. They are 'perfecters', while members of the orders are in the position of being perfected. He actually forms a hierarchy of the state of perfection, wherein bishops come first, the religious orders second, parish priests and arch-deacons third.[1] And in the *De perfectione* (c. xii) he attempts to prove that 'that man merits far more from God who acts under vow than he who is not under any such obligation'. This introduction of the notion of merit from God in virtue of a vow is far from the former description of perfection as love infused by the indwelling Spirit of God.

Of course, no Protestant writer should ever ignore the fact that St. Thomas considered that all human beings could attain to perfection, apart from vows and orders. And he expressly states that bishops who are in a state of perfection themselves may be most deficient in the perfection of love. Their real guilt is not that they are imperfect after they have entered on 'the state of perfection', but through withdrawing their minds from the intention of reaching perfection. But the impression left by the reading of the *De perfectione* is irresistible. The 'religious state' is the short cut to perfection. Any one who is wise will take the vows. His very concessions to the inferior clergy leave the same impression on the mind. It is more difficult to lead a good life together with the exercise of the cure of souls, on account of outward dangers, and to keep oneself innocent in face of a greater peril is proof of greater virtue. Nevertheless, the sacred orders are better.[2]

The effect of a doctrine such as this is to discourage the quest for perfection on the high places of the field, in the throng and press of life. It ignores the old truth

> Es bildet ein Talent sich in der Stille
> Sich ein Charakter in dem Strom der Welt.

---

[1] *S.T.* II. ii, q. clxxxiv, a. 7 and 8.　　　　[2] II. ii, q. clxxxiv, a. 8.

III. The third main thesis is that *God must be loved for His own sake*. St. Bernard had expounded this. St. Thomas takes up the truth and handles it with his usual balance and sanity. It is true that he does not include any discussion of Pure Love in that passage in the *Secunda Secundae* where he definitely deals with perfection. But it is obviously vital to any attempt to set forth the richness of the idea of perfection in his thought.

There is a distinction between perfect and imperfect love. Perfect love is that whereby a man is loved for his own sake (*secundum se*). If a man, for example, loves a friend, he will wish his friend some good for his own sake. On the other hand imperfect love is that whereby a man loves something, not for its own sake, but that he may obtain that good thing for himself. For example, a man may be said to love what he desires. The true love of God (*caritas*) is perfect love, which adheres to God for His own sake. The other kind of love has more of the element of hope in it.[1] The love which springs from desire cannot be a perfect love. It is a result of self-love.[2]

The question may be asked how we can be said to wish good to God, as a man, in his disinterested love, may wish good to his friend. God is the source and fount of all good; in His infinite fullness there is no deficiency. Caietan (Comm. in II. II, q. xxiii, a. 1) answers this in a way of which Aquinas would have approved.[3] There is a distinc tion in the meaning of this good that we can will God to have; it may mean 'the good that is in Him and the good that is simply referred to God. The good that is in Him is His Life, His Wisdom, His Righteousness, His Mercy.' Strictly speaking this is God Himself, and we can by Love will Him to have that good when we find our delight in the fact that God is what He is. The good that is simply referred to God is His Kingdom, the obedience due to Him. This good we can will for Him, not only by finding our delight

---

[1] *S.T.* II. II, q. xvii, a. 8.
[2] I. II, q. xxvi, a. 4; q. xxvii, a. 3.
[3] Quoted by Deharbe, *Die Vollkommene Liebe Gottes*, 89. Compare von Hügel, *Mystical Element*, ii. 162.

in it, but by working with all our powers at its maintenance and increase.

This is perfect Love according to St. Thomas. It is 'the most excellent of all the virtues' because more than Faith or Hope it attains to God.[1] It is true, of course, that the good towards which Hope yearns is God. 'We hope for nothing less from God than Himself,'[2] when we hope for the supreme good of eternal happiness. But 'Love attains God Himself that it may abide in Him (*ut in ipso sistat*), and not that something may accrue to us from Him'.[3] Faith and Hope, on the other hand, do attain to God Himself, but to God as the source from which the knowledge of the truth and the acquisition of the good come to us.[4] So it is that

> Faith will vanish into sight,
> Hope be emptied in delight.

But because Love implies an abiding in God, it is more immediate than Faith or Hope in its attainment of its end.

The same characteristic is noted by Aquinas in his analysis of the effects of Love.[5] He shows how union and divine indwelling result from Love, and his firm insistence is all the more noteworthy because, unlike the Mystics, he does not naturally or readily employ metaphors of union in speaking of the relationship of the soul to God. In discussing union his language is guarded and precise. The union of lover and beloved is twofold. The first is real union, for example, when the lover is present with the beloved; the second union is the union of affection. In this case love itself is the union or bond. The real union is the result of perfect love; it is to live together, to speak together, and be united in other like things.

The mutual indwelling which is the effect of love may refer both to the apprehensive and to the appetitive power. The beloved may abide in the apprehension of the lover, just as the Philippians were in the heart of St. Paul. The

---

[1] *S.T.* II. ii, q. xxiii, a. 6. [2] II. ii, q. xvii, a. 2.
[3] II. ii, q. xxiii, a. 6.
[4] Compare *S.T.* II. ii, q. xxviii, a. 1, ad 3.
[5] I. ii, q. xxviii, a. 1.

lover is in the beloved, in this sense, inasmuch as he strives to gain an intimate knowledge of everything pertaining to the beloved, so as to penetrate into his very soul. From the point of view of the emotions, the object loved is said to be in the lover when it is in his affections, *per quandam complacentiam*. He takes pleasure in it or in its good. The lover is in the beloved by the love of desire (*per amorem concupiscentiae*) or by the love of friendship. The love of desire seeks to possess the beloved perfectly, by entering into his very heart. In the love of friendship the lover is in the beloved, inasmuch as he reckons what is good or evil to his friend as being so to himself; and his friend's will as his own, so that it seems as though he felt the good or suffered the evil in the person of his friend.[1]

The foregoing description of the meaning of mutual indwelling is in reality the exposition which St. Thomas gives of the Johannine text: *He that abideth in love abideth in God, and God in him.* We notice first, that even in commenting on such a text he never blurs the distinction between man and God. And, second, that the possibility of a pure or disinterested love of God is everywhere implied. Elsewhere[2] Aquinas endorses Augustine on this very point. *Frui est amore inhaerere alicui propter seipsum* (*De doctr.* i. 4). God is to be enjoyed. Therefore God is to be loved for Himself. God may be loved immediately, and other things may be loved through God.[3] God may be loved wholly (*totaliter*), according to the powers of finite creatures. No creature can love God infinitely, because all power of creatures is finite.[4]

IV. *Full perfection is in the Life beyond the grave.* We have already seen that the full development of the soul's powers is only possible in the life to come.[5] The finality of Scripture for St. Thomas[6] is seen in his treatment of the Beatific Vision, *We shall see Him as He is. We now see as in a mirror, darkly, but then face to face.*[7] These are the

---

[1] *S.T.* I. ii, q. xxviii, a. 2.   [2] *S.T.* II. ii, q. xxvii, a. 3.
[3] Ibid., a. 4.   [4] Ibid., a. 5.
[5] Ibid., q. clxxxiv, a. 2.   [6] Cf. Harnack, vi. 156.
[7] *S.T.* III, q. xcii, a. 1.

promises on which his theology depends. God will not be seen with the bodily eyes.[1] The soul will see God but will not see all that God sees.[2] The distinction of the creature from the Creator is preserved in the future life. But the most interesting position of St. Thomas for our present purpose is his affirmation of the reality of the heavenly body. The happiness of the saints will be greater after the Judgement than before 'because their happiness will be not only in the soul, but also in the body'.[3] After the resurrection all in the body that hampers the full perfection of the soul will be removed. The union of the body with the soul adds a certain perfection to the soul.

Now the more perfect a thing is in being, the more perfectly is it able to operate: wherefore the operation of the soul united to such a body will be more perfect than the operation of the separated soul. But the glorified body will be a body of this description, being altogether subject to the spirit. Therefore, since happiness consists in an operation, the soul's happiness after its reunion with the body will be more perfect than before.[4]

The distinction of this statement is that St. Thomas thereby escapes from that tendency in his teaching which emphasizes abstraction from the things of sense, and conceives of the ideal life as more or less purely intellectualist and contemplative.[5]

Can we say that the social bliss of the redeemed in heaven is dwelt upon and emphasized as though it were congenial to the mind of our Angelic Doctor? It must be regretfully admitted that he seems to contemplate a *solus cum solo* beatitude.

If we speak of the happiness of this life, a happy man needs friends . . . that he may do good to them; that he may delight in seeing them do good; and again that he may be helped by them in his good work. . . .

But if we speak of perfect happiness which will be in our heavenly

---

[1] *S.T.* III, q. xcii, a. 2.   [2] Ibid., a. 3.   [3] Ibid., q. xciii, a. 1.
[4] Ibid., a. 1.
[5] See von Hügel, *Eternal Life*, 106–9 on the two contradictory tendencies in the ideal of St. Thomas. Cf. *S.T.* I. ii, q. iv, a. 6.

Fatherland, the fellowship of friends is not essential to happiness; since man has the entire fullness of his perfection in God. But the fellowship of friends conduces to the well-being of happiness. . . .

Perfection of charity is essential to happiness, as to the love of God, but not as to the love of our neighbour. Wherefore if there were but one soul enjoying God, it would be happy, though having no neighbour to love.[1]

So far as I can discover there is no passage in the *Summa Theologica* which neutralizes the anti-social affirmation of this article. There are passages in his works which imply another and a more Christian doctrine.

A thing is most perfect when it can make another like unto itself. That shines perfectly which can illuminate other things.[2]

It pertains to the nature of the will to communicate as far as possible to others the good possessed; and especially does this pertain to the divine will, from which all perfection is derived in some kind of likeness.[3]

Love, joy, delight . . . are in God . . . Love causes the lover to wish the beloved good, . . . Love is the unitive force, even in God. . . . So far love is a binding force since it aggregates another to ourselves and refers his good to our own.[4]

God, the cause of all things, by his abounding love and goodness is placed outside himself by his providence for all existing things.[5]

These passages imply a doctrine of heaven which would allow for the perpetuation of human friendship and a real *communio sanctorum*. But the consequences of this more Christian idea seem not to have been realized by St. Thomas. We have a curious result. The ideal which he sketches as realizable in the present life is, in this one respect at least, superior to the fuller beatitude in the life beyond.

[1] *S.T.* I. ii, q. iv, a. 8.
[2] *Summa contra Gentiles*, iii, cap. 21, *ad fin.*
[3] *S.T.* I, q. xix, a. 2.   [4] Ibid., I, q. xx, a. 1.   [5] Ibid., a. 2.

CHAPTER XIII

THE REFORMATION

The whole being of any Christian man is Faith and Love. . . . Faith brings the man to God, Love brings him to men.—Luther.

IN the country which gave birth to the Reformation the word *Perfektionismus* is used by theological writers almost always as a term of reproach. It would seem at a first review of Reformation doctrine that there was no room for any doctrine even of a relative perfection in this world. The Augsburg Confession firmly condemns the Anabaptists for contending that some men may attain to such a perfection in this life that they cannot sin.[1] Luther's *pecca fortiter* is still a formidable weapon when handled by stalwart Catholic apologists.[2] *Peccandum est quamdiu sic sumus; vita haec non est habitatio iustitiae.* Is it possible that in a legitimate protest against a one-sided ideal of monastic perfection, the Reformers neglected to develop any doctrine of their own?

As far as Calvinism is concerned, the answer can be given in a single quotation from the Institutes. Calvin does not deny that the integrity of the believer, though partial and imperfect, is a step to immortality. But he dismisses the Pauline prayers for perfection in believers (quoting 1 Thess. iii. 13).

These words were strongly urged by the Celestines of old in maintaining the perfection of holiness in the present life. To this we deem it sufficient briefly to reply, with Augustine, that the goal to which all the pious ought to aspire is to appear in the presence of God without spot and blemish; but as the course of the present life is at best nothing more than progress, we shall never reach the goal until we have laid aside the body of sin, and been completely united to the Lord. If any one choose to give the name of perfection to the Saints, I shall not obstinately quarrel with him, provided he defines this perfection in the words of Augustine, 'When we speak

[1] Art. xii. Schaff, *Creeds of the Evangelical Protestant Churches* (London, 1877), 14.
[2] See Pourrat, *Christian Spirituality*, iii, 64 (E. tr. 1927).

of the perfect virtue of the saints, part of this perfection consists
in the recognition of our imperfection both in truth and in
humility.'[1]

But the problem is not so easily settled for Lutheranism,
and in the light of the contentions of Ritschl[2] it is impossible to dismiss the Reformation doctrine as negligible.
The classical statements are not numerous, and may be set
out here.

First we have the scattered utterances of Luther.

The state of perfection is to have a lively faith, to be a despiser
of death, life, glory and all the world, and to live in glowing love
as the servant of all men.

Perfectionis status est, esse animosa fide, contemptorem mortis,
vitae, gloriae, et totius mundi, et fervente caritate omnium servum.

(*Werke*, Weimar ed. viii. 584, *De votis monasticis.*)

Better and more perfect is the obedience of son, wife, servant,
captive, than the obedience of a monk, if we are to go on from
imperfection to perfection.

Melior et perfectior est obedientia filii, coniugis, servi, captivi,
quam monachi obœdientia. (Ibid.)

Faith and love—these are the whole being of a Christian man. . . .
Through his faith God does good to him. Through his love he
does good to men.

(*Werke*, Weimar ed. viii. 355.)

'Perfection and imperfection do not depend on works,
. . . but are in the heart, and depend on a man believing
more and loving more. He is perfect, whether he be
outwardly man or woman, prince or peasant, monk or
layman.'

A Christian says: to be perfect means to fear God, and to do all
good to your neighbour. For God has commanded nothing else.

---

[1] *Institutes* (E. tr. 1845), ii. 412. See also Hodge, as quoted by Platt,
E.R.E. ix, art. 'Perfection', 732.
[2] *Geschichte des Pietismus,* i. 38–43; *Rechtfertigung und Versöhnung,* iii
(E. tr. 1902), 168–82, 333–4, 646–70. Seeberg's view has been influenced
by Ritschl; see his inaugural address at Dorpat (*Vom Lebensideal,* 1886)
and *Lehrbuch der Dogmengeschichte,* iv. 268 ff., 409.

These sayings are rare in the writings of Luther. They are mere *obiter dicta*, only drawn from him when he is tilting against monasticism.[1] They do not constitute a doctrine. He acquiesced in the continuance of sin in this life, with more tameness than we should have expected from such a bonny fighter. But the subject is not neglected in the Augsburg Confession. Probably Melanchthon felt that something needed to be said to the world, and some trenchant sentences of Luther were included.[2]

Christian perfection is this, to fear God sincerely, and again to conceive great faith, and to trust that for Christ's sake God is pacified towards us; to ask, and with certainty to look for, help from God in all our affairs, according to our calling; and meantime outwardly to do good works diligently and to attend to our calling. In these things doth consist true perfection and the true worship of God; it doth not consist in celibacy, or mendicancy, or in vile apparel.

In his *Apologia Confessionis Augustanae* Melanchthon takes a line which is not pursued by the theologians of the subsequent age. He says that justification enables a man to fulfil the commandments of the first Table of the Decalogue. These are beyond the ability of the natural man, whereas he may be able to perform the external duties of the second Table. The Christian virtues which a justified man can fulfil are those already quoted in the Augsburg Confession.[3] The first three Commandments are defined as (i) true reverence, faith, and love towards God, (ii) true invocation of God, (iii) true judgement that God hears our prayers.[4] We are to trust in God under all sufferings and have patience in them. Ritschl points out that Luther's exposition in his Catechism agrees with that of Melanchthon.[5] But it should be noticed that Melanch-

[1] Cf. Ritschl, *Gesch. des Pietismus*, i. 39.

[2] Art. 27; Schaff, op. cit., 57. Lindsay, *Hist. of Reformation*, i. 367, assigns these sentences to Luther.

[3] *Apol. Conf. Aug.* in *C.R.* xxvii. 443, 448.

[4] See also *Loci communes* (*Corp. Ref.* xxi. 688–711), where the third commandment is *caeremonia divinitus instituta.*

[5] *Justification and Reconciliation*, iii (E. tr.),170; see Schaff, 74, 75.

thon in his *Apologia* goes farther than Luther. He does see that the law requires perfection,[1] and that in Christ we have power to fulfil the law.

Two salient characteristics of the Lutheran doctrine are noticed by Ritschl. First, it distinguishes between the irreligious and the immoral aspect of sin, and subordinates the latter to the former. 'It is possible for Luther to do so, because when explaining the perfection of the first man, he lays more stress on his free and spiritual religion than upon all his other *sapientia et iustitia*.'[2] Second, that the perfect life of a Christian consists in the freedom and kingship which he can enjoy over all outward circumstances in this present world.[3]

Ritschl calls the first note of Luther's doctrine epoch-making, inasmuch as the Scholastics and Augustine had not laid more stress on the religious aspect of perfection than on the moral. In the light of our previous discussions of St. Augustine and St. Thomas, this view is unjustifiable. Further the 'subordination of morality to religion' is an ambiguous phrase. If it means that religion is never to be identified with morality, or that religion provides power for the fulfilment of the moral law, we may accept it gladly. But if it means that the moral aspect of perfection is insignificant or unimportant, the phrase is untrue and dangerous. The second point which Ritschl makes is valid, and we shall return to it later on.

We have not yet done justice to the ideal of life for the present world which Protestantism set before its adherents. If Luther's ideal was defective, if he neglected as Lutheran theologians after him have neglected the problem of sin in the life of believers, there were certain positive elements in his religious teaching which go far to fill the gap.

---

[1] *Lex enim requirit a nobis opera nostra, et perfectionem nostram.* So far as I know this point has escaped notice hitherto. Ritschl does not take account of it. The language of Melanchthon is much more respectful to the law than that of Luther. He evidently felt the pressure of our problem as Luther did not. See *C.R.* xxvii. 435 (*De iustificatione*).

[2] *J. and R.* iii (E. tr.), 171.

[3] Ibid. 646, 647; cf. i. 184 (3rd ed. 1889).

I. The Rediscovery of the Historical Jesus.

In the first place, he rediscovered for piety the humanity of our Lord. Apart from the Gospels and the Epistle to the Hebrews there is nothing in Christian literature before him quite like his vividness, his profound religious feeling for the human life of Jesus Christ. It is there, in that human life, that he finds God. Even Harnack's appreciation of this point does not do justice to Luther. It is a doubtful eulogy to say that 'the great reform which Luther effected, both for faith and theology, was that he made the historical Christ *the sole principle of the knowledge of God*'.[1] But it was a sign of his deep religious insight when Luther's faith held to the human figure of the Gospels and there found God. Even St. Bernard whom Luther so much admired, deserted the humanity of our Lord at the higher stages of contemplation.[2] But the following passages are not easily paralleled in devotional literature.

When I thus imagine Christ, then do I picture Him truly and properly, I grasp and have the true Christ as He pictures Himself; and then I let go utterly all thoughts and speculations concerning the Divine Majesty and glory, and hang and cling to the humanity of Christ; and then there is no fear there, but only friendliness and joy, and I learn thus through Him to know the Father. Thus arises such a light and knowledge within me that I know certainly what God is, and what is His mind.

Quoted by Herrmann, *Communion with God*, E. tr. 143.

For just as the sun shines and illuminates none the less brightly when I close my eyes, so this throne of grace, or this forgiveness of sins, is always there, even although I fall. And just as I see the sun again when I re-open my eyes, so also I have forgiveness of sins once more when I look up and come back to Christ. Wherefore we are not to measure forgiveness so narrowly as fools dream.

Quoted by Herrmann, *Communion with God*, E. tr. 249.

It is hardly possible to exaggerate the significance of this fact in the history of spirituality. All the religious life

[1] *History of Dogma*, vii. 199. See the massive criticism of von Hügel, *Mystical Element*, ii. 263–5, 332–4. Here we have one of the chief defects of Ritschlianism; cf. Mozley, *Ritschlianism*, 90.

[2] Hence Harnack is not quite accurate. *History of Dogma*, vii. 200.

is centred on the Perfect Figure of the Gospels. The usual
Roman Catholic reproaches of subjectivity 'anthropocen-
tric religion'[1] and the like, fall away. Luther knew that this
piety was distinct from that of the Contemplatives.

No one shall taste Deity save as He wills to be tasted; and thus
He wills: to wit, that He shall be looked on in the humanity of
Christ. If thou dost not find the Deity thus, thou shalt never rest.
Hence let them go on speculating and talking about contemplation,
how everything is a wooing of God, and how we are always having
a foretaste of eternal life, and how spiritual souls set about their life
of contemplation. But do not thou learn to know God thus,
I charge thee.

Werke (Erlangen ed.), xxxv. 334.

II. The Mystical Element in Luther's Teaching.

In the second place, Luther's love for the Mystics and
especially for Tauler, gave him an answer to the question:
How can Faith make man holy?[2] His devotion to the
historical Figure of Jesus was thus reinforced by a moral
purification. The best example is to be found in the
treatise, *On Christian Liberty*. He is expounding how
impossibilities become possible for the man who has faith.
The promises of God give that which the precepts exact,
and fulfil what the law commands, so that all is of God
alone, both the precepts and their fulfilment.[3] How is this
done? First, the word of God is united with the soul;
'such as is the word, such is the soul made by it; just as
iron exposed to fire glows like fire, on account of its union
with the fire'.[4] The image is derived from St. Bernard,[5]
who uses it of the transformation of human affection into
the love of God's will. Here Luther explains how Christian
virtues become part of the soul's life. The second office
of faith is that it honours God by ascribing to Him the
glory of being faithful to His promises. In doing this the

[1] See e.g. Pourrat, *Christian Spirituality*, iii (E. tr.), 70.
[2] The influence of the Mystics on Luther is traced by H. Hering, *Die Mystik Luthers* (Leipzig, 1879). I am indebted to this book for the suggestions of this paragraph.
[3] Wace and Buchheim, *Luther's Primary Works*, 109.
[4] Ibid., 110.   [5] *De diligendo Deo*, x.

soul shows itself prepared to do His whole will. It gives itself up to be dealt with as it may please God. Then follows the answer to faith, in truth and righteousness: 'The third incomparable grace of faith is that it unites the soul to Christ, as the wife to the husband; by which mystery, as the Apostle teaches, Christ and the soul are made one flesh.'[1] Whatever belongs to Christ the soul can claim. Christ is full of grace, life, and salvation. Let faith step in, and there is a delightful prospect of victory and redemption.

Thus the believing soul, by the pledge of its faith in Christ, becomes free from all sin, fearless of death, safe from hell, and endowed with the eternal righteousness, life, and salvation of its husband Christ.[2]

The ideal which is realized in Christ is comprised in two dignities. The first is spiritual freedom. The Christian man is by faith in Him granted spiritual power, so that he is completely lord of all things.[3] 'This is a spiritual power, which rules in the midst of enemies, and is powerful in the midst of distresses. And this is nothing else than that strength is made perfect in my weakness.'[4] Luther is here almost trembling on the verge of the New Testament teaching on perfection. But the freedom of which he speaks is more readily interpreted as mastery over affliction and hostility than freedom from sin. The second dignity is that of priesthood. By this priesthood we are worthy to appear before God, to pray for others, and to teach one another the things of God.

Luther's threefold answer to the question 'How can Faith make us holy?' gives us an ideal for the Christian life which is high, but not high enough. Luther guards himself against antinomianism. 'If faith does everything, why are good words commanded?' Those who say this are impious men. 'Are we to be content with faith?' 'That would indeed be the case if we were thoroughly and completely inner and spiritual persons, but that will not happen till the last day.' In the place of the possibility of a

---

[1] Wace and Buchheim, 111.　　　　　　　　　[2] Ibid., 112.
[3] Hering shows (op. cit., 185) how Luther owes this thought to Tauler.
[4] Wace and Buchheim, 115.

present deliverance from sin, Luther sets a doctrine of progress.[1] And this progress is primarily progress in faith.[2]

III. The Meaning of Vocation.

The most decisive and fruitful element in the Reformation conception of the ideal was that the full Christian life could be lived in any of the ordinary callings. The Augsburg Confession, as we have already seen, set this truth in its definition of Christian Perfection. Elsewhere the Confession insists that God ordained these callings.[3] The very words, 'calling' and 'Beruf' to describe the professions of men in the ordinary business of the world, owe their religious connotations to the Reformation.[4]

Luther taught with the greatest possible emphasis that this life was sacred and that the common human relationships were holy.

What you do in your house is worth as much as if you did it up in heaven for our Lord God. For what we do in our calling here on earth in accordance with His word and command He counts as if it were done in heaven for Him.[5]

It looks like a small thing when a maid cooks and cleans and does other housework. But because God's command is there, even such a small work must be praised as a service of God, far surpassing the holiness and asceticism of all monks and nuns. For here there is no command of God. But there, God's command is fulfilled, that one should honour father and mother and help in the care of the home.[6]

Even in such simple homiletical passages as these the Lutheran identification of the Decalogue and the *Lex Naturae* is evident.[7] We have already seen the identifica-

---

[1] Wace and Bucheim, 118.   [2] Ibid., 126, 127.

[3] Schaff, op. cit., 43, 51. Negatively, i. 16; Schaff, 17.

[4] For the proof of this see Max Weber, *The Protestant Ethic and the Spirit of Capitalism* (E. tr. 1930), 79–92. See also the masterly treatment of the subject in Troeltsch, *Die Soziallehren der christlichen Kirchen und Gruppen* (Tubingen, 1912), 442 ff., 473 ff. and for Calvin, 643–56; E. tr. 472 ff., 494 ff., 602–12.   [5] *Werke* (Erl. ed.), v. 102.

[6] *Werke* (Erl. ed.), v. 100. Other passages are quoted in McGiffert, *Protestant Thought before Kant* (1911), 33–4. The effect of the idea on Luther's conception of life is outlined, 32–40.

[7] Cf. Troeltsch, op. cit., 493 ff.; E. tr. ii. 503 ff., 844 ff.

tion presupposed in the thought of Melanchthon.[1] But both Decalogue and *Lex Naturae* are baptised with a Christian meaning, and are interpreted in the light of the two great commandments of our Lord. So Melanchthon says:[2] 'All men, in whatever vocation they are, ought to seek perfection, i.e. to increase in the fear of God, in faith, in brotherly love, and similar spiritual virtues.'

It must be admitted that Luther did not follow out the implications of his revolutionary view of the common life as a 'calling'. Indeed no sect unless it be the Society of Friends, no large religious communion, has ever yet held unflinchingly to the idea. It was left to Calvinism to discover the close connexion between the actual callings with the work they entailed, on the one hand, and the love and the wisdom of God on the other. To Lutheranism these vocations were forms, within which a man did his Christian duty. To Calvinism they were the very means through which love and faith could become realized. As Max Weber says, Luther sees the Christian serving God *in vocatione*, not *per vocationem*.[3]

But Luther's ideal had begun the revolution in men's minds which is not yet complete. In the course of his life he himself tended, though unconsciously, to recede from his high doctrine. The reason was his repeated reading of St. Paul, in the light of the troubles of the sixteenth century. Owing to the primitive eschatological hope, the Pauline Epistles, while enjoining 'work' for daily bread, are indifferent as to the meaning of that work for society. *Let every man remain in the condition of life where he was called.* Even slavery becomes a matter of comparative indifference in view of the near advent of the end.[4] As Luther fought the fanaticism and insurrections which had followed in the train of his stirring ideas, he became more traditional in his outlook; he taught men to remain

---

[1] See Herrlinger, *Die Theologie Melanchthons* (1879), 249–51.

[2] *Apol. Conf. Aug.* in *C.R.* xxvii. 634 (*De votis monasticis*).

[3] Op. cit., 215; see Troeltsch, 609–11, for a fuller statement of the distinctive contribution of Calvinism.

[4] 1 Cor. vii. 20–4. See Max Weber, 84, 85.

unquestioning in their daily work, and identified the will of Providence with the concrete economic situation.[1] Their virtue was not in the actual work they did, but in the obedience to God which they showed in doing it.

But a new conception of an ideal within the world had entered into the minds of men, and was carried forward by Calvinism to victory. The faith which in the *Liberty of a Christian Man* had meant kingship over death, life, and sin, and freedom from tradition, which had replaced the soul afresh in Paradise and created it anew,[2] was applied to the inward life of men who lived and moved in the ordinary business of life; their goal was to be found there, in the storm and stress of life; it was an inward haven, a Paradise within the world. Contrast the end of Dante's *Divina Commedia* with the end of *Paradise Lost.* The soul is left by Dante in Paradise, at the summit of contemplation; all speech fails; the vision itself is the momentary intuitive gaze of a soul laid to rest and despoiled of its own powers.[3] But at the end of the 'Divine Comedy of Puritanism' the Archangel spreads an active ideal before the gaze of fallen Adam.[4] The wide domains of knowledge are to be his; the spiritual virtues are described in terms that recall the very wording of the *Augsburg Confession.* Michael concludes:

> *then wilt thou not be loth*
> *To leave this Paradise, but shalt possess*
> *A Paradise within thee, happier far.*

And at last the two look back and see

> the gate
> With dreadful faces thronged and fiery arms:
> Some natural tears they dropped, but wiped them soon;
> The world was all before them, where to choose
> Their place of rest, and Providence their guide:
> They, hand in hand, with wandering steps and slow
> Through Eden took their solitary way.

[1] Max Weber (215–16) quotes illustrative passages from Expositions of Genesis.   [2] Wace and Buchheim, 120.   [3] *Paradiso*, xxxiii. 97–102.
[4] Cf. Max Weber, 87–8, from whom the idea of this contrast is borrowed.

We cannot imagine such words on the lips of a scholastic writer.[1] The ideal of the Puritan is far different from that of the medieval Catholic; yet both agree in finding their rest in the arms of God.

The foregoing discussion has left us with one duty unperformed. Can we weave together these threads and call the result a doctrine of perfection? Till the days of Ritschl no one dreamed of finding such a doctrine in the writings of the Reformers. And in Ritschl's day, and after, his critics have declined to follow him in attaching any importance to his discovery of a Lutheran doctrine of perfection. He admitted that the references to it were meagre enough, but insisted that without such a doctrine, Lutheranism was unintelligible. His reasons [2] were interesting and I will venture to analyse them.

1. Monasticism is the ideal of perfection in Catholicism; Protestantism, in order to exist, must have its own standard of a 'qualitative' perfection. This is an 'imputed' perfection, such as is defined in the Augsburg Confession.

2. Granted that such an ideal is seldom alluded to by the Reformers, it is implied in Luther's doctrine of the fall of Adam.

3. Suppose that the Reformers had no such doctrine, no real interest in an ideal realizable in this life. Then they would have been without any stimulus to portray as a whole their ideal of life, and they would have only been able to give fragmentary rules of life. In that case Protestantism would be at an immeasurable disadvantage as compared with Catholicism. This is unthinkable to the mind of Ritschl.

The first consideration starts from an *a priori* supposition: that an epoch-making event such as the Reformation with an enduring influence upon history must have at the heart of it a definite doctrine of perfection, an ideal

---

[1] Ritschl himself in the first volume of his *Justification* lays stress on Luther's doctrine of the *imperfection* of good works in believers, as differentiating Luther from Catholicism. See *Rechtf. u. Versöhnung*, i. 156, 157; E. tr. (1872), 137, 138.

[2] Ritschl, *Geschichte des Pietismus*, i. 38, 39.

regarded as realizable in time. But this supposition needs
to be proved in each historical case. Lutheranism did not
grow and flourish as we might have expected. And we
might be justified, on Ritschl's assumption, in claiming
that the arrested growth of that form of Protestantism has
been due to the absence of such a definite ideal. In any
case all the allusions in the Reformation writings, all the
fresh and living religious ideas which we have sketched,
only provide us with fragments of a doctrine, not with a
dominating conception which moulds the thought of the
Reformers.

The second argument is no more convincing. In many
patristic writings we find allusions to the Fall, with a
doctrine of original perfection.[1] Yet we cannot on that
account conclude that they are equipped with a positive
doctrine of Christian Perfection.

Ritschl's third argument, his *reductio ad absurdum* of the
arguments of his Protestant critics, does not sound so convincing to-day as it might have done to his readers forty-
five years ago. For the question which he regards as
unthinkable is being posed. It is for those Christians outside the Roman Communion to tell us whether they have
any convincing doctrine of an ideal attainable in this world.
If we ask Lutheranism whether it has any teaching comparable to that of the New Testament on this theme the
answer according to Troeltsch, himself a Lutheran, is that
Luther's doctrine is a divergence from that of St. Paul.
Luther taught that sin was unconquerable in this life.
St. Paul assumes that the Christian need not sin.[2]

We have already allowed this much of Ritschl's contention, that Luther was the pioneer of a new Christian piety.[3]
He flung abroad new religious ideas which were like guiding stars for the generations after him. But he failed to
produce a doctrine just at the point where Ritschl insists

---

[1] See H. H. Wendt, *Die christliche Lehre von der menschlichen Vollkommenheit* (1882).

[2] *Die Soziallehren*, 484; E. tr. ii. 498 and 840.

[3] Cf. Dilthey, *Archiv für die Geschichte der Philosophie*, vi. 373; R. Seeberg, *Vom Lebensideal* (Dorpat, 1886), 13–23.

that it was imperative for him to have one. Melanchthon saw more clearly than Luther here. In a letter[1] he says that his chief reason for playing the part of theologian was the reformation of life. Dilthey has pointed out in a masterly study[2] that the goal which Melanchthon set before him was the progressive moralization of the world.[3] 'As in the engravings of Dürer the Christ-child illuminates the plain narrow home and all the hard work in it, so from the pure teaching of antiquity and Holy Writ, according to Melanchthon's heartfelt faith, there streams a light of insight and moral power filling all life and work and banishing all barbarity, rendering irresistible all that is best in the world.' In the light of the Gospel Melanchthon saw the culture of the ancient world united with the new scientific spirit of the Renaissance, and both transformed by a new moral power. He was disillusioned before he died,[4] but the dawn of the Reformation is all the brighter for the glory of his ideal. He believed that the ethical teaching of Aristotle and Cicero was in full agreement with the divine law of the Decalogue.[5] What the Gospel brought was no sentence of Judgement, but power, power for the fulfilment of the ideal implanted in human nature and visible in the teaching of ancient Israel and ancient Greece.

Melanchthon stopped there. He did not inquire whether God had set limits to the operation of this power, nor whether the new ideal could be portrayed and filled out in detail. He was Christian Humanist more than theologian.[6] He made it possible for the educated classes

---

[1] C.R. i. 722.

[2] Archiv für die Geschichte der Philosophie, vi (1893), 225–56, 347–79 (Das naturaliches System der Geisteswissenschaften im siebzehnten Jahrhundert). [3] Ibid., 228. [4] Ibid., 231–2.

[5] So C.R. xii. 691. The divine law and philosophy are in agreement. But the Decalogue contains a clearer teaching on the submission of the heart to God. Cf. C.R. xi. 425.

[6] So Herrlinger, Die Theologie Melanchthons (1878); C. E. Luthardt, Melanchthon's Arbeiten im Gebiete der Moral (1884); cf. Dilthey, Archiv für Gesch. d. Philos. vi. 232, 233. 'Er ist der Geist des christlichen Humanismus', &c.; Dorner, Prot. Theol. (E. tr. 1871), i. 116–17.

to see that there was room for their love of literature and art in the new ideal.[1] He saw no unbridgeable gulf between Nature and Grace. His conception of marriage was finer than that of Luther:[2] 'the marriage union is the highest degree of friendship'. But in spite of his endeavours to correct Luther's theology he found little support and no successor. The humanistic impulses by which he had been influenced were excluded. 'Lutheranism repelled Philippism . . . and had to pay dearly for the renunciation.' And our conclusion must be that of the Ritschlian Harnack:[3] 'Through having the resolute wish to go back to *religion* and to it alone, [the Lutheran Church] neglected far too much the moral problem, the *Be ye holy, for I am holy*.'

[1] Dilthey, op. cit., 364.
[2] Cf. Dilthey, op. cit., 362 with Dorner, i. 269. Luther always sees something of sin in any sexual desire, even in marriage. The effect of this dualism has been traced by von Hügel, *The German Soul* (1916), 168, 169.
[3] *History of Dogma* (E. tr.), vii. 266, 267.

CHAPTER XIV

ST. FRANÇOIS DE SALES; QUIETISM

The Heart which is filled with love of God will love all else in Him.—
Of the love of God, x. 3.

THE Reformation brought the ideal of perfection out into the open. St. Francis of Assisi had, it is true, by the formation of the *Tertius Ordo*, brought the ideal within the reach of those who were married, or performing the ordinary social duties. The aim of the Poverello was 'to awaken in Christian souls everywhere a striving after holiness and perfection, to keep the example of a direct following of Christ before the eyes of the world as a continuous living spectacle, and by self-sacrificing devotion to become all things to those who were spiritually abandoned and physically destitute'.[1] Implicit, therefore, in the aim of the Friars Minor was the belief that perfection was possible for all men. The chasm between monk and layman was at least diminished.[2] But the Reformation was needed in order to assert the possibility of attaining sanctity in ordinary life. Nowhere is the new conception of the ideal more immediately apparent than in the writings of St. François de Sales.

The ideal of St. François de Sales was not altogether new. Before his time hundreds of introductions to the devout life had been written in French and addressed to all.[3] But St. François was original as all genius is original. 'Genius and saintliness alike recreate all they touch.' And he achieved what others had tried to achieve. He protests that his intention is 'to instruct those who live in towns, in

[1] Werner, *Duns Scotus,* 2 (quoted by Harnack, vi. 88).
[2] Cf. Ritschl, *Gesch. des Pietismus,* i. 16.
[3] See other facts assembled by Bremond, *Hist. litt. du sentiment religieux en France* (Paris, 1924), i. 19; (E. tr. London, 1928), 16; see also 56. I quote the English translation of Bremond. Cf. Lindsay, *History of the Reformation,* ii. 543. 'The Reformation had made the world democratic; and the Counter-Reformation invited the mob to share the raptures and the visions of a St. Catharine or a St. Teresa.'

households, and at Court, whose circumstances oblige them to lead *outwardly* an ordinary life.'

It is an error, nay rather an heresy, to wish to banish the devout life from the army, from the workshop, from the courts of princes, from the households of married folk.[1]

And by 'the devout life' he means perfection.[2]

His doctrine of the ideal is contained in his *Treatise on the Love of God*.[3] He begins with a psychological discussion, in which he develops his doctrine of the 'two parts' of the soul.

That is called inferior which reasons and draws conclusions, according to what it learns and experiences by the senses; and that is called superior, which reasons and draws conclusions according to an intellectual knowledge not grounded upon the experience of sense, but on the discernment and judgement of the spirit. This superior part is called the spirit and mental part of the soul, as the inferior is termed commonly, sense, feeling, and human reason.[4]

Just as in Solomon's temple there were three courts, so in the mystical temple of the soul there are three different degrees of reason. In the first 'court' we reason according to the experience of sense, in the second according to the human sciences, in the third according to faith. But there is a fourth place, the sanctuary, a certain eminence or supreme point of the reason and critical faculty, which is not guided by the light of argument or reasoning, but by a simple view of the understanding and a simple feeling of the will, by which the mind acquiesces and submits to the truth and to the will of God.

In the sanctuary there were no windows to give light: in this degree of the soul there is no reasoning which illuminates.[5]

---

[1] *Introduction to the Devout Life*, i. c. 3.   [2] Ibid.

[3] *Œuvres de Saint François de Sales* (Annecy, 1894), vol. iv. The English translation used is that of Dom H. B. Mackey (1884). The translation of Canon Knox Little (1902) is useless for theological purposes. The arrangement is misleading, and no warning is given in the Introduction either that the Treatise has been abridged or that the chapters have been scattered.

[4] *Treatise*, i. 11; *Œuvres*, iv. 63; Mackey, 45, 46; cf. *Introduction to the Devout Life*, iv, c. 3.   [5] Ibid., c. 12; *Œuvres*, iv. 68; Mackey, 49.

The faculties of the mind do not enter the holy place. St. François heaps up his similes to prove that the perfection of the soul is a simple resignation. In the superior part of the soul which alone is concerned with God at the supreme moment of attainment, there are two degrees of reason.

In the one those discourses are made which depend on faith and supernatural light, in the other the simple acquiescences.[1]

It is in this latter degree that the soul enjoys contemplation.[2]

Little bees are called nymphs or *schadons* until they make honey, and then they are called bees: so prayer is named Meditation until it has produced the honey of devotion, and then it is converted into Contemplation.[3]

In these divine mysteries, which contain all others, there is food provided for *dear friends* to eat and drink well, and for *dearest friends* to be inebriated. . . . To eat is to meditate . . . to drink is to contemplate, . . . but to be inebriated is to contemplate so frequently and so ardently as to be quite out of self to be wholly in God. O holy and sacred inebriation which . . . does not alienate us from the spiritual sense but from the corporal senses; does not dull or besot us, but *angelicizes* and in a sort deifies us.[4]

These few extracts are enough to show that the ideal now opened to all sorts and conditions of men is that of the great Contemplatives. It belongs to the Neoplatonic tradition. St. François makes use of St. Teresa, but 'we miss in him that steady devotion to the Person of Christ, and to Him alone, which gives the Spaniards, in spite of themselves, a sort of kinship with evangelical Christianity'.[5] The new thing is that such an ideal is looked on as possible for those engaged in 'the lawful occupations'[6] of a busy life. And that very fact has shed about the writings of our

---

[1] *Treatise*, i, c. 12; *Œuvres*, iv. 69; Mackey, 50.
[2] Ibid., vi, c. 3; *Œuvres*, iv. 312; Mackey, 239.
[3] Ibid.; *Œuvres*, iv. 312; Mackey, 240.
[4] Ibid.; *Œuvres*, iv. 324, 325; Mackey, 250. Cf. many similar passages in *Treatise* vii; Mackey, 281–324.
[5] Inge, *Christian Mysticism*, 231.
[6] *Treatise*, xii, c. 4; Mackey, 538–9.

Saint an added tenderness. He is concerned to awaken within all men the slumbering echoes of the divine Voice.

As soon as man thinks with even a little attention of the divinity, he feels a certain delightful emotion of the heart, which testifies that God is God of the human heart . . . so that when startled by calamity, forthwith he turns to the Divine, confessing that when all else is evil, It alone is good towards him. . . . This pleasure, this confidence which the human heart has naturally in God can assuredly proceed from naught save correspondence existing between Divine goodness and our souls; a correspondence absolute but secret, of which everyone is aware, but which few comprehend.[1]

Thus his spirituality is more human, although the goal of it is ecstasy. 'Doubtless we are His; you have all you need.'[2] There is a hint here, as often in his writings, of another possible doctrine. For if the soul can be sure that all things necessary are given of God here and now, without that rapture of the mind which is the goal of contemplation, then to be with God, to taste His peace, to be free from vain attachments, is a relative perfection.

I leave you the spirit of liberty . . . the liberty of children beloved. It is the setting free of the Christian heart from all things, to follow the will of God once made known.[3]

In virtue of such passages as these, Henri Bremond calls St. François de Sales 'the most perfect incarnation of Devout Humanism', and 'an influence which is no isolated phenomenon, but on the contrary connected with the immense movement of the Renaissance.'[4]

QUIETISM

Molinos published his *Guida Spirituale* in 1675, in Italian.[5] He distinguishes sharply between meditation and contemplation. Meditation is for beginners. It is an

---

[1] *Treatise*, i, c. 15; *Œuvres*, iv. 74; Mackey (corrected), 54.
[2] Letter to Ste. Chantal, *Œuvres*, xii. 385.
[3] *Œuvres*, xii. 359, 363.
[4] *Hist. Litt.* (E. tr.), i. 99–100.
[5] Quotations are made from the English edition of Mrs. Lyttelton (1907).

'exterior road'. The soul must tread it to gain knowledge, but it can never lead to perfection.[1] Contemplation has two stages, the lower and the higher. It is the higher stage with which we are here concerned.

Those who tread the interior way have withdrawn into the inner part of their souls, and resigned themselves wholly into the hands of God. They have forgotten and despoiled themselves of everything, even of themselves. They go with uplifted spirit into the presence of God, by the means of pure faith, without image, form, or figure.[2] Then the supernatural grace is 'infused'.[3] They rise from external actions to the love of God. They take no pleasure in anything in the world, except in contempt and in solitude, and in being forsaken and forgotten by all.[4] Trials they will have in abundance, but they are masters of themselves and live in great repose.[5] The inner peace means that 'we engulf and lose ourselves in the immeasurable sea of His infinite goodness, and in it abide steadfast and immovable'.[6] The best kind of prayer is the prayer of silence. There are three silences, that of words, that of desires, and that of thought. 'The first is perfect; the second more perfect, and the third most perfect. By not speaking, not desiring, and not thinking, the true and perfect Mystical Silence is reached', wherein God speaks with the soul and communicates Himself to her.[7] This attainment is spoken of as deification.[8]

So far we have traced two main characteristics of the ideal. The first is that the activities of sense and intellect are to be left behind; no longer is there a place in the ideal for meditation, even on the truths of the Christian religion. The second is that the ideal is a silence of love. God operates most effectively on the soul when it has lost itself in His immeasurable sea. We can add a third note—that of holy indifference, an *ataraxy* that 'far surpasses the boldest of the ancient Stoics'.[9] Not only must the soul

[1] *Guida Spirituale*, iii. 1; E. tr. 139.
[2] iii. 2; E. tr. 140.　　[3] iii. 4; E. tr. 141.　　[4] iii. 5; E. tr. 141.
[5] iii. 3; E. tr. 141.　　[6] iii. 61.　　[7] i. 128.　　[8] iii. 195.
[9] Rufus M. Jones, 'Quietism' (*Harvard Theol. Review*, x, 1917), p. 12.

learn to be dead to desire, to earthly affection, 'willing, as
if she did not will, desiring as if she did not desire . . .
welcoming equally contempts and honours, benefits and
corrections.'[1] There must also be a walking in the dark
and desert paths of prayer, where no comfort obtrudes,
where no light comes from above, and where the heaven
is as brass. 'Thou canst not think so much as to conceive
a good thought of God'.[2] Only in such desolation can the
divine Presence work without disturbance or disquiet.

A fourth mark of perfection is that there is only one
unbroken act of communion with God. When any one
goes to prayer, he must make an act of faith, and then
remain in that holy repose. He must endeavour for a
whole day, a whole year, a whole life, to continue that first
act of contemplation by faith and love.[3] Any attempt to
multiply acts of aspiration will only hinder the purity of
that act of the will. Elsewhere Molinos uses an illustration. If a man begins a journey to Rome, it is not necessary that at every step he should say, 'I wish to go to
Rome'. So with the contemplative soul. 'If the soul has
once determined to do the will of God and to be in His
presence, she still continues in that act so long as she
recalls it not, although she be occupied in hearing, speaking, eating, or in any other external good.'[4]

In such an uncompromising way the mystical ideal is
stated. And whoso essays the task of criticism finds, first,
the same defects in this more fully developed doctrine as
were discernible as far back as St. Augustine. There is the
same closing of the door on all the things of the senses, on
all the activities of the mind, on all the human loves that
beautify this life of ours. There is the same forgetfulness
of the central historic truths of the Christian Religion.
Even Love Incarnate must be forgotten, just because that
love is Incarnate. On the whole I must regretfully agree

---

[1] iii. 195.

[2] i. 48. The purification is achieved by two spiritual martyrdoms, that
of the bitter waters of affliction, and that of the burning fire of inflamed
love (iii. 21). This love annihilates the soul. It kills as death kills (iii. 50).

[3] i. 85; cf. 86.   [4] i. 112.

with Heppe and Dean Inge that the piety of Molinos cannot be viewed as an isolated aberration.[1] Molinos adds nothing that is new. He renders more explicit what has been taught by a series of great mystics. With all his rejection of 'external acts' in his ideal of prayer, he insists on the necessity of a spiritual director, and thus is less indifferent to institutional religion than St. John of the Cross himself.[2]

There are two qualifications to be made in this verdict. The first is that in one of the predecessors of Molinos we have a most healthy insistence on the humanity of Our Lord. Santa Teresa shows her usual balance and sanity in correcting the common tendency of mystical piety.[3]

What I would say is, that the most Sacred Humanity of Christ is not to be counted among the objects from which we have to withdraw. . . . That would be making the soul, as they say, to walk in the air. For it has nothing to rest on, how full soever of God it may think itself to be.[4]

But even this magnificent retractation is a personal discovery of our Saint. It is the exception and not the rule, in the mystics preceding Molinos.

Another qualification is that in Molinos, more clearly than in previous Mystics, we have the doctrine of the one unbroken Act of the soul. Stated as Molinos states it, this is a psychological blunder. And yet this very blunder is due to the Neoplatonic influence on the mystical tradition of the Church. 'That Neoplatonic constituent, always present in those ancient Mystics, had ever tended to conceive the soul's unity at any one moment, as a something outside of all multiplicity whatsoever. Hence this character of the simultaneous unity had only to be extended to the successive unity—and the literally One Act, as in the present so throughout the future, became a necessary postulate.'[5]

---

[1] Heppe, *Geschichte der quietistischen Mystik*, 21, 125, 126; Inge, *Christian Mysticism*, 230, 231; cf. von Hügel, ii. 143, and the article by R. M. Jones already quoted.   [2] von Hügel, ii. 147.

[3] *Life, written by herself*, ch. xxii (E. tr., D. Lewis, 5th ed. 1924), 184–97. See von Hügel, ii. 365.   [4] Ibid., 190.

[5] von Hügel, *Mystical Element*, ii. 147.

CHAPTER XV

FÉNELON

The very perfection of Christianity is Pure Love.
Lettres de M. de Cambrai; Œuvres, iv. 168.

THE controversy on Pure Love does not occupy much space in modern English theological writings.[1] The heresy which was suspected in the *Maximes* of Fénelon is not a danger into which the Christians of the West are likely to fall. But at a time such as this, when Christians in the East are ambitious to express their new found faith in the forms of their own indigenous culture, the issue may come alive more quickly than we dream. It must be admitted that the controversy between the eagle of Meaux and the saintly courtier of Cambrai is not altogether a pleasant theme. To most of us outside the Roman Church it seems certain that Fénelon should never have been condemned at all.[2] Even Roman Catholic writers in reviewing the evidence are forced to explain away the condemnation of the *Maximes* as not implying any disapproval of the doctrine which Fénelon always avowed he held.[3] Even more emphatically they have to maintain, what Bossuet's triumph at the Vatican makes it indeed difficult to maintain, that the doctrines held by Bossuet were not endorsed by authority. But apart from these difficulties, which are a domestic question for Roman Catholic theologians, we may discern a real value in the controversy. It ensured the full discussion, among all sorts and conditions of religiously minded people, all over Europe, of the true goal of the Christian life. Both the protagonists in the course of the

[1] But see the admirable brief discussion in Kirk, *Vision of God* (1931), 451–63.

[2] The case made out by H. Heppe, *Geschichte der quietistischen Mystik in der katholischen Kirche* (Berlin, 1875), that Rome executed a *volte-face* on the whole question of Quietism, is very strong.

[3] So Bishop Hedley, *The Spiritual Letters of Fénelon* (London, 1892), I. xi, xii; von Hügel, *Mystical Element* (1908), ii. 161; Deharbe, *Die vollkommene Liebe Gottes* (1856).

controversy repeatedly assume that perfection is possible for all classes of the faithful. The governing distinction is no longer between monk and the rest of the world, but always between 'beginner' and 'perfect'.[1] In his *Instruction Pastorale* to his diocese, Fénelon insists that the way of perfection is no secret tradition for the few, although in practice the higher reaches can only be for those who have a true thirst for the ideal.[2] In giving advice he assumes that even those who are children in the faith may pray for the vast ideal of disinterested love.[3]

For the best exposition of the doctrine of Fénelon we shall not go to the *Maximes des Saints*, but rather to the second Epistle to Pope Clement XI, the date of which (1712) is thirteen years after the condemnation of the *Maximes* by Innocent XII. The heat of the battle is past. The letter is 'extraordinarily compact and balanced',[4] and reviewed in the light of some of the richest and most sober pieces of the writings of the earlier period will give us the clue to guide us through the controversial maze.[5]

The main contentions of Fénelon are three.

I. The Highest Love is Disinterested Love.

The love which is the principal 'theological' virtue is a love of God which is independent of the motive of reward, although those who are in the most perfect state of love always desire the reward.[6]

In proprio charitatis theologicarum virtutum principis actu, potest amari absoluta Dei in se spectati perfectio, sine ullo adjecto promissae beatitudinis motivo.[7]

It was this statement that was vehemently contradicted by

---

[1] Cf. Articles of Issy, No. xxxiv; *Œuvres de Fénelon* (1820), iv. 21, 22. Cf. Art. xiii (*Œuvres*, iv. 15).   [2] *Œuvres*, iv. 180, 181.

[3] *Œuvres*, iv. 306. Cf. 308.

[4] von Hügel, *Mystical Element*, ii. 161.

[5] I have used below the writings which are especially recommended by Baron von Hügel; *Première Réponse aux Difficultés de M. l'Évêque de Chartres* (*Œuvres*, iv. 119–32); *Instruction Pastorale* (ibid., 179–308); *Lettre sur l'Oraison passive* (*Œuvres*, viii. 3–82); *Lettre sur la Charité* (*Œuvres*, ix. 3–56); *Epistle II* (ibid., 617–77).

[6] *Instruction*, *Œuvres*, iv. 180.

[7] *Epistola II de Amore Puro*. *Œuvres*, ix. 632.

Bossuet. Already we have seen authoritatively expounded by St. Thomas Aquinas the view which Fénelon champions.[1] And it would be possible to find in St. François de Sales expressions as strong as any ever used by Fénelon.[2] But as usual, the critic fastened on the illustrations of the expositor in order to assail the exposition. The prayer of Moses, the prayer of St. Paul (*I would that I were accursed for the sake of my brethren*) are the illustrations used by Fénelon. The soul may say to God: 'if thou wouldst condemn me to the eternal pains of hell, without losing your love (though the supposition is impossible), I would love Thee none the less'.[3] It is clear that the sacrifice of eternal beatitude is a purely hypothetical sacrifice. The sacrifice cannot be absolute. But there can be an absolute sacrifice of the 'mercenary' or 'interested' love of eternal beatitude. The ideal of the Christian life is so to love God that our own beatitude is subordinated to the love of God as our true and ultimate end. We should love God for His own sake, and not for our own; and we should keep His design for us before our minds for God's sake, since our beatitude is His good pleasure.

Much of the controversy centred round the word 'disinterested'. Fénelon had said that the soul united with Christ 'makes the absolute sacrifice of its own interest for eternity'. If by 'its own interest' we mean the *Summum Bonum* itself, any such a sacrifice would be an act of despair, the very height of impiety. But if by 'its own interest' we mean that selfish or 'mercenary' affection which comes from our own natural love of ourselves, such a sacrifice has been made and taught by the saints in all ages. Such a sacrifice of our own self-love is possible and should be made.[4]

Fénelon claims that his use of the word is that which was established and authorized by the mystical tradition of the Church. His case here was overwhelming.[5] It is true

---

[1] Cf. von Hügel, *Mystical Element*, ii. 161, 162; for the ignorance shown by Bossuet, see Bremond, *Apologie pour Fénelon*, 349 ff.; Fénelon, *Œuvres*, ix. 668.

[2] See e.g., *Instruction* (iv. 277).   [3] Gosselin in *Œuvres*, iv. cv, cvi.

[4] *Instruction Pastorale*, iv. 198.   [5] Ibid., 221–92.

that the 'disinterested' soul is content to have all sensible
comforts withdrawn in order that all selfishness should be
purged away, but the one thing that could not be sacrificed
or lost is the attachment to the promise of God Himself.
In a single verse Rothe[1] put the position of Fénelon:

> Though waves and storms go o'er my head,
>   Though strength, and health, and friends be gone,
> Though joys be withered all and dead,
>   Though every comfort be withdrawn,
> On this my steadfast soul relies,—
> Father, Thy mercy never dies!

This is almost a transcript of the words of Fénelon.[2]

The final demonstration of the main assertion of Fénelon
does not lie in the appeal to tradition, nor even in the
utterances of the saints, but rather in a consideration of the
essence of love at its highest.[3] This point was seized and
expressed by Leibniz, in a work on International Law.
'To love', he said, 'is to find one's pleasure in the felicity
of another. *Amare est felicitate alterius delectari.*' It follows
from this that Love is for man essentially an enjoyment,
although the specific motive of love is not the pleasure or
the particular good of him who loves, but the good or the
felicity of the beloved object.[4] 'This love cannot but give
us the greatest pleasure of which we are capable when
God is the object. And though this love be disinterested,
it already constitutes, even thus simply by itself, our
greatest good and deepest interest.'[5]

II. The possibility of a state of Pure Love.

The second assertion of Fénelon was that we must
recognize a *state* of perfect charity, where this virtue
reigns, animates all the other virtues and commands all the
acts of the life, and brings them to perfection without
depriving them of their own motives, or their own inherent

---

[1] The hymn was translated by John Wesley.
[2] *Instruction Pastorale*, iv. 198, 199.
[3] Cf. Bremond, *Apologie pour Fénelon*, 443.
[4] Quoted by Gosselin, iv. clxxvii, clxxviii.
[5] Quoted by von Hügel, ii. 176.

distinction. In this state acts done from the lower motive of mercenary or interested affection are reduced to the minimum and sometimes cease altogether.[1]

The first point on which Fénelon lays stress is that in this habitual state love is the very bond of all virtues, but never excludes the operation of any. In the thirteenth of the *Articles d'Issy*, the bishops agree that in the most perfect state of life and prayer all the acts of the interior life are united by love alone, in so far as love inspires all the virtues and commands their exercise.[2]

In the second place, Fénelon insists, again and again, that the state of pure love is liable to change and loss. *Habituel et point invariable* is the reiterated phrase. If any one says 'habituel' he does not mean 'un état inadmissible, ni inaltérable, ni invariable, ni entièrement uniforme'.[3] In the common usage of the term 'habitual' means the ordinary state, although transient acts and those only infrequently may interrupt the acts proper to such a state. The word *plerumque* in his Latin definition is chosen as the equivalent of the phrase *d'ordinaire*, to describe the acts which make up the state of pure love. But when the soul finds itself in violent temptations, recourse may be had to all the motives of interested love in order to beat the passions down—and in particular to the 'interested' motive of hope. God may even allow the soul in such dire need to call upon the motives proper to the state of servile fear.

---

[1] *Instruction Pastorale*, iv. 180. See especially *Epistola II de Amore Puro*, ix. 652. Compare John Wesley's favourite summary of the doctrine of Perfect love, in the hymn by his brother:

> Lord, I believe a rest remains
>   To all Thy people known,
> A rest where pure enjoyment reigns,
>   And Thou art loved alone:
>
> A rest, where all our soul's desire
>   Is fixed on things above;
> Where fear, and sin, and grief expire,
>   Cast out by perfect love.

[2] Cf. *Instruction*, iv. 191.

[3] *Première Réponse donnée aux Difficultés de M. l'Évêque de Chartres*, iv. 120.

The third main point of emphasis in his description is the place of 'hope'. Following St. Thomas Aquinas, Fénelon claims that hope is rendered more perfect by the presence of love.[1] But there are some virtuous acts, acts even of a supernatural virtue, which are done from the motive of hope and are not commanded by love.[2] These too may interrupt the habitual state of pure love.

Fourthly, Fénelon says repeatedly that this state may be interrupted by venial sins. On that account every Christian prays daily, *Dimitte nobis debita nostra*. Moses himself, standing at the summit of perfection for mortal man, hesitated in his faith, and was excluded from the promised land.[3] There are innumerable examples of the venial sins committed by other saints, including Peter himself.[4]

The fifth point, to which Fénelon constantly returns, is that in the exalted state of pure love the deliberate acts of self-love are reduced to a minimum and hardly recur. Involuntary acts of such love do recur.[5] But as a general principle, it is possible that the concupiscence remains in the most perfect souls to be diminished, so that the flesh may be entirely subdued to the spirit.[6]

III. Continuous contemplation impossible in this life. The passive state of prayer.

Nullus est perfectiorum iustorum status, in quo ipsi iugi et continua contemplatione fruantur; nullus in quo absoluta impotentia ligatae iaceant animi potentiae, ne discursivos christianae pietatis actus edere possint; nullus in quo verae libertatis arbitrio careant ad eliciendos eiusmodi actus; nullus denique in quo a legibus Ecclesiae sequendis, et ab omnibus superiorum mandatis adimplemendis eximantur.[7]

We come now to the problem of Quietism. The other

---

[1] *S.T.* II. ii, q. xvii, a. 8. *Epistola II de Amore Puro, Œuvres de Fénelon*, ix. 653.

[2] *Epistola II*, ibid., 663–8.   [3] *Epistola II*, ibid., 653; cf. 673.

[4] Ibid., 653. Cf. *Première Réponse aux Difficultés de M. l'Évêque de Chartres*, iv. 122.   [5] *Epistola II*, ibid., 654.

[6] See *Les Principales Propositions du Livre des Maximes justifiées, Œuvres*, viii. 277, and the array of authorities cited, Clement of Alexandria to Blosius, 278–87.   [7] *Epistola II de Amore Puro*, ix. 668.

two assertions of Fénelon are really distinct from the points
at issue in the Quietist controversy.[1] Fénelon was condemned on questions relating to Pure Love. On the subject of Passivity in prayer he was always far more orthodox
than Bossuet. The two problems are linked together because
if the main Quietist position is accepted, that perfection
diminishes the number of the soul's acts, the next step in
thought must be to ask what is the nature of those few
acts or of that single act. The answer would inevitably be
that it must be an act of Pure Love. The problem whether
the soul is active or not at the highest moment of communion with God is in a sense far deeper and more searching than the questions of pure love to which Fénelon,
following the mystical tradition of the Church, has already
given his answer. Fénelon had explained that the state of
pure love was a 'passive state'. But even in the *Maximes* he
was careful to limit this ambiguous and misleading expression. By 'passivity' he meant the opposite of 'natural
activity', and by 'activity' he included the acts of hurry and
distraction—*les actes inquiets et empressés*—whereby the
soul impedes the action of God upon it.[2] Bossuet understood Fénelon to teach that pure love must be a perpetual
passive contemplation, that the soul must be passive in the
sense of inactive, and without any of the deliberate virtuous
acts which the Christian ought to perform.

It can hardly be denied that the word 'passive' is unfortunate, especially in the English language. But behind
him once more Fénelon had the mystical tradition of which
Bossuet was ignorant.[3] Bossuet had confused 'passive contemplation' with 'the passive state'. He himself fell into
an error more obstinate and pernicious. He maintained
that, in its highest state, the human mind was entirely
intuitive in its one unbroken act, that this was wrought by
a miracle of God whereby the ordinary discursive acts were
superseded and replaced.[4] Fénelon, on the contrary, insists

[1] So, e.g., von Hügel, ii. 141.
[2] *Lettre à M. l'Évêque de Meaux, Œuvres*, viii. 6, 7.
[3] See Gosselin, *Analyse*, iv. ccxxi–ccxxiii.
[4] Cf. von Hügel, *Essays and Addresses*, i. 279.

that the mind in this life remains discursive in its operations, that it is never without its own characteristic liberty
of choice (*verae libertatis arbitrio*), that the virtuous action
which Christianity prescribes can be carried out without
the 'activity' which vainly seeks to anticipate the action of
God. This activity is the worried distraction of a Martha,
the 'restless will which hurries to and fro, seeking for some
great thing to do or greater thing to know', while all the
time the springs of life are within reach.[1] On the other
hand Fénelon's insistence on 'action' is a true description
of the ideal. It has been pointed out by von Hügel that
there are two currents in Christian mysticism. The one
tends to emphasize the soul's simple receptivity. The
other lays stress on the awakening by Divine Grace of the
soul's energy. The one tends to use words such as Passivity, Fixity, Oneness. The other has Action, Growth,
Harmony, as its characteristic words. The one type often
speaks as though nature had to be supplanted or expelled
before Grace could do its perfect work. The other type
realizes that Grace purifies, stimulates, awakens, and completes Nature. And so 'every divine influx is ever a stimula-
tion of all the good and true energy already, even though
latently, present in the soul. . . . That great, indeed all
but central, term and conception of "Action" has been
wisely generalized by most Christian Mystics as the truly
Christian substitute for the strongly Neo-Platonist term
"Passivity": that term and conception . . . was first fixed
and elucidated by Aristotle.'[2]

Fénelon does not make the value of his own assertion
apparent. Indeed the full value of his assertion could
hardly have been evident even to himself, otherwise he

[1] It was the doctrine of *abandon* which attracted Fénelon in the teaching
of Mme Guyon. See the shrewd remarks of Abbé Huvelin, *Bossuet,
Fénelon, et le Quiétisme*, ii. 151–4.

[2] *Mystical Element*, ii. 131, cf. 133. The illustrations of von Hügel
(drinking in the unity of a varied landscape, absorbing the Parthenon
sculptures, Raphael's Madonnas) are most apt. 'In all these cases the mind
or soul energizes or develops in precise proportion as it is so absorbed in
the contemplation . . . of these countries of the spirit, as to cease to notice
its own overflowing action.'

would not have continued to use the term 'passive' for the highest state of disinterested love.[1] But in his refutation of the Molinist errors, he is splendidly convincing. The first error condemned was: 'Oportet hominem suas potentias annihilare: et haec est via interna'. He points out that when the Mystics spoke of the annihilation of the soul's powers they did not mean complete annihilation. 'Ce qui paroît les anéantir n'est autre chose que les simplifier et les perfectionner.'[2] The dark night of the soul spoken of by St. John of the Cross is not a period of blindness and stupidity, but a lofty state wherein 'interested' love yields to pure love.

As against the doctrine of the One Act, Fénelon was right as against Bossuet. Molinos had taught that perfection consisted in one unbroken act of contemplation, and that this act once produced could subsist even during sleep, provided that it were not expressly revoked.[3] This is a psychological delusion. The soul's acts may 'overlap and interpenetrate one another', and yet it is 'the renewal, however peaceful and unperceived, of these acts which keeps the soul in existence'.[4]

It is almost needless to say that Fénelon did not deny, but most passionately affirmed, the tradition of the mystics that the final beatitude of the saints in heaven was contemplation, and that foretastes of that beatitude could be and were granted to the saints in the present world. The inspiration of the man in the 'passive state' is only an habitual inspiration for his interior acts of evangelical piety.

---

[1] On the other hand he is always (cf. *Œuvres*, iv. 30) most tenacious of and respectful to terms used by the great mystics.

[2] *Explication et Réfutation des LXVIII Propositions de Molinos.* *Œuvres*, iv. 29, 30.

[3] Gosselin, *Œuvres*, iv. lxxviii. Cf. Molinos, *Spiritual Guide* (E. tr. by Kathleen Lyttleton, 1907), 5, 28, 100, 106, 119. Compare the quotations from Petrucci given in Heppe, *Geschichte der quietist. Mystik*, 139, 140, 141. Petrucci was made a cardinal eighteen months after the beginning of the trial of Molinos. Innocent XI was delighted to have read Petrucci's book (Heppe, 144), and made him a bishop soon after. The Inquisition condemned his works in 1688 (Heppe, 282).

[4] See von Hügel, ii. 135, 136.

It does not render the man passive, or infallible, or impeccable, or independent of the Church.[1] Even the passive contemplation which is distinct from the 'passive state' is not absolutely necessary for the attainment of perfection in this life.[2]

As a whole, the doctrine of Fénelon in his later writings merits all the eulogy which Baron von Hügel, Canon A. L. Lilley, and Dr. Kenneth Kirk, have bestowed upon it. But his influence inevitably suffered in his own communion owing to his condemnation. On the other hand he was studied far beyond the borders of the Roman Church. Both William Law and John Wesley quote him, but in all probability Wesley was not familiar with the better and later writings. It is through his spiritual letters that his teaching has touched countless souls. Thus it was, as Evelyn Underhill has said, that he 'reached and affected the eighteenth-century Quakers, the leaders of the Evangelical revival, the Tractarians; and, in his own country, taught and still teaches, those who continue the great Gallican tradition of the spiritual life'.[3]

---

[1] *Mémoire à M. l'Évêque de Châlons. Œuvres*, iv. 5. Cf. *Instruction, Œuvres*, iv. 216.

[2] *Instruction, Œuvres*, iv. 216.

[3] *Mystics of the Church* (1926), 210-11.

CHAPTER XVI

THE PIETISTS

Each moment draw from earth away
My heart, that lowly waits Thy call:
Speak to my inmost soul, and say,
I am thy love, thy God, thy All!
To feel Thy power, to hear Thy voice,
To taste Thy love, be all my choice.
Tersteegen.

Pietism leaves the world and secular civilization severely alone.—*Troeltsch.*

BETWEEN the doctrines canvassed in the Quietist controversy of the seventeenth century and the evangelical movement of the eighteenth there is one most interesting link. It is the movement in Holland and Germany known as Pietism.[1] Its impulse came from the desire for personal holiness. Those who were dissatisfied with the hardness and objectivity of the prevailing Lutheranism found a leader in P. J. Spener.[2] Ritschl will hardly allow Spener the title of Pietist because he was against all separation from the Lutheran Church, and because he had no trace of the quietistic tendencies which characterized the later stages of the movement.[3] The first reason is not convincing. As well deny to Wesley the name of Methodist because he lived and died a member of the Church of England, and advised his followers never to separate. And the quietistic, mystical teaching is not the essential characteristic of the movement, though for our present purpose it is a significant fact. The essential mark of Pietism is its quest for individual holiness.[4] It arose, inevitably, as a reaction against a type of religion which laid no stress on

[1] Heppe, *Gesch. der quietist. Mystik.* 490.

[2] J. Jüngst, *Die Pietisten* (1906), is right (as against Ritschl) that there is no such thing as a standard Pietism and that it is better to speak of Pietists.

[3] *Geschichte des Pietismus*, ii. 163; cf. i. 190. My indebtedness to Ritschl in this section, as elsewhere in this book, is great. But as will be seen below, the point of view is different.

[4] Cf. Dorner, *Hist. of Protestant Theology* (E. tr. 1871), ii. 210, 214–19.

a high attainment in the present life and had no doctrine of the goal.[1]

The chief contribution of Spener to the movement was his organization of the seekers after holiness into *collegia pietatis*. Emphasis was laid on devotion rather than on doctrine; true knowledge of Christianity was to be shown in good works rather than in theological skill. His teaching on the goal of the Christian life is hardly distinguishable from that of the Augsburg Confession. The real proof of any one's standing in grace and justification by faith lies in love and obedience, in the passion for practical holiness. These good deeds will spring from the feeling of gratitude for the forgiveness mediated by Christ. Melanchthon had taught this.[2] But Spener went farther. He taught that it was necessarily possible for the regenerate to fulfil all the divine commands. Those who have faith are perfect in so far as they are sincere, honest, and striving after perfection like St. Paul (Phil. iii). Spener disowns the idea of a 'quantitative' perfection. However we strive we shall come short of our goal. Those good works are perfect which are done in self-denial with a view to the glory of God.[3]

As Ritschl points out, this is a vague and ambiguous test. The danger of self-deception is ever present. We do not always know what works of ours are done to the glory of God. But the teaching of Spener was not far away from orthodox Lutheranism, and he could satisfactorily answer the criticism of Alberti that the inevitable result of the Pietistic stress on holiness was self-satisfaction.[4]

That there was no uniform doctrine of perfection among the Pietists is proved by an essay of A. H. Francke, written in 1690–1, on *The Perfection of a Christian*. Here Francke taught that there were three stages in the progress towards the goal, corresponding to the growth in human life from childhood to youth and youth to manhood. He did not

---

[1] Ritschl does not like this reading of the history (i. 43). It seems to me to be the true reading of the facts. Analogies are the rise of the monastic ideal when the surrounding level of church life was deplorably low, and the new ideals of Law and Wesley.　　[2] *Apol. Conf. Aug.* in *C.R.* xxvii. 478–9.

[3] Ritschl, ii. 115.　　　　　　　　　　　　[4] Ibid., ii. 213, 214.

claim that sinlessness was a mark of maturity. Rather was the decisive sign the ability to distinguish between good and evil (Hebrews, v. 14).

It was Francke who translated[1] into Latin the *Guida Spirituale* of Molinos, in 1687. But in his teaching there is hardly any trace of quietistic influence. The purpose of his translation of Molinos was to let his countrymen know the teaching of the famous mystic.[2] Both Spener and Francke had found great spiritual aid in the writings of Arndt. It was to the book *Vom wahren Christenthum* that Spener owed his early deep impressions of religion. But he did not tread in the footsteps of that mystic.[3] Francke defined the goal after the way of the mystics, as *arctissima coniunctio cum deo*; this perfection could be reached in prayer.[4] It is doubtful whether his knowledge of mystical literature was wide, but in his writings the tendency towards the mingling of mystical ideas with Pietist devotion is discernible.[5] In the later stages of the movement, the mysticism which invaded it came in a quietistic form. Singularly enough, the condemnation of Molinos meant much for Pietism. 'Spener, Arnold, Francke, and Vitringa were of the opinion that whatever within the Roman Church seemed dangerous must be allied to Protestantism.'[6] A few years later the romantic story of Madame Guyon's imprisonment and sufferings gave her fame, and the discussion of the controversy between Bossuet and Fénelon secured an audience for the exposition of Quietist ideas everywhere. Schortinghuis and Tersteegen brought a quietistic piety into the Reformed Church as Poiret and Gottfried Arnold did for Lutheranism.[7]

The theology of Zinzendorf does not bear many traces of Quietism in the strict sense but among the Moravians the quietistic error of abstaining from religious observances

---

[1] Heppe, op. cit., 500.　　　　　　　[2] Ritschl, ii. 262.
[3] Ritschl, ii. 98. See the account of Arndt's book in Ritschl, ii. 42–61. On perfection, see esp. 47–50. Cf. the analysis of Sachsse, *Ursprung und Wesen des Pietismus* (1884), 198–200.
[4] Ritschl, ii. 263.　　　　[5] Ibid., 264.　　　　　　[6] Ibid., i. 474.
[7] Heppe, *Gesch. der quietist. Mystik*, 491–506.

is found in the strange doctrine of 'stillness' which caused the break between the Moravians and the early Methodists.

Zinzendorf himself distinguishes two types of union with God. The first is a union wherein God allows the faculties of the intellect to rest and then works in a supernatural way upon the soul. Zinzendorf regards this as a dangerous doctrine. The second type is a union of will, wherein the heart is filled with love to the Creator and empties itself to receive God; so the heart will love nothing so much as God and the fulfilment of His will. This, says Zinzendorf, is the true *Theologia Mystica*.[1] Ritschl maintains that this statement is free from Quietism, but the metaphor of 'self-emptying' makes us pause. His doctrine of sanctification equates perfection with $\pi\lambda\eta\rho o\phi o\rho\iota a \ \pi\iota\sigma\tau\epsilon\omega s$.[2] If the Saviour has once won His place in our hearts, if we are flesh of His Flesh, incorporated into His spiritual body, if we have partaken of His Spirit, then we shall remain true to Him like all souls who are loved. He interprets the doctrine of the Augsburg Confession to mean that in conversion the soul is absolved from all sin.[3]

An interesting illustration of Zinzendorf's doctrine may be quoted from the *Journal* of John Wesley.[4] Wesley met him on 3 September 1741, in Gray's Inn Gardens, and noted down the conversation afterwards in Latin.[5] The following are the chief passages on Perfection:

Z. I acknowledge no inherent perfection in this life. This is the error of errors. I pursue it through the world with fire and sword. . . . Christ is our sole perfection. Whoever follows inherent perfection, denies Christ.

W. But I believe that the Spirit of Christ works this perfection in true Christians.

Z. By no means. All our perfection is in Christ. All Christian perfection is Faith in the blood of Christ. Our whole Christian Perfection is imputed, not inherent. We are perfect in Christ, in ourselves we are never perfect.

W. I think we strive about words.

---

[1] Ritschl, iii. 407, 408.   [2] Ibid., 436.
[3] Ibid.   [4] Standard ed., ii. 487–95.
[5] 'To spare the dead'; A translation is given in Moore, *Life of Wesley*, i. 481–8.

Most readers will agree with the last remark of Wesley. But a real difference emerges later:

W. I mean nothing else by perfection than [loving God with all his heart].

Z. But this is not his holiness. He is not more holy if he loves more, or less holy if he loves less.

W. What! Does not every believer while he increases in love, increase equally in holiness?

Z. Not at all. In the moment he is justified, he is wholly sanctified (*sanctificatur penitus*). From that time he is neither more nor less holy, even unto death. . . .

W. Do we not, while we deny ourselves, die more and more to the world and live to God?

Z. We reject all self-denial. We trample on it. . . . No purification precedes perfect love.

After this strange conversation, it is a pleasure to note that Wesley, while separating his followers from the Moravian meeting-house, could so acknowledge his debt to them to the end of his days, that a Moravian testimony is adduced in the *Plain Account* as 'the first account I ever heard from any living man of what I had before learned myself from the oracles of God, and had been praying for (with the little company of my friends) and expecting for several years'.[1] The testimony is that of Arvid Gradin.

Requies in sanguine Christi. Firma fiducia in Deum, et persuasio de gratia divina; tranquillitas mentis summa, atque serenitas et pax, cum absentia omnis desiderii carnalis, et cessatione peccatorum etiam internorum. Vero, cor quod antea instar maris turbulenti agitabatur, in summa fuit requie, instar maris sereni et tranquilli.

We notice, too, that Wesley does not protest against the identification of the moment when saving faith is fully received with the moment of entire sanctification.

A survey of the various teaching of the Pietistic movement reveals certain defects.[2] In the first place, the doctrine is narrowly individualist. There is no ideal of the world

---

[1] *Works*, xi. 369, 370. See also *Journal*, Standard ed. ii. 49.
[2] A full discussion is found in Dorner, *History of Protestant Theology* (E. tr. 1871), ii. 218–27.

inspired in all its life by the spirit of religion. Secondly, the ethical ideal is negative and narrow. Art and science hold but a precarious place in its view of life.[1] Thirdly, the statements of the ideal show how easily an anxious scrupulosity might enter into the mind of its adherents.[2] But in extenuation of these failures must be urged the missionary impulse which Pietism gave. Judged by missionary enthusiasm alone, the *Unitas Fratrum* is the greatest communion in the world.[3] What would Lutheranism itself have to show in the cause of world-evangelization if it were not for the work of the Pietists?

[1] Troeltsch, *Leibniz und die Anfänge des Pietismus; Gesammelte Schriften* (1925), iv. 516.

[2] I have not thought it necessary to refute Ritschl's disparaging criticisms of Pietism. On this point see R. Mackintosh, *The Theology of Albrecht Ritschl*, 193–218, for some admirable remarks.

[3] See art. 'Moravians' in *E.R.E.* viii.

CHAPTER XVII

QUAKERISM[1]

I saw also, that there was an ocean of darkness and death; but an infinite
ocean of light and love, which flowed over the ocean of darkness.—
Geo. Fox.

The little seed of light groweth up even to perfection and then knoweth
and receiveth the light of the day in its full strength.—*Isaac Penington.*

QUAKERISM is one of the most significant facts in
the history of the Church. The value of its main
tenets for the religion of the future may well be vaster than
its achievements in the past. Yet until the twentieth century few writers outside the Society of Friends have attempted any estimate of Quaker doctrines. In these latter
years some of the arrears of neglect have been made up;
yet even in 1913, the date of the publication of the article
on the Society in Hastings's *Encyclopaedia*, no writings by
non-Quakers could be deemed worthy of inclusion in the
bibliography.[2]

On the one hand, the teaching of George Fox may be
regarded as the logical outcome of the Lutheran conception of faith. Faith for the Protestant was a man's conscious attitude of trust in God. 'The doctrine of the inner
light is not exactly the same thing as justification by faith
but it does apotheosize, one might almost say, the sense
of personal responsibility enshrined in the heart of Protestantism. The anti-sacerdotal principle assumes its most
logical form in Quakerism.'[3] But on the other hand, in

[1] The primary sources are George Fox, *Journal*; the eighth and
bicentenary edition (London, 1891) has been used, with references to the
Cambridge edition (ed. N. Penney, with introduction by T. E. Harvey,
2 vols. 1911); Isaac Penington, *Works* (4 vols, London, 1784); William
Penn, *Select Works* (3 vols., London, 1825).

[2] By far the most sympathetic and discriminating of all non-Quaker
writers are Baron von Hügel, *Essays and Addresses*, ii. 59–88, and (if he
may now be classed among them) Mr. H. G. Wood, *Quakerism and the
Future of the Church* (1920); *George Fox* (1912). See the masterly chapter
of C. J. Cadoux, *Catholicism and Christianity*, 117–44.

[3] H. G. Wood, *George Fox*, 146.

religious and ethical insight, George Fox went far deeper than the Reformers, and he did so precisely in virtue of his teaching on perfection. The holiness which he taught was not imputed but real.[1] The Quaker doctrine has this distinction among all the types of teaching from the third century to the eighteenth, that it returned whole-heartedly to the attitude of the New Testament.

In two ways Quakerism is related to the spirituality of the past. (1) In the first place the movement arose out of the comparison between the prevailing poverty of the contemporary religion and the riches of the New Testament experience. It is significant that he dates the first crisis in his history to a time when he was shocked by the inconsistency of 'religious professors'.[2] He was constant in his solitary study of the Bible and he saw that which was creative in the New Testament.[3] He had great 'openings of the Scriptures'.[4] And at last the awakening came. The famous passage which follows would have an honoured place in any anthology of the first-hand experiences of the soul.[5]

But as I had forsaken the priests, so I left the separate preachers also, and those esteemed the most experienced people; for I saw there was none among them all that could speak to my condition. When all my hopes in them and in all men were gone, so that I had nothing outwardly to help me, nor could I tell what to do; then, O! then I heard a voice which said, 'There is one, even Christ Jesus, that can speak to thy condition' and when I heard it, my heart did leap for joy.... And this I knew experimentally.... For though I read the Scripture that spake of Christ and of God; yet I knew him not but by revelation as he who hath the key did open, and as the Father drew me to his Son by the spirit.

That this result was not isolated is proved by the parallel experience of Isaac Penington.[6] Again we mark the

---

[1] This characteristic has been emphasized by von Hügel, *Essays and Addresses*, ii. 73.   [2] *Journal*, i. 3; cf. the incidents related in i. 6.

[3] Cf. his insight into the meaning of the Cross (5), his abstinence from Church and his reading of the Bible (7), the results of his study (8, 9, 10).

[4] *Journal*, i. 9.   [5] Ibid., 11.

[6] *Works*, i. xliii–xlvii (summarized). *Relation of his spiritual travail*, written in Aylesbury Prison, 1667, and printed in Thomas Ellwood's Testimony.

contrast between the powerlessness of contemporary religion and the sense of God in New Testament days.

My soul was not satisfied with what I met with, nor indeed could
be. . . . For I saw plainly that there was a stop in the streams, and
a great falling short of the power, life, and glory which they partook
of. We had not the Spirit, nor were so in the faith, nor did so walk
and live in God as they did. . . .

At last . . . when I came [to a Quaker meeting] I felt the presence
and power of the most High among them, and words of truth from
the Spirit of Truth reaching to my heart and conscience, opening
my state as in the presence of the Lord. Yea, I did not only feel
words and demonstrations from without, but I felt the dead
quickened, and the seed raised; insomuch as my heart, in the certainty of light and clearness of true sense, said: 'This is He; this is
He; there is no other; this is He whom I have waited for and sought
after from my childhood, who was always near me, and had often
begotten life in my heart, for I knew Him not distinctly, nor how
to receive Him or dwell with Him.' I have met with the true peace,
the true righteousness, the true holiness, the true rest of the soul,
the everlasting habitation which the redeemed dwell in.

The last sentence carries with it a doctrine not of imputed
but of real holiness. This relative perfection was for every
one who was illuminated by the Inner Light, and had
entered into the true knowledge of God.

The Quakers did not hesitate to declare that the history
of the Church from apostolic times till George Fox was a
'great apostasy'. One of the best read of them all declares
this roundly in his literary masterpiece.[1]

Well! but what has been the success of those ages that followed
the apostolical? any whit better than that of the Jewish times? Not
one jot. They have exceeded them; as with their pretences to
greater knowledge, so in their degeneracy from the true Christian
life.

(2) In the second place Quakerism was indebted, far
more than its leaders were aware, to the mystical tradition
of the Church.[2] The debt of the founder to the Johannine

---

[1] Penn, *No Cross, No Crown*, Part I, c. vii, 14. *Select Works* (1825),
i. 392.

[2] See Baron von Hügel, *Selected Letters* (1927), 234-5, 272-3;
Essays and Addresses, i. 14, 231.

theology is everywhere evident. But till recently it had scarcely been recognized that George Fox was indebted to many previous spiritual movements for the success of his mission. Fox received his inward illumination in 1646, when he was twenty-two. In 1647 he began his work among the 'shattered' Baptists. In the next year the new community arose among them, under the title of 'Children of the Light'. This name had been used before by some continental Baptists.[1] It is not possible to adduce any proof that George Fox consciously derived his characteristic ideas from the continental mystics. But there is a remarkable similarity between his main tenets and those of Schwenckfeld.[2] It is probable that he was far more indebted than he knew to the mystical tradition of the Church. In any case his own spiritual convictions were nourished and deepened by the new religious fellowship into which he entered in 1647 and 1648. The solitary prophet had now become the spokesman of a community. How much added strength that brings to a preacher can only be known by any one who after long solitary strivings has found his own discoveries shared.

The teaching on the goal of the Christian life is nowhere in the writings of the early Quakers set out as a connected whole. But from the beginning Fox saw that his doctrine of the Inner Light must mean emancipation from sin. We notice this, first, in his own experience. The opening chapter of the *Journal* contains no confession of personal sin. This is a most singular fact. It has been suggested[3]

---

[1] Professor Cornelius wrote to R. Barclay (1876) that the designation of the Baptists as *Kinder des Lichtes* was found in the document 'Brüderliche Vereinigung' in the State Library at Munich. The date is 1527. The title was often used by the Baptists. John Goodwin (the Independent) wrote a book in the early seventeenth century entitled *The Child of Light* '*Walking in Darkness*'. See Barclay, *Inner Life of the Religious Societies of the Commonwealth* (1876), 262, 273. Margaret Fell was the great granddaughter of the famous martyr, Anne Askew. It is significant that Anne Askew had embraced Melchior Hoffman's opinions (Barclay, op. cit., 267). Thus from the beginning the Friends had much in common with the continental Baptists.

[2] Barclay, op. cit., 237. See the whole of this valuable discussion, 227–52.   [3] H. G. Wood, *George Fox*, 18, 19.

that the cause of his early distress was not a consciousness of sin and guilt but rather the pressure of temptation. 'Temptations grew more and more, and I was tempted almost to despair.'[1] But surely the temptations must have vanquished him, else why should he despair? His problem was: 'Is there no overcoming life for the believer here and now?' Perhaps the explanation of his reticence is that his problem was always wider than the individual struggle. Was there no remedy for the disorder in a so-called Christian kingdom? Could not Christians be expected to find victory over sin, within and without? This suggestion is supported by the answer he gave[2] to 'Priest Stevens' concerning the cry from the Cross, *My God, my God, why hast thou forsaken me?*

I told him that at that time the sins of all mankind were upon Him, and their iniquities with which He was wounded, which He was to bear. . . . This I spoke being at that time in a measure sensible of Christ's sufferings, and what He went through.

The last sentence is a hint that the struggle in which he found victory was vicarious; his own conflicts were individual but never merely individual.

A second interesting fact is that he rejected the Puritan pre-occupation with sin. Nowhere is his point of view better expressed than in a letter he sent in 1658 to Lady Claypole, the Lord Protector's daughter, who had been a seeker.[3]

This then is the word of the Lord God unto you all; whatever temptations, distractions, confusions, the light doth make manifest and discover, do not look at these temptations, confusions, corruptions: but look at the light, which discovers them, and makes them manifest; and with the same light you may feel over them, to receive power to stand against them.

This extract shows that for Fox the discovery of sin and the illumination of Christ form one inseparable revelation. 'He that shows a man his sin is the same that takes it away.' But it was the release that Fox stressed. In his

---

[1] *Journal*, i. 4.   [2] Ibid., i. 5.   [3] Ibid., i. 433.

imprisonment at Derby in 1650, he said to 'divers professors' who 'came to plead for sin and imperfection':

If your faith be true, it will give you victory over sin and the
devil, purify your hearts and consciences (for the true faith is held
in a pure conscience), and bring you to please God, and give you
access to Him again. But they could not endure to hear of purity,
and of victory over sin and the devil: for they said they could not
believe that any could be free from sin on this side the grave.[1]

The accepted doctrine of the time could not make room
for a message like that of Fox. To the Puritans the natural
life of man belonged to an undivine order. This was a lost
world. And the miracle of the Quaker message is the more
evident when we recognize that Fox shared these presuppositions of his age. One more extract[2] must be given
which illustrates how he cut the knot. The experience
belongs to the year 1648, when he was twenty-four years
old.

Now was I come up in spirit through the Flaming Sword, into
the Paradise of God. All things were new, and all creation gave
another smell unto me than before, beyond what words can utter.
I knew nothing but pureness and innocency and righteousness,
being renewed into the image of God by Christ Jesus, so that
I say I was come up to the state of Adam, which he was in before
he fell. . . . But I was immediately taken up in spirit to see into
another or more steadfast state than Adam's in innocency, even into
a state in Christ Jesus that should never fall. And the Lord showed
me that such as were faithful to Him, in the power and light of
Christ, should come up into that state in which Adam was before
he fell, in which the admirable works of the creation and the virtues
thereof may be known, through the openings of that Divine Word
of wisdom and power by which they were made.

Fox regards the new experience that has come to him as
a change in the substance of his soul. He is renewed into
the condition before the Fall, and kept by the power of
Christ in a state of perfection even 'more steadfast' than
that of Adam in Paradise. It has been pointed out that on
his favourite seal there was a device—G. F. and the Flaming Sword; this was a perpetual reminder to him of the

---

[1] *Journal*, i. 56.   [2] Ibid. i. 28 (corrected to 1694 edn.).

experience by which he had entered into the realm of abiding victory.

The Quakers were careful to guard the teaching of Fox from fanaticism, and doubly careful after James Nayler's fall. The following extract from William Penn will prove this.

Because we have urged the necessity of a perfect freedom from sin, and a thorough sanctification in body, soul, and spirit, whilst on this side the grave, by the operation of the holy and perfect Spirit of our Lord Jesus Christ, according to the testimony of the holy scripture, we are made (i.e. represented as being) so presumptuous, as to assert the fullness of perfection and happiness to be attainable in this life: whereas we are not only sensible of those human infirmities that attend us, whilst clothed with flesh and blood; but know that here we can only 'know in part, and see in part': the perfection of wisdom, glory, and happiness, being reserved for another and better world.[1]

William Penn tries to work out the connexion between the inward light and the consequent gifts of God. First comes a sight of sin; secondly, a godly sorrow for sin; then justification, which is forgiveness. But this is useless unless it means the fulfilment of the end for which Christ came —'to save his people from the nature and defilement, as well as the guilt of sin'.[2]

The teaching of early Quakerism was expounded in the most systematic form to which it ever attained by Robert Barclay who is regarded by Friends as the greatest of Quaker theologians.[3] But unfortunately Barclay did not carry through the emancipation of Quakerism from the bondage of the doctrine of the total depravity of human nature. He was well read in the works of the Reformation divines. He knew the Fathers and the Schoolmen. But he did not know the spiritual predecessors of Quakerism. He had not read the Cambridge Platonists.[4] His aim was

[1] *A Testimony to the Truth of God* (1698), xi; *Select Works*, iii. 521.
[2] *Select Works*, iii. 430.
[3] Cf. Braithwaite, *Beginnings of Quakerism*, 226.
[4] Rufus M. Jones in the Introduction to *The Second Period of Quakerism*, xxxiii. His judgement is endorsed by Edward Grubb, *Holborn Review* (July 1924).

to adjust the new in Quakerism to the old of Reformation
Theology. And therefore, in the *Apology for the True
Christian Divinity*, for all its intellectual power, we are
moving in a narrower world than that of Fox, and we must
be on our guard lest by accepting the formulation of
Barclay as the true expression of the Quaker teaching, we
do an injustice to the originality and genius of the
movement.

Barclay sees that the essential fact in Quakerism is the
staking of everything on the supreme end of man. 'The
height of all happiness is placed in the true knowledge of
God.'[1] The revelation to the soul of man is immediate and
divine. There is no knowledge of the Father but by the
Son. There is no knowledge of the Son but by the Spirit.
And by the Spirit God reveals Himself to His children.[2]
But in the fourth proposition Barclay returns, as Wesley
did after him, to the crudest statement of the doctrine of
Total Depravity, based on the words of Genesis vi. 5: *God
saw that every imagination of the thoughts of his heart was
only evil continually*.[3] Barclay is able to hold side by side
with the old dogma the existence of a spiritual nature,
proceeding from the seed of God in man.

He parts company with the prevailing view of good
works:

We believe that such works as naturally proceed from this
spiritual birth and formation of Christ in us are pure and holy even
as the root from which they come; and therefore God accepts
them, justifies us in them.[4]

The Eighth and Ninth Propositions contain the doctrine of Perfection.

In whom this pure and holy *birth* is fully brought forth, the body
of death and sin comes to be crucified and removed, and their hearts
united and subjected to the *truth*; so as not to obey any suggestions
or temptations of the evil one, but to be free from actual sinning and
transgressing of the *law of God*, and in that respect *perfect*: yet doth
this *perfection* still admit of a growth, and there remaineth always

---

[1] Prop. i.   [2] Prop. ii. 5–12.   [3] Prop. iv. 2.   [4] Prop. vii. 3.

in some part a possibility of sinning, where the mind doth not most diligently and watchfully attend unto the Lord.[1]

Although this gift and inward grace of God be sufficient to work out salvation, yet in those in whom it is resisted, it both may and doth become their condemnation. Moreover, they in whose hearts it hath wrought in part to purify and sanctify them in order to their further perfection, may, by disobedience, fall from it, *turn it to wantonness, make shipwreck of faith, and after having tasted the heavenly gift, and been made partakers of the Holy Ghost, again fall away*; yet such an increase and stability in the truth may in this life be attained, from which there can be no total apostasy.[2]

On this doctrine we may observe, first, that the Divine Light is infused into the soul by a purely miraculous act. The Light or Seed is a *vehiculum Dei*.[3] By this device God is able to operate in the soul which by itself has no spiritual capacity. 'This light of which we speak is not only distinct, but of a different nature from the soul of man, and its faculties.'[4] It is a substance which exists even in the hearts of wicked men, 'as a naked grain in the stony ground'.[5] It is even distinct from conscience.[6] We see how a false doctrine of man has entangled Barclay in a vicious dualism when he tries to explain the operation of divine grace.

In the second place, the Light or Seed is totally different from the rational soul of man and is incapable of any correlation with reason. It is not a product of human experience; the mind cannot test it. Barclay explains that man possesses a rational principle which may order and rule men in things natural. We do not deny, he says,

but by this rational principle man may apprehend in his brain, and in the notion, a knowledge of God and of spiritual things; yet that not being the right organ, . . . it cannot profit him towards salvation, but rather hindereth; and indeed the great cause of the apostacy hath been that man has sought to fathom the things of God in and by this natural and rational principle, and to build up a religion in it, neglecting and overlooking this principle and seed of God in the heart.[7]

---

[1] Prop. viii. [2] Prop. ix.
[3] Prop. v, vi. 15; Quest. 5.
[4] Prop. v, vi. 16. [5] Prop. v, vi. 14.
[6] Prop. v, vi. 16. [7] Ibid.

On these principles it is difficult to see how there can be any co-operation on the part of man with the working of divine grace. As Barclay says,[1] man is wholly unable of himself to work with the grace. Dr. Rufus Jones has maintained that these positions are not those of the first period of Quakerism, and that largely owing to the theology of Barclay, 'its mysticism was shifted from the dynamic affirmation mysticism of the first period to a passive and negative life.'[2] It is evident that Barclay's statements are quietistic. Man's only act is a decision to be passive, and not resist the visitation of grace. It comes at certain times and seasons and he must wait for it.[3]

It may be questioned whether the distinction between the teaching of George Fox and the formulation of Robert Barclay is as sharp as Dr. Rufus Jones maintains. Granted that the quietism of Barclay is new, the 'Flaming Sword' passage already quoted from Fox is a proof of the difficulty which any one in that age felt in reconciling the doctrine of the Inner Light with the accepted dogma of the Total Depravity of man's nature. And three defects are patent in Quakerism from the first: 'the tendency to distrust the intellect, to suspect the outward and to neglect the historical'.[4]

We may turn now to the more congenial task of pointing out the distinctiveness of the Quaker contribution.

1. Through all the early Quaker testimonies there runs a sense of enhanced personality. Human nature has been lifted on to a new level of life. Victory is in the air. Moral effort has not been superseded, but the struggle is no longer hopeless. In this we trace a return to the New Testament teaching. There is no longer any acquiescence in the presence of sin in the life of a believer.

2. There is a concentration upon the life of holiness as the life for which man was destined. But this holiness was recognized as obligatory in the social life of man in the fixing of wages for farm-labourers and the reform of national abuses, as well as in the individual moral life.

---

[1] Prop. v, vi. 17.   [2] *The Second Period of Quakerism*, xli.
[3] Loc. cit., sect. 16.
[4] H. G. Wood, *Quakerism and the Future of the Church*, 70.

'The enforcement of these principles was a definite part of Fox's mission to England.'[1]

3. The Quakers taught that there was that in man which would lead, without the following of any external authority, to the perfect life. It is true that for reasons already discussed the nature of man was misinterpreted. But the recognition of the divine seed in every man, the stress on the light which lighteth every man, was an emancipation for the Christian mind. It led at once in men like William Penn and Isaac Penington to a catholicity of spirit, a desire to discover the good in other races and other faiths, and to a new sense of the sacredness of human personality.[2]

4. The chief distinction of the Quaker doctrine of perfection was that its centre was in the Cross of Christ. There George Fox found the power for that unwearying love which is the perfect life. For him and for his friends the Atonement was no transaction, carried on outside a man, no paying of a debt, no enduring of a punishment which left his heart unchanged. The favourite sentence of Fox was: 'The Cross is the power of God'. The Atonement was inward.

Now that ye know the power of God and are come to it—which is the Cross of Christ, that crucifies you to the state that Adam and Eve were in, in the Fall, and so to the world, by this power of God ye come to see the state they were in before they fell, which power of God is the Cross, in which stands the everlasting glory; which brings up into the righteousness, holiness, and image of God, and crucifies to the unrighteousness, unholiness, and image of Satan.[3]

Fox knows, like his later follower, that the Cross is no 'dead fact, stranded on the shore of the oblivious years', but an inward living experience in the heart of the believer, refashioning his life into perfect love.

'You that know the power and feel the power, you feel the Cross of Christ, you feel the Gospel which is the power of God unto salvation to every one that believeth.'[4] Out of

---

[1] W. C. Braithwaite, *The Beginnings of Quakerism*, 49.

[2] See Professor Elbert Russell in the *Holborn Review*, *George Fox Tercentenary Number* (July 1924), 335–42.

[3] *Journal*, i. 345.   [4] *Journal*, i. 191.

this conviction came the Quaker way of humility and non-resistance, of overcoming evil by the sole force of love.

The most harmonious expression of this truth is to be found in the dying words of one[1] who fell and who was brought back to the humility of Christ.

There is a spirit which I feel that delights to do no evil, nor to revenge any wrong, but delights to endure all things, in hope to enjoy its own in the end. Its hope is to outlive all wrath and contention, and to weary out all exaltation and cruelty, or whatever is of a nature contrary to itself. It sees to the end of all temptations. As it bears no evil in itself, so it conceives none in thoughts to any other. If it be betrayed, it bears it, for its ground and spring is the mercies and forgiveness of God. Its crown is meekness, its life is everlasting love unfeigned; and takes its kingdom with entreaty and not with contention, and keeps it by lowliness of mind.

---

[1] James Nayler; a summary of his life and this last message may be found in *Christian Life, Faith and Thought*, 25–26.

CHAPTER XVIII

WILLIAM LAW[1]

God is Love, yea, all Love, and so all Love, that nothing but Love can come from Him.—Works, v. 156.

'IT is possible,' said Dr. Bigg, 'to dally with the literary charm of Pascal or à Kempis or Augustine, but few can read the *Serious Call* without great searchings of heart.' It is in virtue of this searching of the conscience that William Law has won his immortality in devotional literature. He was indeed a man of genius: he was a witty controversialist, undefeated in argument by Hoadly, or Wesley, by Warburton or Tyndal; his style alone on the testimony of Gibbon would have lifted him to a place 'among the most agreeable writers of our language'; in the depth and power of his religious life he stood out far above most of his contemporaries in an irreligious age. Yet he owes his influence primarily to his appeal to the conscience of mankind. His life of purity and self-denial is of one piece with his devotional writings. Both as saint and as maker of books he recalled the Anglican Church to the pursuit of the ideal.

We may divide his writings on Christian perfection into the two main classes, which correspond to the earlier and the later periods of his religious life. The first class includes the Treatise on Christian Perfection and the Serious Call. The second embraces the mystical writings of his later years when he had fallen under the influence of Jacob Behmen. In spite of the severe animadversions of John Wesley, there is a certain unity of message, as I hope to show, in both these periods of Law's life.[2]

[1] The edition of the *Works* in nine volumes, 1893, has been used, but the *Serious Call* is cited from the standard edition of Overton (English Theological Library, 1898). The two modern monographs are those of Overton (1881) and Stephen Hobhouse (1927). I must apologize for the lengthy quotations by quoting the words of F. D. Maurice, who calls Law 'the most continuous writer in our language, each of his sentences and paragraphs leading on naturally and, as it were, necessarily, to that which follows'. Cf. Overton, 267.   [2] Cf. Overton, 293.

THE EARLIER WRITINGS OF WILLIAM LAW

The *Treatise on Christian Perfection* was published in 1726 when William Law was forty years old. It was the first of all his distinctively spiritual writings, but it is the product of a mind experienced, penetrating, and mature. No summary can do justice to its wealth of spiritual wisdom. The attempt of Canon Overton in his *Life and Opinions of William Law*, the most complete and indeed, till recently, the only modern monograph on Law, fails to render an account of the ideal which Law sets before the Church in that indifferent and unenthusiastic age. Indeed the very opening of the Treatise is unintentionally misleading. In his anxiety to disprove the prejudice against the word Perfection in the minds of his readers, Law defines it 'the right and full Performance of those Duties which are necessary for all Christians, and common to all States of Life'. It might seem from this definition that there was a *prima facie* case for Wesley's subsequent charge against Law's practical treatises that they taught a Pharisaic doctrine of works.[1] But in the light of the second chapter, such a charge is found baseless. In the first place, the Perfection which Law expounds is founded on a thorough doctrine of conversion, and this conversion is wrought by God. Christianity requires a change of Nature: 'There is but this one Term of Salvation, *He that is in Christ, is a new Creature*'.[2] Law's conclusion is as evangelical as any teaching of Wesley.

If Religion has raised us into a new World, if it has filled us with new Ends of Life, if it has taken possession of our Hearts, and altered the whole Turn of our Minds, if it has changed all our Ideas of Things, given us a new Set of Hopes and Fears, and taught us to live by the Realities of an invisible World, then may we humbly hope that we are true Followers of the Holy Jesus.[3]

Only by divine grace, he says in a later chapter,[4] 'are we disposed towards that which is good, and made able to perform it'. He does not give as much prominence as

---

[1] Cf. Hobhouse, 313.   [2] *Treatise*, 35.
[3] Ibid.   [4] c. ix. 134.

Wesley gives to saving faith. But since his aim in the Treatise is to set forth the moral ideal to which all Christians without distinction are called, he uses the doctrine of grace to prove his main thesis, that self-denial is perpetually necessary. Because the aim of our religion is to bring us into union with God into a Life lived in and by the Spirit of God,

it must be necessary, that we deny ourselves all those Tempers and Ways of Life, which may make God withhold his Grace from us; and likewise all those Enjoyments and Indulgences, which may make us less able and less disposed to improve and co-operate with those Degrees of Divine Grace, that are communicated to us.[1]

The turn of argument is curiously and characteristically neat, but it is irresistible.

In the second place, the chief characteristic of the positive teaching of Law's Christian Perfection is the emphasis on taking up the Cross. *Entbehren sollst du, sollst entbehren* is written wide over almost every page. No less than six chapters out of fourteen are devoted to this one theme. It would be as unfair to censure Wesley for Pharisaic insistence on good works, because among his famous forty-four 'Standard' sermons thirteen are based on the ethical demands of the Sermon on the Mount, as it would be to censure Law for Wesley's reasons.

But the true reason for the insistence of Law and Wesley on the ethical teaching of Jesus lies deeper. There is a chasm between the temper of the world and the spirit of Christ. Law sees this. He rests his teaching of self-denial on the parable of the pearl of great price. 'I suppose it means, that a great deal is to be given for it, and when it says, that the Merchant went and sold all that he had and bought it, I suppose this is to teach us, that it cannot be bought at any less Price.'[2] Law sees that the duty of self-denial is grounded in the very constitution of the world, in the facts of life.[3]

The consequences deduced from this main principle are drastic enough. He rightly singles out the use of wealth

[1] c. ix. 135.　　　　　　[2] c. iv. 49.
[3] Cf. c. vi. 80.

as a crucial test of practical Christianity. 'The peaceful, pleasurable Enjoyments of Riches is a State of Life everywhere condemned by our Blessed Saviour.'[1] There is no 'other lawful way of employing our wealth (beyond our bare necessities) than in the assistance of the poor'.[2] He goes so far as to say that suffering is to be sought. 'For if there is a Reasonableness between Sin and Suffering, every Christian acts against the Reason of Things, that does not endeavour to pay some part of that Debt which is due to Sin.'[3] His appeal to the Reason of Things is characteristic of his age. But his earnestness, his power of focusing his message into a startling image is all his own. 'He that is proud offends as much against Truth and Reason, and judges as falsely of himself, as the Madman who fancies himself to be a King, and the Straw to which he is chained to be a Throne of State.'[4]

If a Person was to walk upon a Rope across some great River, and he was bid to deny himself the Pleasure of walking in silver Shoes, or looking about at the Beauty of the Waves, or listening to the Noise of Sailors, if he was commanded to deny himself the Advantage of fishing by the Way, would there be any Hardship in such self-denial? Would not such self-denials be as reasonable as commanding him to love Things that will do him good, or to avoid Things that are hurtful? . . . So they who think that Pleasures and Indulgences are consistent with their keeping this narrow Way, think as reasonably as if the Man upon the Rope should think that he might safely use silver Shoes, or stop in his Way to catch Fish.[5]

The *Serious Call* owes its greatness to the sense of the need for renunciation in every Christian life. The summary of the ideal of perfection in the opening chapter is characteristic of the whole.[6]

Our blessed Lord and His apostles are wholly taken up in doctrines that relate to common life. They call us to renounce the world, and differ in every temper and way of life from the spirit and the way of the world; to renounce all its goods, to fear none of its evils; to reject its joys and have no value for its happiness. . . . This is the common devotion, which our blessed Saviour taught, in order to make it the common life of all Christians. . . . If we

---

[1] *Treatise*, c. iv. 49.   [2] c. v. 65.   [3] c. vi. 80.
[4] c. vii. 104.   [5] Ibid., 104.   [6] Overton's ed., 6.

are to follow Christ, it must be in our common way of spending every day.

In the third place, we notice how William Law sets Christian perfection on the common ways of life, in the daily duties, amid the throng and press of men. He who was to retire to Kingscliffe would have 'no cloister'.[1] 'Christian perfection is tied to no particular form of life.'[2] 'Religion turns our whole life into a Sacrifice to God.'[3] This is the note sounded at the beginning of the *Treatise*. The same music is heard at the end.[4] In company with the saints and doctors of the Church, William Law knew the inner meaning of that great cry of St. Paul: *Pray without ceasing*. Devotion is 'a State and Temper of the Heart'.

Friendship does not require us to be always waiting on our Friends in external Services. . . . It is not to begin and end as external Services do, but is to persevere in a Constancy like the Motion of our Heart, or the Beating of our Pulse. It is just so in Devotion. Prayers have their Hours, their Beginning, and Ending. But that Turn of Mind, that Disposition of the Heart towards God, which is the Life and Spirit of Prayer, is to be as constant and lasting as our own Life and Spirit.[5]

There must be no compromise at this point. The dedication must be absolute. 'Christianity does not consist in any partial amendment of our Lives, any particular moral Virtues, but in an entire Change of our natural Temper, a Life wholly devoted to God.'[6] But Law takes care to safeguard his words. In expounding 1 John iii. 9, he says:

This is not to be understood as if he that was born of God was therefore in an absolute State of Perfection, and incapable afterwards of falling into anything that was sinful. It only means that he who is born of God is possessed of a Temper and Principle that makes him utterly hate and labour to avoid all sin: he is therefore said *not to commit Sin*, in such a Sense as a Man may be said not to do that, which it is his constant Care and Principle to prevent being done. . . . When Holiness is such a Habit in our Minds, so directs and forms our Designs, as Covetousness and Ambition directs and governs the Actions of such Men as are governed by no other

[1] *Treatise*, c. i. 5.   [2] *Serious Call*, c. xxiv; Overton's ed., 298.
[3] *Treatise*, c. i. 15.   [4] Ibid., c. xii. 196.   [5] Ibid., 196.
[6] Ibid., c. ii. 29.

Principles, then are we alive in God, and living Members of the mystical Body of his Son Jesus Christ.[1]

In his earlier years John Wesley objected to William Law that such a view of Christian duty was too high to be attainable.[2] But Law both silenced and satisfied him for the time by saying: 'We shall do well to aim at the highest degree of perfection, if we may thereby attain to mediocrity.' Whatever measure of truth this answer conveys, Wesley could not be satisfied or silenced by it for many years. As we shall see, the facts of religious experience in the Evangelical Revival drew him to a more advanced view.

But Law never faltered in his insistence that this absolute devotion was for all Christians and was no mere vocation for the few. The *Treatise* owes the strength of its appeal to this one fact. No evangelist will be granted much success unless he can see the saint in any sinner. No religious writer can awaken the souls of men as Law did, unless he can believe so passionately that every one is called to Perfection. The charge may be brought against him with some justice that he did not make sufficient allowance for the varieties of human nature. An amusing illustration is found in the *Serious Call* where he urges the rash opinion that every one can sing. But not quite so rash is the opinion that every one is called to a communion with God. Is any child utterly incapable of recognizing and loving his Father? Law uses another line of argument to prove his point.

As all Christians are to use the same holy and heavenly devotions, as they are all with the same earnestness to pray for the Spirit of God, so is it a sufficient proof that all orders of people are, to the utmost of their power, to make their life agreeable to the one Spirit for which they are all to pray.[3]

The argument rests on the assumption that prayer is a universal obligation. This was not an axiom for 'Fulvius', to whom Law gives some notable pages in this very chapter. Fulvius has no religion, no devotion, no pretences to piety. But Fulvius is a rational creature and is as much

---

[1] *Treatise*, c. ii. 27.   [2] See Overton, *Life*, 80.   [3] *Serious Call*, c. x. 96.

obliged to live according to reason as a priest is obliged to attend at the altar, or a guardian to be faithful to his trust. And by neglecting the holiness of the Christian religion Fulvius is as the man who disregards the most important trust. He is like one who puts out his eyes or murders himself. He abuses his own nature, because the very nature of man is to be dependent on God and obedient and devoted to God. Thus Law founds the necessities of a reasonable and holy life 'not in the several conditions and employments of this life, but in the immutable nature of God and the nature of man'.[1]

The fourth characteristic of William Law's ideal is that Christian Perfection is likeness to Jesus Christ. Law here is one with the tradition of the Church Catholic. He is never a mere literalist. His imitation is not a blind reproduction of the outward acts. But 'we may as well expect to go to a Heaven where Christ is not, as to go to that where He is, without the Spirit and Temper which carried Him thither'.[2]

Law lays down the principle that Perfection consists in the Christ-like use of *My Station and its Duties*. Some of the passages in which he develops his view might have served as illustrations for Mr. F. H. Bradley's famous essay. 'Then are they true followers of Christ when they are doing that in their several States which Christ did in His.'[3] We may notice one particular application of this *Imitatio Christi*, because it will conduct us to a point whence we can survey both the strength and the weakness of Law's delineation of the ideal. In his treatment of prayer he bases his view of human duties on the articles of our religion, on the nature of our Lord. We are to pray constantly because 'our Blessed Saviour is now at the Right Hand of God, there making perpetual Intercession for us'.[4]

The Necessity and Reason of Prayer is founded in the Nature of God, as He is the sole Fountain and Cause of all Happiness; it is

---

[1] *Serious Call*, c. x, 89–90.   [2] *Treatise*, c. xiii. 217.
[3] Ibid., c. xiii, 218, 224.   [4] Ibid., c. xii. 195.

founded in the Nature of Man, as he is weak and helpless, and full of
Wants. So that Prayer is an earnest Application or Ascent of the
Heart to God, as to the sole Cause of all Happiness.[1]

Undoubtedly we are brought by a contemplation of
Jesus to the ultimate truth of Christian Prayer. There is
a profound distinction between God and Man; we can
never be to God all that He is to us; therefore the true
Christian attitude in prayer must be humility, receptive-
ness, adoration. And William Law then produces another
truth of the spiritual life. We sometimes exhort people to
be fervent in devotion. This is to as little purpose as to
exhort people to be merry, or to be sorry. But our tempers
always follow the judgements and opinions of our minds.
It is we ourselves who must be changed if we are to be
humble and devoted in prayer and altogether like our
Lord.

Law conducts us to this point, and leaves us there. He
says that 'Devotion is an earnest Application of the Soul to
God as its only Happiness'.[2] And he believes that to state
such ideals is enough to awaken them in other hearts. 'For
these truths cannot be believed without putting the Soul
into a State of Prayer, Adoration, and Joy in God.'[3]

Law does not exercise his mind on the problem of conversion. He can be searching and simple enough, but he
lacks the definiteness and the simplicity of an evangelist
at the very point where definiteness and simplicity are
imperative.

The defects of his doctrine are perhaps due to Law's
remoteness from ordinary human life. He lacked that last
touch of divine sympathy that makes the persuasive evangelist. 'No one can read the *Serious Call* without great
searchings of heart.' But it is possible to read the *Serious
Call* without feeling the appeal of the grace of God.

This is the first and most pervasive defect in his early
treatises. The ideal he erects must have seemed vast and
unattainable to the men of the eighteenth century. We do
not wonder that the youthful Wesley, at a time when Law

---

[1] *Treatise,* c. xii. 197.   [2] c. xii. 203.   [3] Ibid., 204.

was his 'oracle', objected that the view of duty was too
high. It was not too high, of course. But it was too high
if we forget that emphasis on the divine power and its
availability which makes the New Testament with its even
higher ideal a joyous and not a depressing book. *I can do
all things through him who strengthens me.* Though he
quotes St. Paul so often in his *Treatise*, Law never once
quotes that comfortable word. *So run that ye may obtain* is
much more congenial to the habit of his mind. At the end
of the *Treatise* he promises the seeker after perfection the
glories of heaven. There is not a word about present
power to conquer here on earth. In the light of some of
the passages already quoted it would not be fair to say that
Law only makes demands, and never offers Christ. In the
Serious Call he does dwell with attractiveness and force on
the peace and happiness enjoyed by those whose lives are
one continued course of devotion.[1] He hardly sounds this
note in his previous *Treatise*. But on the whole he is more
at ease in aiming his shrewd shafts of satire at Coelea or
Flatus, or Feliciana, than he is in directing his readers to
the Delectable Mountains.[2] As Overton says, 'the work is
more calculated to alarm than to attract. . . . There is still
a certain austerity about the Serious Call which has a
tendency to break the bruised reed.'

The second defect of his doctrine of the ideal is that he
does not see any meaning in the actual business of life.
He has not grasped Luther's conception of ordinary life
as a genuine vocation. For him 'Christianity is a Calling
that puts an End to all other Callings. We are no longer
to consider it as our proper State or Employment to take
care of Oxen, look after an Estate, or attend the most
plausible Affairs of Life, but to reckon every condition as
equally trifling and fit to be neglected for the Sake of the
one thing needful.'[3] This is his exegesis of the Parable of the
Great Supper, and the excuses of the guests. He exhorts
'men of serious Business and Management' to consider
'that the Business of the World, where they think they

---

[1] e.g. c. xi. 108, 114.   [2] Cf. Overton's criticism, 115–16.
[3] *Treatise,* c. iii. 37.

show such a manly Skill and Address, is as vain as Vanity
itself.'[1]

He does grant that some worldly cares are made necessary by the necessities of nature. But they must be bounded
by the just Wants of Nature. Our care must not seek 'to
add an imaginary Splendour to the plain demands of
Nature, or it will be vain and irregular, it is the Care of the
Epicure, a longing for Sauces and Ragouts.' It is to be
feared that aeroplanes and motor-cars, Polar exploration
and the climbing of Everest, the conquests of fresh ter-
ritories in the large domain of science, and the discovery
of new realms of beauty, would all be dismissed by Law
as Sauces and Ragouts! With the same defective sense of
all that is good in the ordinary occupations of human life,
Law will not allow any 'spare time' to the Christian.[2] Not
for him is the motto *Dulce est desipere in loco*. He must
only have 'spare time to spend in the Study of Wisdom,
in the Exercise of Devotion, in the Practice of Piety'.[3] He
must never read a play,[4] but only books that are religious
and moral. The character sketches in which Law excels
prove how lightly he valued human learning. As Canon
Overton says: 'The most illiterate of Methodist preachers
did not express a more sublime contempt of mental culture
than this refined and cultured scholar'.[5] He does not
understand the honourable motive behind the lives of men
of learning. 'If a man asks why he should labour to be the
first mathematician, orator, or statesman, the answer is
easily given, because of the fame and honour of such a distinction'.[6] The answer is easily given, and like most of such
swift condemnatory judgements passed by stern moralists
it is unjust. An ideal of the Christian life which cannot
make room for the disinterestedness of Newton or Kepler,
of Burke or many of the Renaissance humanists, is
definitely a defective ideal.

The defect is due to the habit of his mind to see grace as

---

[1] *Treatise*, c. iii, 37.   [2] Ibid., c. x. 168.   [3] Ibid., 169.
[4] There was of course justification for the extremely rigid Puritan
attitude which Law adopted to all stage entertainment. Cf. *Treatise*, 154.
[5] Overton, 46.   [6] *Treatise*, c. xiv. 233.

that which supplants Nature. Christianity and the world, nature and grace, are found in unrelieved opposition. His picture of life is in white and black.

Nothing therefore can be more plain than this, that if we are to fill our Soul with a new Love, we must empty it of all other Affections, and this by as great a Necessity as any in Nature.[1]

This is asceticism back again, even though it be inner-worldly asceticism.[2] It was the same spirit as that of the nun Antoinette Bourignon:

> Come Saviour Jesus from above!
>   Assist me with Thy heavenly grace;
> Empty my heart of earthly love,
>   And for Thyself prepare the place.

Law strongly believed in clerical celibacy, but he will not have it that perfection is any particular state such as celibacy or virginity. Yet the mistake of his ideal of perfection is precisely that of the nun's hymn. As the Baron von Hügel used to say, Grace is not the cuckoo that drives the other bird out of the nest. But Law means by Nature a state of soul which is hopelessly corrupt and devoid of God. In an unpublished fragment of Law occur these statements: 'No Religion can be true and good that is merely natural': 'Mere nature in the creature is mere want'. He dismisses the self-condemnation of poor Fanny Henshaw as the working of 'meer nature'.[3]

Lastly, the ideal held up by Law is purely individualistic. There is a sense in which individualism in religion is imperative and justifiable. No other appeal in the eighteenth century would have been warranted. An individualistic appeal which awakened the consciences of men like John Wesley, Samuel Johnson, George Whitfield, Henry Venn, Thomas Scott, has done a greater work in the world than is given to most religious writers to accomplish. But in two particulars the individualism is excessive. First, the

---

[1] *Treatise*, c. v. 69.
[2] The term is Max Weber's; see *Gesammelte Aufsätze*, i. 84. Cf. Troeltsch, *Protestantism and Progress*, 80, 140.
[3] Stephen Hobhouse, *William Law and Eighteenth-Century Quakerism* (1927), 57, 58.

motive adduced for aiming at Christian Perfection is that
it is your only chance of happiness, here and hereafter.[1]
Second, there is an apparent depreciation of religious fellowship and institutional religion.[2] To this objection it
may be answered that Law was presupposing the associations of Christians in the Church. But the fact remains
that nowhere is the thought of the *communio sanctorum*
dwelt upon and drawn out as though it were congenial to
the writer's mind.

THE LATER WRITINGS OF WILLIAM LAW

The later writings were not so influential as the *Serious
Call.* Yet it may well be doubted whether they have not
more to say to the twentieth century. Unfortunately, the
message is constantly entangled in the difficult language
and fantastic theories of Jacob Behmen. There is no contradiction between the earlier period and the later period
of Law's literary activity. He himself saw no discord
between his own doctrines, even his doctrine of the Atonement, and the official formularies of the Church of England.
But the garb in which his thought came clothed was unat-
tractive to English taste. For all that, Law is perhaps
the greatest of all our English mystics.

God is Love. From this axiom of Christian spirituality
Law was led to ask how could evil arise in God's universe.
God could not bring any creature into existence but by
breathing into it the self-existent, self-moving qualities of
His own being. The only difference between those qualities in the creature and those qualities in God is that in the
creature they exist in a state of limitation. The power of
self-motion was essential to man's original perfection. Yet
in virtue of that power he separated himself from God.[3]

This separation was the sin of the fallen angels. Separa-

---

[1] Overton, 48.

[2] This was the defect noticed by Charles Wesley: 'Do you not think
that a palpable mistake in Mr. Law's *Serious Call* that there is no command
for public worship in Scripture?' See Overton's note in his edition of the
Serious Call (Preface, xii–xiii), and *Life,* 115.

[3] *Works,* vi. 69; cf. vi. 18.

tion is the Fall; separation is sin; separation is death.[1] But
the ruin caused by the revolt of the fallen angels was not
confined to themselves. It affected the outward and visible
world. Sun, moon, and stars, fire, air, water, and earth—
all these had been the glorious kingdom of Lucifer and his
Angels. They were created to dwell here. They must live
here, in the place of their sin and fall, in the defilements
and disorders of their spoiled kingdom.[2] All visible things
are polluted, and have in them some grossness owing to
that Fall; that is why they must some day be dissolved,
and pass through a purifying fire. The fall of man was of
the same nature as the fall of the angels. By the creation
of the six days described in Genesis, the world had been
changed temporarily into a certain, but low resemblance of
its first state, and man had been introduced 'as Lord and
Prince of it, to have power over all created things, to discover and manifest the wonders of this new created world,
and to bring forth a holy offspring such as might fill up
the place of the fallen angels'.[3] But again the desire of
separation stirred within him. He began to will contrary
to the will of the Deity. The life of the Triune God was
extinguished within him.[4]

Had Law been content to stay his hand here, it would
have been easier to descry his ideal for mankind, even
amid all the mythological trappings of his theory. But he
saw the specific motive for this separation in the wandering
curiosity of the first man.[5] Before his fall man had a power
of looking with the eyes of his understanding either in-
wards or outwards; upwards or downwards. He had a
power of acquiescing and rejoicing in that which he found
himself to be, and adoring the Power and Goodness which
had brought him into the possession of such a nature. He
had too a power of wandering into conjectures and reasons
about that which he was *not*. As an intelligent creature he

---

[1] Compare the work of a modern mystic, T. S. Gregory, *They Shall
See God* (1926).   [2] *Works*, vi. 16, 17, 18.

[3] Ibid., 17, 18.   [4] Ibid., 74.

[5] Overton does not notice this side of Law's doctrine of the Fall. For
the reason given below it seems to me to be significant.

could not be without this power of wandering; it was no
defect, but a necessary part of his first perfect state:

The Eye of his new inexperienced Understanding, beginning to
cast a wandering look into that which he was not, was by an unsus-
pected Subtlety or Serpent, drawn into a Reasoning and Conjectur-
ing about a certain Good and Evil, which were no part of his own
created State.[1]

The Fall then was due to a false curiosity, to a desire for
knowledge of those things in the visible world which
should not be known. Therefore was Adam swallowed up
by this earthly life and earthly knowledge.[2] It is not fanciful to connect with this theory the distrust of all human
learning and human intellect which we have already
noticed, and which grew upon Law in his later years.[3]
Whatever the motive which led to this self-will and
separation from God, the result was disastrous enough.
Man lost his original perfection. This does not merely
mean that he lost his moral perfection, or the natural acute-
ness of his rational powers. Adam lost his first life. He
died to all the influences and operations of the Kingdom
of God on him, as we die to the influences of this world
when the soul leaves the body. At the same time the
influences of this world became opened in him as they are
in every animal at its birth into this world.[4]
From this view of the Fall we see what Redemption
must be. It must involve a restoration of the original perfection, a revival of the First Life. Such life could only be
produced by a new birth in man of the life which was lost.[5]
The Spirit of this new life was breathed into Adam soon
after the Fall. This was the meaning of the promise of the
bruising of the serpent. The Word of Life was *in-spoken*
into the first fallen Father of Man. It is this alone that

[1] *Works*, vii. 171.
[2] Ibid., 173.
[3] Ibid., 185–95, esp. 192, 193. Cf. the comments of Overton, *Life
and Opinions of Wm. Law*, 319. 'Rusticus is an utterly impossible
rustic. Law had very little knowledge of the poor except as recipients of
his bounty.'
[4] *Works*, vi. 74, 89–92.   [5] Ibid., 96, 97.

gives to all the race of Adam their power of being again
sons of God.[1]

Here we encounter a doctrine of the Seed, the light
which lighteth every man, which is hardly distinguishable
from that of the Quakers. Law says in his *Animadversions
upon Dr. Trapp's late Reply* that he had never read any of
the writings of George Fox.[2] But the resemblances between
his later teaching and that of the eighteenth-century
Quakerism have recently been investigated and made
clear.[3]

Any such doctrine must face this question. Wherein
lies the difference between Christians and non-Christians,
if both are illuminated by an inward light? Law's answer
is a good statement of his later doctrine of perfection.

> When the Son of God had . . . finished all the wonders that belong
> to our redemption . . . then a heavenly kingdom was set up on earth,
> and the Holy Spirit came down from heaven or was given to the
> flock of Christ in such a degree of birth and life as never was, nor
> could be, given to the human nature till Christ, the Redeemer of the
> human nature was glorified. . . . The heavenly life . . . of the Holy
> Spirit was the gift which He gave to His brethren, His friends and
> followers. . . . This was . . . Gospel Christianity, a thing as different
> from what was Christianity before, as the possession of the thing
> hoped for is different from hope.[4]

The goodness now made possible is angelic goodness.[5] It
is often said that we are poor, infirm men and must be
content with the poverty and infirmity of human virtues.
Law answers that 'to be content with our infirmities is to
be content with our separation from God'.[6] Not to aspire
after the one angelic goodness is to be carnally-minded,
and is death. Angelic goodness is perfectly expressed in
the two great commands of Christ; in sentences such as
these—*Whether you eat or drink or whatever you do, do all
to the glory and praise of God.*[7] This is the perfection which
had been lost;[8] the complete change of nature which is the

---

[1] *Works*, vi. 101.   [2] Ibid., 182.
[3] See Stephen Hobhouse, *William Law and Eighteenth-Century
Quakerism.*   [4] *Works*, vii. 181.   [5] Ibid., 154.
[6] Ibid., 154, 156.   [7] Ibid., 155.   [8] Ibid., 166.

effect and fruit of Christ's glorification in heaven.[1] It is possible on this earth to dwell in heaven, within the love of God.[2]

There can be no meaning in the Atonement of Christ unless the Wrath which is between God and man is removed.[3] This wrath cannot be in God,[4] for God cannot will the alteration of anything that is in Himself. The wrath is nothing else but sin or disorder in the creature.[5] Therefore Christ is the Atonement of our sins when by and from Him, living in us, we have victory over our sinful nature.[6] Our inborn natural essential state is our own hell, and cannot be anything else unless all sin be separated from us, and righteousness itself be again made our natural state, by a birth of itself in us.[7]

Divine Love is perfect peace and joy, it is a freedom from all disquiet, it is all content and mere happiness; and makes everything to rejoice in itself. Love is the Christ of God: wherever it comes, it comes as the blessing and happiness of every natural life, as the restorer of every lost perfection, a redeemer from all evil, a fulfiller of all righteousness and a peace of God which passeth all understanding. Through all the universe of things, nothing is uneasy, unsatisfied, or restless, but because it is not governed by Love, or because its Nature has not reached or attained the full birth of the Spirit of Love. . . .

Divine love is a new life and new nature, and introduces you into a new world. It puts an end to all your former opinions, notions and tempers, it opens new senses in you, and makes you see high to be low, and low to be high; wisdom to be foolishness and foolishness wisdom.[8]

In passages such as these the later mystical writings give us that which was lacking in the *Serious Call*, and the *Treatise on Christian Perfection*. He describes the new life with God which renders possible the moral transformation involved in the Christian ideal. He had always known that 'the masters of morality and human discipline' could only tame and civilize, but not transform mankind.[9] But now,

---

[1] *Works*, vii. 182.   [2] Ibid., 149, 155.
[3] *Works*, viii (*The Spirit of Love*), 70.   [4] Ibid., 71.
[5] Ibid., 70.   [6] Ibid., 74.   [7] Ibid., 81.   [8] Ibid., 108, 109.
[9] *Works*, vii. 158. Cf. the earlier part of this chapter.

as one familiar with the varied aspects of the heavenly country, he dwells on the grace whereby men are born anew. If we ask how we are to give opportunity to God to change us, he has his answer. It is not always direct and pointed. With all his exquisite style Law did not excel as a director of souls. He could not give the plain answer which plain people need. He could diagnose the need more easily than prescribe the healing. But now he has something to say which he did not say in his earlier writings.

Our need is to have the life of eternal Nature (i.e. the Nature of God) re-kindled within us.[1] If it is kindled we become capable of the Kingdom of Heaven and nothing can keep us out of it.[2] If a man in one instance can act disinterestedly, and solely from this principle, that from his heart he embraces Christ as his suffering Lord and pattern, he helps to kindle the heavenly life within the soul.[3] He must have a sense of the vanity and misery of this world, and a prayer of faith and hope to God, to be raised to a better state.[4] If a man cannot be brought to this sensibility, we are to leave him to himself in his natural state, till some good providence awakens him out of it. What we are not to do is to attempt to teach him theology, to reason with him about the Trinity or the Incarnation.[5] But when once he cries out in need, in that moment the Mercy of God and the misery of man are met together. There the Fall and the Redemption kiss each other.[6] For the Word of God is not the word printed on paper, no, not even in the Bible itself, but the universal Teacher who from the beginning to the end of time, and without respect of persons, stands at the door of every heart of man, calling and knocking by the inward stirring of an awakened divine life.[7]

Or, as he puts it in a still later writing,[8] there is 'one true, simple, plain, immediate and unerring way. It is the

---

[1] *Works*, vi. 97 (*Appeal to all who Doubt*).   [2] Ibid., 99.
[3] Ibid., 100.   [4] *Works*, vii. 180 (*Way to Divine Knowledge*).
[5] Ibid., 176.   [6] Ibid., 180, 181.
[7] Ibid., 216.   [8] *Works*, viii. 122 (*The Spirit of Love*).

way of patience, meekness, humility, and resignation to
God.' He does not mean virtues which need length of
time and variety of method for their attainment, but 'a
turning of the mind' to Christ, whereby any one may have
all the benefit of those virtues, as publicans and sinners by
their turning to Christ, could be helped and saved by Him.

When it is objected that this is too short a way, and has
too much of miracle in it, Law explains in a singularly
beautiful passage:[1]

Suppose, he says, I had given you a form of prayer in these words,
O Lamb of God that takest away the sins of the world, help me to a
living faith in Thee, would not this be a prayer of faith in Christ?
Just so when I tell you to give yourself up to patience and meekness,
I am turning you directly to the Lamb of God. 'The Lamb of God
means the Perfection of Patience, Meekness, Humility and Resignation to God. Consequently every sincere wish after these virtues,
every inclination of your heart, that presses after these virtues, and
longs to be governed by them, is an immediate direct application to
Christ, is worshipping and falling down before Him, is giving up
yourself unto Him, and the very perfection of faith in Him.' 'For
Christ is nowhere but in these virtues, and where they are, there is
He in His own kingdom.'

In these words Law has achieved a statement of the ideal
which unifies the moral and spiritual elements of Christian
perfection and which is possible at any moment for ordinary
men and women. Most of our criticisms of the earlier
treatises of Law may be advanced against his later statements. He never saw the meaning of the ordinary business
of human life. He was still fiercer against human learning
and science in his later treatises than in the earlier. He has
not overcome his sense of the impassable gulf between the
state of nature and the state of grace. If anything, it is
wider than before, owing to his eccentric doctrine of the
Fall. His piety is still individualistic. But he is now full
of such a sense of the nearness of the grace of God, the
swiftness of the divine succour, as makes our first criticism
now obsolete.

[1] *Works*, viii. 124, 125.

One more magnificent consequence of his doctrine of the inner light remains to be stated.

He has interpreted the spirit of the life of Christ as universal love. The supreme passage in which William Law's eloquence finds wings and takes flight into a pure realm far beyond the controversies of the eighteenth century is actually to be found in his controversial reply to Dr. Trapp. This gentleman, first Professor of Poetry at Oxford, and Rector of Christ Church, Newgate Street, had taken objection to Law's statement of the necessity of an inner birth in the soul: 'Salvation wholly consists in the incarnation of the Son of God in the soul or life of men'. Such teaching was labelled as Quakerism by Dr. Trapp. No other refutation was deemed necessary. In his indignant reply to such a method of discussion, William Law dares to track down this sectarian spirit to its origin, in the divisions of the Church. The greatest evil wrought by the rending of Christendom into sects is the raising in every communion of a selfish partial orthodoxy. Each sect defends all that it has, and condemns all that it has not. Had Bossuet been born in England and owned Oxford for his Alma Mater he would have written as many learned folios against Romanism as Stillingfleet. Anglicans are afraid of commending celibacy (in which Law believed) for their clergy, for fear of seeming to condone the errors of Rome. The most pious parish priests are afraid to assert the sufficiency of the Divine light and leading of the Holy Spirit, because the Quakers have made this doctrine their cornerstone. Then Law breaks out:

If we loved truth as such; if we sought it for its own sake; if we loved our neighbour as ourselves; if we desired nothing by our religion but to be acceptable to God; if we equally desired the salvation of all men; if we were afraid of error only because of its hurtful nature to us and to our fellow-churches, then nothing of this spirit could have any place in us.

There is therefore a catholic spirit, a communion of saints in the love of God and all goodness, which no one can learn from that which is called orthodoxy in particular Churches, but is only to be had by a total dying to all worldly views, by a pure love of God, and by such an unction from above, as delivers the mind from all selfishness, and makes it love truth and goodness with an equality of affection in every man, whether he be Christian, Jew, or Gentile.

That universal love, which gives the whole strength of the heart to God, and makes us love every man as we love ourselves, is the noblest, the most divine, the God-like state of the soul, and is the utmost perfection to which the most perfect religion can raise us; and no religion does any man any good, but so far as it brings this perfection of love into him. . . .

We must enter into a Catholic affection for all men, love the spirit of the Gospel wherever we see it, not work ourselves up into an abhorrence of a George Fox, or an Ignatius Loyola, but be equally glad of the light of the Gospel wherever it shines, or from what quarter it comes; and give the same thanks and praise to God for an eminent example of piety wherever it appears, either in Papist or Protestant.

This passage[1] is not yet obsolete.

[1] *Works*, vi. 183–4, 188.

CHAPTER XIX

METHODISM[1]

That I Thy mercy may proclaim,
    That all mankind Thy truth may see,
Hallow Thy great and glorious name,
    And perfect holiness in me.
                                        C. Wesley.

A CERTAIN river on the Continent rises from a mysterious spring which wells up from beneath an ancient
cathedral. Within a quarter of a mile of its source the
river has become so strong and forceful that a great mill is
worked by it. It was with such a mysterious suddenness
that the stream of Methodism appeared in the world. In
an incredibly short space of time that stream had become
a practical force. The man whose heart was strangely
warmed in Aldersgate Street in 1738 was flinging ecclesiastical propriety to the winds and winning illiterate miners
to Jesus Christ in 1739. If there are any spiritual laws to
be discerned behind the swift movement of this sudden
force, we ought to know them. John Wesley himself
thought he knew. He says that the law was to preach
Perfect Love to those who already know something of the
rule of Christ in their own lives.

There were two great influences on the mind of Wesley
as he formed his characteristic teaching on Christian Per-

[1] The primary sources are first-hand religious documents. Before all
the simple, artless autobiographies of the *Early Methodist Preachers*, 3 vols.
1837–8; 6 vols. 1865; *Wesley's Veterans*, ed. John Telford, 1912–14.
There is a further store of material in the *Arminian Magazine*, 1778 and
following years; the *Works of John Wesley*; W. B. Pope, *Compendium of
Christian Theology* (London, 3 vols., 1879), iii. 28–99; O. A. Curtis, *The
Christian Faith* (London, 1905), 371–93; F. Platt, 'Perfection (Christian)',
Hastings, *E.R.E.* ix. 728–37; W. J. Moulton, 'John Wesley's Doctrine
of Perfect Love' (in *London Quarterly Review*, July 1925); Benjamin
Hellier, 'The Scriptural Doctrine of Holiness' (essay in his *Life*, by his
son and daughter); E. H. Sugden, in his edition of *The Standard Sermons
of John Wesley* (2 vols. 1921), ii. 147–77, 442–60; J. A. Beet, in *London
Quarterly Review*, January 1920.

fection. The first was the influence of earlier writers and
saints of the Church, and the second was study of the
experience of individual Christians, first among the Moravians, and then within the fold of the Methodist Societies.

I. The foundation of the Doctrine in the mystical tradition of the Church.

Of all the earlier writers whom Wesley studied, William
Law was incomparably the most influential. The two first
biographers of John Wesley, writing a year after his death,
already recognized this.[1]

> By his excellent pen Mr. Law was the great forerunner of the
> revival which followed and did more to promote it than any other
> individual whatever; yea more perhaps than the rest of the nation
> collectively taken.

John Wesley himself had asserted something like this
in a sermon[2] preached long after his breach with his former
mentor. Speaking of the origin of the Methodists he says,
'There was some truth in Dr. Trapp's assertion that Mr.
Law was their parent.' In the introduction to the *Plain
Account of Christian Perfection*, Wesley expressly mentions
Thomas à Kempis, Jeremy Taylor, and William Law, as
the three writers who had helped him most in his quest.

But his debt was far deeper than he acknowledges in
that tract. He mentions Clement of Alexandria and the
portrait of the Perfect Christian in the seventh book of the
Stromateis as the inspiration of his own endeavour to portray such a character.[3] The hymns of both the Wesleys
contain frequent reminiscences of the very words of St.
Augustine. Not only the great passages of the *Confessions*,
but the *Soliloquies* and the *Tractates on the Gospel of John*
are quoted in the hymns. There are also probable reminiscences of Plotinus, the hymn of St. Thomas Aquinas in

---

[1] Coke and Moore, *Life*, 7.

[2] No. 107 on 'God's Vineyard', *Works*, vii. 203; cf. the same vol.,
Sermons 93. 9; 95. 3; 118. 1.

[3] *Journal*, Standard ed., v. 197. In 1774 he criticizes the 'Apathy' of
Clement's ideal as Stoic. 'I do not admire that description as I did formerly.'
Works, xii. 297–8.

the Roman Breviary, and a hymn of Adam of St. Victor.[1]
In early life John Wesley studied the *Theologia Germanica*
and some of the writings of Tauler; he greatly admired
the writings of the Cambridge Platonists; his abridge-
ment of the *Guida Spirituale* of Molinos was the only
edition issued in England between 1699 and 1775. Before
the Revival began he had studied Antoinette Bourignon
and Madame Guyon. He read the *Homilies* of Macarius
the Egyptian in Georgia.[2] He published an extract from
the *Homilies* in the first volume of the *Christian Library*.[3]
He quotes Macarius in the Sermon which more than any
other may be regarded as the epitome of the message of
the Evangelical Revival.[4] These facts are overwhelming
proof of his debt, whether avowed or unconscious, to the
mystical tradition of the past.[5] As the great nineteenth-
century theologian of Methodism says, the doctrine of
Christian Perfection was presented to the Wesleys at first
in its mystical and ascetic form, as an object of ethical aspiration;
it never afterwards lost this character; the grandeur and depth of
Thomas à Kempis and the best Mysticism of antiquity are reflected
in the hymns of Charles Wesley, and in all the writings of John
Wesley, even the most controversial, on this subject. To this preparatory discipline the Methodist doctrine owes much; the foundations of its future highest teaching were laid before the first elements
of it were clearly understood.[6]

II. The Experiences of the Early Methodists.

The doctrine of the Wesleys was not fashioned out of
the religious history of John Wesley alone. This fact is
often ignored in the histories of the Evangelical Movement. But the *Journal* of John Wesley affords proof
enough of the eager curiosity and acute observation which
he showed in recording the details of the experiences of

[1] Details are given in the learned and attractive volume of Henry Bett,
The Hymns of Methodism in their Literary Relations (1913, 2nd ed., 1920),
45–58.   [2] *Journal*, Standard ed., i. 254.
[3] The extract covered no fewer than sixty pages.
[4] *Works*, vi. 45, Sermon 43, 7.
[5] Cf. the essay by the present writer on 'Methodism and the Catholic
Tradition' in *Northern Catholicism* (1933), ed. N. P. Williams and C. Harris.
[6] W. B. Pope, *A Compendium of Christian Theology*, iii. 88.

those who had entered into new life. To his care in securing autobiographies and biographies we owe one of the most interesting spiritual treasures which the Christian Church possesses—the *Lives of the Early Methodist Preachers*. In addition to the seven volumes containing these thirty-six 'lives', there is a wealth of material in the *Arminian Magazine*. These records bear the stamp of life. There is an artlessness, a simplicity, a sincerity and force about them, that make the collection unrivalled in devotional literature. Singularly enough, in spite of the admiration for the 'Lives' avowed by men as dissimilar as Matthew Arnold and Charles Gore, the records are as yet an almost unworked quarry for the student of religion.[1]

It must be premised that the preaching of 'Entire Sanctification' or 'Perfect Love' was part of a particular schematization of the religious life, which is parallel to the various degrees in the doctrine of the mystics. The experience of 'conversion' precedes the experience of the 'Great Salvation'.

The word 'experience' did not mean for those early Methodists merely a lofty moment in the soul's past, but a communion with God. Experience means consciousness, and consciousness can only be real in individuals, and the appeal to experience means of course an appeal to a consciousness of God which individuals enjoy. But not only was the individual's apprehension of God to be tested in fellowship and verified by the moral conduct of daily life. Their experience was based on the objective facts of an historical revelation. There were three stages in the process of revelation, in the Christian sense of the word, if we may analyse what is implicit in their own accounts. First, there is one historical figure, the Perfect Revelation of God, Jesus in His Life and Death. Secondly, there is Revelation in the continuation of the work of Jesus, in the religious consciousness of the primitive Church, the experience

---

[1] But see S. G. Dimond, *The Psychology of the Methodist Revival* (1926); Caldecott, *Proceedings of the Aristotelian Society*, vol. viii ('The Religious Sentiment: an Inductive Inquiry'). W. James (*Varieties*) uses only Nelson's *Journal*.

which the New Testament calls the Spirit. And thirdly, there is this Revelation as it is appropriated and made real and vivid in the daily consciousness of the individual Methodist himself, in mind and heart and conscience.

The appeal to experience, then, for any Methodist meant that he put his seal to it that God was true; that is, that the facts of revelation in the New Testament were verified in his own case. But at no point is the verification independent of the life of the Jesus who was born in Bethlehem and died outside the gates of Jerusalem on a cross.

In all these records five or six points are noticeable.

1. This experience and the faith which enables the recipient to secure it are always described as a *gift*. The language of achievement is absent. This spontaneous witness of vocabulary to the essential 'givenness' of religion is the more remarkable inasmuch as there is no attempt to reproduce the phraseology of the New Testament. So in W. Delamotte's letter to Charles Wesley,[1]

God hath heard your prayers. Yesterday about twelve, He put His fiat to the desires of His distressed servant; and, glory be to Him, I have enjoyed the fruits of His Holy Spirit ever since. The only uneasiness I feel is want of thankfulness and love for so unspeakable a gift. But I am confident of this also, that the same gracious Hand which hath communicated will communicate even unto the end.

There too we may notice that the gift is usually (though not in Charles Wesley's own case) given instantaneously. Delamotte's testimony is striking, for he had long been hindered from receiving the gift (says Charles Wesley, four days before) because he could not believe that faith could be given in an instant.[2] In the Methodist revival in its first and most spontaneous appearances, sudden conversions are not the exception but the rule.

2. Secondly, this experience is usually entwined with the thought of the gracious Figure of the Gospels, and something He said or did. Often the gift is received during the reading of a miracle story, as in the striking case of Mr. Chapman who cried out 'I believe' when he heard how the

---

[1] *The Early Journal of Charles Wesley* (ed. J. Telford, 1910), 179.
[2] Ibid., 175.

woman with an issue of blood touched the hem of the garment.[1] More often the gift of faith is connected with the thought of the death of Jesus Christ.

3. The experience is communicable, but only by those who already have it. In fact there always seems some human intermediary to break the bread of God. This does not mean that the gift is always bestowed at group gatherings, during the period of united prayer. Often faith is given for the first time in solitude. But in every case some one illuminated individual seems appointed to lead the seeking soul into the expectation and desire of the light. In the case of Charles Wesley it was the poor ignorant mechanic, Mr. Bray; in John Wesley's case Peter Böhler; in the case of Delamotte, Charles Wesley himself.

4. In nearly every case conversion is preceded by a preliminary period of acute distress; of earnest seeking and prolonged prayer; sometimes of blackness and desperate struggles of soul.[2]

5. A fifth fact to be noted is that the deliverance which is given is not mere feeling, and therefore Pusey's reproach of Methodism as 'justification by feeling', falls to the ground. The consciousness of God is not an ecstasy and often does not even include a feeling of gladness or joy. The experience is not merely an emotional individual and evanescent something, comparable to the waves of feeling that in a crowd or a quarrel or a recital of good news may beat upon the heart. It is a consciousness *of Some one*; the first moment is like the commencement of an intimacy between two who had known one another casually before. The communion given to the soul is as a friendship about which definite things may be said. In our modern phrase, the experience has an intellectual content.

It is not as if the intuitive emotional element in religion

---

[1] *The Early Journal of Charles Wesley*, 178, 186, 187.

[2] Thos. Tennant, in *Wesley's Veterans*, vi. 236–8. The most striking example is the long agony of John Haime who, after three years of conscious communion with God, passed through a period of despair which lasted twenty years. In all this time he still preached and his word was fruitful. But this story is exceptional and was a standing perplexity to Wesley himself (vi. 49).

were here having full and unfettered play, while the rational, scientific element came along afterwards and worked upon the data already supplied. The mind is vitally concerned and active throughout as in the loftiest friendship between two human beings. Even in the period of distress which preceded the bestowal of the great gift, we see a movement of the mind. And when the day of emancipation dawns, it brings a true φωτισμός, an intellectual as well as a moral and emotional illumination, and enables the liberated soul to say new things about God— or rather as in the word of Jesus, things that at once are new and old, new because only just learnt by the soul thus illuminated, old because seen by elect souls before. The mind is enabled to discriminate between truths then first firmly grasped, and truths not yet apprehended. Charles Wesley says:

I now found myself at peace with God, and rejoiced in hope of loving Christ. My temper for the rest of the day was mistrust of my great, but before unknown, weakness. I saw that by faith I stood; by the continual support of faith, which kept me from falling, though of myself I am ever sinking into sin. I went to bed still sensible of my own weakness (I humbly hope to be more and more so), yet confident of Christ's protection.

And the next day (Whit Monday) he says:

To-day I saw Him chiefly as my King, and found Him in His power; but saw little of the love of Christ crucified, or of my sins past; though more, I humbly hope, of my own weakness and His strength.[1]

6. A further fact which is evident on every page of all our records is that the experience is followed by ethical results. The immediate result is described by John Wesley, who here, at least, may be allowed to speak for all his helpers.

After my return home, I was much buffeted with temptations; but cried out, and they fled away. They returned again and again. I as often lifted up my eyes, and He 'sent me help from His holy place'. And herein I found the difference between this and my

[1] *Journal of Charles Wesley*, 149.

former state chiefly consisted. I was striving, yea, fighting with all my might under the law, as well as under grace. But then I was sometimes, if not often, conquered; now, I was always conqueror.[1]

A hymn echoes the same thought:

> I wrestle not now, but trample on sin,
> For with me art Thou and shalt be within,
> While stronger and stronger in Jesus's power
> I go on to conquer, till sin is no more.

So James Rogers says 'I had power also over inward and outward sin', though 'the fountain of corruption was not dried up'.[2]

Some of them confess to a relapse, but unhesitatingly attribute their fall to lack of discipline and watchfulness; and in nearly every case the renewal of the communion experience is speedy and complete. The soul walks for ever in another world; not indeed liberated from temptation, for newer and subtler temptations unknown before are wont to attack; but the battle is waged from a new vantage ground and on a higher plane, with infinitely brighter prospects of victory.

It is only in the light of such a preparatory 'experience' of the grace of God that the 'Great Salvation' can be fully understood. Entire Sanctification is the perfection of the regenerate state. Wesley is at pains to distinguish conversion from the 'Great Salvation'. 'We do not know a single instance, in any place, of a person's receiving, in one and the same moment, remission of sins, the abiding witness of the Spirit, and a new, a clean heart'.[3]

We now proceed to set out some typical testimonies. This experience is that of Alexander Mather,[4] Wesley's right hand man in all administrative work, who was considered at one time likely to succeed to Wesley's autocracy

---

[1] *Journal*, standard ed., i. 476–7.

[2] See W. B. Pope, *Compendium*, iii. 89, with the passages quoted to prove that this was Wesley's doctrine.

[3] Preface to the second volume of *Hymns* (1741). *Works*, xi. 380. But he is not quite consistent here. See Sugden, *Standard Sermons*, ii. 148.

[4] *Wesley's Veterans*, ii. 112–15.

in the government of the societies. Mather was a calm balanced Scot; by temperament he was remote from all extravagance in religion, and reluctant to express the inner experiences of the soul's life.

With regard to the time and place, it was at Rotherham, in the year 1757, that I enjoyed it in a far larger degree than I ever did before, or do now. . . . What I had experienced in my own mind was an instantaneous deliverance from all those wrong tempers and affections which I had long and sensibly groaned under, an entire disengagement from every creature, with an entire devotedness to God: and from that moment I found an unspeakable pleasure in doing the will of God in all things. I had also a power to do it, and the constant approbation both of my own conscience and of God. I had simplicity of heart and a single eye to God at all times and in all places, with such a fervent zeal for the glory of God and the good of souls as swallowed up every other care and consideration. Above all, I had uninterrupted communion with God, whether sleeping or waking. O that it were with me as when the candle of the Lord thus shone upon my head! While I call it to mind, my soul begins to wing its way towards that immediate enjoyment of God. May it never be retarded, but press into the glorious liberty, which is equally free for all the sons of God.

As to the manner wherein this work was wrought: After I was clearly justified I was soon made sensible of my want of it. For although I was enabled to be very circumspect, and had a continual power over outward and inward sin, yet I felt in me what I knew was contrary to the mind which was in Christ, and what hindered me from enjoying and glorifying Him as I saw it was the privilege of a child of God to do.

He goes on to mention how inadequate he felt to his work, when called to preach, and how the promises of Scripture surpassed anything he already possessed, and then says:

Having a full assurance of the power and faithfulness of the Promiser, my soul often tasted of their sweetness, and though unbelief prevented my immediate possession, yet I had a blessed foretaste of them . . . I was inflamed with great ardour in wrestling with God, and determined not to let Him go till He emptied me of all sin and filled me with Himself.

This I believe He did when I ventured upon Jesus as sufficient to save to the uttermost. He wrought in me what I cannot express, what I judge it is impossible to utter.

Thomas Rankin, also of Scottish birth, writes:[1]

After labouring as in the fire, from the month of June to September, the Lord gave me such a discovery of His love as I had never known before. I was meeting with a few Christian friends who were all athirst for entire holiness, and after several had prayed, I also called on the name of the Deliverer. . . . While these words were pronounced with my heart and lips 'Are we not O Lord the purchase of Thy blood? Let us then be redeemed from all iniquity', in a moment the power of God so descended upon my soul, that I could pray no more. It was

> That speechless awe which dares not move,
> And all the silent heaven of Love!

I had many times experienced to the power of redeeming love and in such a manner as I scarce knew whether in the body or not. But this manifestation of the presence of my adorable Lord and Saviour was such as I never had witnessed before, and no words of mine can properly describe it. . . . The language of my heart every moment was 'Oh what has Jesus done for me!'

Thomas Walsh has been called Wesley's typical helper.[2] Certainly Wesley looked on him with especial admiration.[3] For a man of his years, Walsh had extraordinary learning, especially in Hebrew. 'I do not know any preacher', said Wesley, 'who in so few years as he remained upon earth, was an instrument of converting so many sinners from the error of their ways'.[4] He died in April 1759 in the twenty-ninth year of his age. His Journal is written with piercing sincerity; it is full of broken cries for perfection, for uninterrupted communion with God. Sometimes we light upon days when the intercourse is unbroken. But even when in his remorseless dealings with himself he confesses his spiritual darkness, we are aware of one who is continually advancing.[5]

---

[1] *Wesley's Veterans*, vi. 151–2.
[2] R. Green, the author of a modern biography of Walsh (1906).
[3] *Works*, xii. 206.   [4] *Works*, xiii. 336.
[5] *Wesley's Veterans*, v. 144, 160.

It is notable that, like Wesley himself, he never claimed to have attained the goal. Two years before he died a report was spread that he 'professed to be cleansed from all sin'. Morgan wrote to him to inquire. In his reply Walsh asked that his words might not be quoted, and the letter was not published till after his death. He said:

(1) I feel the constant witness of the Spirit of God, that I am forgiven, and that I love God and my neighbour. (2) I do not feel any evil tempers. (3) I firmly believe that God will eternally save my soul. But whether all sin is taken out of my heart, and the possibility of grieving the Spirit of God, I do not determine; neither do I think that I love either God or my neighbour as I ought, or as I shall. I am helpless, but God is my strength. I live by faith. I am ashamed. I have no wish that anyone should believe I am saved from all sin.[1]

His Journal after this letter shows struggle, aspiration, attainment, with frequent 'dry seasons'. He discerns fresh depths and heights of holiness, attainable in this world.[2]

These experiences all display the same marks.

(i) The goal is uninterrupted communion with God. It is also described as Love, including both Love to God and love to man.

(ii) The attainment is the gift of God, just as the entrance on the Christian life (conversion) is His work.

(iii) The entrance on this larger experience is instantaneous, i.e. it is given in a moment, and can be dated.

(iv) There is a process of struggle and quest leading to the decisive moment.

(v) There is full consciousness of the need for progress in love and growth in the spiritual life after the Great Salvation has been received.

(vi) The experience includes a deliverance from all conscious sin. The recipients believed that indwelling sin had been rooted out of them. They were conscious of a liberty beyond anything previously experienced.

(vii) But all of them are most careful not to claim perfection, or sinlessness, or even enjoyment of that Great Salvation, at the time at which they write.

[1] *Wesley's Veterans*, v. 145. [2] Ibid., 150.

EXPOSITION OF THE DOCTRINE OF JOHN WESLEY.

1. *The necessity of aiming at perfection.* This is where Wesley begins. In 1725 he had read Jeremy Taylor, and 'was exceedingly affected' by the part of the book which discusses purity of intention. He saw that every part of his life must be dedicated to God. In reading Thomas à Kempis 'I saw that simplicity of intention and purity of affection, one design in all we speak or do, and one desire ruling all our tempers are indeed the wings of the soul, without which she can never ascend to the mount of God'. Then Law's *Christian Perfection* and *Serious Call* convinced him more than ever of the absolute impossibility of being half a Christian.

2. *This perfection is love.* In the first of all his published writings, the Sermon preached in St. Mary's on 1 January 1733, he says:

> Let your heart be filled with so entire a love to Him, that you may love nothing but for His sake. . . . Desire other creatures so far as they tend to this; love the creature as it leads to the Creator.[1]

In his translation from Gerhardt he sees the same ideal:[2]

> O grant that nothing in my soul
> 　　May dwell but thy pure love alone!
> O may thy love possess me whole,
> 　　My joy, my treasure, and my crown;
> Strange fires far from my heart remove;
> My every act, word, thought be love!

3. *Love includes the keeping of all the commandments.* The Christian 'cannot lay up treasures upon earth, no more than he can take fire into his bosom'.[3] He cannot speak evil of his neighbour, nor utter an unkind word. He cannot speak idle words.[4]

Love hath purified his heart from envy, malice, wrath and every unkind temper. It has cleansed him from pride.[5] He prays without ceasing. . . . In this he is never hindered, much less interrupted, by any person or thing. In retirement or company, in leisure, business or conversation, his heart is ever with the Lord. Whether he

---

[1] *Works*, xi. 368.　　　　[2] Ibid., 369.　　　　[3] Ibid., 373.
[4] Ibid., 373; but see *Works*, xii. 207.　　　　[5] Ibid., 372.

lie down or rise up, God is in all his thoughts: he walks with God continually; having the loving eye of his soul fixed on Him, and everywhere seeing Him that is invisible.[1]

4. *Perfection is freedom from sin.* It does not mean freedom from ignorance, nor from mistake. Christians may fall into a thousand nameless defects, either in conversation or behaviour—such as impropriety of language, ungracefulness of pronunciation. They are not free from infirmities such as weakness of understanding, heaviness of imagination. No one can expect to be freed from temptation. Wesley appeals to the first epistle of St. John and declares: 'A Christian is so far perfect, as not to commit sin'.[2]

The above categorical statement occurs in the *Plain Account* which received various revisions and enlargements, the last being in 1777.[3] It is singular to find that in a letter of 12 May 1763 he had written: 'Absolute or infallible perfection I never contended for. Sinless perfection I do not contend for, seeing it is not scriptural.'[4] He had repudiated the phrase twenty years earlier in the controversy with Whitefield.[5] But in 1767 he says: 'I do not contend for the term *sinless*, though I do not object against it'.[6] It is difficult to reconcile his statements on this point. In the same letter in which he says that sinless perfection is not scriptural, he continues:

A perfection such as enables a person to fulfil the whole law, and so needs not the merits of Christ—I acknowledge no such perfection; I do now and always did protest against it. 'But is there no sin in those who are perfect in love?' I believe not. But be that as it may, they feel none; no temper contrary to pure love, while

---

[1] The quotations under this head are all taken from *The Character of a Methodist* (*Works*, viii. 339–47). All of them are repeated in the *Plain Account* (*Works*, xi). It will be noted that *The Character of a Methodist* was the work inspired by Clement's Seventh Book of the *Stromateis*.

[2] *Works*, xi. 376.

[3] So Thomas Jackson in *Works*, xi. 366.

[4] *Works*, xii. 257. He must mean that the actual adjective 'sinless' is never used in the New Testament to qualify perfection.

[5] Simon, *John Wesley and the Methodist Societies*, 45.

[6] *Works*, xi. 446. *Brief Thoughts on Christian Perfection.*

they rejoice, pray, and give thanks continually. And whether sin is suspended or extinguished, I will not dispute. It is enough that they feel nothing but love.[1]

Evidently Wesley is using the word sin in two distinct senses. Sin means either any falling short of the divine ideal for humanity, or it means a voluntary transgression of a known law of God which it was within our power to obey.[2] It was only in the latter sense that Wesley maintained we could be free from sin.

5. So far we have not yet encountered the old *distinction between voluntary and involuntary transgressions*. It would seem that Wesley had deliberately avoided it. He had explained away the passage of St. James[3] (πολλὰ γὰρ πταίομεν ἅπαντες) as not having reference to any real Christian.[4] But a discussion in the Bristol Conference of his preachers in 1758 forced the distinction upon his mind.[5]

Q. Have they that are perfect need of the merits of Christ? Can they pray for forgiveness?

A. (1) Every one may *mistake*, as long as he lives.

(2) A mistake in *opinion* may occasion a mistake in *practice* (as in Mr. de Renty).

(3) Every such mistake is a transgression of the perfect law.

(4) Therefore every such mistake, were it not for the blood of atonement, would expose to eternal damnation.

(5) It follows that the most perfect have continual need of the merits of Christ, even for their actual transgressions, and may well say for themselves, as well as their brethren, 'Forgive us our trespasses'.

Q. What does Christian perfection imply?

A. The loving God with all the heart, so that every evil temper is destroyed; and every thought and word and work springs from and is conducted to the end by the pure love of God and our neighbour.

---

[1] *Works*, xii. 257.

[2] See the discussion of this ambiguity by the late Principal Wilfrid J. Moulton, *London Quarterly Review* (July 1925), 20–1.

[3] iii. 2.

[4] *Works*, xi. 375. The date of the publication of the Sermon quoted is 1740. See *Works*, xi. 374. But see the very different exposition in an unpublished sermon, Moore, *Life of Rev. John Wesley*, ii. 216, quoted below.

[5] See Simon, *John Wesley the Master Builder*, 49–50.

The mistake in the conduct of Mr. de Renty was his wearing an iron girdle! This, of course, was due to the mistaken opinions occasioned by his papistical upbringing.[1] In 1759, the distinction between sin as the voluntary transgression of a known law and sin as the involuntary transgression of a divine law, known or unknown, is clearly stated as part of the doctrine which the Methodists believed. 'A person filled with the love of God is still liable to these involuntary transgressions. Such transgressions you may call sins, if you please; I do not, for the reasons above mentioned.'[2]

It is difficult to carry through such a distinction without contradictions. In 1761 Wesley preached a sermon from the words of St. James (In many things we all stumble) in which one of his main divisions was: 'A mistake may occasion my loving a good man less than I ought; which is a defective, that is, a wrong temper.'[3] It is impossible to harmonize this with the oft-repeated statement that entire sanctification is a deliverance from all 'evil tempers', 'all tempers contrary to pure love'. We must acquiesce in the verdict of one of the most sympathetic modern students of Wesley's doctrine: 'I have found no way of harmonizing all of Wesley's statements at this point; and I am inclined to think that he never entirely cleared up his own thinking concerning the nature and scope of sin.'[4]

6. *The reception of the experience is instantaneous.* Ordinarily, says Wesley, inward sanctification is not given till a little before death.[5] That is because men do not expect it sooner. The work itself is always wrought in an instant.[6]

[1] See Simon, op. cit., 61; *Works*, xi. 394–5; xi. 364; xii. 293, 294, 344, 352, 447; xiii. 127; viii. 190–1.   [2] *Works*, xi. 396.

[3] Henry Moore, *Life of Rev. John Wesley* (London, 1825), ii. 216.

[4] O. A. Curtis, *The Christian Faith* (1905), 378.

[5] *Brief Thoughts* (1767), *Works*, xi. 446; *Plain Account*, *Works*, xi. 387, 393, 402.

[6] The evidence for this is the testimonies to entire sanctification which Wesley had examined. He gives an account in Sermon 83. *Works*, vi. 490–1. But in his Sermon on 'The Scripture Way of Salvation' he says, 'Perhaps it may be gradually wrought in some; I mean in this sense, they do not advert to the particular moment wherein sin ceases to be.' *Sermons*, Standard ed. ii. 459; see Sugden's notes ad loc.; *Works*, vi. 53.

'But I believe a gradual work, both preceding and following that instant.'[1]

7. *The Assurance of the Great Salvation.* We now come to the supreme difficulty in any exposition of Wesley's doctrine. Has it been realized in life? Unfortunately this question was not put in such general terms. Wesley's question is:

Q. When may a person judge himself to have attained this?

A. When, after having been fully convinced of inbred sin, by a far deeper and clearer conviction than he experienced before justification, and having experienced a gradual mortification of it, he experiences a total death to sin, and an entire renewal in the love and image of God, so as to rejoice evermore, to pray without ceasing, and in everything to give thanks. Not that 'to feel all love and no sin' is a sufficient proof. Several have experienced this for a time, before their souls were fully renewed. None therefore ought to believe that the work is done, till there is added the testimony of the Spirit, witnessing his entire sanctification, as clearly as his justification.

Q. But whence is it that some imagine they are thus sanctified when in fact they are not?

A. It is hence; they do not judge by all the preceding marks, but either by part of them, or by others that are ambiguous. But I know no instance of a person attending to them all, and yet deceived in this matter. I believe, there can be none in the world. If a man be deeply and fully convinced, after justification, of inbred sin; if he then experience a gradual mortification of sin, and afterwards an entire renewal in the image of God; if to this change, immensely greater than that wrought before he was justified, be added a clear, direct witness of the renewal; I judge it as impossible this man should be deceived therein, as that God should lie. And if one whom I know to be a man of veracity testify these things to me, I ought not, without some sufficient reason, to reject his testimony.[2]

With his usual sanity and candour, Wesley recognized at once the immense danger of Pharisaism[3] and spiritual pride in any claim to the attainment of entire sanctification.[4] If he had seen no peril, the events of 1763 would

[1] *Works*, xi. 446; cf. 426.   [2] *Works*, xi. 401–2.
[3] See above, p. 7, and below, pp. 333–4.
[4] Some of his language is unguarded: e.g. *Works*, xi. 405, 'But he is deceived. What then? It is a harmless mistake, while he feels nothing but love in his heart'. But when Wesley deals with particular claims, he can

have forced him to utter warnings.[1] At the same time it is significant that he nowhere claims the experience which he so often describes.

Dr. Curtis believes that he has found the moment when Wesley became conscious of the Great Salvation. In the *Journal* (for 1744, Standard ed. iii. 157) we read:

Dec. 24. In the evening I found such light and strength as I never remember to have had before. I saw every thought as well as every action or word, just as it was rising in my heart; and whether it was right before God, or tainted with pride or selfishness. I never knew before (I mean not as at this time) what it was 'to be still before God'. . . . *Tuesday*, 25, I waked by the grace of God in the same spirit; and about eight, being with two or three that believed in Jesus, I felt such an awe and tender sense of the presence of God as greatly confirmed me therein: so that God was before me all the day long. I sought and found Him in every place; and could truly say, when I lay down at night, 'Now I have *lived* a day'.[2]

It is impossible either to prove or to disprove the theory of Dr. Curtis. But this passage is one indication among others that he himself had entered into the supernatural realm of conquest and abiding peace.[3] If he did not know, in his own soul, at least in some measure, what Perfect Love was, he could hardly with any candour have recommended all his preachers to preach that doctrine. And in whatever particular John Wesley failed, he never failed in candour.

But the difficulty still remains. How did it come to pass that the apostle of the Evangelical Revival, convinced that the movement only prospered so far as Perfect Love was preached, positing, as he did, that sanctification, like justification, must be attended by the inward witness, encouraging those who believed that they had attained to bear their

be plain-spoken, as ever. *Works*, xi. 424–6. On the danger of pride and its effects, see *Works*, xi. 429–43; Simon, *John Wesley the Master Builder*, 123 f.

[1] For an account of these, see Simon, *John Wesley the Master Builder*, 106–7, 119–20, 121–8; Tyerman's *Life of John Wesley*, ii. 432–4; Moore, *Life of John Wesley*, ii. 217–31.

[2] *Journal*, Standard ed. iii. 157.

[3] I agree with W. J. Moulton, *London Quarterly Review* (July 1925), 22.

testimony to the attainment—himself never bore such testimony? Was it some fastidiousness, some half-unconscious suspicion that avowal would be perilous to the health of his soul?[1]

We turn from this insoluble question to a more detailed examination of the doctrine. This is no esoteric message for the few. Thousands of ordinary men and women have lived by the teaching which we have analysed. The section in the Methodist Hymn-book headed 'For Believers Seeking Full Redemption' has been that to which five generations of Methodists have most naturally and readily turned. The sanctification expected has been an ideal possible of attainment in the struggle and suffering of ordinary human life. This is the first mark which distinguishes the doctrine from others which have preceded it.

In the second place, we see in this doctrine the attainment of the Christian ideal connected more directly with the believer's experience of Christ Crucified than in any other teaching of perfection (Quakerism perhaps excepted, see pp. 291–2) since the New Testament. Space has been lacking to recount the examples of this centrality of the Cross in the experiences of the early Methodists.[2]

But the same story is told even more winningly in the hymn-book.

> Thou didst undertake for me,
>   For me to death wast sold;
> Wisdom in a mystery
>   Of bleeding love unfold;
> Teach the lesson of Thy cross,
>   Let me die with Thee to reign;
> All things let me count but loss,
>   So I may thee regain . . .

---

[1] Dr. Sugden's answer does not fully meet the difficulty. 'Wesley came more and more to see that it *was* an ideal, to which the believer approximates ever more closely, though it may be impossible to say that he has absolutely attained it.' *Standard Sermons of John Wesley*, ii. 150.

[2] See especially the experience of Sampson Staniforth, a soldier in the campaign of Fontenoy (*Wesley's Veterans*, i. 74–5), Matthew Arnold says (*St. Paul and Protestantism*, 36) that this is of precisely the same order as

Thine in whom I live and move,
  Thine the work, the praise is Thine;
Thou art wisdom, power, and love,
  And all Thou art is mine.[1]

Other spiritual writers before the eighteenth century had
let down their anchor in the thought of the grace of God.
Few had seen so gratefully the prize offered by the hand
of goodness stretched out from the Cross. Even St. Bernard himself, as we have seen, recommends those who have
advanced some way in the progress towards perfection to
let go the thoughts of the death of the Man Jesus Christ.

The third distinctive mark of the ideal is that it is not
merely individualistic. Even Troeltsch, whose generalizations are usually so just, calls Methodism 'the revivifica-
tion of the primitive faith of Christianity in a sharpened
individualistic form'.[2] The phrase may be true of Bunyan
and the Puritans.[3] It is not true of the early Methodists.
To them conversion meant immediate entrance into a fellowship unknown before. They felt their experience to be
altogether incomplete without it: 'Our own individual life',
says one nurtured within the tradition,[4] 'comes to its true
blossoming and fruitage, not in its separate unity, but as
a part of this great company, membership of which is
absolutely essential to the growth, and finally to the
existence, of our own personality.'

The Great Salvation was sought in the early band
meetings and society classes of Methodism. For example,
George Shadford, the Lincolnshire soldier, says: 'In a fort-
night after (i.e. after his conversion) I was joined in society.
. . . It is really marvellous that all who are awakened have
not resolution enough heartily to unite in fellowship with
the people of God. It is very rare that such make any

the conversion of St. Paul. Cf. also the experience of James Rogers
(*Wesley's Veterans*, vii. 140).
  [1] No. 348 in Wesley's book (1780); 358 in the book in use till 1904;
424 in the 1904 Methodist Hymn-book; and 465 in the new 1933 edition.
  [2] *Die Soziallehren der christlichen Kirchen und Gruppen* (Tübingen,
1912), 836–7; E. tr. ii. 721.
  [3] R. H. Coats, *Types of English Piety* (1912), 152.
  [4] W. Bradfield, *Personality and Fellowship* (1914), 92.

progress'.[1] C. Wesley's hymn, often quoted by Fletcher, and selected by John Wesley as the authentic word of Methodism, is full of the longing for the communion of saints.

> Call them into thy wondrous light,
> Worthy to walk with thee in white;
> Make up thy jewels, Lord, and show
> The glorious, spotless church below.
>
> From every spot and wrinkle free,
> Redeemed from all iniquity,
> The fellowship of saints make known;
> And, O my God, might I be one!

The missionary motive was explicitly connected with the pursuit of holiness.

> That I Thy mercy may proclaim,
>   That all mankind Thy truth may see,
> Hallow Thy great and glorious name,
>   And perfect holiness in me.

This is no merely individualistic piety.

What are the defects in this doctrine? Professor Clement Webb suggests that the Methodist ideal is defective if the aspirant after holiness takes the mere feeling of assurance in abstraction from the particular acts in which such a holy life expresses itself.[2] However the doctrine may have been reduced or misconstrued in the hands of lesser men, that criticism is not valid against the teaching of John Wesley. As we have seen, at every point, in every turn of his thought, he lays all possible stress on the fulfilment of the moral law. That there are defects in Wesley's doctrine is undeniable. But their root is to be found elsewhere.

I venture to suggest that they spring from an inadequate analysis of the nature of sin. According to his definition, sin is a voluntary transgression of a known law. Dr. F. R. Tennant would have us use the word 'sin' only in this narrower sense. But the word has too long a history behind

---

[1] *Wesley's Veterans*, ii. 185; cf. ii. 24.

[2] See the whole of his careful comparison of the ideals of the Evangelical and Tractarian movements, *Religious Thought in the Oxford Movement* (1928), 112–23.

it for such a limitation to be possible. Indeed the narrower
sense is not even desirable. Our worst sins are often those
of which we are unconscious. The stress on the consciousness and deliberate intention of the agent is the most
formidable defect in Wesley's doctrine of the ideal. If
only those transgressions are overcome which are recognized to be transgressions by the agent, the degree of
sanctification attained by him will depend on his previous
moral development, on his own insight into motive, and
on his knowledge of himself. And γνῶθι σεαυτόν is an
infinitely difficult ideal. Many otherwise good people are
unconscious of their own selfishness. The quarrelsome
man genuinely thinks that every one is unreasonable but
himself. The revengeful man believes that he is animated
only by a proper self-respect. 'Moral evil', says Martineau,
'is the only thing in the creation of which it is decreed that
the more we are familiar with it, the less we know of it.
. . . The blindness which is induced by all deliberate injury
to our moral nature, and which thickens its film as the
habit grows, is one of the most appalling expressions of the
justice of God.'[1] Such blindness may affect a whole community, accustomed to a moral evil which no conscience
has ever challenged.

These considerations which hold good even of the com-
moner vices, the more flagrant sins,[2] are true of the subtler
and more deadly sins of the spirit. Pride in all its forms,
vanity, egotism, spiritual complacency, a self-centred religion, the Pharisaism which is goodness, and yet is false
goodness—all these forms of moral evil are most likely to
appear in those whose lives are disciplined and virtuous.
'The selfish principle does not require vice as its instrument; so long as it can get behind the last erected class of
virtues, can dominate the situation, and dictate the motive,
it is enough. It retreats then behind the last ground gained,
whether of truth or morals, and uses the latest virtues as
its fulcrum and leverage'.[3] This type of evil necessarily

[1] *Endeavours after the Christian Life.*
[2] See von Hügel, *Essays and Addresses,* i. 4–5.
[3] J. B. Mozley, *University Sermons* (1895), 42.

goes with a high level of moral and religious attainment. The essence of the vice we now call Pharisaism is that it is unconscious hypocrisy; it may even hide behind a man's penitence for his past. As a reviewer once said of the biography of a famous Evangelical pietist: 'The prayer of the publican may be no better than the prayer of the Pharisee, if it be written carefully in a Journal and published by his literary executor.'

These considerations make it impossible for us to acquiesce in the distinction between voluntary and involuntary, conscious and unconscious, which, as we have seen, plays a prominent part in Wesley's doctrine. It is only fair to point out that in the less formal and more intimate teaching which we meet in the hymns there are many hints at such a sense of the subtlety, ingenuity, hiddenness of moral evil as we have been attempting to convey. The Wesleys dreaded the doom which follows on moral evil, the doom of 'hardness'; and hardness meant insensibility, an inability to repent, an incapacity to see.

> Show me, as my soul can bear,
>   The depth of inbred sin;
> All the unbelief declare,
>   The pride that lurks within.
>
> With softening pity look,
>   And melt my hardness down;
> Smite with Thy love's resistless stroke,
>   And break this heart of stone!

But what becomes of the instantaneous deliverance from every evil temper, if sin be seen as thus ceaselessly menacing our very virtues, our spiritual attainments? It would seem that this stress on the instantaneous nature of the deliverance masks a deficient analysis of the nature of moral evil in traditional theology. Strange as it may seem, one might write over many a theory, even of those who thought they emphasized the malignity and heinousness of sin, the Anselmic motto from the *Cur Deus Homo*, the words which were the turning-point of the argument: *nondum considerasti quanti ponderis sit peccatum*. Inheriting

as he did the Augustinian doctrine of original sin,[1] Wesley
tends to speak of sin as a *quantum*, or hypostasis; as a
substance which might be expelled, or rooted out, or as an
external burden which might be taken away. As Dr. Sugden has pointed out, he never quite shook off the fallacious
notion 'that sin is a *thing* which has to be taken out of a
man, like a cancer or a rotten tooth'.[2] In the 1768 *Minutes*
he says: 'From the moment we are justified there may be
a gradual sanctification, or a growing in grace, a daily
advance in the knowledge and love of God. And if sin
ceases before death, there must in the nature of the thing
be an instantaneous change. There must be a last moment
wherein it does exist, and a first moment wherein it does
not.'

But sin is not a mere *thing*. From a mere bundle on the
back however burdensome a man may be delivered in an
instant. How can he be delivered in an instant from that
which he himself is?[3] The man himself must be changed;
and we are changed by the companionship of the Indwelling Spirit of God.

It is singular that the sweeping condemnation of human
nature into which Augustine, and Wesley after him, had
fallen, actually tends to ignore the real strength and
subtlety of moral evil as it appears in self-will. It is because
sin is the depravation of faculties and instincts which are in
themselves good, that sin is so hard to fight. And there is
a constant tendency in any theory which goes back to
Augustinianism to identify sin too exclusively with concupiscence. While it is therefore possible, and even likely,
that a complete emancipation from certain lower and
easily recognizable kinds of sin will be gained by any one
who has entered into a new and transforming experience
of God, it is not so likely that the subtler sins of Pharisaism

[1] Cf. Sermon 38 (Standard ed., ii. 207–25) with the passages quoted by
N. P. Williams from Augustine and Luther, *The Ideas of the Fall and of
Original Sin*, 364–74, 428–31.
[2] *Standard Sermons*, ii. 459; 148–9. Cf. N. P. Williams, *Ideas of the
Fall and of Original Sin*, 429.
[3] See Moberly, *Atonement and Personality* (1901), 31–2.

will be once and for ever uprooted in that same spiritual crisis. Here, as so often, the later thoughts of Wesley are better than much of his earlier expositions. In the *Minutes* of 1770 he asks: 'Does not talking of a justified or a sanctified *state* tend to mislead men? Almost naturally leading them to trust in what was done in one moment? Whereas we are every hour and every moment pleasing or displeasing to God according to our works; according to the whole of our inward tempers and our outward behaviour.'[1]

A second defect in Wesley's doctrine of perfection has already been touched upon in the previous exposition. It lies in that characteristic word 'assurance'. We have noticed that Wesley himself never laid claim to the blessing of 'entire sanctification', and yet he spoke and wrote about the experience as though he fully appreciated, as if from the inside, the gift to which others laid claim. The dangers of laying claim to such an experience are sufficiently obvious. Nothing has more discredited the whole subject of 'sanctification' than the unlovely self-sufficiency of many who have testified to the possession of holiness. Is it not possible that the defect lies in a confusion latent in Wesley's use of the word 'assurance'? He started from the principle that in all matters affecting the Christian salvation, perfect faith is attended by its interior evidence.

Q. 16. But how do you know that you are sanctified, saved from your inbred corruption?

A. I can know it no otherwise than I know I am justified. *Hereby know we that we are of God* in either sense *by the Spirit that He hath given us.* We know it by the witness and by the fruit of the Spirit. And, first, by the witness. As when we were justified, the Spirit bore witness with our spirit that our sins were forgiven; so when we were sanctified, He bore witness that they were taken away. . . .

Is not the same thing implied in that well-known Scripture, *The Spirit itself beareth witness with our spirit that we are the children*

---

[1] See Sugden, *Standard Sermons*, ii. 458. It must be noted that the foregoing discussion does not deny the possibility of supreme crises, great moments in the spiritual life. The sole question is the claim of Wesley that believers may be in an instant freed from all indwelling sin.

of God? (Romans viii. 16). Does He witness this only to those who are children of God in the lowest sense? Nay, but to those also who are such in the highest sense. And does He not witness that they are such in the highest sense? What reason have we to doubt it?[1]

The word 'assurance' carries within it one of the marks of the Christian life. The New Testament offers to those who repent and believe an awareness of God, a conscious communion. The consciousness is of the very essence of the new relationship. Just as every child was meant to know its father, so every man was meant to know God. But if our criticism of Wesley's doctrine of sin is valid, the word 'assurance' is inapplicable to the uprooting of all indwelling sin. A man may bear testimony to his awareness of a God who is willing and able to 'destroy the last remains of sin'. He cannot know himself well enough to claim that God has already done it. He can be aware that he is in the hands of One whose presence floods his heart with the spirit of supernatural love. But he cannot without pride believe that he is now no longer on a permanently lower level, but on a permanently higher level. The first kind of assurance is a conviction about God. The second kind of assurance is a conviction about himself. The emphasis in such a trust will be upon a particular deliverance in the past rather than on the experienced Deliverer in the present.

John Henry Newman made the most searching and, if it were valid, the most fatal criticism of Protestantism when he said:

A system of doctrine has risen up during the last three centuries in which faith or spiritual mindedness is contemplated and rested on as the end of religion instead of Christ. . . . Stress is laid rather on the believing than on the Object of belief, on the comfort and per-suasiveness of the doctrine rather than on the doctrine itself. And in this way religion is made to consist in contemplating ourselves instead of Christ; not simply in looking to Christ, but in ascertaining that we look to Christ, not in His Divinity and Atonement, but in our conversion and our faith in those truths.[2]

As a criticism of the Methodist teaching in the eighteenth

---

[1] *Plain Account, Works,* xi. 420, 421.
[2] J. H. Newman, *Lectures on Justification* (3rd ed. 1874), 324, 325.

century Newman's strictures are easily refutable. The paragraph could not have been penned if the author had first sat down to read the hymns of the Wesleys. The songs on which the Methodists nourished their souls were such as these:

> Christ, from whom all blessings flow,
> Perfecting the saints below,
> Hear us, who Thy nature share,
> Who Thy mystic body are.
>
> Centre of our hopes Thou art,
> End of our enlarged desires;
> Stamp Thine image on our heart,
> Fill us now with heavenly fires;
>
> .   .   .   .
>
> Lead us through the paths of peace,
> On to perfect holiness.

But the criticism of Newman would be valid against the claim to have attained entire sanctification at some date in the past, and the resting in that past experience as a proof of its own permanence. Fortunately, as we have already shown, Wesley's own reluctance to bear any public and explicit testimony to the uprooting of all sin from his own heart, proves that he was not quite happy about this element in his teaching.

One more defect in the Methodist doctrine of the ideal remains to be noticed. We have already criticized various doctrines of the pre-Reformation age for turning away from the common things of human life in their quest for God. The pervasive defect in the Protestant ideal was an asceticism curiously similar and yet distinct, an intra-mundane asceticism, if we may use the expressive phrase coined by Max Weber.[1] The Reformers had rejected the ascetic practises of monasticism, but another subtler and even more pervasive asceticism was admitted as if by a back door. For the Protestants renounced the world inwardly and from inward motives, even if they do not outwardly abandon it; their fundamental religious idea is redemption from a corrupted and God-abandoned natural

[1] *Gesammelte Aufsätze*, i. 84-163; E. tr. 95-154.

condition of things. So it was that the puritans came to
regard the secular life as an inevitable, but fortunately
transient, scene for man's activity; an opportunity for
endurance, or even a howling wilderness,[1] or a vale of tears.

In nothing is this intra-mundane asceticism[2] more strik-
ingly apparent than in the attitude of the early Methodists
to art. As human beings most of them could not help
loving the beautiful and enjoying it. But in their enjoyment they were suspicious of themselves. Wesley delighted
in architecture, and it is pleasant to read his enthusiasms,
though his judgements are often wrong. After describing
Beverley Minster he adds, as a pious afterthought: 'But
where will it be when the earth is burned up and the
elements melt with fervent heat?' At the close of an enjoy-
able afternoon in the British Museum where he saw books
and art treasures and fossils, he adds: 'But what account
will a man give to the Judge of quick and dead for a life
spent in collecting all these?'[3] He resolved to be a man of
one book—*homo unius libri*, and, to his credit be it said,
never kept his rule. He enjoyed Shakespeare to the end.
But his preachers followed the way of inner asceticism only
too closely; John Pawson burnt Wesley's copy of Shakespeare with all Wesley's copious notes. Joseph Cownley,
whom Wesley thought one of his ablest preachers, admired the beauty of Edinburgh—but at once reflects,
'After a while all this pomp will perish.'[4] I understand
that even our great nineteenth-century theologian, William Burt Pope (who only died in 1903), would never
dream of quoting Shakespeare in the pulpit, though he
diligently read through the plays every year, and knew
them almost by heart.

The result of this inward asceticism was a sharp division
of life into sacred and secular. In some continental cities,

---

[1] *Wesley's Veterans*, iii. 160; in the autobiography of John Nelson.

[2] From the second *Minutes* of Conference, 2 August 1745, it appears
that Wesley and his preachers were not sure that an 'entirely sanctified'
person would ever get married. This must be due to 1 Cor. vii. 7–8. The
most accessible reference is *Proceedings of the Wesley Historical Society*
(1896), i. 23.   [3] *Journal*, v. 176; vi. 301.

[4] *Wesley's Veterans*, iv. 158; cf. 143.

there is an almost complete contrast between cathedral and market-place; a heavy leathern curtain hangs over the doorway of the cathedral; hardly any hint of the traffic or talk of the world outside may enter in. So in the mind of the evangelicals a subtle barrier is flung between man's worship and man's work; a curtain of separation hangs between the life of the soul with God and the life of man with man.[1]

The hymns of the Wesleys are far wider in their range over life than is realized by those who sing the fragmentary masterpieces in modern services. They had caught a glimpse of the truth that religion was meant to hallow every incident of the life of man. But owing to their defective view of human nature they were unable to Christianize the manifold realms of human life. Those hymns do most wonderfully explore the intercourse of the soul with God. But they do not explore with any success the relations of men with one another.

Bunyan had seen man as a pilgrim, accomplishing an arduous journey through a perishing world, whose beauties were temptations, and whose pleasures were snares. The Methodist modified and enlarged the picture. Christian was one of a happy band of the pilgrims of eternity. But he and his companions were always viewed as 'purely spiritual beings, entangled for reasons of discipline in earthly pursuits, and encumbered for some inscrutable reason by a body'.[2] The Evangelicals did not see men as human beings. The ultimate reason for their failure was theological. The doctrine of total depravity governed their thought, and their idea of God was not rich enough.

The vision of God which was granted to the men of Wesley's day was not equal to the revelation of Him in the first three Gospels, if it be true that God is what Jesus is, in His inexhaustible interest in human life.

Our theological coat [says a modern Methodist] was cut for the figure of Total Depravity, but when it was tried on, it was found

---

[1] See the account of Thomas Walsh in *Wesley's Veterans*, v. 113–17 —an amazing document.

[2] W. R. Maltby; cf. his manual, *To Serve the Present Age*.

not to fit any kind of human nature. Accordingly we let out a seam
in the back, as far as it would go, and the margin thus gained, with
the stitches still showing, we called prevenient grace. Still the coat
does not fit, for it is not by any afterthought that we can do justice
to that boundless patience and holiness of God, which loves goodness everywhere, labours for it, and delights in it everywhere. We
have often thought of God as though it were 'all or nothing' with
Him. But it is not true. In His mysterious humility He tends the
last smouldering lamp in every rebellious heart. . . . It is He who
defends the last strip of territory against the invasion of passion,
when all the rest is gone, and raises mysterious defences about
beleaguered virtues whose doom seemed sure. When He is denied
or unrecognized in His own person, He still lingers about a man,
dimly apprehended as a sense of duty, or as some indestructible
principle, some notion of what is 'not cricket', some code of thieves,
or He returns upon us in some New Thought, some shadowy
Infinite, some impersonal Life-Force, some half-crazy system like
Christian Science, worshipping its fragment of the truth—and so
men entertain Him unawares. These vast tracts of the unbaptized
human life we make over to poets, and novelists, and dramatists,
who explore them with inexhaustible interest and sympathy. Yet
that interest and sympathy comes from God, Who loves this human
life of ours, not only as a moralist approving where it is good, and
disapproving where it is bad, but as a poet or artist loves it, because
he cannot help loving a thing so strange, piteous, and enthralling as
the story of every human soul must be.[1]

[1] Dr. W. R. Maltby, quoted (in part) by Miriam Gray, *God in Everything* (1917), 18; originally in *Methodist Recorder*, Dec. 1916.

CHAPTER XX

SCHLEIERMACHER[1]

Nur das Vollkommne vor Gott bestehen kann.—Der christliche Glaube,
104. 3.

TWO months after Wesley's long life closed, a young
tutor in the family of a Prussian count was planning
a visit to Koenigsberg. There he met Kant, whose writings
his Moravian father had bidden him to study some four
years before. Before the century closed the private tutor
was preacher at the Charité Institute in Berlin, and a member of the Romanticist circle which traced its intellectual
paternity to Goethe. It is hardly too much to say that
during that decade the new ideal which was destined to
create modern theology was born in that one man's soul.
His passionate aspiration after a richer, fuller life, his
emancipation from the tyranny of the Moravian dogma of
the total depravity of human nature, the vision of the
Universe seen by Goethe as a glorious and progressive
Whole, all combined to give meaning and life to the ideal
of the *Summum Bonum* to which he had been brought by
his earlier intellectual struggles with the philosophy of
Kant.

It was a richly gifted and impressionable nature in
which modern theology came to its birth. Fortunately, the
first and most enduring influence was that of Moravian
evangelicalism. The earliest and the last periods of his
life were bound each to each by his youthful piety. 'Christ
alone is my stay; the God who died for me on the cross.'[2]
So wrote the boy before he was seventeen years old. On
the day of his death, his last act was to hand round the

---

[1] There are now translations of his three great works: *Speeches on
Religion*, tr. John Oman, London, 1893, out of print; *The Soliloquies*,
tr. H. L. Friess, Open Court Pub. Co., 1926, cited as M. in the following
pages; *The Christian Faith*, E. tr. of the second German edition, 1830,
ed. by H. R. Mackintosh and J. S. Stewart, Edinburgh, T. and T. Clark,
1928. See also *Selected Sermons*, tr. Mary F. Wilson, London, 1890.

[2] *Life and Letters*, E. tr. by F. Rowan (1860), i. 37.

bread and the wine, repeating the words of institution. *'This is my blood of the new covenant, which is shed for many for the remission of sins.* Upon these words of Scripture I take my stand; they are the foundation of my faith.' His wife tells us that he pronounced the benediction, and said to her, 'In this love and fellowship, we are, and ever will remain, one.'

The religious genius of Schleiermacher was akin to that of Zinzendorf. Wendland[1] has described it as an expression of the feminine side of religion. Certainly, fifty years before Goethe, Zinzendorf had discovered how to enrich religion with the warmth of personal feeling, and had shown how in this sense 'the eternal womanly' could draw us on towards God. It may be granted that many pages of the *Monologen* read exactly as though they had been written by a woman. Whether either the modern feminist or the modern student of feminine psychology would agree, that the distinctive characteristics of the 'eternal womanly' are in the passive virtues, is another and a more dangerous question. Enough for our present purpose to point out that both Zinzendorf and Schleiermacher laid their religious emphasis on peace, on receptivity, on dependence, on the immediate touch of God on the human heart. But the debt of Schleiermacher to the Moravians went deeper. He had learnt to dissociate religion from mere acceptance of dogma. The doctrine of the unity of the divine and human natures in the one person of Christ, the doctrine of the legal satisfaction paid to God by the sufferings and death of Christ— these and other dogmatic formularies 'cannot possibly lead to the distinguishing characteristic of religion'. Zinzendorf did not break with these formularies, but he laid all the stress on the religious experience which those formularies should explain and guard. Ritschl[2] correctly describes the introduction of this method of regarding dogmatic formularies as an epoch in evangelical Christianity, because

[1] *Die religiöse Entwicklung Schleiermachers* (1915), 15–20.
[2] *Schleiermachers Reden über die Religion, und ihre Nachwirkungen auf die evangelische Kirche Deutschlands* (1874), 54; cf. *Speeches*, E. tr., 87, 160.

not only was Lutheranism influenced through Zinzendorf and Schleiermacher, but the origin of Methodism was due to the application of the same method. It is a further and not irrelevant reflection that in his appeal to sentiment and to the direct experience of the individual, Zinzendorf was a forerunner of Goethe and the Romanticists.[1] It was no accident that in his middle years, Schleiermacher, the pupil of the Moravians, found a home in the Romantic movement in Berlin.

Among the Moravians at Gnadenfrei, Schleiermacher was converted in his fourteenth year. He was a true spiritual son of Herrnhut. He could name the place and time of his conversion. In the *Reden* he says that the man who can point to the birthday of his religious life and tell the wondrous story of the working of God upon his soul is an individual, characteristic and special. There are no doublets in the kingdom.[2] He was always grateful to the Moravians. In a letter of 1805, he says of their love-feasts, 'there is not throughout Christendom, in our day, a form of public worship which expresses more worthily, or awakens more thoroughly, the spirit of true Christian piety'.[3] His debt to them has been traced[4] in the enhancement of the value of feeling in religion, the joy that suffused all his religious experience, the influence of their *cultus* on his mind, and his conviction of the necessity of the freedom of the Church from State control. But an even deeper debt may be observed if we read the *Reden* and the *Monologen* in the light of the following quotations from Zinzendorf.[5]

A Christian wants nothing else than to be holy. He holds it as an honour to be like Christ in all things, in His shame, poverty, and lowliness. . . . It is his element, his life, his joy.

What is Perfection? How many years must one wait for it? All

---

[1] Cf. Wendland, op. cit., 16, on the debt of Klopstock, Herder, and Goethe to the Moravians.

[2] *Reden*, 268 (Otto's ed. 165); *Speeches*, E. tr., 228.

[3] Rowan, *Life and Letters*, ii. 23; cf. ii. 321 and *Speeches*, E. tr. 151 and 189; E. R. Meyer, *Schl. u. Brinkmanns Gang durch die Brüdergemeinde* (1905), 259–68.   [4] Wendland, op. cit., 26–31.

[5] I owe these to Wehrung, *Schleiermacher in der Zeit seines Werdens*.

moralists unite to say that from year to year one becomes more perfect. But I and those like me and the Apostle and the Saviour are not of that opinion. We believe that there is no other Perfection than that given in the first minute.

The morality of the Child who is begotten of the Spirit and the morality of the servant of God who has served fifty years in the ways of the Lord are equally perfect. . . . More experience is added . . . but in itself holy is holy, and unholy is always unholy. There is no plus or minus.

For Zinzendorf holiness is more than morality. It is a looking upon God. In morality there are grades. The man who is striving after morality is never at the end of his task. There are always new difficulties to overcome, new problems to solve. But in religion

> Faith lends its realising light,
> The clouds disperse, the shadows fly;
> The Invisible appears in sight,
> And God is seen by mortal eye.

This verse of Charles Wesley is almost an echo of the saying of Zinzendorf:

> The eye of the soul must see Him.

I demand the essential thing—that a man should be certain that his spirit has seen, that his heart has seen and felt.

There are many echoes of the same music in the *Reden*.

When religion moves in a man with all its native force, when it carries every faculty of his spirit imperiously along on the stream of its impulse, we expect it to penetrate into the hearts of all who live and breathe within its influence.[1]

Schleiermacher knows the passion, and also the disappointment, of the evangelist. Believing as he does in conversion, as involving both a crisis and an imperceptible progress, he chiefly defends the cause of those who refer the beginning of their religious life to one definite moment.[2] He maintains that in conversion the distinctive character of the individual is given, the quality that renders him a 'new man'.

[1] *Speeches*, E. tr., 119 (an autobiographical passage).
[2] Ibid., 258.

This character and tone of the first childhood of his religion are borne by the whole subsequent course of his views and feelings, and are never lost, however far he may advance in fellowship with the Eternal Fountainhead.[1]

It is only a step to his characteristic doctrine that redemption is a communication to the believer of the sinless perfection of Christ. And this doctrine he owed to Zinzendorf. *Desinunt ista, non pereunt* is the apt motto adopted by the historian of Schleiermacher's sojourn in the Moravian fold.[2]

After his break with the community, Schleiermacher passed to the study of the chief representative of the *Aufklärung* in Germany, Immanuel Kant. He never became a Kantian. In a letter[3] written to his father on 23 December 1789, he says that his 'thinking began with doubting', and he does not think he can ever form a system of thought; he has had much intercourse with the firmest adherents of various systems, but has 'remained pretty much in the same stage'. But it was the study of Kant that taught him how to think. Dilthey[4] has given us a youthful essay of Schleiermacher which shows astonishing critical acumen. The main point of it is the untenability of Kant's definition of the supreme good as the combination of virtue and happiness. Happiness is conditioned by time and sensation, and therefore cannot be a conception of the pure reason. But in spite of his independence his thought displays throughout his life traces of Kant's influence. He derives his famous distinction between philosophical and historical theology from Kant.[5] He always takes his starting point from the self-consciousness; and he discovers an *a priori* principle of reason in the idea of perfection which he traces in the self-consciousness.

The German *Aufklärung* was distinguished from the parallel movements in France and England by its theo-

---

[1] *Speeches*, 228.
[2] E. R. Meyer, op. cit., 257.
[3] *Life*, i. 79.
[4] *Leben Schleiermachers* (1870); *Denkmale* (in an Appendix), 6–19.
[5] *Kurze Darstellung*, § 23, § 26; *Sämmtliche Werke*, i. 13, 14.

logical character.[1] The German people had not forgotten
the Reformation. The existence of a personal God, the
creation of the world through His wisdom and power, the
immortality of the soul, the binding necessity of fulfilling
the moral law—all these conceptions were part of the
mental furniture of the chief representatives of the new
intellectual movement in Germany. On the other hand,
Hume and Gibbon, Diderot and Voltaire, were Deists.
For them the First Cause of all things remained in ob-
scurity, and uttered no intelligible tones in the human
conscience. Kant called himself a Theist and found that
the moral law within filled him with wonder. It was, therefore, easier for one so acute and at the same time so profoundly religious as was Schleiermacher, to perceive that
the traditional rationalist theology, with its proofs of the
existence of God, had suffered a deadly blow at the hands
of Kant. Religion, he saw, could not be appropriated by
purely intellectual means. In fact the central point of
religion was not in the intellect at all.

The third influence which played upon him, ere he
developed his distinctive doctrine, was that of the Romanticists who were drawing water from new wells of life. To
us in England, Romanticism means the whole poetic movement of the time, with Wordsworth and Coleridge as well
as Schiller and Goethe, as the hierophants of the new
mysteries. In Germany the word is more often applied in
a narrower sense to a particular literary school with its
centre in Berlin. Goethe was the high priest of this coterie,
and to Schleiermacher the writings of Goethe seemed like
the revelation of a new ideal of life.[2] 'The school bore all
the marks of an extreme reaction. Individuality was often
driven to whim and self-pleasing, and the sacred rights of
feeling were too often conferred upon the shallow claims
of sentimentality. Its special appeal was to the artistic
intuition, and its special task was to expound that great

[1] Dilthey, 78 ff.
[2] See Wehrung, *Schleiermacher in der Zeit seines Werdens* (Gütersloh,
1927), 74 ff.; *Briefe*, i. 141, on Goethe's *Wilhelm Meister*. See the
following passages in *Wilhelm Meister*, viii. 1, ii. 9, viii. 3, viii. 5, viii. 7.

work of art, the Universe, with its boundless variety in closest unity of design.'[1] There was more than a touch of Pantheism in the outlook of the school. Spinoza's doctrines gave satisfaction to Goethe. Schleiermacher himself came for a time under the same spell. The world-spirit was conceived as unfolding itself in a genetic development from unconscious Nature to the highest forms of self-consciousness. Out of this conception grew the new Pantheism apparent in the systems of Schelling and Hegel.[2] But the chief contribution of Romanticism to the development of the ideal of Schleiermacher was its new conception of individuality and freedom. Frederick the Great had spoken of the feeling of duty as the supreme good of the human race. The Romanticists would rather have spoken of the duty of feeling. But the feeling was that expansive intuition of the universe as an organized, creative, and developing whole, and of themselves as possessing individuality because of the presence in each one of them of the variety of the Eternal Soul. Each person might be 'a sort of quintessence of the Universe, but with a character all his own'.[3] Schleiermacher drank deeply of the new wine of Romanticism. But amid that brilliant circle in Berlin, he stood a little apart. He was with them, but not of them. He saw that they made no place for religion in their new ideal of life. From this insight sprang the *Reden*, the *Addresses on Religion to its Cultured Despisers*. But the English translation 'Addresses' (or 'Speeches') gives no hint of the warmth and intimacy of the word *Reden*. Schleiermacher 'talks' to his brilliant eager audience as a man to men. He knows them. And the *Reden* can never be understood except as a missionary appeal. It is the superb Tract to Romanticists, by one of themselves. Like the *Protrepticus* of Clement of Alexandria it is enthusiastic, flowing, passionate, intense—even rhetorical. But the rhetoric itself is always subordinated to his desire to win

[1] J. Oman, *The Problem of Faith and Freedom in the Last Two Centuries* (1906), 204.
[2] Cf. Dilthey, op. cit., 181.
[3] Oman, op. cit., 209.

his readers to religion. In this his first great work we see Schleiermacher as evangelist.[1]

I. Analysis of the Ideal as described in the *Reden* and *Monologen*.

For our present purpose it is unnecessary to give any detailed summary of the *Reden*. Schleiermacher's main motive is to prove that religion is an original and vital element both in human nature and in history. It is not *knowing* doctrines, neither is it morality. It is *feeling*. It is an intuition of the Infinite.

A study of the *Monologen* (1800) is essential to an understanding of the *Summum Bonum* as conceived by Schleiermacher. But the *Monologen* ought not to be isolated from the *Reden* (published only a year earlier), nor indeed from the work of Schleiermacher as a whole. They form a stage in his mental development. Ritschl has observed[2] that Schleiermacher's most valuable contribution was that he applied to theology the ethical conception of the *Summum Bonum*.

In the *Monologen* we see the new forces which demand inclusion in the ideal of a perfect human life, so far as such a life can be lived on this side of the grave.

This ideal goes far beyond that of his contemporaries, whether Romanticist or rationalist. The fact is indubitable, though some modern criticism[3] has tended to assume the contrary. In the first place, Schleiermacher is opposed to the ideal of the amelioration of the outward and visible world. 'This perverse generation loves to talk of the improvement of the world.'[4] 'It plumes itself more shamelessly than any previous generation, and reviles every one

[1] The proof of this is in the *Erstes Sendschreiben an Lücke*, Mulert's critical edition (Giessen, 1908), 27. Mulert justly calls these letters 'Schleiermachers theologisches Testament'. For the actual reception given to the *Reden* see Dilthey, *Leben*, i. 427–46, and especially 445–6, Neander's estimate of the effect of the book on the younger generation.

[2] See Otto Ritschl, *Albrecht Ritschl's Leben*, ii. 84; *Rechtf. u. Vers.* i. 490; E. tr. 446 ff., especially 452.

[3] See Brunner, *Die Mystik u. das Wort* (2nd ed. 1928).

[4] M. 69 (Schiele, p. 49), E. tr. 50.

who seeks a better future, simply because the true goal of mankind, towards which the age has risked scarcely a single step, lies unknown to it in the dim distance.'[1] It is not enough that man should control the material world, tapping all its powers for his own service, and conquering space. The true ideal is more inward, more spiritual, and more social. In the second place, Schleiermacher's ideal is centred not in man's activities at all, but in religion and in God. This dominating principle is proved by his Sermons. It is unjust to discover a gap between his utterances before a congregation and his theological works, and to accuse him of inconsequence or insincerity.[2] The truth lies in a deeper insight into the presuppositions which are common both to the *Reden* and the *Monologen* on the one hand, and to the *Predigten* on the other.[3] In a sermon on prayer[4] he does battle against the self-centred view that God will do whatever man asks, because man asks it. 'To have found God is first of all to have found His will.'[5] So too the condition of the realization of the ideal of the *Monologen* is the feeling of absolute dependence on God enjoined in the *Reden* and in the *Glaubenslehre*.

1. The first mark of the ideal is freedom to be one's true self. 'The hours of happiness I have deserved, the results achieved by my efforts, . . . these are of the world; they are not myself.'[6] The essential worth of the inward deed cannot depend upon outward accomplishment or success, or else the inward and spiritual would depend on the external world. But, as we see from the *Reden*, the fact of this freedom depends on the relationship of the human spirit to the Infinite. Man is not free by being self-contained. He is free because he is in a conscious relationship to the Eternal Spirit who dwells in all things. The prevalent idea of duty was that of obedience rendered

[1] M. 70, E. tr. 51.
[2] D. F. Strauss accused him of insincerity.
[3] Wendland, 95–7.
[4] *Predigten*, i. 32; E. tr. 42, 43.
[5] *Predigten*, i. 159. This sermon (154–69), though an early one, contains a magnificent statement on the transcendence of God. See 157.
[6] M. 19 (Schiele, p. 18); E. tr. 19.

by all to the same legal injunction.[1] But Schleiermacher
now sees that each man is meant to represent humanity in
his own way. 'This thought alone has uplifted me, and
set me apart from everything common and untransformed
in my surroundings; it has made of me an elect creation
of the Godhead, rejoicing in a unique form and character.
The act of freedom which accompanied this inspiration has
assembled and integrated the elements of human nature to
make a unique existence.'[2]

One consequence of this new conception of religious
freedom has not often been drawn, but it is vital for any
modern doctrine of the ideal. The feeling for art is an
element in the complete life of the individual.[3] This does
not mean that every man is called upon to be a creator.
Schleiermacher excluded himself 'from the territory sacred
to artists'.[4] But he saw that the capacities for appreciating
nature's free artistry and for creating other forms of art
come alike from the supreme Artist, God Himself.[5] Ritschl
criticized Schleiermacher on this very ground that he made
art and religion 'lie down in one bed in order to bring
religion to perfection'.[6] Religion, thought Ritschl, had
thus been made into a variety (*Abart*) of artistic feeling for
the universe.[7] But Schleiermacher says expressly (166)
that the artistic sense can pass over into religion. It is,
therefore, not to be identified with religion. This conclusion is fortified by a letter[8] to Sack, which contains a
defence of his position against this misunderstanding.

But the true thought of Schleiermacher is that in looking

---

[1] See Oman, *Problem of Faith and Freedom*, 214, with the quotation
from Fichte expressing this view.   [2] M., E. tr. 31, 32.

[3] *Speeches on Religion*, E. tr. 138, 139.

[4] M. 49 (Schiele, p. 36), E. tr. 37.

[5] M., E. tr. 34–36; *Speeches*, E. tr. 142. It was no accident, says Kattenbusch, *Die deutsche evangelische Theologie seit Schl.* (revised ed. of *Von Schl.
bis Ritschl*, Giessen, 1924), p. 23, that S. was also the translator of Plato.

[6] *Schleiermachers Reden und ihre Nachwirkungen auf die evangelische
Kirche Deutschlands* (Bonn, 1874), 26. So Kattenbusch, op. cit. 27; and
Lipsius, *Schls. Reden*, 173.   [7] Op. cit., 28.

[8] In 1799. *Br.* i. 238. See Huber, *Die Entwicklung des Religions-
begriffs bei Schleiermacher* (Leipzig, 1901), 32.

within his own deepest being a man finds the Infinite. Thus he finds Eternal Life present in the midst of time.

As often as I turn my gaze inward upon my inmost self, I am at once within the domain of eternity. I behold the spirit's action which no world can change, and no time can destroy, but which itself creates both world and time.[1]

Every act should be accompanied by an insight into spiritual mysteries, and in every moment man can dwell beyond the moment, in the higher world.[2]

Thus even in the fleeting moment we are eternal. Individuality enters the realm of eternity. Schleiermacher called this conception of freedom his 'mysticism'. The term was misleading. This is not the mysticism of the Middle Ages, when the soul closes its eyes upon all that is human, upon all the images of the outward and visible world. Rather is it a consciousness of kinship with all humanity and an insight into Nature as the ordered realm of God. 'He saw in her the mother-soil of the higher life, and saw, too, how rich are the impulses that flow to us from her.'[3]

But lest any one should think that this liberty spells licence and should fear lest the Art, to which Schleiermacher gives honour, should become procuress to the lords of Hell, it is to be noticed that the life of individuality is impossible without love.

The highest condition of individual perfection in a limited field is a general sensitiveness. And how can this subsist apart from love? ... Love, thou force of gravitation in the spiritual world, no individual life and no development is possible without thee! ... Thou art the alpha and omega. No development without love, and without individual development no perfection in love; each supplements the other, both increase indivisibly.[4]

2. The second mark of Schleiermacher's ideal is that it is essentially social. His ultimate indictment of the ideal of his own time was that it took no account of the need for 'a higher, more intimate, spiritual community'.[5] He sees the possibility of 'a pervasive love drawing all humanity

---

[1] M. p. 22, E. tr.　　[2] M. p. 23, E. tr.　　[3] Wendland, op. cit., 115.
[4] M. pp. 38, 39, E. tr.　　　　　　　　　　　[5] M. p. 55, E. tr.

into miraculous relationships ever productive of new and marvellous fruit'.[1]

From the beginning onward Love need not be tainted. Indeed, it is natural that Love, the source of all virtues and perfections, like them should be a growth.[2]

A family can be the . . . truest picture of the Universe. When quietly and securely all things work together, all the powers that animate the Infinite are thus operative; when all advances in quiet joyousness, the high World-Spirit rules in it; when the music of love accompanies all movements, the harmony of the spheres resounds, resounds in the smallest space.[3]

It follows from these quotations that Schleiermacher's ideal preserved the balance between individuality and freedom on the one hand, and the life of society on the other. The perfect life of the society cannot be reached without the development of the individual. And the life of the individual essentially demands human intercourse, love, and an organic social life for any full attainment of its powers.

These forms of life are essential for the highest manifestation of the ideal—Friendship, Marriage, and the State. But all three are seen by Schleiermacher as deformed and stunted, unable to express the true inner fellowship of the spirit, because they all aim merely at a strengthening of man's power over things.

Friendship is open to all. But the sacrifice shown rarely issues in something greater than each could achieve independently. 'Each ought to grant the other full play to follow the promptings of his spirit, offering assistance only where the other feels a lack, and not insinuating his own ideas in place of his friend's. In this wise each would find strength and life in the other, and the potentialities within him would be fully realized.'[4]

So, too, marriage is usually a compromise of two wills. They take turns in governing. Its true significance remains

---

[1] M. p. 50, E. tr.

[2] *Predigten*, i. 220, 221. See also iv. 488–90 (All true love of our neighbour is love to God).

[3] *Speeches*, 178; Otto's ed., 141–2.   [4] M. p. 56, E. tr.

a closed secret to those that enter into it. Mere happiness
is regarded as the end towards which they must strive.
But each home ought to have its unique characteristics, and
to be the fine embodiment of a beautiful soul.

Schleiermacher's selection of Marriage as needing a
new and ideal exposition was justified. 'Kant and Fichte
could give no positive meaning to the bodily side of marriage, and so it seemed to them something of which man
must be ashamed.'[1] In this relationship, if anywhere in
this world, there is the possibility of a harmony between
body and soul, and Schleiermacher believed that through
married love the human soul could live the ideal life.

His criticism of the third main form of human society,
the State, has been amply justified by events. The theory
that the State is a necessary evil must regard State action
as always a fettering of individual freedom.[2] The reason
for such a pessimistic view is that men have no regard for
anything but visible external association. Did they but
measure life by the pursuit of spiritual ends, they would
see how the State could be moralized. 'Neither in art, nor
in the realization of human perfection is there community
of talent, such as was instituted long ago for the service
of man's external needs.'[3] But Schleiermacher was lonely
in this dream, and knew himself to be alone.[4] Lonely, too,
in these days, are those who cherish the same dream.

But Schleiermacher holds to his hope. 'It is coming!
. . . The blessed time when a true and spiritual society
shall arise cannot be remote from this present childhood
of humanity. . . . I am a prophet citizen of a later world,
drawn thither by a vital imagination and strong faith. To
it belong my every word and deed.'[5]

The reproach of self-centredness which has been cast
upon the *Monologen* will not bear examination. At first
sight the literary form of the book lays it open to such
a charge. But the same reproach would apply to all 'Con-

---

[1] Wendland, op. cit., 111.   [2] M. p. 59.   [3] M. p. 55.
[4] Cf. Dilthey, i. 461; Wehrung, *Schl. in der Zeit seines Werdens*, 233,
237, who gives some anticipations from Schiller and Novalis.
[5] M. pp. 61, 62.

fessions'. The critic would be daring who dismissed in
the same breath St. Paul's personal outpourings and St.
Augustine's prayers. And the *Monologen* are 'confessions in
the grand style'.[1] Such documents are not merely individual but typical. They speak home to the common heart,
and speak of an ideal open to all mankind.[2] And the ideal
of the *Monologen*, whatever be the expression of it in literary
form, preserves a marvellous poise between the development of the individual and the life of the community. From
the beginning of his literary activity to the end, there is no
break in the continuity of the thought of Schleiermacher
as to the place of the corporate life in his ideal. When he
comes to speak of the Church in his *Christian Faith* he says:[3]

> Here our attention is focussed on the most definite thing in our
> whole self-consciousness, where we always distinguish and combine
> both things—our independent personality in living fellowship with
> Christ, *and our life as an integral constituent of a whole.*

So too in the *Reden*[4] he speaks of the blessed time of the
complete manifestation of infinite Spirit in finite human
life, when all communicate to one another, because all are
taught of God. This overwhelming sense of the fellowship
with all mankind will enable us to understand his startling
word that 'we find the proper sphere of conscience in corporate life'.[5]

3. The Principle of the unity of the moral ideal. From
the supreme discovery which Schleiermacher made, his
'higher intuition' (M. 31), there follows a third characteristic of his ideal. It is one. This principle he learnt
from Plato.[6] He says that all virtue is contained in every

---

[1] The phrase is Hans Reuter's; *Zu Schleiermachers Idee des 'Gesamt-
lebens'* (1914), 15.   [2] See the defence of Dilthey, i. 457.
[3] § 114, 2. Ritschl, I think, misreads this passage (*Justif. and Reconciliation*, E. tr. i. 475–6). He says that Schleiermacher gives to the idea
of life fellowship with Christ as an individual, the pre-eminence over
participation in the Church. On the contrary Schleiermacher intends to
preserve a necessary balance.   [4] E. tr. 7–8.
[5] Ibid., § 83, 2. Hans Reuter, *Zu Schleiermachers Idee des 'Gesamt-
lebens'*, 30. This writer has proved what has been said above as to the
continuity of Schleiermacher's thought.
[6] *Protagoras*, 349; *Gorgias*, 507.

manifestation of righteousness; the whole of piety is in every act of obedience to the divine law; the whole of bravery in every victory over suffering and temptation.[1]

In the *Monologen*, Schleiermacher goes farther. 'Each of my acts reveals the whole of my being, undivided; each of its manifestations goes with the rest.'[2] This difficult saying must mean that a morally good act is a display of the whole personality, because the doer of it knows himself to be in touch with the Infinite Good, and does that act in that confidence. Compare the following saying:[3]

I live always in the light of my entire being. My only purpose is ever to become more fully what I am; each of my acts is but a special phase in the unfolding of this single will; and no less certain than my power to act at all is my ability to act always in this spirit.

There are two distinctions which are fundamental in the ethics of Schleiermacher. 'Every morally ordered being and every special action of the reason is ordered with a double character. It is like itself, always and everywhere, in so far as it *is* related to the reason, which everywhere is one and the same. And it is everywhere different, because the reason is always ordered in variety.'[4] Just as 'each man is meant to represent humanity in his own way, combining its elements uniquely, so that it may reveal itself in every mode,'[5] so too each action of each man who lives on this high plane of being will be unique, and will yet be in harmony with the whole personality. It follows that when a man does one action in the spirit of absolute dependence he is fulfilling the purpose of his being in that act.

The second distinction is that between man's outward mastery over nature and his cultivation of his inward life.[6]

---

[1] *Predigten*, i. 22. See the *Denkmale* at the end of Dilthey, *Leben Schleiermachers*, 90 fr. (No. 10, 16); Schleiermacher, *Kritik d. bisherigen Sittenlehre* (O. Braun's ed., Leipzig, 1910), 232–4.

[2] M. p. 22.   [3] M. pp. 71, 72.

[4] *System der Sittenlehre* (Schweizer's ed., Berlin, 1835), 94.

[5] M. p. 31.

[6] *System der Sittenlehre*, § 124 ff.; Schweizer's ed., 88–94. This is first expressed in a most interesting fragment in the *Denkmale* (Dilthey's *Leben*, 90, No. 15). There are, says Schl. only two virtues: (1) the philosophical virtue, the pure love of humanity, whose aim it is to build up the humanity

The control of the material world is only valuable if it enables the spirit to put forth all its powers. Schleiermacher sometimes speaks as though these two grades of life were two distinct historical stages in the development of mankind. But this is not true to the facts. The gains of the material mastery of life may be transmitted from one generation to another. But every generation has to win its own battle with materialism. The victory cannot be passed on as a spiritual inheritance, compact and complete.[1] The weakness of all Millenarianism is the tendency to ignore the freedom of the human will in the supposed interests of the establishment of the ideal society.

But, with Schleiermacher, we must hold to it that one side of the moral ideal is that mastery over nature which has been slowly achieved through the centuries. The value of the struggle is partly in the sense of comradeship promoted by it, but most of all in the ultimate goal to which all the victories of mankind over space and the world must be made subservient. That goal is seen by Schleiermacher in the kinship and commerce of the human soul with the Infinite and the Eternal.

Thus are reconciled and united the two essential movements in moral action,[2] the outward activity, the power of the will to do and to achieve on the visible plane, in the world of men; and on the other side, the inward activity, the mastery over self, the bowing down of the soul in humility before the Infinite. In his own personality Schleiermacher displays this synthesis. His ideal was no mere passive contemplation. Few lives have been more crowded with activities. Yet the secret of his concentrated will-power was a deep inner dependence upon God. Because God is creative activity, the calling of every man who

in human beings; (2) the heroic virtue, the pure love of freedom, which goes out to extend the mastery of man over nature. See also Dilthey, 458–60; Süsskind, *Der Einfluss Schellings auf die Entwicklung von Schleiermachers System*, 46.

[1] Cf. the discussion of this question in Wehrung, *Schl. in der Zeit seines Werdens*, 240, 241, 246.

[2] Wendland, op. cit., 84. There are illustrations of this unity in his sermons. See *Predigten*, i. 113, 121, 164 f.; cf. Süsskind, op. cit., 39–41.

is aware of God at the centre of his own personal life is a calling to activity within the kingdom of God.[1]

4. The Dependence of the ideal upon God. We now come to the central citadel. Piety is the 'feeling of absolute dependence'. For our present purpose it is unnecessary to examine the adequacy of this definition. The fact of supreme value for us is that the realization of the moral ideal in this life is the gift of God. It is more than that. The moral ideal itself includes at the heart of it the sense of this absolute dependence upon God. For, as Principal Oman has justly said, this absolute dependence is really dependence on the Absolute.[2]

Is this piety specifically Christian, or not? The debate is still proceeding. The central question would seem to be whether in Schleiermacher's developed thought any specifically Christian character is given to the Absolute. If so, the feeling of absolute dependence would have a positive content. It would not be mere emotion. It would be the sense of dependence for all the gifts of life and nature, for every vision and victory in the moral realm, on the God revealed in Christ. It may farther be suggested that in this debate the true method is not to interpret the later work of Schleiermacher (especially *The Christian Faith*) by reference to the *Reden* and the *Monologen*, but rather to interpret, and if necessary supersede, these earlier writings by the later. There are many volumes of Sermons to aid in the decision. If we follow this method there can be little doubt as to our answer. In the *Reden* and the *Monologen*, there is a tendency to use the pantheistic language of Romanticism. But for Schleiermacher, at any rate after 1805, the new life which is the gift of God was connected explicitly in his thought with the Person of Christ.[3] Schleiermacher's outlook, like that of St. Augustine, became more specifically Christian as the years went by. If

---

[1] *The Christian Faith*, § 108. 6. § 9. 2. See Stephan, *Die Lehre Schleiermachers von der Erlösung* (Tübingen, 1901), 18, 19.

[2] *Problem of Faith and Freedom*, 243. Contrast Brunner, *Die Mystik u. das Wort*, 111.

[3] See Wendland, op. cit., 170–1.

we must speak of 'evolutionary pantheism',[1] it is but a description of one stage in his thought. It is that 'preliminary pantheism', whose services to religion have been set out with discrimination and clarity by Baron von Hügel.[2] At a later stage in his spiritual development, Schleiermacher took the utmost care to repudiate the pantheism with which he was charged. He said that in order to guard against any such impression he had long hesitated about reversing the order of the two main sections of his *Christian Faith*, so that the discussion of the historical redemption wrought by Christ should precede the preliminary analysis of the religious self-consciousness. This change he had declined to make, as involving an anti-climax.[3]

II. The Doctrine of Perfection in *The Christian Faith*.

There are two moments in the later, systematic thought of Schleiermacher where we see the idea of Perfection governing his thought. (1) The first is in his stress on the original perfection of the world, and also on the original perfection of man. (2) The second is in his description of redemption as a communication of the sinless perfection of Christ.

1. The two doctrines of the original perfection of the world and the original perfection of man.

His doctrine of the original perfection of the world is derived immediately from his central principle. 'The universality of the idea of absolute dependence includes in itself the belief in an original perfection of the World' (§ 57, E. tr. 233). By the perfection of the world he means that the totality of finite existence, as it influences us (including also those human influences upon the rest of existence resulting from our place in the same), works together in such way as to make possible the continuity of the religious self-consciousness. At the beginning of his great work he has explained that the highest self-consciousness is an uninterrupted intercourse with God, and that this

---

[1] Süsskind, op. cit., 31, 32.   [2] *Mystical Element*, ii. 329–34.
[3] *Erstes Sendschreiben an Lücke* (Mulert's ed., 1908), 23 ff. See *The Christian Faith*, § 8; E. tr. 38, 39.

can be required of us (§ 5. 4–5; E. tr. 24). The possibility of this is confirmed every time a religious soul laments over a moment of his life which is quite empty of the consciousness of God, since no one laments the absence of anything which is recognized to be impossible. Since then we are to expect communion with God to be constant, we must suppose that the higher self-consciousness which is not dependent on outwardly given objects can always be conjoined with the consciousness of sensible objects (§ 5. 3; E. tr. 21). The conclusion is drawn as inevitable—that since it is the will of God that perfect human awareness of Himself can co-exist with awareness of the natural world, and the world of human beings, that world must be regarded as originally perfect.

It may be objected that the conclusion does not follow inevitably. An uninterrupted intercourse with God may be possible for one who is forced to be aware of disease or of the sinfulness of men. This was true of Christ, save only once, when He cried an exceeding bitter cry. Does Schleiermacher mean that the world of nature was perfect at a certain point in the past and that human beings are created perfect? He answers by declaring that by *original* he does not refer to any definite condition of the world or of men, nor of the God-consciousness in men. He disclaims the fable of a Golden Age previous to actual history (§ 59. 3; E. tr. 241–4).

The question is rather of self-identical perfection prior to all temporal development, and based on the inner relations of the temporal finite existence. Such perfection is affirmed in the above sense, i.e. it is laid down that all finite being, so far as it co-determines our self-consciousness, is traceable back to the eternal omnipotent causality, and all the impressions of the world we receive, as well as the particular way (consequent on human nature) in which the predisposition towards God-consciousness becomes realized, include the possibility that the God-consciousness should combine with each impression of the world in the unity of a moment (§ 57. 1; E. tr. 234).

Such an answer makes us pause. In what sense can perfection be predicated of the outward and visible world if this means merely that God uses it to aid, rather than hinder, the perfect and unbroken communion of human beings with Himself? Is it possible that Schleiermacher has taken over into his own thought, unexamined and without due recognition of the grave difficulties in the way of any complete theodicy, the optimistic doctrine of Leibniz, that this is the best of all possible worlds? Again he has his answer. He has deliberately rejected the doctrine of the best world (§ 59. 3). 'We must stop at the affirmation that the world is *good*, and can make no use of the formula that it is the *best*; and this because the former expression signifies far more than the latter.' The idea of the 'best' world implies that there were many worlds all originally equally possible with the one which actually came into existence. 'The whole productive activity of God is assumed to be selective, and therefore secondary.' This answer must mean that it is vital to Schleiermacher's ideal of the Christian life that God should be conceived as directly acting on the human soul through the outward and visible world. The soul may be set amid unfavourable relations of bodily life, and it has often been maintained that piety flourishes best in sickness or poverty. We must follow back the reasons for this till we see that, behind such a result of the stimulus of such outward circumstances to the development of the human spirit, there is all the omnipotent causality of God. The world being as God has made it, those circumstances, favourable or apparently unfavourable to the God-consciousness in man, can be so apprehended by man as to combine with his awareness of God which is the secret of all true piety.

Every moment in which we confront externally given existence involves the implication that the world offers to the human spirit an abundance of stimuli to develop those conditions in which the God-consciousness can realize itself, and at the same time that in manifold degrees the world lends itself to being used by the human spirit as an instrument and means of expression (§ 59. E. tr. 238).

This is Schleiermacher's considered expression of his doctrine of the original perfection of the world. Man on his inner side, as spirit, is aware of God. Originally his bodily side belongs to this material world into which the spirit enters. 'Only gradually does it become for the spirit instrument and means of expression—as later, mediately through it, all other things likewise become instrument and means of expression—but first of all and primarily it mediates the stimulating influences of the world on the spirit.' The original perfection of the world means, first, that in the world there is given for the spirit such an organism as the human body in living connexion with all else—an organism which brings the spirit into contact with the rest of existence. Secondly, existence is knowable (§ 59. 1; E. tr. 239). Even if there are realms of existence not yet known, those realms are capable of being apprehended by the human spirit. This, too, is the original intention of God.[1]

There are thus two ways in which the doctrine of the original perfection of the world is related to Schleiermacher's moral ideal. On the one hand the organizing ability of the spirit of man can only achieve mastery over the world by the use of the physical. The human body which brings his spirit into contact with the rest of existence is the medium by which he masters the world. And this mastery is a perpetual reminder to him of God, inasmuch as it is based upon the divine omnipotence. Any simple victory of the human spirit over nature is possible because, through and in God, spirit everywhere in nature is supreme. On the other hand, the spirit of man craves expression. The world because it is knowable gives expression to spirit. The perfection of the world means that it provides such a receptivity for the influences of the spiritual self-activity of man, as is, considered in itself, unlimited. Because 'the simple activity of spirit is expressed through the medium of space and time, . . . it awakens, as a copy thereof, the consciousness of the divine causality' (§ 59. 2).

The doctrine of the original perfection of man follows closely in the wake of the doctrine of the original perfec-

---

[1] From the human side we should prefer to say that the perfection of which Schleiermacher speaks is potential rather than actual. But he will not allow the use of the distinction. It does not exist for God (§ 54. 2; E. tr. 213).

tion of the world. Schleiermacher has rejected (§ 60, *ad fin.*; E. tr. 244) the traditional doctrine that man was created immortal, as also the view that, with alteration in his nature, the whole arrangement of the earth relatively to him was altered as well. He deduces the doctrine of the original perfection of man from his central principle that this tendency to God-consciousness, to the feeling of absolute dependence upon God, is a living impulse, and that the God-consciousness is meant to be unbroken (§ 60; E. tr. 244).

The predisposition to God-consciousness, as an inner impulse, includes the consciousness of a faculty of attaining, by means of the human organism, to those states of self-consciousness in which the God-consciousness can realize itself; and the impulse inseparable therefrom to express the God-consciousness includes in like manner the connexion of the race-consciousness with the personal consciousness; and both together form man's original perfection.

The first care of Schleiermacher is to set forth the thesis that, in the Christian ideal, communion with God is meant to be unbroken. The living impulse towards God-consciousness can only proceed from the true inner nature of the being which it goes to constitute. Hence religious men must reckon the whole range of those states with which the God-consciousness can unite as belonging to this true inner nature. 'It is an essential element in the perfection of human nature that those states which condition the appearance of the God-consciousness are able to fill the clear and waking life of man onwards from the time when the spiritual functions are developed.' We should be essentially imperfect if the emergence of the feeling of absolute dependence were confined to separate and scattered moments.

Next Schleiermacher sets out the three main ways in which the God-consciousness combines with the other forms of consciousness. First, there are 'the excitations of self-consciousness' which arise out of the physical basis of spiritual life. These may express enhancements of life or hindrances to life. But both have one and the same bearing on the excitation of the God-consciousness. Second, there is the intellectual basis of spiritual life. By means of sense-impressions the spirit may obtain knowledge. This knowledge leads to the consciousness of a natural order which involves the idea of the comprehensive inter-connexion of all being. This consciousness must co-exist with a consciousness of God. Third, there is in spiritual life the impulse to express the God-consciousness in external act, and in particular, to express in act the longing for fellowship. This line of thought leads naturally to an assertion of the inner union of the race-consciousness and the personal self-consciousness. All the outward life of man is social, and his actions are thus a communication of his inward consciousness. 'In every kind of fellowship, whatever its object, a man's acts, because accompanied by a sensible excitation of self-consciousness, may contain at the same time a communication of his God-consciousness' (§ 60. 2; E. tr. 246).

Whatever criticisms philosophers may cast on this account of the human consciousness, the closely reasoned argument, which has just been summarized, contains a notable contribution to the doctrine of the ideal. In the first place, all the conscious life of man is claimed for God. Science, leisure, all his activities belong to the ideal life and may be ruled by religion. In the second place, a *solus cum solo* beatitude is implicitly repudiated. It belongs to the essential nature of religion to propagate itself and express itself in a fellowship. Thirdly, his new formulation of the doctrine involves the supersession of old ideas such as 'original righteousness' and the like; ideas which have been ambiguously interpreted in the theologies of the past and have given rise to false theories of perfection.[1]

2. The Doctrine of Redemption as a communication of the Sinless Perfection of Christ.

For Schleiermacher, Christianity is a teleological religion. By this he means that 'a predominating reference to the moral task constitutes the fundamental type of the religious affections' (§ 9. 1; E. tr. 42). The *telos* is holiness. 'In the realm of Christianity the consciousness of God is

[1] Cf. Carl Clemen, *Schleiermachers Glaubenslehre in ihre Bedeutung für Vergangenheit und Zukunft* (Giessen, 1905), 60–1.

always related to the totality of active states in the idea of a Kingdom of God' (§ 9. 2; E. tr. 43). Or, to quote his famous definition,

Christianity is a monotheistic faith, belonging to the teleological type of religion, and is essentially distinguished from other such faiths by the fact that in it everything is related to the redemption accomplished by Jesus of Nazareth (§ 11; E. tr. 52).

Only through Jesus has redemption become the central point of religion (§ 11. 4; E. tr. 57). There is no other way of obtaining participation in the Christian communion than through faith in Jesus as Redeemer (§ 14; E. tr. 68), and to belong to the Church involves a desire to seek after the ideal of unbroken communion of God. The essence of redemption is that 'the God-consciousness already present in human nature, though feeble and repressed, becomes stimulated and made dominant by the entrance of the living influence of Christ' (§ 106, 1; E. tr. 476).

Schleiermacher sees that some of the Protestant Confessions err in putting the complete state of blessedness into the conception of forgiveness (§ 109. 1; E. tr. 496). He defines justification as a change in his relationship to God; and conversion makes itself known in each individual by Repentance which consists in the combination of regret and change of heart; and by Faith which consists in the appropriation of the perfection and blessedness of Christ. (§ 108; E. tr. 480, 481). The Faith so exercised must persist, and the perfection thus initially appropriated in Conversion becomes the sanctification of the believer. 'In living fellowship with Christ, the natural powers of the regenerate are put at His disposal, whereby there is produced a life akin to His perfection and blessedness; and this is the state of Sanctification' (§ 110; E. tr. 505).

The Sinless Perfection of Christ is therefore appropriated at every stage of the Christian life. This is made clear in Schleiermacher's examination of the consciousness of grace (§ 88). 'In this corporate life which goes back to the influence of Jesus, redemption is effected by Him through the communication of His sinless perfection.' In harmony with the ideal developed in his previous writings, communion with Christ is regarded as mediated through the Christian community. The prominence of the living fellowship of believers in the doctrine of Schleiermacher has rightly been regarded[1] as one of his greatest services to theology.

But if it is perfection that is communicated, why is that perfection never complete in us? This is the paradox that remains for us in the exposition of his thought. 'The individual life of each one of us is passed in the consciousness of sin and imperfection' (§ 100. 1; E. tr. 425). This consciousness is referred to the corporate life of general sinfulness which still has a place in the life of the redeemed man (§ 101. 2; E. tr. 432). But in the same paragraph we read that *the redeemed man, since he has been assumed into the vital fellowship of Christ, is never filled with the consciousness of any evil, for it cannot touch or hinder the life which he shares with Christ.* The stress is on the word *filled.* The consciousness of sin is pain and suffering to him, but it reaches him only as an indication of what he has to do; consequently there is in it no misery. The consciousness of evil, as existing in the corporate life round about him, remains. The consciousness of personal sin has gone.

The state of union is the real possession of blessedness in the consciousness that Christ in us is the centre of our life, and this in such a way that this possession exists only as His gift, which since we receive it simply by His will that we should have it, is His blessing and His peace.

Schleiermacher proceeds (§ 101. 3; E. tr. 434) to criticize those who relegate the enjoyment of the unclouded blessedness of Christ to the life beyond time. It is, he says, contrary to the word of Christ Himself (John v. 24). *Verily, verily, I say unto you, he that heareth my word and believeth him that sent me, hath eternal life, and cometh not into judgment, but hath passed out of death into life.* There is growth in our fulfilment of the divine will. 'Indeed Christ's highest achievement consists in this, that He so

---

[1] e.g. by Ritschl, *J. and R.* i, § 62, 63; E. tr. (1872) 443–8.

animates us that we ourselves are led to an ever more perfect fulfilment of the divine will.'[1]

Schleiermacher repudiates the view that any superfluity of goodness in Christ could be distributed among men to cloak their failure to please God. *Nur das Vollkommne vor Gott bestehen kann.* Only that which is perfect can stand before God (§ 104. 3; E. tr. 456).

This is perfectionism with a vengeance! And at the centre of the thought of the Father of modern theology! The wonder grows that so little attention has been paid to it by German theologians who have admired their great precursor. The statements quoted above do not occur in any appendix to his systematic thought, not even in his specific treatment of the doctrine of sanctification, but in his exposition of Redemption wrought by Christ, the governing idea of his dogmatic system.

(α) This perfection begins with conversion at the beginning of the Christian life. It is then manifested in regret for sin that is past. Where regret is, the regretted condition has been abjured (§ 108. 2; E. tr. 484). 'The regret that goes with conversion, relating not to particulars but to a general condition, and abjuring that condition finally, is . . . the purest and most perfect pain, which if allowed to reach its limit, might bring life to an end.' Before conversion there was a legal repentance. It was concerned with particulars. The outcome of such regret is death or despair. But the true conversion-regret must always arise out of the vision of the perfection of Christ. 'Christ awakens a wholly perfect regret just in so far as His self-imparting perfection meets us in all its truth, which is what happens at the dawn of faith.'

(β) The communication of the perfection of Christ needs time for its complete fulfilment. The reason for this is that the strength of the God-consciousness is not an original possession of the redeemed man. It is a gift which becomes his only after sin has already developed its power. What has emerged in time, can only be removed in time, by its opposite. Even if there are intermittent lapses,

[1] E. tr. 456. He quotes here John xv. 2, 5, 8, 11.

the certainty of faith is always increasing. Sin cannot win
fresh ground, now that all the powers of the life are just at
the disposal of Christ. All the time sin is being dislodged
from its former positions (§ 110. 2; E. tr. 507, 508).

(γ) One far-reaching qualification is made to the perfection attainable in this life. 'There is a boundary line
which it is not given to us to overstep.' The development
of our Lord in His earthly life was natural, but constant
and uninterrupted. There was no cleft in Him between
His actions and the indwelling of His life. To no other
who has shared the common life with its sinfulness is this
vouchsafed. This difference from Christ must, strictly
speaking, be there at every moment, even in moments
involving an advance in likeness to Christ. 'But this does
not prevent union with Christ from being operative in
every moment of the state of sanctification' (§ 110. 3;
E. tr. 508, 509).

The explanation of the sins committed by the regenerate
does not concern our present theme (see § 110. 2; E. tr.
506; and § 111; cf. § 148, 149). Suffice it to say that like
his earliest master, Plato, Schleiermacher is forced by the
imperfections of the visible society to fall back on the
society of the Invisible Church, the infallible undivided
unity wrought by the Spirit, where Christ is. And his discussion of his ideal might fitly have ended with Plato's
final word on the ideal he had reared.[1]

The city of which we are the founders . . . exists in idea (ἐν λόγοις)
only; for I do not believe that there is such an one anywhere on earth.

In heaven, I replied, there is laid up a pattern of it, methinks,
which he who desires may behold, and beholding, may set his own
house in order. But whether such an one exists, or ever will exist
in fact, is no matter; for he will live after the manner of that city,
having nothing to do with any other.

III. Criticism and Estimate of Schleiermacher's Doctrine.

Carefully guarded as are the affirmations of *The Christian
Faith*, it must be said that Schleiermacher reaches his

[1] *Republic*, ix, *ad fin.* (Jowett's tr.).

synthesis too easily. (1) The first and most serious defect
is an inadequate doctrine of sin. A great modern theologian has declared that the motive of his work has been
to bring home to the conscience of his pupils and himself
the meaning of sin and guilt.[1] That could not be said of
Schleiermacher. *Sanctus, Sanctus, Sanctus.* The Vision of
God brings the sense of sin. And if the sense of sin is
deficient we suspect some defect in the vision of God. It
may well be, as some have argued, that Schleiermacher
never entirely escaped from the early influence of Goethe's
work. It is possible to find a partial explanation in his
sheltered early life, or his singularly balanced and equable
temperament. Like Clement of Alexandria, he does not
seem to have known the full blast of temptation. But whatever the explanation, the defect is there. There are few
expressions which betray a genuine terror and pity for the
tragedy wrought in human life through moral evil. Emil
Brunner quotes the words whose melancholy music sounds
through all the theology of Calvin, 'Conscientia infelicita-
tis, miserabilis haec ruina, in quam nos dejecit primi
hominis defectio', and says that of this consciousness there
is not a single trace to be found, either in the young
Romantic or in the sixty-year old Church leader and prince
of thought.[2] Even in his message that God speaks to us all
through the outward and visible world, he gives no sign
that he had faced the problems of earthquake, or epidemic,
of idiocy, or the sufferings of animals. The argument[3] used
to refute Leibniz proves the essential optimism of his
thought. His work is a theodicy, and like most theodicies,
unsatisfying. When he treats of human nature, the contrast between God and man is that of power and weakness,
wisdom and ignorance, rather than that of holiness and
impurity.[4] This explains why his description of Christ is

[1] Rudolf Otto. See Heinrich Frick's introduction to the *Festgruss,
Marburger theologische Studien* (Gotha, 1931), Heft 3, v–vii.

[2] *Die Mystik und das Wort* (1928, 2nd ed.), 271. But there *are* some
traces in the *Predigten*. See *Selected Sermons* (E. tr. 1890), 254–6.

[3] See above, pp. 361–2; *The Christian Faith*, § 59. 3.

[4] See the contrast between Luther and Schl. drawn out by Wendland
op. cit., 92; also Wendland, 185–7.

always *Erlöser* (Redeemer) rather than *Versöhner* (Reconciler). Evil becomes a stage on the way to the consummation of all things in God. As a listener to his lectures wrote in his journal a hundred years ago, the black colour of sin is exchanged for grey!—'nach dieser Lehre das Böse seine schwarze Farbe mit der grauen vertäusche'.[1] Thus he needed no special theory of forgiveness. All the Christian life was a re-birth and a renewal, and the moment of forgiveness was only one moment in this whole.

2. It follows that in his theory of the ideal there is an absence of any feeling for a supreme meaning in the Death of Christ. He rejected all the older ideas of propitiatory sacrifice, and sees in the cross merely 'the seal of His previous activity'.[2] On this view the Cross of Christ would have no particular significance for piety. Schleiermacher is unable to appropriate the devotion of Zinzendorf to the Crucified, and to find a place for such a religious experience in his systematic thought. But in his own personal piety Schleiermacher was greater than his doctrine. At the last he declared that the foundation of his faith was in the words *This is my blood . . . shed for many for the remission of sins*. And in many later sermons[3] that faith kindled into flame.

The absence from his theology of any sense of a supreme and concentrated meaning in the Cross may be accounted for in two ways. On the one hand, his optimistic view of human nature, and his remoteness from any form of asceticism made him more at home with the thought of self-development than with that of self-sacrifice. On the other hand, he was not able, even in the later developments of his system, to give an adequate place to the historical facts of the life of Christ. His theology was Christocentric, but Christ was always regarded by him as the unique personifi-

[1] Wichern, in April 1831. *Ges. Werke*, i. 125. I owe this quotation to Wendland, 186, 187.

[2] *Predigten*, ii. 118. So in *The Christian Faith*, § 104. 4; E. tr. 462: 'His persistence in redemptive activity'.

[3] *Predigten*, iii. 242; E. tr. 372–84 (The death of Christ was for our perfection), esp. 379–82. This sermon was preached on Good Friday, 1832. Cf. E. tr. 250–65. *Predigten*, ii. 666.

cation of the supreme ideal,[1] rather than as an historical
Person who spoke certain words and died a shameful death
upon a Cross. Significant, above all, is his disparagement
of the first three Gospels. As late as 1821 he could speak[2]
of the Synoptic Jesus as 'a Jewish rabbi of philanthropic
disposition, somewhat Socratic morals, a few miracles, or
what others took for miracles, and a talent for striking
apophthegms and parables'.

It was the Fourth Gospel which according to Schleiermacher revealed the true meaning of the life of our Lord.
The Christian Faith, he said,[3] was written in elucidation of
one fundamental text—John i. 14. *The Word became flesh
and dwelt among us . . . full of grace and truth*. But those
were strange days, in which Novalis could write: 'For our
delight and instruction it is no matter whether the persons
in whose fate we trace our own really lived or not,' and in
which Kant thought of the Christ-idea as the representative
of the Humanity-idea! At all events the Person of Christ
won a new place[4] in the mind of Schleiermacher after
1807, and he saw that progress in holiness, insight into
the divine message, power of illuminating others—all these
gifts were given to those who lived in a personal relationship with their Redeemer.[5]

3. There is a deficiency in his account of Prayer, the
intercourse with God which takes place at the summit of
the Christian ideal. It is impossible to bring all such
prayer under the one formula to which it is reduced in *The
Christian Faith*. Here prayer is traced to the common consciousness of the Church that there are obstructions and
fluctuations in the accomplishment of the task of the Church
in history. This is a consciousness of imperfection, and
therefore is the work of the Divine Spirit. This consciousness moves to and fro between the present and the future;

---

[1] Cf. Lipsius, *Dogmatik*, 494–8 (507, 3rd ed.); Süsskind, *Der Einfluss
Schellings*, 278–83; Bleek, *Die Grundlagen der Christologie Schleiermachers*,
213–15; Storr, *Development*, 241, 245, 246.

[2] *Reden*, 3rd ed., Note 14 to the fifth Speech, E. tr. 262.

[3] *Zweites Sendschreiben an Lücke*, Mulert, 34.

[4] Proof is in the *Predigten*, and is set out by Wendland, 163–9. See
i. 317; ii. 138–50.   [5] iii. 157. Sermon of 1832.

sometimes success is attained in the accomplishment of its
end, sometimes failure is registered. But since success is
due not only to human activity but also to the divine
government of the world, prayer will take two forms. If
the average result of human effort is surpassed, prayer
takes the form of thankfulness. If the average result is
unachieved, prayer takes the form of resignation (§ 146.
1; E. tr. 668, 669). On the other hand, his sermons
recognize the need of the human heart to make known its
requests unto God;[1] and prayer is recognized as a genuine
intercourse between the soul and God.[2] But both in his
popular teaching and in his systematic work, he tends to
imprison God within the laws of the Universe. Prayer as
an active energy of the soul, inspired and used by God for
the release of new spiritual forces; prayer as addressed to
a God Transcendent and therefore adored—these conceptions, though occasionally allowed, are not congenial to
Schleiermacher's system. 'He failed to develop any clear
doctrine of God's Personality.'[3]

There can be little doubt as to the importance of Schleiermacher in the development of the doctrine of the Christian
ideal. In the first place, it was he who before all other
theologians in modern times defined Christianity as a teleological religion. What Christianity is must be judged by
what it does, and what it does in the imperfect earthly
society must be judged by its living ideal of all that God
can do for us in this world. Secondly, his doctrine is a
synthesis of the natural good in human nature and in
the world with the supernatural and specifically Christian
redemption which is given in Jesus Christ. Room was
thus made in Christian piety for modern scientific research,
for the creative work of the artist, for the speculative
systems of the philosopher; the dualism between God and

[1] See the eminently characteristic sermon in *Selected Sermons* (E. tr. by
M. F. Wilson), 38–51, summarized in Ménégoz, *Das Gebetsproblem im
Anschluss an Schls. Predigten und Glaubenslehre* (1911), 3.

[2] Ménégoz, 20, and reff.

[3] V. F. Storr, *Development of Theology*, 246; cf. F. Ménégoz, *Le
Problème de la Prière* (Strasbourg, 1925), 62–72, esp. 69.

the world which had wrecked previous systems was over-come.[1] Thirdly, Schleiermacher blended the idea of free individuality with that of the mediation of the community. The solitariness of the mystical ideal was transcended; the fullness of the salvation brought by Christ was not restricted to the individual. For Schleiermacher the individual is nothing if he be severed from the community.[2] The achievement of eighteenth-century Methodism in the everyday life of the Church was now carried over into the realm of systematic theological thought.

[1] See Wernle, *Melanchthon und Schleiermacher*, 52–4, on the difference of Schl.'s outlook from that of the recent resuscitation of dualism in the Barthian theology.

[2] Wehrung, *Schleiermacher in der Zeit seines Werdens*, 221, 222.

CHAPTER XXI

RITSCHL

In his formulation of 'Christian Perfection' Ritschl hit the nail on the head. But this 'Christian Perfection' admits, and indeed demands, a number of elements which Ritschl has rejected as 'pietistic'.—Harnack: *Reden u. Aufsätze*, ii. 359.

IN the book which has been described as his theological 'Last Will and Testament', Schleiermacher expressed his belief that a dogmatic theologian would come after him who would govern his work by the thought of Redemption.[1] In part, but only in part, Ritschl fulfilled this prophecy. He often recalled the occasion on which he met Schleiermacher.[2] Ritschl was then a little boy, nine years old; his father was Bishop of Pomerania, and was living in Stettin. Schleiermacher came to visit him, and the parents took their distinguished guest and their little boy for a drive. The boy sat on the box seat, and ever afterwards remembered his childish pride that he was with Schleiermacher, and yet, from the box, had a view of the surrounding country which was freer and farther reaching than the view of Schleiermacher himself. It was, he dared to think, a parable of his theological work.

Schleiermacher's theology had been hampered, as well as enriched, by the pantheistic tendency of his earlier thought. There was never any trace of pantheism in Ritschl. He was an independent and vigorous personality, with his thought clear and sharp cut. 'There is a refreshing sense of the natural man in all his criticism.'[3] If we dared to find something of the 'eternal womanly' in the piety of Schleiermacher, we could find nothing save virility in that of Ritschl. He was always a man, take him for

---

[1] *Zweites Sendschreiben an Lücke*, Mulert's critical ed., 35. See Ritschl, *J. and R.*, iii. 332; this is quoted from the E. tr. of 1902.

[2] Otto Ritschl, *Albrecht Ritschls Leben*, i. 11; see also ii. 246, in connexion with the publication of Ritschl's book on Schleiermacher in 1874.

[3] James Denney in *Expository Times*.

all in all; and such natures are slow in coming to full maturity.[1]

It is probable that Ritschl took over the central idea of his system, that of the Kingdom of God as the *Summum Bonum*, from the thought of Schleiermacher. Kant had already seen in the moral idea of the Kingdom of God the final cause of the world, but Schleiermacher was the first to use this teleological idea to characterize the Christian religion.[2] As we have already noticed, that was one of his greatest merits in the eyes of Ritschl. It is easy for us to-day, who have passed through a generation of debate on the meaning of the 'kingdom' in the teaching of our Lord, to underestimate the insight of these nineteenth-century theologians in setting the idea at the centre of Christian doctrine. Ritschl's exegesis was, no doubt, at fault. 'The idea of the kingdom of God is interpreted not at all eschatologically, and not only ethically, but soteriologically. . . . Ritschl's use of the idea is quite unhistorical.'[3] None the less, his combination of the two conceptions of Kant and of Schleiermacher was an act of astounding originality, in an age when leading theologians, such as Rothe and C. H. Weisse, could assign the kingdom to an indeterminate future, or to beings scattered in infinite space.[4]

The second influence which played on Ritschl's mind was that of Ferdinand Christian Baur. He passed under the yoke of Tübingen, only to shake himself free of it, not without pain. The symbol of his emancipation was the second edition (1857) of *The Origin of the Ancient Catholic Church*, which after three-quarters of a century remains a very great book. Its importance for our present purpose

---

[1] See Harnack's characterization in *Albrecht Ritschl; Gedenkfeiern der Universität Bonn*, 1922, p. 4. Reprinted in *Erforschtes u. Erlebtes*, 328, 329.

[2] The question of the indebtedness of Ritschl to his predecessors is well handled by H. Schoen, *Les Origines Historiques de la Théologie de Ritschl* (Paris, 1893), 87–99. Cocceius had in some sense anticipated both Kant and Schleiermacher. Ritschl, *Gesch. d. Pietismus*, i. 142. The *Panegyricus de regno Dei* of Cocceius appeared in 1660.

[3] Garvie, in *E.R.E.*, x. 816*b*.   [4] Schoen, 89–90.

is due to its recognition that Christian piety centres round
a historical Person. 'It abides in value because it does not
deal with bloodless categories but with living men, and
because it sees that the supreme concern is the Person of
Christ.'[1] Ritschl set up a new standard of reality for dogmatic theology by appealing to the Second Gospel as prior
to St. Matthew and St. Luke.

The *magnum opus* of Ritschl was *Justification and Reconciliation*; the first volume was published in 1870, the second
and third in 1874. The final chapter contains an explicit
doctrine of Christian Perfection. For the first time a theologian whose reputation and influence were destined to be
world-wide had deliberately dared to place such a doctrine
at the climax of his work. And in Germany! The position
of his discussion was carefully chosen. Just as Schleiermacher[2] would not reverse the order of the two parts of
The Christian Faith because he desired to avoid an anti-
climax, so Ritschl kept to the last his discussion of the
teleology which according to his mind dominated the
Christian revelation. This is made clear not only in this
chapter, but in the other two sources which we shall use.
One of these was the address given on 'Christian Perfection' in January 1874, before the *Frauenverein* in Göttingen. The manuscript of the last chapter of his *Justification*
was nearing completion. But the address was no mere
summary of the chapter. Rather did the necessity which
was laid upon him of expounding his ideas before a public
audience serve to clarify his mind as to the main themes of
his book. He says himself[3] that the book gained mightily
(*erheblich*) because of this address. The other source for
our exposition of his doctrine is his small volume *Instruction in the Christian Religion*. One quotation for the moment
will suffice. 'Membership in the Evangelical Church is
rather to be determined by what constitutes Christian
Perfection according to evangelical teaching.'[4]

---

[1] J. Oman, *Problem of Faith and Freedom in the last Two Centuries*
(1906), 314, where the best account of Ritschl's book is to be found,
314–24.   [2] *Sendschreiben an Lücke*.   [3] *Leben*, ii. 156.
[4] § 86. Translation by A. T. Swing, p. 279. For the importance of the

A. EXPOSITION OF RITSCHL'S DOCTRINE

In the main, Ritschl follows Luther, though, as we have pointed out, Luther does not, like Ritschl, regard the idea of perfection as governing his thought. Apart from his systematic exposition of the doctrine, Ritschl scatters observations throughout his work, as his custom is, on a theme so congenial to his mind. Thus in the conclusion to his chapter on the doctrine of God, he says:[1]

The conception of God which is given in the revelation received through Christ and to which the trust of those who are reconciled through Christ attaches itself, is that of a loving will which assures to believers spiritual dominion over the world, and perfect moral fellowship in the kingdom of God, as the *summum bonum*.

Or again, in the chapter on the doctrine of sin, he insists that the only way in which an idea of sin can be formed at all is by comparison with an idea of the good. The more or the less complete the latter, the deeper or the shallower will be our conception of the worthlessness of sin.

The Christian ideal of life, as the opposite of which we have to conceive sin, includes two different kinds of functions, the religious and the moral—trust in God by which we rise superior to the world, and action prompted by love towards our neighbour, and tending to produce that fellowship which as the *summum bonum* represents at the same time the perfected good.[2]

I. The Kingdom of God.

The *Summum Bonum* is the Kingdom of God. In this thought is expressed the divine purpose for humanity, and all the work of Christ.

Jesus saw in the kingdom of God the moral end of the religious fellowship He had to found. He understood by it not the common exercise of worship, but the organization of humanity through action inspired by love.[3]

---

doctrine in Ritschl's thought which has not always been recognized, see Fabricius, in his critical ed. xiv, xv, and Harnack, *Albrecht Ritschl* (Bonn, 1922), 14: 'In allen Religionen und Konfessionen, lässt sich ihre Eigenart am besten an dem Ideal, das sie sich von der vollkommenen Frömmigkeit gebildet haben, erkennen' (*Erforschtes* 341).

[1] *J. and R.* iii, E. tr. 326.   [2] Ibid., E. tr. 333.   [3] Ibid., 12.

The Kingdom of God is the reign of love. 'The complete (perfect) Christian conception of God is love.'[1] 'In Christianity everything is related to the moral organization of humanity through love-prompted action, but at the same time everything is also related to redemption through Jesus.' Thus Christian life has a double character. The (private) end of the individual is freedom from sin, freedom in God, the freedom of the children of God, but the Kingdom of God is the final end of all.[2] This is the meaning of the much criticized *dictum* of Ritschl that Christianity is an ellipse with two foci.

The *dictum* may still stand, inasmuch as there is in practice a real distinction between the private struggle of the solitary Christian against sin and the service which he can render to the community. But ideally, and ultimately in practice also, the two are closely inter-related. It would be just to say with Garvie that in reality Ritschl subordinates the doctrine of redemption to the doctrine of the Kingdom as the means to the end.[3] But this does not mean that the Kingdom of God is merely a moral end, or that religion has become subordinated to ethics. Dr. Kenneth Kirk has criticized Ritschl's use of the conception on the ground that in it the law remains primary, because the idea of redemption is subordinated to the moral ideal of the kingdom.[4] But in Ritschl's later work the Kingdom is essentially supernatural.[5] It is the highest good because the community founded by Christ is founded through the revelation of Himself which God has made in Christ. Christianity is the perfect religion because it gives a perfect knowledge of God.[6]

II. The Meaning of Perfection for the Individual.

Let us take the second focus of the ellipse. In what sense is the end of the individual Christian attainable in this life? And how does Ritschl justify the word 'perfect' as applied to the believer?

---

[1] *Instruction*, § 11 (ed. Fabricius).   [2] *J. and R.* iii, E. tr. 13.
[3] *E.R.E.* x. 816*b*.   [4] *The Vision of God*, 428.
[5] *Unterricht*, § 8.   [6] Ibid., § 2; Swing, 171.

He appeals to the use of the word in the Gospels and by James. He holds fast to the passage in Philippians which describes those as perfect who press on to the goal. He will have it that those who are conscious that they have not attained, and yet who, with all their powers, are earnestly and incessantly pressing forward, are actually attaining. The nature of the individual ideal is expounded in contrast with the ideal of monasticism. Not in flight from family life and earthly possessions is perfection to be found, but in the common life of mankind. All these delimitations of the doctrine we have met before. But then there comes the genuine, the highly individual and masculine Ritschl himself. The chief mark of perfection is that the Christian 'exercises dominion over the world'. All Ritschl's thought on our doctrine starts from this point, and is summed up in it. 'The lordship over the world possessed by believers is the aim of reconciliation with God in the Christian sense.' So he begins his supreme chapter in his *magnum opus*.

The sentence echoes Luther, of course. But it means far more than a restatement of Luther's prophetic word. The word needs interpretation as sympathetic as Roman Catholics have a right to ask for in our assessment of the monastic ideal. Harshly treated, the thesis might seem but another example of the 'metaphysical ego-centrism, something much subtler, much deeper, and much more serious than egoism'[1] which some modern Romans find in Luther.

We notice first that this dominion over the world is religious, through and through. It is given by God, it is the believer's destiny as willed by God, it is only attained by the identification of the end of the individual with the world-end willed by God which is the Kingdom of Heaven.

The confidence with which, whether in favourable or adverse positions in life, men cast themselves on the guidance and help of God, regarding themselves as enjoined by Him to seek the one highest goal, dominion over the world in the fellowship of the kingdom of God, is in reality a product of the Christian religion. For

[1] Maritain, *Three Reformers*, 14 (E. tr.).

the God who is Lord over the world and our Father, who cherishes no envy and wrath against His children, gives them the assurance that all things serve for their good. And this truth stands firm only when based upon our reconciliation with God.[1]

As usual, Dr. Garvie is here a safe and sympathetic guide to Ritschl's meaning.

Let all that is implied in this statement be very carefully noted. (1) The sinner has been forgiven, and his estrangement from, and enmity to, God has been removed. (2) He has accepted as the end of his life and work, not any earthly goods, but the highest good, the kingdom of God. (3) He trusts in God's care, and surrenders himself to God's will. (4) As having his portion not in this world, the circumstances of his earthly life are significant to him only as the means of spiritual discipline and development.[2]

But while admitting that the phrase 'dominion over the world', as thus interpreted, expresses a worthy element in Christian experience, Dr. Garvie goes on to say that the place assigned to it by Ritschl is in no way justified by religious experience.

But another view is possible. Ritschl is not attempting to analyse the religious experience of most Christian lives. He would rather set up an everlasting mark of the Christian victory as it may be known in this world. He is re-interpreting the call to holiness which (as Dr. Garvie says) is heard by most Christians. Holiness means for Ritschl that every man is called to completeness of life. 'Perfection' as Jesus, James, and Paul describe it and maintain it has this meaning, that every Christian ought to be or to become a whole, every man after his own kind. *Jeder ein Ganzes in seiner Art.* Religious faith and moral conduct are to be blended into an indissoluble unity.[3] Ritschl explains his meaning with greater force and lucidity in his address to the ladies of Göttingen than in his *magnum opus.* If the light of the doctrine of Christian Perfection is placed under a bushel, Christianity is not fully understood or propagated.[4]

The ultimate problem of religion, as indeed of every

[1] *J. and R.* iii, E. tr. 625.   [2] *The Ritschlian Theology,* 350.
[3] *Die chr. Vollkommenheit* (ed. Fabricius), p. 8.   [4] Ibid., p. 8.

human being, is that in man Nature has produced a being
nobler than herself. Man is at once a diminutive fragment of the world and the image of God. His worth is
other and higher than that of the whole natural realm.
God has so created man that he strives to overcome this
contradiction at the heart of his being. In no other religion
is the struggle accomplished, but in Christianity man is
integrated; he is recognized as a soul of higher worth than
the whole world. The development of character is a supernatural task; it is a task imposed on us both by religion
and by ethics, and it can only be fulfilled in a community
which acts on the assumption that spirit dominates flesh,
that things unseen are more considerable than things seen,
that the whole world is no equivalent for the spiritual life
of man. Ritschl goes so far as to say that any faith in the
scttled order of the whole world depends on this valuation
of the individual spiritual life as higher than all the natural
visible things. Those who hold such a faith in the rationality
of the universe and yet have abandoned the vessel of
Christian belief, are still clinging to a plank of that very
ship.[1] But for Christians, faith in the orderly moral government of the universe is the corollary of the faith expressed
in that word of Jesus, *What shall it profit a man if he gain
the whole world and forfeit his life?* Our conclusion, therefore, as against that of Dr. Garvie, is that Ritschl is right
in the place assigned to the idea of dominion over the world.
The problem of man's lower nature includes not only his
sinfulness, but his weakness.[2] Victory over moral evil must
be joined with a mastery of natural frailty in face of the
appalling happenings of life. We have already seen the
same mark of the triumphing life at the climax of St. Paul's
exposition of the ideal.[3]

III. The Expression of the Ideal Life.

'The form in which religious lordship over the world is
exercised is *faith in God's providence*.'[4] As we have already

[1] *Die chr. Vollkommenheit*, 10.
[2] See the clear statement of this attitude to the task of religion in the
writings of a very different thinker: von Hügel, *Essays and Addresses*,
i, p. xiii, and 43.   [3] See above, pp. 67–9.   [4] *J. and R.*, iii, E. tr. 617.

seen, Ritschl regards this belief as only firm when it is based upon our reconciliation with God.[1] Under the stress of the experiences of life, faith in God's providence produces two 'functions' or 'organs',[2] patience and humility; to these, later on, Ritschl adds prayer and fidelity to one's vocation. In the sense in which Ritschl uses the words, none of these can appear without the others. They are the expression of the Christian Perfection which belongs to the believer, reconciled as he is with God.

(*a*) Patience is distinguished as a Christian virtue from the patience whose classical model is found in Stoicism. The Stoic ideal is apathy, the suppression of pain. In Christian patience the pain continues. But the sting is withdrawn from it.[3] The sting disappears precisely when the sufferer knows that God's providence is above all, that God Himself guarantees to us dominion over the world and participation in the ideal life of His kingdom.[4] The Christian 'is raised to such a height that he can glory in the afflictions and persecutions which he undergoes for Christ's sake (Jas. i. 2; Rom. v. 3), while the Stoic who resigns himself to the course of the Cosmos, deadens his sensibility to the feeling of evil.'[5] Ritschl's view of the close connexion between the Christian ideal in face of suffering and the sense of lordship over the world is illustrated by his characteristic treatment of the doctrine of the work of Christ. In the sixth chapter of his third volume, when labouring at the summit of the dogmatic edifice which he has constructed, he asserts[6] that

Christ's patience under suffering . . . is the real test . . . of His unique power over the world.

By the patience which springs from the religious motive, men lift themselves above their misfortunes and the world. From this point of view their sufferings even become for them a helpful yoke

---

[1] *J. and R.* iii. 625; *Die chr. Vollkommenheit,* 13.

[2] *Funktionen* is the word used in the *Christian Perfection,* and as the title for the last chapter of *J. and R. Organe* is used in the text of all editions of *J. and R.,* iii. 554 (1st ed.), 592 (3rd ed.).

[3] *J. and R.,* iii. 627.   [4] Ibid., 628.   [5] Ibid., 629.

[6] *J. and R.* iii, E. tr. 460, 463 (interpreting Matt. xi. 28–30).

which brings them experience of the guiding of God. This is the proof Jesus Himself offers us of the supremacy over the world which belongs to Himself through the mutual knowledge existing between Himself and God.

I have ventured to linger over this element in Ritschl's teaching not only because it is so central in his thought, but also because his insight has penetrated to the true characteristic of Protestant saintliness. The ideal life may be lived in the world, by dominion over it. As the foregoing chapters have shown, it was only at the Reformation that this truth was firmly grasped. The ideal life had commonly been conceived as an anticipation of the bliss to come. As Ritschl often says, it was a *vita angelica*. But there is an ideal for life in this world. It is a human ideal, and patience such as that whereby Christ wrought out His unique vocation is essential to it. What is sought in this way is not aesthetic enjoyment, not ecstacies or visions, but religious strength for victory over the world. Such piety is disclosed in the prayers of the *German Passional of our Lord Jesus Christ* (Nuremberg 1548). Here the contemplation of the separate acts of the Passion leads to petitions congruous with the ideal of Ritschl:[1]

That Thou wouldst for Thy Passion's sake protect us from every snare of the devil and from all the assaults of sin;

That I may be strengthened to overcome all afflictions, sufferings, and sickness in Thy Passion;

That I may entirely surrender all my will to Thy most perfect will, so that my walk in life may ever be found in Thy service;

That I may not be moved by wicked slander, but may possess my soul in Christian patience.

(*b*) Hand in hand with patience, goes the sister of patience, humility. Humility is directed to God, as patience to the world.[2] The two are but the different sides of the shield which the Christian carries.

> And, wheresoe'er they went, like Juno's swans,
> Still they went coupled and inseparable.

---

[1] *J. and R.*, iii. 597.
[2] *Die chr. Vollkommenheit* (ed. Fabricius, 1924), 16.

Humility is a frame of mind not possible except to faith.
It rests on a deep sense of God's unspeakable gift. Ritschl
interprets the New Testament references as pointing to
'deliberate submission to the dispensations of God' as the
common meaning of them all.[1] The occasion for this
temper of soul is furnished in most cases by the sufferings
of life, or the social pressure under which we stand against
our will. But in the Publican's prayer (Luke xviii. 14) the
occasion falls out of sight. It is self-abasement to secure
Divine forgiveness. It is the 'fear of God', which in the
Christian sense is 'the impulse accompanied by blessedness
to an open acknowledgment of God's glory. . . . It signifies (Phil. ii. 12; 1 Peter i. 17) the acknowledgment that
we are dependent on God throughout the whole range of
our moral activity.'[2] Characteristically enough Ritschl
cannot describe humility without discharging some stray
shots (not always missing the mark!) against perversions
of humility in Catholic monasticism, in puritanical Calvinism, or in Pietism. 'Arrogant humility' he calls it.[3] But
his best piece of ammunition is borrowed from the ascetic
writer, Christian Scriver. 'Humility is the eye which sees
everything except itself.'[4] By the side of this definition
I may set another aphorism from a writer (to me) unknown.
'When Humility says "I am here," it is gone.'

(c) A third expression of faith in the fatherly Providence
of God is found in Prayer.[5] The duty of prayer must not
be based upon divine command. It is the natural language
of a soul redeemed. In every religion it is the sacrifice of
praise, the fruit of lips which acknowledge the name of
God (Heb. xiii. 15). In Christianity it springs out of the
wonder of reconciliation, and refers that act of God to His
fatherly care. It is a special manifestation of the resolve
to win humility; for in prayer that vague longing becomes
articulate. Ritschl dismisses Schleiermacher's doctrine of
prayer, together with the common Pietistic belief in the
efficacy of petition and the Pietistic stress on 'answers to
prayer', and reduces all prayer to the general form of

---

[1] *J. and R.*, iii. 634.			[2] Ibid., 636.			[3] Ibid., 640.
[4] Quoted ibid., 635.						[5] Ibid., 641–2.

Thanksgiving. Petition, he says, is merely a modification
of thanksgiving to God. The misplaced ingenuity by
which he excises petition from the Lord's prayer need not
detain us.[1] He is clearly recoiling from the extravagant
claims of certain types of Pietism. In the only passage of
real insight in his slight exposition of Prayer he notices
how the note of joy resounds throughout the New Testament. *Rejoice evermore!* says St. Paul. Even in tribulation
these men rejoice. '*Die Freude aber ist das Gefühl der
Vollkommenheit.* But Joy is the feeling of Perfection.'[2]
That is Ritschl's homage to the spiritual law which forbids
the Roman Church to recognize the saint unless his life
has shown the mark of joy.

(*d*) A fourth element in Ritschl's ideal is moral fidelity
to one's vocation.[3] Here Ritschl follows the Augsburg
Confession, but notes that such a conception, wrought out
as it was in opposition to the monastic ideal, seems to be
entirely out of relation to the New Testament.[4] No stress
can be laid on the scanty Pauline references (1 Cor. vii.
20, 24; 2 Thess. iii. 10; 1 Thess. iv. 11; 1 Cor. iii. 13), for
the hallowing of daily work is merely implicit. The fidelity
to a vocation 'does not appear to find a place among the
marks of perfection' either in the teaching of Jesus or in that
of St. Paul.[5] But, in the first place, it springs directly out of
the Christian view of the common ideal which is set before
men in their social relationships. 'The universal task of
the kingdom of God and the law of universal love to man,
which Christ has made operative, oblige us to aim at an all-
embracing supernatural union of men with one another.'[6]
But the universal is only always real in the particular, and
therefore the Christian rule is to honour the particular
relationships and hallow the common duties by raising
them from the natural to the spiritual plane. Thus the law
of love will be fulfilled; so will the kingdom of God be

---

[1] *J. and R.*, iii. 645.

[2] *Die chr. Vollkommenheit*, 17 (and 1st ed. of *R. und V.*, iii. 578).

[3] Ibid., (ed. Fabricius, 1924), 10–13; *J. and R.*, iii. 445 ff., 589,
635, 661–70.   [4] *J. and R.*, iii. 661.

[5] Ibid.   [6] *Die chr. Vollkommenheit* (ed. Fabricius), 12.

made real among men. 'Our special calling, in fact, is seen
to be the field of moral action to which we are summoned,
because we appropriate it as subordinate to the universal
final end of the good, or as an integral part of the kingdom
of God.'[1] Ritschl here has rendered a great service to
Christian thought by interpreting the universal law in
terms of 'My Station and its Duties'.[2] In the second place,
the prominent place assigned to 'fidelity to one's vocation'
in the Christian ideal is vindicated by an appeal to the
example of Christ. His vocation was unique. Our true
Imitatio Christi is to be as faithful to our several vocations
as He was to His.[3]

In the third place, Ritschl defends his limitation of
moral perfection to the vocation by another line of argument. If there is no such limitation, then 'one has to be
bringing forth good works in every moment of time in all
the possible relationships of life.' That would mean that
a Christian would be torn asunder, separated into fragments.[4] It is an impossible conception of Christian duty.
If the duty to which a Christian is called in any given
moment is impossible even with the grace of God, then it
is no duty. The very demand on a man implies that there
is grace available to fulfil it. Ritschl explicitly disclaims
the lax view to which the impractical rigorism, which he
is refuting, has given birth, both in the theology of the
Aufklärung and in the thought of Calvin.[5] He sees the
danger of narrowing the sympathies of men involved in his
own view. But he sets before the Christian the ideal of
the kingdom as the community of blessedness. 'In the
particular sphere of his regular activity every man is to act
not only for his own, but also for the common good in the

---

[1] *J. and R.*, iii. 666.

[2] The reference in the text is to F. H. Bradley's famous chapter in
Ethical Studies. The view of Ritschl's service to Christian thought agrees
with that of Dr. Garvie, *The Ritschlian Theology*, 359. See *infra*, 404–5.

[3] See *J. and R.*, iii. 589. For Christ's vocation, and the importance of
this idea in Ritschl's system see *J. and R.*, iii. 445–52. He recognized that
the idea had been used by theologians before him. See iii. 445; i. 510
(A. Schweizer); i. 543–6 (Hoffmann); i. 572, E. tr.

[4] *Die chr. Vollkommenheit*, 11.   [5] *J. and R.*, iii. 662–3.

widest sense.'[1] Every man is expected 'to round his life to
a whole in faithful service in his own moral calling, whether
it be exalted or limited.'[2] If he knows himself condemned
unconditionally to imperfection in any activity, he is
crippled from the beginning. 'The possibility of perfection must be held out in prospect if we are to expend our
industry on any branch of action.'[3] One more quotation[4]
is necessary to prove how distinct is Ritschl's doctrine
from the Methodist, or the monastic, doctrine.

The conception of moral perfection in the Christian life ought
on no account to be associated with the idea of a fruitless search for
actual sinlessness of conduct in all the details of life. It rather means
that our moral achievement or life-work in connexion with the
kingdom of God should, however limited in amount, be conceived
as possessing the quality of a whole in its own order.

Perfection, as thus conceived, is qualitative, not quantitative. It does not mean sinlessness nor infallibility of
judgement. The Christian is intended by God to be a
whole in his spiritual kind; to be conscious of his own
worth as a child of God; to serve the present age, and to
fulfil his calling.

B. CRITICISM OF RITSCHL'S DOCTRINE

The doctrine which we have expounded is by far the
most systematic of any of those which have been noticed
in our journey through the centuries. Little criticism has
so far been given to it. Harnack may call the pamphlet
on *Christian Perfection* a 'marvellous discourse'.[5] Yet the
traditional dread of any 'Perfektionismus' is so strong that
most of his fellow countrymen who write monographs on
Ritschl's thought, pass the doctrine by on the other side.
The following defects in Ritschl's doctrine must be pointed
out, though perhaps some of them may be remediable in
the light of the thought of his followers.

[1] *Die chr. Vollkommenheit,* 12.   [2] Ibid.
[3] *J. and R.,* iii. 662.
[4] Ibid., 665.   [5] *Erforschtes u. Erlebtes* (1923), 336.

I. The Denial of any place to Metaphysics in Theology.

The first main defect in Ritschl's ideal is closely connected with his emphasizing of religion as a function of a moral being capable of envisaging and of attaining his moral destiny, in spite of all the hindrances experienced in the world. This moral destiny is man's true end. So anxious is Ritschl to lay stress on the practical side of religion that he denies any place to metaphysics in theology. Theology, he thought, should not be concerned with any theoretical explanation of the universe. The world only comes within the scope of theology because God has placed human beings in a certain relationship to it, and that with a moral end in view. This conception is too narrow. It is not merely only an impoverishment of theology but of the Christian ideal. Theology can never surrender its belief that, in the ideal to be realized in this life, religion and science can meet. If the human soul is to be at unity with itself, it must reach that integration on the territory of truth. Into our conception of the Christian ideal must enter the searchings of the mind after the meaning of the universe. Here Harnack saw farther than his master. Ritschl, he said, had vanquished the speculative rationalism which gave itself out as true Christianity. Theology had conquered—but in virtue of its greater historical sense. 'But speculative rationalism will one day appropriate history. Then it will return with seven other spirits, no demons, but luminous and powerful.'[1] We may add that if the activity of the mind on ultimate questions is banished from our conception of the ideal for the life of man on this earth, the ideal itself cannot be kept sweet or pure. Just because its problems are ultimate, metaphysics may conduct the soul to humility and reverence. Thinking, also, may be worship. *Das Denken ist auch Gottesdienst*.

II. Defective Doctrine of Sin.

Ritschl regards the quest for sinlessness as fruitless, yet that quest can never be given up. Let it be granted that his doctrine is a healthy reaction from a type of piety which

[1] Harnack, *Reden und Aufsätze*, ii. 363.

has often fallen into the snares of morbidity and excessive scrupulousness. His ideal is positive and not negative, active and not passive. But it does not satisfy the cries of penitence, and the yearnings after complete freedom from sin, which have proceeded from the solitary shrines of the saints. *Grant us, O Lord, to pass this day in gladness and peace, without stumbling and without stain, that, reaching the eventide victorious over all temptation, we may praise thee, the Eternal God, who dost govern all things.* There is nothing unhealthy in such a prayer. Yet in Ritschl's theory there is little room for it. We may trace this defect partly to his recoil from Pietism, partly to his defective doctrine of sin. He denies original sin. He seeks to explain sin as an acquired tendency instead of an inherited bias. He ignores the truth to which the Church has always borne witness that evil springs from within.[1] He describes pardonable sin as ignorance though he does not intend to deny or minimize the reality of sin. He continually leaves the impression that he does not enter into those searching analyses of man's misery when sold under sin which are in all ages the foundation for the Christian message. There is one key to unlock the mystery of the gospel, and that is despair. Ritschl's disciple, Herrmann, understood this,[2] but the master had not used that key.

III. Defective Doctrine of Grace.

It must be admitted that in Ritschl's explicit formulation of his doctrine of the kingdom, too much stress is laid on human activity, too little mention made of the divine aid.[3] Yet without continual appeal to the grace of God, no doctrine of perfection is other than futile and ridiculous. It is true, of course, that Ritschl does justice to the initiative of God in the founding of the Kingdom. It is equally true, at least in his *magnum opus*, that the commonest use of the phrase 'Kingdom of God' is in its exclusively ethical

[1] See Wendland, *Ritschl und seine Schüler*, 108; Garvie, *The Ritschlian Theology*, 306.

[2] See the passages quoted by Garvie, *The Ritschlian Theology*, 312. 'The gospel to Herrmann means a great deliverance from a great distress.'

[3] Garvie, *The Ritschlian Theology*, 244–5, 251.

sense. He wavers between the religious and the ethical sense of the term, and in a later work finally sets the religious meaning in the foreground. But even in his later editions of the *Justification and Reconciliation* he keeps unchanged his phraseology. 'The kingdom is the moral unification of the human race, through action prompted by universal love to our neighbour.'[1] He endorses the Kantian definition—'an association of men bound together by laws of virtue.'[2] On the other hand he limits the doctrine of God by the idea of the kingdom of God. 'All the attributes of God are confined to their relation to the kingdom of God.'[3] There is no stress on God's transcendence, and it is easy for us at this time of day to understand how reaction from Ritschlianism would produce a 'Theology of Crisis', with its God stretching His hand out of darkness and mystery to rescue perishing man. But even in his doctrine of God immanent, Ritschl gives no satisfactory place to the Spirit who comes to the aid of our human frailty.

IV. Defective Doctrine of Communion with God.

The doctrine of prayer is altogether inadequate to the facts of Christian experience, and to the practice and teaching of our Lord as recorded in the Synoptic Gospels. Ritschl seems uncomfortably aware of this. He is undoubtedly right in the view that thanksgiving, as an acknowledgement of God, stands higher than petition.[4] But petitionary prayer may be subordinated without being banished. It is impossible to carry through the thought of the Fatherhood of God into the life of prayer, unless all our desires are made known in that innermost colloquy which proceeds between the soul and God. But it is the possibility of that colloquy in this life which Ritschl denies. He interprets St. Paul's injunction to 'pray without ceasing' as denoting 'that transformation of prayer back into the voiceless feeling of humility and patience which, as accompanying the

[1] iii. 280; cf. H. D. Wendland, *Die Eschatologie des Reiches Gottes* (1931), 138, 139.
[2] iii. 11; cf. Wendland, *Ritschl und seine Schüler*, 94–5.
[3] Garvie, op. cit., 260.
[4] *J. and R.*, iii. 644. See also 202–3, on adoration.

whole active life, is equivalent to prayer as the normal
form of the worship of God'.[1] Prayer is reduced to a state
of mind. Most of us are familiar with the temptation to
excuse ourselves from that difficult and formidable exercise
of all our faculties which is genuine prayer by the excuse
'All the life ought to be prayer'. The ideal is misused as
an evasion of the way to the ideal. The misuse is natural,
but it is temptation, and Ritschl has yielded to it.

But this defect in the doctrine of prayer is not a mere
intellectual misreading of the New Testament, nor is it
merely due to the reluctance of the natural man. Ritschl
denies that in this life any communion between God and
the soul can take place, except in the form of what he calls
Faith. 'Faith is a new direction of the will to God, evoked
by reconciliation. . . . It belongs as a special class to the
general idea of obedience.'[2] Faith is 'trust in God and
Christ, characterized by peace of mind, inward satisfaction, and comfort'.[3] Faith is trust in God, exercised in all
situations of life, in the production of humility and prayer;
and by this exercise of faith the believer experiences his
personal assurance of reconciliation.[4] So far will Ritschl go,
but not one step farther. His greatest disciple, Wilhelm
Herrmann of Marburg, has disclosed how deeply Ritschl
was shocked by the title of Herrmann's book *The Communion of the Christian with God*.[5]

Perhaps the most acute criticism levelled against Ritschl
in his lifetime came from Lipsius, who pointed out that
the mystical element was the chief element in religion, and
that Ritschl's tendency was to deny or ignore it. He
admitted that since Ritschl's system acknowledged the
internal witness of the Spirit as constituting the ground of
that knowledge of God and that moral life which exist in
the Christian community, it would be wrong to say that
the mystical element was entirely absent.[6] But Ritschl

---

[1] Ibid., 646.   [2] Ibid. iii, E. tr. 100.   [3] Ibid., 142.   [4] Ibid., 670.
[5] *Festgabe für Harnack* (Göttingen, 1921), 405. Yet Herrmann himself says (*Verkehr*, 8) that the idea of communion with God is not Christian.
[6] R. A. Lipsius, *Dogmatische Beiträge* (Leipzig, 1878), 16, 17; *J. and
R.*, iii. 471–2.

often means by fellowship with God no more than the agreement of the human will with the divine purpose. The thought of any real indwelling of the Spirit of God in believers does not appear. The idea of the presence of God within, not only as directing the human will to conform to the divine, but also as giving the power to fulfil all the will of God, never comes to its own.

He could describe the religious experience as a relation of person to person; 'what we religiously affirm as the operation of God or Christ in us, assures us not of the distance, but of the presence of these authors of our salvation.'[1] He attacks the mystical notion of 'immediate' communion with God, but he is careful to explain that the intercourse with God is none the less genuine and personal, because remembrances of the historical Jesus, or of the law and promise contained in God's word, are used as *media* of the operation of God. But his attention is absorbed in the psychological process in the historical mediation. He forgets the living Person who communicates Himself in that process, through that History. In first-hand religious documents like the letters of Paul or the testimonies of the Quakers, we see souls aware of a Presence apprehending them, constraining them, enabling them, communing with them through the joys and distresses of daily life and passionately loved by them. They can give no other explanation of their religious experiences as a whole than that the same God, whom they see revealed in Jesus in the pages of the Gospels, is alive and speaking (though always speaking through certain *media*) to their own minds. Ritschl never did justice to facts such as these. In his doctrine of perfection, he says much of love to man. He says nothing of love to God or love to Christ. He explains that love to Christ is less definite than faith in Him, and that he fears the medieval language of familiarity with Christ as the bridegroom of the soul.[2] We may answer that not even in the medieval mystics does the experience of communion

---

[1] *Theologie und Metaphysik*, 49–50. I owe this reference to Garvie, *The Ritschlian Theology*, 145.

[2] *J. and R.*, iii. 593–7.

with God and love to Christ necessarily involve 'love-play on an equal footing with the beloved', neither is the erotic language of the Song of Songs the only imagery used. The greatest of the mystics thought of the very passion of love to God as given to them by God Himself. His love it was that entered with reconciling power into the human heart, expanding it and assuring it of communion with God Himself. This was a side of religion to which Ritschl was almost blind.[1] He thinks of the love of God only under the category of the divine Will. His love is to make our destiny His own end.

Fortunately, his followers atoned for his failure. There are few devotional books written in the last fifty years which are comparable to Herrmann's *Communion of the Christian with God* for religious intensity and devotion to Christ. Ritschl himself seems to have advanced in sensitiveness for the more distinctively religious message of Christianity. His son, who gives few details of the end of Ritschl's life, tells one story, which is, perhaps, not without significance.[2] The great theologian had disliked Paul Gerhardt's famous Passion hymn, founded as it is on the meditations of St. Bernard of Clairvaux. He had selected St. Bernard as the typical representative of the mystical piety which he condemned. Yet in full peace of soul, as the end drew near, he asked his son to read the last two verses of Gerhardt's poem.

> What language shall I borrow
>   To praise Thee, heavenly Friend,
> For this thy dying sorrow,
>   Thy pity without end?
> Lord, make me Thine for ever,
>   Nor let me faithless prove;
> O let me never, never
>   Abuse such dying love.

[1] Henri Du Bois, *De Kant à Ritschl* (Neuchâtel, 1925), 112, singles out this defect in Ritschl's conception of religion as the supreme defect. See also an excellent discussion in Garvie, *The Christian Ideal for Human Society* (1930), 203–4.   [2] *A. Ritschls Leben*, ii. 524.

CHAPTER XXII

CONCLUSIONS

Yet when the work is done,
The work is but begun:
Partaker of Thy grace,
I long to see Thy face;
The first I prove below,
The last I die to know.

C. Wesley.

OUR historical survey fitly ends with Ritschl. There were other discussions of the doctrine of Christian Perfection in the nineteenth century, but none so original. Another famous theologian who has since ventured to handle the subject is the late Principal Forsyth.[1] The influence of Ritschl is evident on every page, though the thought is cast in Forsyth's own characteristic, staccato style. Let us taste the flavour of some of his epigrams:

Our perfection is not to rival the Perfect, but to trust Him. Our holiness is not a matter of imitation but of worship. Any sinlessness of ours is the adoration of His. The holiest have ever been so because they dared not feel they were.

Faith is always in opposition to seeing, possessing, experiencing.

Perfection is not sinlessness. The perfect in the New Testament are certainly not the sinless. And God, though He wills that we be perfect, has not appointed sinlessness as His object with us in this world. His object is communion with us through faith. And sin must abide, even while it is being conquered, as an occasion for faith. Every defect of ours is a motive for faith. To cease to feel defect is to cease to trust.

We do not need God chiefly as a means even to our own holiness. But we need God for Himself. . . . He does not offer us communion to make us holy; He makes us holy for the sake of communion.

All life is the holding down of a dark wild elemental nature at our base, which is most useful, like steam, under due pressure. So

---

[1] *Christian Perfection* (1899). Dr. Garvie's great work (1930) is mentioned below, pp. 401, 403.

with sin and its mastery by faith. The pressure from below drives us to God, and the communion with God by faith keeps it always below. . . . It is doubtful if real holiness is possible to people who have no 'nature' in them, no passion, no flavour of the good brown earth.

Peter Forsyth is like William Law, at least in this, that when you begin quoting him you hardly know when to stop! He is exhilarating. His sentences dance across the page. But we may take leave to doubt whether he is fair to Protestant piety when he says that 'communion with God is possible along with cleaving sin'.[1] A sharpened epigram may deal a wound to doctrine, and a death-blow to holiness itself. 'Love, and not sinlessness, is the maturity of faith.'[2] To which we may reply that a love which is not holy ceases to be love.

Forsyth follows Ritschl in his emphasis both on the Christian community as God's end in Christ,[3] and on the active nature of sanctity.[4] He distinguishes between a sinful perfection and a sinless perfection, by which epigram he means that a man is to be judged by his verdict on his own sins.

The final judgement is not whether we have at every moment stood, but whether having done all we stand—stand at the end, stand as a whole. Perfection is wholeness.

It is not sins that damn, but the sin into which sins settle down.[5]

There is sin as the principle of a soul, and sin as an incident, sin which stays and sin which visits. Visitations of sin may cleave indefinitely to the new life.

Perfection is not sanctity but faith.

It is better to trust in God in humiliated repentance than to revel in the sense of sinlessness.[6]

The trouble with these epigrams is that they ignore the main problem and at least half the facts. The facts are that for most believers their sins are not fleeting visitations, but

---

[1] Op. cit., 13.   [2] Op. cit., 16.   [3] Op. cit., 17–20.
[4] 'To hang upon Christ, and to do no more than hang, is to be a drag on Christ and a strain on man' (op. cit., 30).   [5] Op. cit., 36, 45.
[6] Op. cit., 46, 84, 135.

expressions of some habit. A church dignitary may be irritable; a lifelong Christian deplorably egoistic. The main problem is whether the Christian religion is to promise release from such ingrained habits of mind, or whether, under cover of some fine phrase or delusive epigram, it is to acquiesce.

Like Ritschl, Forsyth lays stress on dominion over the world.

Incessant growth is a condition of perfect living personality.

Our perfection is in coming to ourselves in Christ.

Growth is progress, not *to* Christ but *in* Christ.

Happiness is a power of the soul to find its joy amid the constant change of experience and to grow in mastery of a growing world.[1]

The elements in Christian Perfection singled out by Forsyth are Humility, Patience, Thankfulness, Prayer, Duty, Love. The very list shows the debt of Forsyth to his great forerunner. But Forsyth has his own gift to add to Ritschl's analysis; it is his overwhelming sense of the power of the Cross.

Humility is not possible where the central value of the Cross is forgotten, where the Cross is only the glorification of self-sacrifice instead of the atonement for sin. . . . It is very hard, unless we are really and inly broken with Christ on the Cross, to keep from making ourself the centre and measure of all the world.

Do not think that patience is a way of bearing trouble only. It is a way of doing work. . . . It is a way of carrying success. . . . It is the intense form of action which made the power of the Cross.

What we need is the personal impression of Christ, the personal sense of His cross, the fresh, renewing, vitalizing, sweetening contact of His soul in its wisdom, its tenderness, its action for us—and all so freely for us, so mercifully, so persistently, so thoroughly. What we need is the touch, the communion of that kind of perfection. We need to realize how in the Cross the defeat of that sort of goodness is really its victory, its ascent to the throne of the world.[2]

[1] Op. cit., 119, 112, 109.
[2] Op. cit., 137, 139–40, 149–50.

The foregoing summary of the little treatise of Dr. Forsyth aids us in the proof not only of the influence of Ritschl's teaching, but also of the attraction of the doctrine for the great minds of the Church. This, indeed, is the first main conclusion reached, after our survey of Christian thought throughout the centuries. The doctrine of Christian perfection—understood not as an assertion that a final attainment of the goal of the Christian life is possible in this world, but as a declaration that a supernatural destiny, a relative attainment of the goal which does not exclude growth, is the will of God for us in this world and is attainable—lies not merely upon the by-paths of Christian theology, but upon the high road. To this declaration some of the greatest theologians have set their seal. Theirs was no mere formal assent, but a conviction which dominated their thought. In the New Testament St. Paul and St. John are as one in that faith. St. Basil and St. Augustine, St. Thomas Aquinas and the Mystics, George Fox and John Wesley, form a fellowship that is not easily broken. We have seen two theologians, perhaps the greatest and certainly the most influential of the nineteenth century, placing variations of this doctrine at the centre of their systems. Is it too much to ask that the mind of the Church shall once again be addressed to the question which lies behind all variations of the doctrine—how much may we expect God to do for us as individuals and in society in this present world?

A second consideration may be mentioned. This essay has dealt in some fullness with varieties of Protestant doctrine. But Protestants cannot afford to neglect that at the heart of Roman Catholicism is a doctrine of perfection. The word itself is part of the Catholic heritage. By Protestants it is usually dismissed as an irrelevance. It ought to be accepted as a challenge. So far in Protestantism the aspirations after 'perfect love' have been more prominent in sects and coteries than in the teaching of the great church. Will there come a time when sanctity, and no mere average standard of goodness, is enthroned as the practical ideal in all the sections of Christendom? In art and in science the ultimate good is unattainable in this world. Yet precisely because artist or scientist is deliberately working with that goal in view, a relative and partial attainment is possible.

We reach, then, this broad conclusion, that the seeking of an ideal that is realizable in this world is essential to Christianity. It is essential to the corporate life of the Church that this principle should be enshrined at the heart of its doctrines, its hymns, its confessions of faith, its institutions. It is essential for the individual Christian that the goal set before him should be not merely conversion, not merely a life of service, but perfection. Or if the term is disliked, let it be Wesley's phrase—'perfect love', or 'sanctity', or 'holiness'. 'If we have no hunger and thirst after that righteousness which is Christ, we are not Christians . . . at all.'[1] Christianity is not Christianity unless it is aiming at Perfection. Certain corollaries may be drawn from this principle. One is that the true practical method for the winning of converts is that Christians should be aiming after complete personal sanctity. *Ask and ye shall have.* And they shall have more than they ask. Personal influence is 'the means of propagating the truth'.[2] There is a strange and attractive contagion clinging to sanctity. This method of influence is deducible both from the Old Testament doctrine of the Remnant, and from the practice of Jesus Himself. *Let the children first be filled.*

For Protestants there is one conclusion that may be less welcome. A recent liberal and learned Protestant apologist says that Protestantism is inferior in a certain ethical intensity which may truthfully be predicated of the Catholic character.[3] This generalization unduly simplifies the facts. I would suggest another reading of English religious life since the Reformation. We must begin with Harnack's reluctant admission that the Lutheran church neglected far too much the moral problem, the *Be ye holy for I am*

---

[1] W. R. Inge, *Personal Religion and the Life of Devotion*, 38.

[2] Newman, *Oxford University Sermons*, 91–7.

[3] C. J. Cadoux, *Catholicism and Christianity*, 77. See a kindred, but different, generalization in C. C. J. Webb, *Religious Thought in the Oxford Movement*, 35.

holy.[1] It would be difficult to claim for the English Reformation that a passion for personal holiness was its predominant motive and driving power. But just because the New Testament was opened, the desire for holiness blazed up in three reactions against the ordinary, comfortable standards which were commonly accepted in the English Church. Singularly enough each of these fires was kindled in the middle years of each century since the Reformation; Quakerism in the seventeenth, Methodism in the eighteenth, the Oxford Movement in the nineteenth. We have already proved for Quakerism and Methodism that the driving power was a doctrine of holiness and that both arose in the form of a reaction against the conventional piety of the day. It is not always recognized that both generalizations are true of the Tractarian movement. 'The desire of holiness was its grand inspiration from first to last; and this is the central truth about it.'[2] The kinship of this inspiration to that of the Methodist movement has been traced by a sympathetic and detached observer,[3] and the connecting link found in the work of Alexander Knox. Dr. Brilioth writes that Knox was the heir of Methodist evangelicalism in its Wesleyan form, especially in its 'perfectionist ethics, which hold up the ideal of complete holiness, instead of the compromises he saw and lamented in the various forms of Protestantism'.[4] One of the sublimest passages in Newman's writings is that wherein he takes his stand on holiness as the single mark of the true Church.[5]

[1] See above p. 257. Harnack, *History of Dogma*, vii. 266, 267.

[2] C. C. J. Webb, *Religious Thought and the Oxford Movement*, 53; Brilioth, *The Anglican Revival; Studies in the Oxford Movement*, 128.

[3] Brilioth, 46–52.

[4] Op. cit., 46. The influence of Alexander Knox on the Oxford Movement was probably not direct. See Appendix I (331–3) in Brilioth's work. But Newman fully acknowledged the work of Knox in preparing the way for the Oxford Movement (*Essays Critical and Historical*, i. 268–71). For a due estimate of the importance of Knox in the history of Anglican Theology see Storr, *Development of English Theology in the Nineteenth Century*, 85–91.

[5] *Letter to ... Richard Lord Bishop of Oxford on the occasion of the Nineteenth Tract* (ed. of 1841, pp. 43–6), *Via Media*, ii. 395–424. Brilioth, 159, says he is 'led for a moment up to a spiritual height which has too

Pusey was carried over into the Tractarian camp primarily by his longing for holiness.[1] In spite of many noble prayers in the Liturgy, in spite of Lancelot Andrewes and Jeremy Taylor in the seventeenth century, was there always burning at the heart of traditional Anglican piety this passionate flame?

So far we have gathered certain historical and practical conclusions after our long journey through the centuries. It remains to formulate a number of constructive conclusions for any positive doctrine of the ideal, so far as it is attainable in this world. Of the following eight principles, the first two may be regarded as primary and determinative; the next five concern the content of the ideal; and the last deals with the tension caused by the fact that the Christian ideal is intended both for this world and for the life beyond.

1. The full Christian ideal must span both worlds, the present life and the life to come. It is only completely realizable in the life beyond the grave. *Here we have no abiding city, but we seek that which is to come.* As St. Thomas Aquinas said, 'the final felicity of man is not to be attained in this present life'. The doctrine of immortality is essential to any Christian doctrine of relative attainment in this life. The argument might run thus. If in this life only we have trusted in Christ, our trust is vain unless His perfect goal for us is reached in this life. We see that it is not reached. We must, therefore, either lower the ideal, or pronounce it altogether unattainable. In either case Christ's ideal is not attained. *Christ died for naught.*

This principle of the constant recognition of the life beyond, in all our strivings after holiness in this, is essential if we are to avoid presumptuousness and Pharisaism. Presumptuousness may be found both in the aberrations of certain sects which claimed full attainment here below, and in the attempts of certain mystics to anticipate the bliss of the life beyond. It would seem to be the wisdom of mortal man to expect for this life the relative attainment

seldom been reached in the history of Neo-Anglicanism'. Cf. *Apologia*, 61, and the first of *Parochial and Plain Sermons*.

[1] Liddon, *Life of Pusey*, i. 144. Cf. Brilioth, 126, 174.

possible for those who live in the body. 'The earthly life has its own intrinsic values; and there is a purpose of God on earth for which we may anticipate a fulfilment which will satisfy the Creator of it.'[1] It follows that it is a mistake to force the soul away from human concerns to the *vita angelica*.[2] But, at the same time, the recognition of the principle of St. Thomas carries with it a choice of a life that will differ from a mere this-worldly ideal, however altruistic, as the light differs from the dark. 'If the Platonic and Christian view is true, it must follow "as the night the day", that we dare not lose our hearts to any temporal good. The rule of detachment will be the obvious supreme rule of successful living; the moral task of man will be to learn so to use and prize temporal good as to make it a ladder of ascent to a good which is more than 'for a season', *ita per temporalia transire ut non amittamus aeterna*.'[3] The acceptance of this principle as our guiding rule in any doctrine of perfection will give us all that Ritschl sought to win by his governing conception of 'dominion over the world'.

2. The Christian Life is the gift of God. Whether in this world, or the next, the Christian life at its completion, as at its inception, is supernatural, and is the gift of God. Such is the voice of Christian tradition. But this principle carries with it theological admissions which are not being made unless the problem of attainment in this life is faced. Robert Browning saw this, the supreme practical difficulty in the way of the acceptance of Christianity. Those who are running the heavenly race with the grace of God to assist them are often not demonstrably holier than those who lay claim to no such supernatural aid.

> Do not these publicans the same? Outstrip!
> Or else stop race you boast runs neck and neck,
> You with the wings, they with the feet,—for shame!

Of what avail is the grace of God unless God's end is reached? 'Is the thing we see, salvation?' It is a 'dreadful

---

[1] Garvie, *The Christian Ideal for Human Society*, 462.

[2] So Ritschl, *passim*.

[3] A. E. Taylor, *The Faith of a Moralist*, i. 283.

question', as Browning makes the old Pope say.[1] Every one can feel the force of it in practical life. But the bearing of it on theological teaching is not so clearly seen. If God's grace can accomplish the miracle and lift poor sinning human beings to a supernatural plane to walk with Him in the light, may we not speak of an attainment of His purpose as complete as is possible in this world? The answer to this question is often put in a peremptory challenge (as though it settled the problem): 'Have you ever known a perfect Christian?' But this retort is irrelevant if our principle is admitted. The ultimate consideration is not whether human beings have ever attained, but whether it is God's will that they should. Even if we grant (as we must) that in the lives of Christians, God's will is continually thwarted, we are moving in a clearer moral air if we may be sure that it is God's will for Christians to be more than conquerors in the present life.

3. From the two preceding principles we may advance to a third. No limits can be set to the moral or spiritual attainments of a Christian in the present life. Two results follow from this principle. First, the possibility of continued and unlimited growth in spiritual apprehension is preserved, both for the life of the individual and for the life of society. Second, reverence is maintained for the infinite resources of God. The ultimate sin is unbelief. *Repent, and believe in the gospel.* If the Church fails in its great task of sanctity, it must be because the Church is not taking God to be what He is.

These two results are ignored when any one professes to have attained the goal of the Christian life. The one person who cannot be perfect is the person who claims to be. Can we go farther in any doctrine of the content of the ideal attainable in this world than this bare assertion that no limits can be set? Surely the foregoing historical study warrants us in laying down certain other principles.

4. The Inclusion within the Christian ideal of the various realms of the good life. It was the merit of Schleiermacher, as we have already shown, to expand the

---

[1] R. Browning, *Poetical Works*, ii. 238, lines 1585, 1630.

traditional Christian ideal. Herein he was true to the thought of Jesus. The Kingdom is never merely an individual good. Therefore the Christian ideal must be the life of a society, and the perfect life of that society will include the pursuit and partial attainment of truth and beauty as well as of moral goodness.[1] The vast expansion made possible in modern times for Christian thinking on the ideal may be best traced in the masterly treatise of Principal Garvie. 'The comprehensive ideal is perfectionism, the highest good, the realization according to the divine purpose, of the whole manhood of all mankind.'[2]

5. Daily work as a divine vocation. This principle follows inevitably from the last. If human activities have a divine meaning, all the legitimate work of mankind may be transfigured. The debt of Christian theory to Ritschl is most apparent in this conception of the doing of the duties of one's vocation as an expression of faith in God. Those who do not share Ritschl's prejudices will naturally prefer to speak of the fulfilment of the duties of our vocation as an integral part of our communion with God. This is an immense advance in the theory of the ideal Christian life, and is as yet a comparatively unfamiliar thought among Christian people. Compare Wesley's view of the ordinary duties of life with that of Ritschl. The early Methodist preachers, true to the tradition exemplified in the monastic ideal, always had a sacred and a secular.[3] There were tracts of human life in which they were not interested and others of which they were afraid. They did not, it is true, call men out of their secular employment in order to find God. They 'accepted the common life as inevitable, and urged men to discharge their part in it faithfully, but rather so as to be done with it than as rejoicing in it, and looking to find God's meaning in every part of it'. But if we follow out Ritschl's ideal, every task

[1] See Garvie, *The Christian Ideal for Human Society*, 141 ff.
[2] Op. cit., 166.
[3] See W. R. Maltby, *To Serve the Present Age* (1918), 19, 20, from which the following quotation is taken.

may be seen as service rendered to one's fellows, and therefore to God. Just as those who visit the sick or the prisoner are thereby in communion with Christ (Matt. xxv. 31–46), so the Christian grocer or artisan may hear after every day's work the words: *Inasmuch as ye did it unto one of these my brothers, ye did it unto Me.*

Ritschl published his work in 1874. Two years later a young Fellow of Merton published an incisive criticism of current theories of ethical thought, and advanced to a higher point of view. The theory that the moral end was 'My Station and Its Duties' was a contribution to ethics parallel to Ritschl's contribution to the doctrine of perfection. The value of the view is that it gives content to the abstract conception of duty. It is concrete, it is objective, it enables the individual to realize himself morally by doing the duties of his station for the sake of society. 'The individual's consciousness of himself is inseparable from the knowing himself as an organ of the whole.'[1]

It is true that in his statement of the new theory Bradley fell into exaggeration. Rashdall, for example, criticized strongly and justly the commendation of Hegel's dictum, that 'the wisest men of antiquity have given judgement that wisdom and virtue consist in living agreeably to the Ethos of one's people'.[2] But all moral progress in the history of mankind has been due to those pioneers who were dissatisfied with the Ethos of their people. To acquiesce in the common standard is to fail.

The theory of 'My Station and its Duties' as the end is open to a farther and an unanswerable objection. The goal as thus stated is limited and fully attainable, whereas 'the moralist who is in earnest with life is, necessarily and on principle, an *intransigeant*; he means to aim not at the rather better, but at the absolute best . . . the life of unremitting moral endeavour is an unending aspiration after a *Je ne sais quoi*, just as the life of the profound thinker or the great artist seems often, even to himself, to be one

[1] F. H. Bradley, *Ethical Studies* (2nd ed. 1927), 183.
[2] Rashdall, *Theory of Good and Evil*, ii. 157, 158. See Bradley, *Ethical Studies* (2nd ed. 1927), 187.

perpetual attempt to express the ineffable or "convey the incommunicable".[1]

Valid as these objections are against Bradley's statement of 'My Station and its Duties' as the supreme end, they do not touch the conception of the fulfilment of the duties of one's vocation as a necessary expression of the communion of the Christian with God. But it follows that in part the Christian ideal is realizable in this life. If the carpenter is making tables and chairs, which, though not perfect, are the best he can make at that stage of his life, if he is offering all his powers and his daily work as a sacrifice to God, surely we may speak of him as therein, and at that stage, fulfilling the purpose of God. As Bradley says: 'The narrow external function of the man is not the whole man. He has a life which we cannot see with our eyes; and there is no duty so mean that it is not the realization of this and knowable as such. What counts is not the visible outer work so much as the spirit in which it is done. . . . But here, if so, we *seem* driven to justification by faith.'[2]

> O Master Workman, if Thou choose
> The thing I make, the tool I use,
> If all be wrought to Thy design,
> And Thou transmute the Me and Mine,
> The noise of saw and plane shall be
> Parts in the heavenly harmony,
> And all the din of working days
> Reach Thee as deep and peaceful praise.
>
> (A. M. Pullen.)

6. The principle of concentration on each moment. Since holiness is given in response to faith, and since faith is no mere single response but a continuous succession of responses to the divine Giver, it follows that the ideal life is a 'moment-by-moment' holiness. Enshrined in the Sermon on the Mount (Matt. vi. 25–34), vindicated by the

[1] A. E. Taylor, *The Faith of a Moralist*, i. 139, 140.
[2] Op. cit., 109. The last sentence is an additional note in the second edition. See also 182, additional note, and the famous passage on justification by faith, 325.

practice of the great saints, this principle does not yet seem to have been recognized as affecting the theory of the possible realization of the ideal.

The argument would run as follows. The Christian ideal is a gay sanctity, freed from anxiety and fettering self-consciousness, a holiness unaware of itself, and symbolized by birds and flowers. It can only be achieved by living in the moment, and steadily refusing to be anxious for the morrow. It rests on complete acceptance of Christ's ideal (Matt. vi. 33, *Seek ye first the Kingdom*), and on faith in God's willingness to give it. *Fear not little flock, it is the Father's good pleasure to give you the Kingdom* (Luke xii. 32). The only demand is responsiveness, willingness to receive, faith. Faith can be perfect in any one moment. Therefore holiness, or the perfection congruous with this stage of our growth, is possible at any moment in this world. Our business is to accept the ideal, and to take the gift of God contained in each moment; we may be assured that so we are offering ourselves and our lives moment by moment unto God.

Three observations may be made on this element in the ideal, which has been happily, if daringly, called 'The Cult of the Passing Moment'.[1] In the first place, the 'cult' rests on a cardinal fact of the present life—its transitoriness. The concentration on the moment has commonly been associated with the theory of hedonism. If the scientific doctrine that all things pass and nothing abides becomes the basis of a way of life, the inference is usually made that the only wisdom is to draw from each fleeting moment an immediate pulsation of pleasure. The pleasures are not necessarily gross. Walter Pater preached that they might be exquisite and refined. But the conclusion that pleasure is the end of life does not inevitably follow from the fact of transitoriness. 'The principle of living in and for each moment does not demand an irrational, any more than it implies a gross, attitude to life. . . . It means rather

[1] See *The Cult of the Passing Moment*, by Arthur Chandler, formerly Bishop of Bloemfontein (Methuen, 1914), to which I am indebted in the following paragraph.

that since the passing moment and the passing feeling are all that we have to count on, we must make the most of them. We must educate ourselves to understand the messages which come and go so quickly.'[1] So might an advocate of self-culture speak. He could say also that these impressions of the moment survive as ideas in the memory, or are stored in that uncharted reservoir of the sub-conscious. He will notice that some of the fleeting moments are arrested and given a relative permanence by the genius of Art, and will claim that in a sense the fugitive thing of beauty may be a joy for ever. But, of course, the theory fails.

For ever wilt thou love, and she be fair!

No, that is not true. Not all the music of Keats, nor all the sculpture of Hellas, can give eternal youth to the fair lady on the Grecian urn. All things pass—even the Grecian urn. We ourselves are more enduring than the momentary feelings and impressions that race past us, and we know that we seek something higher and other than these can of themselves afford.

The second step in the argument is that the saints have practised a cult of the passing moment by finding a gift of God in it.[2]

St. Catherine of Genoa . . . would quietly concentrate, each moment, upon that moment's special content—upon God's gift and will of special suffering or joy, of determination, effort, decision, and the like, conveyed within that moment. Such a scheme follows out something similar, within the spiritual life, to the action of the sun upon the sun-dial in physical life. The sun successively touches and illumines this, and then that, and then the next radius of the dial. Or again, the scheme reminds one of Goethe's old mother, Frau Rath, who when one day an acquaintance, ignorant of Frau Rath's condition, called at her house and asked to see her, sent down

[1] Chandler, 6.
[2] Cf. Caussade, *L'Abandon à la Providence Divine*, p. 80 (ed. Ramière, Paris, Gabalda, 1911): 'Les saints des premiers temps ont-ils eu d'autres secrets que celui de devenir de moment en moment, ce que cette action divine en voulait faire?' See the translation of a lengthy passage in Chandler, 212, 213; and E. tr. by Algar Thorold (1933), 45.

a message to the visitor that 'Frau Rath was busy dying'. Indeed a genial, quiet death to self lies in every minute, when the minute is thus taken separately as the dear will and the direct vehicle of God.[1]

In the third place, the separate moments are unified and held together by the God who abides, though the moments and the things of time perpetually pass, who has a connected message to speak to us, and in whose will and gift lies our perfect sanctity. To trust God moment by moment, to attend to that heavenly message, is perfect faith.

Would not the acceptance of this principle modify the confession of sins which English Christians feel by their tradition compelled to make? *We have left undone those things which we ought to have done.* Behind this cry lies, perhaps, a misinterpretation of a saying of Jesus (Luke xvii. 10). *We are unprofitable servants.* That, however, is a different matter. There is behind the daily repetition of the same confession a tacit admission that even by the grace of God we are destined each day to defeat in the moral task. There lurks behind the confession what Ritschl[2] called 'the statutory idea of the moral law, on which depends the intolerable, because boundless, demand for good works'. That 'statutory idea' is responsible for much of the worried, anxious goodness of our day.

7. The consciousness of personal unworthiness. The Communion with the Lord of all, with the resultant sense of victory over the world, can and does co-exist with a deep sense of personal imperfection and unworthiness. It cannot co-exist with what Forsyth called 'cleaving sin'.

We are now faced by the problem of problems, so strangely evaded, as we have seen above, in his doctrine of perfection by the theologian who faced it so magnificently in his doctrine of the Cross. How can the fulfilment of God's perfect will in this world co-exist with the human sense of imperfection? The 'Theology of Crisis', true to its Calvinistic tradition, would repudiate any and every doctrine of perfection. Even while exercising faith, man remains a sinner. He is a Christian by the grace of

---

[1] von Hügel, *Essays and Addresses*, ii. 227, 228.
[2] *J. and R.*, iii. 666.

God, and a sinner at the same time. So in the Heidelberg Catechism we are told that we increase our guilt daily, and that the best works of Christians in this life are defiled with sin. The Lutheran Churches are one at this point with the Reformed. In a modern liturgy Christians are taught to say: 'We transgress Thy divine commandments unceasingly, in thoughts, words, and deeds'.[1]

Our answer to this must lie in a careful analysis of the consciousness of personal imperfection and unworthiness which we are including as an integral element in the ideal life in this world.

(i) First, this must mean the consciousness of our inadequate apprehension of the grace and goodness of God, inasmuch as the final fulfilment of human destiny is in the life beyond.

(ii) Second, it must mean the consciousness of receiving everything from God, that we may render all to Him. As Luther protested, *Nos nihil sumus; Christus solus est omnia*.

(iii) Third, it will include a remembrance of past sin. We dare not exclude from the perfect colloquy of the soul with God entreaties such as that of Charles Wesley:

> Remember, Lord, my sins no more,
> That them I may no more forget;
> But, sunk in guiltless shame, adore
> With speechless wonder at Thy Feet.

This remembrance of sin needs somewhat fuller analysis. The sin is past. That is why the shame can be guiltless. The remembrance of the sin is not a cleaving barrier. If some one has cheated me, has repented, and been forgiven, if I accept him back into the old relationship, then the very memory of that forgiveness will make the restored relationship rather closer than it was before. The remembrance becomes not a barrier but a link.

The tradition of evangelical piety is that the heights of

[1] The above examples are taken from B. B. Warfield, *Studies in Perfectionism* (1931), 119–20. The Reformation tradition is summarized in 113–23.

holiness are signalized by the deepest self-accusations. But it is possible to exaggerate the principle that

> They who fain would serve Thee best
> Are conscious most of wrong within.

A charming illustration has been given in the life of John Denholm Brash. That gay saint was once accused of saintliness. 'No,' he cried out in his dramatic way, 'I'm a Hound of Hell.' There was no pose about this remark; it was the cry of the contrite heart of the holy man. He meant it, but he withdrew it. His daughter in bringing up his breakfast said with such a happy dash of mirth: 'Here's your breakfast, hell-hound!' and he smiled: 'After all, perhaps I am not a hound of hell.' Surely humility may preserve both penitence and the sense of walking in the light. Hell-hounds do not walk in the light. We can admit wholeheartedly the words of Forsyth:

In our perfection there is a permanent element of repentance. The final symphony of praise has a deep bass of penitence. God may forgive us, but we do not forgive ourselves. It is always a Saviour, and not merely an Ideal, that we confess.

But this does not mean that the consciousness of imperfection includes the consciousness of sinning in that moment, or even, necessarily, of having sinned in the recent past. There is wisdom in the criticism passed by Keshab Chandra Sen on English piety: 'He who says always, "I am a sinner," remains a sinner; he who says "I am bound", remains bound.'

(iv) It is probable that this regret for the past will grow in poignancy, as the soul grows in dependence on God.

(v) The consciousness of personal imperfection will include a conviction that a lapse into sin is certain if the hold upon God's grace slackens or be lost. Why is this? Perhaps an answer is more possible now than in previous centuries. We have been familiarized with the conception of the sub-conscious, that deep and mysterious treasury where the thoughts of the past are stored. The believer who will be content with nothing less than the highest must reckon with the possibility that previous habits may

reassume their ancient power. That is the cardinal problem for Christianity, that past sins are not past. There are
instances of those who have preached holiness and soon
after have fallen into the abyss.[1] The reason is probably
that pestilential thoughts have come out of the sub-conscious into the waking consciousness, have been enter-
tained there, and harboured, and dwelt upon. Then they
may be dismissed owing to other and worthier claims on
the mind. But now they have an added tenacity. They
will inevitably come back sometime in the form of temptation. If the will yields those thoughts will some day be
expressed in act. Can this spell be broken? Is salvation
possible for the sub-conscious? That is the real question
for the seeker after holiness in our time.

The answer ought not to be in doubt, if the assurances
of the New Testament are received. Hebrew psychology
had no doctrine of the sub-conscious. Yet the 'heart' was
recognized as the storehouse whence the thoughts were
brought forth. And the Christian benediction promises
that the peace of God Himself shall stand on sentry-duty
at the door of the human 'heart', challenging, and if need
be, rejecting, every thought that issues forth.[2]

(vi) The consciousness of personal imperfection must
include one other element which previous theories of perfection have usually overlooked. The believer must always
reserve the possibility that he is sinning unconsciously.
Indeed it is possible that our worst sins are those of which
we are unconscious. This consideration sweeps away the
optimism with which Ritschl, among others, has treated
the problem of moral evil. Ritschl taught that God
regarded pardonable sin as ignorance.[3] But in real life we
find that our ignorance that we are sinning is often the

---

[1] See, e.g., an example adduced by Dr. Horton, *Mystical Quest of Christ*.

[2] Philippians iv. 7; cf. Haupt (in Meyer, ed. 8, 1902), 165; ed. 6
(1897), 177. Lohmeyer's theory (Meyer, 1928, 171 f.) that St. Paul
in these verses is envisaging the narrower situation of a possible martyrdom
for the members of the Philippian Church is not proven.

[3] I follow here the interpretation of his son, Otto Ritschl (*Leben A.
Ritschl's*, ii. 199–200). Cf. Garvie, *The Ritschlian Theology*, 315, as
against B. B. Warfield, *Studies in Perfectionism* (1931), i. 16.

main problem. The ignorance may be overlooked, but forgiveness in its full Christian sense is no mere passing over of unrecognized sin, and the communion with God, to which He introduces us in forgiveness, cannot be according to His will for us if all the time we are egotists, quarrelsome, selfish. It is a mark of those who are noticeable for such habitual sins as these, that they are unconscious of them. So, too, the very men who planned together to put Jesus to death were not conscious of the sin involved. Indeed they may have been highly religious, thoroughly at home in the piety of the Psalms. 'The deeply spiritual ... author of Psalm cxxxix exclaims: 'Do I not hate them, O Yahweh, that hate thee? I hate them with a perfect hatred,' he adds, quite as if, so far from such a hatred being a weakness, it was rather a feather in his cap.'[1] We can recognize such sins as deadly in others; we are often blind to them in ourselves. If at a certain stage in the development of the race God bears with such unrecognized sins in the regular piety of a community, He may be bearing with such sins unrecognized by the individual in himself. But since it would be sheer unreality if a man confessed unworthiness, admitting thereby the possibility of such unconscious sins, and left it at that, the confession would always include a cry for the searching illumination of inexorable love.

It will be observed that the foregoing analysis of the sense of personal imperfection avoids the traditional Lutheran and Calvinistic assertion that we are bound to sin every day. That does seem to be a denial of the grace of God. On the other hand, our analysis surely avoids the reproach levelled against some theories of perfection, that they minimize the awfulness of moral evil, or deny the supernaturalness of the saving process.[2]

[1] C. G. Montefiore, *The Old Testament and After*, 194.

[2] Cf. B. B. Warfield, *Studies in Perfectionism* (1931), i. 130–3. I have not ventured to discuss the question whether 'inbred sin' can be eradicated. The notion is so ambiguous that it needs further analysis in the light of recent psychological investigation. The acknowledgement that our worst sins may be unconscious opens up a new problem, which cannot be fully discussed here.

8. The dying out of the temporal realm into the eternal. The first principle which we laid down as constitutive of any doctrine of the Christian ideal carries with it another necessary element in the content of the ideal attainable in the present world. The earthly life has its own intrinsic values, but they are relative; if need be, they must yield to the absolute values of the life beyond. The fulfilment of the duties of our vocation, we have said, is an integral part of our communion with God. But the vocation to which we have vowed the sincere service of a lifetime is broken, or comes to an end. Married life may be a sacrament of the divine love. But sooner or later death strikes the ministrant; and the bread is no longer broken, there is wine in that chalice no more. Bereavement, loss, sudden shafts of poverty or unhappiness—these inevitable pains and disabilities of earthly life are capable of being transfigured. If accepted as *media* of our communion with God they become richly contributory to spiritual growth. In a word, the Cross is an integral element in the ideal life in this world.

The Cross, is, therefore, far more than the pain involved in the relinquishing of evil habit. If we may dare to say it, the Cross is even more than the vicarious endurance of suffering for the guilt of others. It is the pathway from the temporal to the eternal world. It is the obedience which even the Holy One learnt through the things which He suffered. It is the condition of ultimate perfection. And therefore, for this life, it is an essential element in the ideal.

. . . That dying out of the temporal into the eternal which writers like Suso spoke of as 'passing away into the high Godhead' must be real, and must be no mere negation, but the final affirmation of the moral self, if morality itself is to be, in the end, more than a futility. What is put off in such an achievement of the moral end must be not personality or individuality, but that inner division of the soul against itself which makes the tragedy of life, and leaves us here mere imperfect fragments of persons.[1]

The chasm between the life of time and the life of

---

[1] A. E. Taylor, op. cit., i. 311.

eternity has sometimes been regarded as unbridgeable. Kierkegaard, for example, who is regarded by the Barthians as their prophet and precursor, has represented this view in its awful, unconditional hopelessness as regards the present world. 'What the conception of God, or of man's eternal beatitude, is to effect in man, is that he shall remodel his entire existence according to it; but by this remodelling man dies to his entire immediacy. As the fish dies out of its element when left upon the strand, so is the religious man caught in his absolute conception of God; for such absoluteness is not directly the element of a finite being. No wonder, then, if, for the Jew, to see God meant death.'[1] The deep religious truth in this statement of the transcendence of God must not blind us to the emptying of the Gospel which ensues. 'Man dies to his entire immediacy.' Kierkegaard followed this out uncompromisingly. All ecclesiastical organization was regarded as essentially compromise and hypocrisy;[2] asceticism is the only true Christianity. Woman is regarded as representing the world and its desire; Luther's glorification of wedded life, and Christ's visit to the marriage feast at Cana in Galilee must be visited with the same condemnation.[3]

But there is a way of preserving the rich values of the present life together with a profound apprehension of the difference of the life beyond and the ultimate other-worldliness of the Christian ideal. There is a bridge between the two worlds.[4] It is that act of surrender which Christ made in His dying. By another route we thus return to the ideal of the author of the Epistle to the Hebrews. Christ's offering of obedience in time was also through the eternal Spirit in the world within the veil. By such an act of dying to the temporal, Christ entered into the eternal, and so may we (Heb. x. 19). The ideal life in this world

---

[1] *Final Unscientific Postscript*, Germ. tr. of *Ges. Werke*, vii. 170, 171. Quoted by von Hügel, *Eternal Life*, 261.
[2] von Hügel, 261; Höffding, *Kierkegaard*, 148–9.
[3] Höffding, 147, 148.
[4] But it involves suffering, as Kierkegaard so clearly saw; Höffding, 119.

is a process of repeated surrenders. Hence there is in Charles Wesley's lines all the adoration of the limitless majesty and holiness of God which inspired the dualistic thought of Kierkegaard, together with a conviction that in Christ the dualism is bridged, and that in this life through Jesus we may look upon God.

> Before us make Thy goodness pass,
>   Which here by faith we know;
> Let us in Jesus see Thy face,
>   And die to all below.[1]

What it is to enter on the fruition of eternal life we cannot so much as imagine: *trasumanar significar per verba Non si poria.* At the most we can only say that such a life would have always and in perfection the quality we experience now, rarely and imperfectly, when we have made one of those surrenders which we find it so hard to make, and have made it heartily and with a will.[2]

A comparison of this last chapter with our first will prove that the main elements in the doctrine of any ideal for the present life are still those of the teaching of our Lord, as recorded in the first three Gospels. 'Beyond Pheidias art cannot go.' The comparison may prove, incidentally, the value of the apocalyptic framework in which that teaching was set. It is still the eschatological movement in the teaching of Jesus that determines the true direction of any this-worldly ideal. But the main conclusion will be that Christianity is impoverished unless it be preached as a Gospel of hope for this world as the next, as a Gospel that all things are possible to faith, because faith is set on a living God who has a purpose for us in this world and in the life beyond. Our religion offers an ideal that is realizable in time, and to beings of flesh and blood, on the condition that the full ideal for human beings is never to be regarded as attained within the limits of this earthly

---

[1] *Poetical Works* (ed. in 13 volumes), i. 238.

[2] A. E. Taylor, *Faith of a Moralist*, i. 314. See the excellent statement of the paradox, 306, 307. 'You cannot overvalue the highest temporal good, nor promote it for humanity too ardently, so long as you care more yourself, and labour as far as is in you that mankind shall care more, for something else.'

life. It is an ideal resting on the grace and the promises of God, a God whose command of holiness is mocked if men regard themselves as for ever destined to moral frustration and defeat in their present battle. It is an ideal involving a series of surrenders out of which the soul (and the Church) will come forth enriched and victorious, and only victorious in virtue of the grace of God. But the purpose of this book will have been lost, unless the supreme conclusion is a prayer for that ideal life, whose origin, content, and goal are perfectly summed up in our Lord Jesus Christ. The words of the Gelasian Sacramentary[1] may serve as a beginning:

O God of unchangeable power and eternal light, look favourably on thy whole Church, that wonderful and sacred mystery; and, by the tranquil operation of thy perpetual providence, carry out the work of man's salvation; and let the whole world feel and see that things which were cast down are being raised up, that those things which had grown old are being made new, and that all things are returning to perfection, through him from whom they took their origin, even through our Lord Jesus Christ. Amen.

[1] Ed. H. A. Wilson (1894), 82: et per ipsum redire omnia in integrum, a quo sumpsere principium.

INDEX

[References to the principal discussions of a subject are given in italic.]